DIVE
RED SEA
THE ULTIMATE GUIDE

DIVE
RED SEA
THE ULTIMATE GUIDE

ULTIMATE®
SPORTS

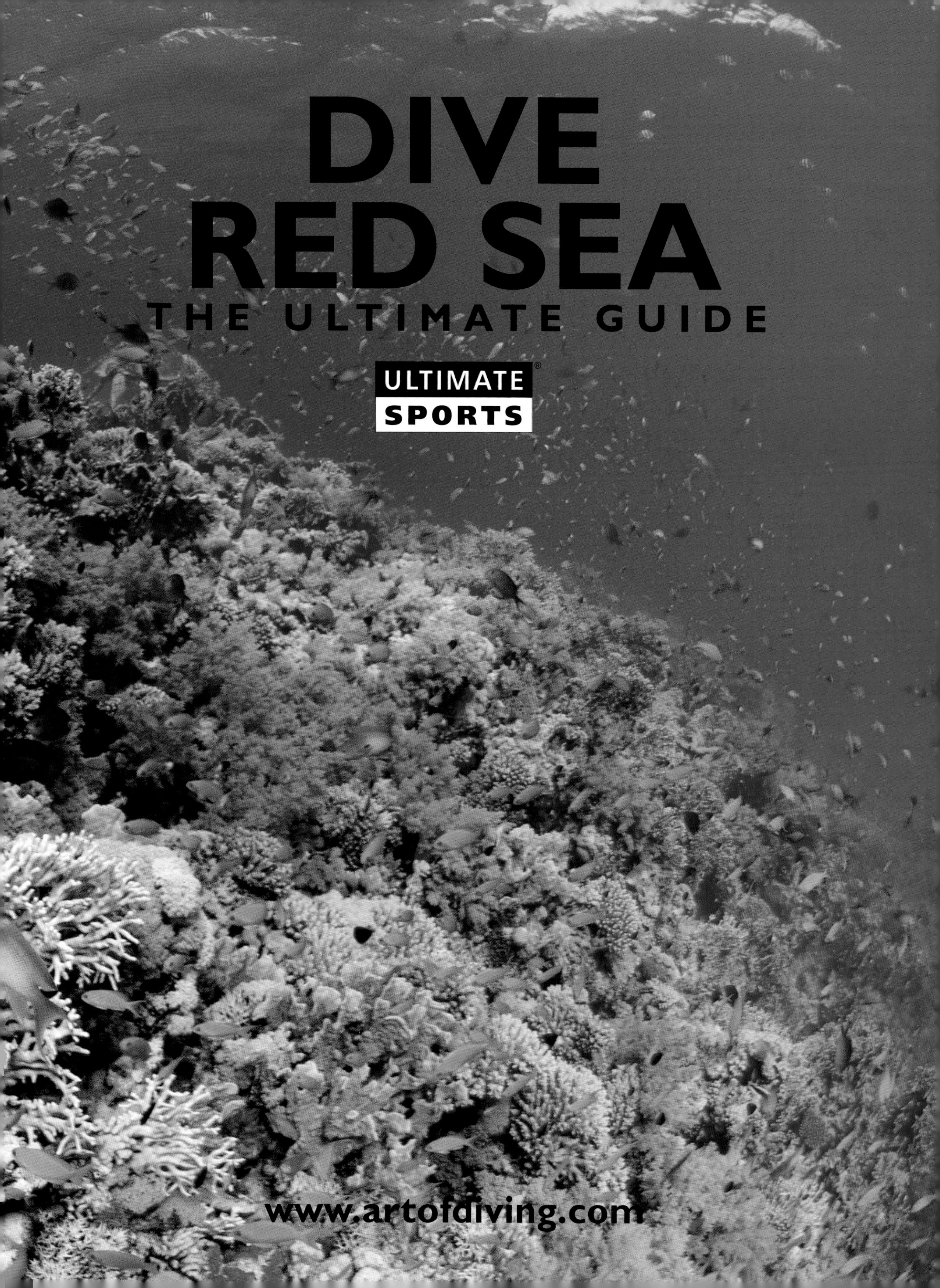

www.artofdiving.com

AN ULTIMATE SPORTS BOOK
Planned and produced by
Ultimate Sports Dive Co Limited.
8 Grange Road, Barnes,
London SW13 9RE,
United Kingdom
E-mail: info@ultimate-sports.co.uk
www.ultimate-sports.co.uk
www.artofdiving.com

PUBLISHER	David Holyoak
PROJECT MANAGER	Richard Watts
DESIGN AND MAPPING	Total Media Services Ltd
ILLUSTRATOR	Ian Legge
EDITOR	Mike Unwin
PROOF READER	Anthony Holley
INDEXER	Julie Dando

Although every care has been taken in compiling this book, using the latest information available at the time of going to press, some details are liable to change and cannot therefore be guaranteed. Neither the publishers, nor the authors, accept any liability whatsoever arising from errors or omissions, however caused.

The representation of frontiers shown on the maps do not imply any recognition or official acceptance on the part of the publishers. The specific marking of any dive site or settlement does not guarantee its existence. The maps are not intended to be used as a navigational aid.

Scuba diving is a potentially hazardous sport to be undertaken only after appropriate training, qualification, experience, and using the correct equipment. Neither the publishers, nor the authors, accept any responsibility for any incident that takes place during the course of diving any of the sites listed in this book.

Reprographics by PDQ Digital Media Solutions Ltd.

Printed in Slovakia by Polygraf Print.

A catalogue for this book can be obtained from the British Library.

ISBN-10: 0-09545199-3-0

ISBN-13: 978-0-9545199-3-3

Cover: Diver photographing a Red Sea reef (Alexander Mustard)
Pages 2–3: A Red Sea reef (Alexander Mustard)
Page 5: Bigeye soldierfish (Simon Rogerson)
Back cover: A Red Sea reef (Alexander Mustard)

ACKNOWLEDGMENTS

Simon Rogerson

First thanks must go to my wife, Anna, for enduring the research and writing phases of this book with remarkable patience. Thanks also to the tour operators and local divers who have facilitated trips, all of which have contributed in some way to my understanding of the Red Sea. They are: Tony Backhurst; Regal; Aquatours; Mosaic; Camel Diving in Sharm; Oonasdivers; Red Sea Diving Safari; Dolphin Diving of Djibouti for torrents of whale sharks; Erik Mason and all at Dream Divers in Saudi Arabia; MV *Royal Emperor* and James Curtis-Smith for the outline sketch of the *Umbria* and general advice on Sudan; Joe Dallison and Karen Von Arx of MV *Hurricane* for advice on St John's and the Fury Shoal; Grant Searancke and Sonia Goggel for general information on southern Egypt and its offshore islands; Yasser El Moafi and the crew of the Royal Evolution; Steve Brown of Tony Backhurst Scuba for thoughts on Sharm's instructor scene; Simon Gardner for expertly herding the oceanic white-tips towards me.

Thanks are equally due to Charles Hood for information on Yemen and to Alex Mustard for advice on natural history (not to mention being the two finest underwater photographers in the UK). Especial gratitude to Peter Collings for contributing a section on the shipwrecks of Suez, in addition to sharing his knowledge of some of Egypt's less-known wrecks. I am similarly grateful to all my colleagues at DIVE magazine, especially Charlotte Boan, David Lloyd and Jane Morgan, all of whom have contributed photographs. A doff of the hood also to JP Trenque for special photographic services, and to Graeme Gourlay for providing inspiration on a routine basis.

Finally, I would like to reiterate my gratitude to all the boat professionals and dive guides who have helped me on my travels – your friendship and hospitality is what makes the Red Sea experience so very memorable.

John McIntyre

Many people have contributed to my years of experience as a Red Sea veteran. Among them is Tony Backhurst of Tony Backhurst Scuba Travel, whose enthusiasm, professionalism and unselfish help as an operator has been invaluable. Tornado Marine and Traveline deserve a mention, too, for provision of excellent dive boats and logistics in Egypt. I'd also like to pay tribute to the superb craftsmanship of Paul Remijan of Fathom Imaging in creating underwater optics to help me capture beautiful pictures, complementing the work of John Ellerbrock of Gates Housings. Thanks also to my brother Phil McIntyre for his good humour and great stills pictures, and my long suffering partner Liz Shaw who has buddied me on many Red Sea dives. I'd like to put on record my special appreciation of the following dive guides for their enthusiasm and wealth of expertise: Grant Searancke, Sonia Goggel, Steve McEwan, Marlin Svedberg, Karim Helal of the Red Sea Association, Ned Middleton, for his research on shipwrecks, and last but not least the incomparable 'Ali Baba'.

For Robin & Sybil Rogerson and Bill & Kathleen McIntyre.

A list of photographers whose images appear throughout the book is provided on page 349.

CONTENTS

Giannis D. Alexander Mustard

SOMALIA

YEMEN

●ADEN

●SAN'A

MOCHA●   KHOR ANGAR●

AL HUDAYDAH●   TADJOURA● ●DJIBOUTI

JIZAN●   ASAB●

DJIBOUTI

AL QUNFUDHAH●

●IDI

TIO●

ETHIOPIA

MASSAWA●

MERSA KAWT●   ●ASMARA   ●ADDIS ABABA

ERITREA   Ethiopian Highlands

Lake Tana

SAWAKIN●
PORT SUDAN●

SUDAN

Blue Nile

Nile

White Nile

●KHARTOUM

Nubian Desert

N

| 0 | | 150 km |
| 0 | | 100 miles |

Note: Mapping convention is for north and south to be positioned at the top and bottom of a page respectively. This map of The Red Sea map is rotated anti-clockwise 90 degrees to allow largest possible reproduction as a double page spread.

DIVE SITES

● novice ● beginner ● intermediate ● advanced

REGION	PAGE	DIVE SITE	TYPE	DEPTH (M)		SKILL LEVEL
AQABA	43	Gorgone One	Reef	15m	●	5 dives
	44	Wreck of the *Cedar Pride*	Wreck	28m	●	20 dives
	46	Wreck of the *Taiyong*	Wreck	60m	●	50 dives
	49	The Tank	Reef	6m	●	1–5 dives
	50	The Power Station	Reef	40m	●	20 dives
EILAT	58	Moses Rock	Reef	10m	●	1–5 dives
	58	Japanese Gardens	Reef	* 40m	●	15 dives
	61	Dolphin Reef	Reef	18m	●	1–5 dives
	61	Eilat wrecks	Wreck	20–30m	●	20 dives
	63	Coral Island	Reef	30m	●	15 dives
NORTHERN SINAI	67	Blue Hole, Dahab	Reef	100m	●	50 dives
	68	Abou Lou Lou	Reef	20m	●	1–5 dives
	68	The Sinker	Reef	35m	●	15 dives
	68	M.F.O. Pipeline	Reef	20m	●	5 dives
	71	The Black Coral Site	Reef	25m	●	5 dives
	71	The Canyon	Reef	32m	●	15 dives
	71	The Fjord	Reef	24m	●	5 dives
SOUTHERN SINAI	76	Shark Reef / *Yolanda* Reef	Reef	40m	●	20 dives
	79	SS *Kingston*	Wreck	19m	●	10 dives
	83	*Dunraven*	Wreck	32m	●	10 dives
	83	The Alternatives / Stingray Station	Reef	30m	●	10 dives
	84	Shark Observatory	Reef	* 40–70m	●	30 dives
	85	The Gardens	Reef	10–40m	●	5 dives
	86	Ras Umm Sid	Reef	* 30m	●	15 dives
	86	Ras Nasrani	Reef	* 40m	●	15 dives
	87	White Knights	Reef	40m	●	15 dives
	87	Amphoras and Turtle Bay	Reef	* 30m	●	10 dives
	88	Pinky's Wall	Reef	* 30m	●	10 dives
	92	Shark Bay	Reef	* 30m	●	10 dives
	92	Temple	Reef	* 20m	●	10 dives
	93	Gordon Reef	Reef	* 30m	●	15 dives
	95	Thomas Reef	Reef	* 40m	●	15–30 dives
	95	Woodhouse Reef	Reef	* 40m	●	25 dives
	96	Jackson Reef	Reef	* 40m	●	30 dives
	97	Lagoona	Reef	* 40m	●	20 dives
	97	The *Million Hope*	Wreck	24m	●	15 dives
SHA'AB ABU NUHAS	105	*Carnatic*	Wreck	27m	●	20 dives
	108	*Giannis D*	Wreck	27m	●	20 dives
	115	*Chrisoula K*	Wreck	30m	●	20 dives
	118	*Kimon M*	Wreck	32m	●	20 dives
THISTLEGORM & ROSALIE MOLLER	124	The *Thistlegorm*	Wreck	30m	●	20 dives
	135	The *Rosalie Moller*	Wreck	25–50m	●	25 dives
HURGHADA TO EL QUSEIR	148	Bluff Point	Reef	* 28–42m	●	20 dives
	150	Giftun Seghir	Reef	* 25–50m	●	20 dives
	151	Careless Reef	Reef	25m	●	20 dives
	153	Erg Abu Ramada	Reef	22m	●	15 dives
	153	Panorama Reef / Abu Alama	Reef	*30–40m	●	15 dives
	154	*Salem Express*	Wreck	31m	●	15 dives
	155	Sha'ab Sheer: eastern point	Reef	20m	●	10–15 dives
	156	Abu Qifan	Reef	40m	●	40 dives
	157	El Kaf	Reef	*18–40m	●	1–5 dives
OFFSHORE ISLANDS	166	Elphinstone Reef: south point	Reef	* 40m	●	50 dives
	168	Elphinstone Reef: north point	Reef	* 40m	●	50 dives

Note:
* These sites have depths in excess of safe diving limits. In each case we have indicated the maximum depth necessary to explore the site. To suggest a suitable skill level for each dive site, we have indicated a number of completed dives as a means of quantifying the experience each of them requires. It should be noted that this is only a rough indication of the likely demands of the sites. Readers should use all the information available for each dive to determine whether it is suitable for their particular level of experience and skill, and bear in mind other factors such as weather conditions, water temperature and personal health.

ACCESS	CURRENT	MUST SEE
Shore dive or dayboat	Slight – None	Lionfish in their den; stonefish atop the reef
Shore dive or dayboat	Slight – None	Large grouper below the wreck
Shore dive or dayboat	Slight – Moderate	Inner workings of the crane where it's joined to the barge
Shore dive or dayboat	Slight – None	Speckled grey morays under the tank tracks
Shore dive or dayboat	Slight – None	Goldies among the black coral
Shore dive	Slight – None	Glassfish, garden eels
Shore dive or dayboat	Slight – None	Table corals, blue-spotted stingrays
Shore dive	Slight – None	Bottlenose dolphins, if they choose to seek you out
Shore dive	Slight – None	Sufa Missile Boat and Yatush Gunboat wrecks, with developing coral growth
Shore dive or cruise boat	Moderate – Powerful	Eagle rays, turtles, anthias schools
Shore dive	None	Yourself – safely back to the surface
Shore dive	Slight – None	Lionfish galore
Shore dive	Slight – Moderate	Boxer shrimps and glassy sweepers
Shore dive	Slight – None	Look out for colourful frogfish
Shore dive	Slight – None	Peppered morays by the handful
Shore dive	Slight – None	Keep eyes peeled for gorgeous pyjama nudibranch
Dayboat	Slight – None	The hole or undersea well-like formation
Dayboat or liveaboard	Moderate – Powerful	Shark Reef's vertical wall; schooling barracuda and snapper in summer; *Yolanda's* toilets
Dayboat or liveaboard	None – Moderate	Swim-throughs on the aft section; twin boilers; vertical struts buzzing with surgeonfish
Dayboat or liveaboard	None – Moderate	Propeller at 32m; glassfish around the boilers; crocodilefish on the sand
Mostly liveaboard	Slight – Powerful	Gorgonian fans; coral pinnacles; blue-spotted stingrays
Mostly liveaboard	Moderate – Powerful	Pelagic action in May and June; caves and overhangs; the reef wall
Shore dive, dayboat or liveaboard	Slight – Moderate	Anemonefish at Near Garden; eagle rays at Middle Garden; black corals at Far Garden
Dayboat or liveaboard	Slight – Moderate	Gorgonian fan coral forest starting at 15m; hunting octopus by night
Shore dive, dayboat or liveaboard	None – Moderate	Moray eels hiding in the coral, eagle rays, Napoleon wrasse
Shore dive, dayboat or liveaboard	Slight – Moderate	The canyon; small wooden wreck of dive boat
Dayboat or liveaboard	None – Moderate	The old anchor from the Turkish shipwreck; tiny globules of mercury from the broken amphoras
Shore dive, dayboat or liveaboard	None – Moderate	Colonies of *Alcyonaria* and *Dendronephthya* corals; moray eels and octopus
Shore dive, dayboat or liveaboard	None – Moderate	Whale sharks and mantas if you're feeling lucky; otherwise, stingrays are common
Dayboat or liveaboard	Slight	The larger of the coral pinnacles; moray eels
Dayboat or liveaboard	Moderate – Powerful	Napoleon wrasse circling below dive boats; schooling surgeonfish on the southern wall
Dayboat or liveaboard	Moderate	The canyon (experience permitting)
Dayboat or liveaboard	Moderate	Reef sharks on the wall; coral wall running to Jackson
Dayboat or liveaboard	Moderate	Schooling hammerheads; hawksbill turtles
Dayboat or liveaboard	Moderate – Powerful	Liner-inflicted reef scars; night dive inside the lagoon
Liveaboard	Moderate – Powerful	Giant propeller and rudder system; vast holds; port hull so giant it looks like a reef wall
Liveaboard or dayboat	Slight – None	Within the wreck behind the metal structure
Liveaboard or dayboat	Slight – Moderate	Try diving at sunset to see bottlenose dolphins actually swimming close to the wreck
Liveaboard or dayboat	Slight – None	Best seen from inside, where you will find the stacks of tiles for which the wreck is best known
Liveaboard or dayboat	Slight – None	Hardened sacks of inedible lentils
Dayboat or liveaboard	Moderate – Powerful	Motorbikes; trucks; guns on stern; bow viewed from seabed; Lee Enfield rifles and wellington boots
Dayboat or liveaboard	Moderate – Powerful	Countless glassfish; damage caused by German bombers; workshop and engine room
Dayboat or liveaboard	Moderate – Powerful	Anthias schools; moray eels out in the open; caverns from 22m; green and hawksbill turtles
Dayboat	Slight – Moderate	Gorgonian fans on the wall; longnose hawkfish; black coral at depth
Dayboat or liveaboard	Moderate	Moray eels everywhere; glassy sweepers in cracks and ledges; jacks and visiting pelagics
Dayboat or liveaboard	Moderate – Powerful	The biggest erg and its resident fish life
Dayboat or liveaboard	Slight	Mixture of soft and hard corals on the reef; anemone city on the southern wall
Dayboat or liveaboard	Moderate	The propellers; the area under the wreck; resident frogfish
Dayboat or liveaboard	Slight	The diversity of reef fish in the shallows
Dayboat or liveaboard	Moderate – Powerful	Barracuda, sweetlips and bottlenose dolphins, if you're lucky
Shore dive or dayboat	Slight	The coral tunnels, where getting lost is a good idea
Liveaboard or dayboat	Moderate – Powerful	Grey reef sharks, soft coral, hunting trumpetfish, oceanic white-tip sharks in season
Liveaboard or dayboat	Powerful	Napoleon wrasse, grey reef sharks, oceanic white-tip sharks

REGION	PAGE	DIVE SITE	TYPE	DEPTH (M)		SKILL LEVEL
	172	Big Brother: *Numidia*	Wreck	10–90m	●	50 dives
	173	Big Brother: *Aida*	Wreck	30–60m	●	50 dives
	176	Big Brother: southern plateau	Reef	34m	●	30 dives
	179	Little Brother: north point	Reef	* 40m	●	50 dives
	180	Little Brother: southern edge	Reef	* 40m	●	30 dives
	180	Daedalus Reef (Abu Kizan)	Reef	* 40m	●	50 dives
	181	Rocky Island	Reef	* 40m	●	50 dives
	184	Zabargad Island: pinnacles	Reef	25m	●	25 dives
	184	Zabargad Island: the 'Russian'	Wreck	24m	●	15 dives
EL QUSEIR TO SUDAN	198	El Shona	Reef	28m	●	5 dives
	199	Abu Galawa tugboat	Reef	17m	●	5–10 dives
	200	Abu Galawa Soraya	Reef	18m	●	5–10 dives
	202	*Adamantia K*, Gotta Abu Galawa	Reef	18m	●	10 dives
	203	SS *Turbo*	Wreck	28m	●	25 dives
	205	Trawler wreck, Mikauwa Island	Wreck	52m	●	50 dives
	206	Sha'ab Samadai	Reef	15m	●	1-5 dives
	207	Sha'ab Claude/Claudia	Reef	18m	●	5–10 dives
	209	Sha'ab Mansour/Maksur	Reef	* 30m	●	25 dives
	209	Sataya (Dolphin Reef)	Reef	* 30m	●	25 dives
	212	*Hamada*, Abu Gosoon	Wreck	15m	●	5–10 dives
	212	St John's: Habili Ali	Reef	* 40m	●	30 dives
	213	St John's: Habili Gafaar	Reef	* 40m	●	30 dives
	214	St John's: Gotta Soraya	Reef	* 30m	●	25 dives
	215	St John's: Dangerous Reef	Reef	24m	●	15 dives
	215	St John's: Umm Kharerim	Reef	20m	●	15 dives
SUDAN	224	Sha'ab Rumi: south plateau	Reef	* 40m	●	20 dives
	227	Sha'ab Rumi: Conshelf II	Reef	12–33m	●	5–10 dives
	230	Sha'ab Rumi: north plateau	Reef	* 40m	●	30 dives
	231	Sanganeb: southwest plateau	Reef	* 40m	●	30 dives
	233	Sanganeb: north plateau	Reef	45m	●	50 dives
	234	Mesharifa	Reef	15m	●	1-5 dives
	238	Sha'ab Suedi: The *Blue Belt*	Wreck	* 40–70m	●	40 dives
	239	Angarosh Reef	Reef	* 30–35m	●	40–50 dives
	241	Sha'ab Ambar	Reef	* 25–30m	●	30 dives
	241	The *Umbria*	Wreck	33m	●	1–5 dives
ERITREA	249	Difnein Island, northern side	Reef	20m	●	15 dives
	251	Norah seagrass	Reef	5m	●	1–5 dives
	251	Russian dock	Reef	15m	●	1–5 dives
	251	Mojeidi Island South	Reef	15m	●	10 dives
DJIBOUTI	259	The Dome	Reef	35m	●	20 dives
	260	Ras Koralai	Reef	34m	●	30 dives
	261	'La Faille'	Reef	50m	●	50 dives
	262	The *Arcon Rafaael*	Wreck	28m	●	20 dives
	262	The Seven Brothers Islands	Reef	* 40m	●	40 dives
YEMEN	269	South-west Rock	Reef	40m	●	40 dives
	270	Ship Rock	Reef	30m	●	25 dives
	270	Williamson Shoal	Reef	* 30m	●	30 dives
	271	Quoin Rock	Reef	* 40m	●	40 dives
SAUDI ARABIA	278	Washing Machine	Reef	* 35m	●	40 dives
	280	Gorgonia Point	Reef	* 35m	●	25 dives
	283	Maluthu East	Reef	* 35m	●	20 dives
	283	Hanging Garden, Muddar Reef	Reef	* 30–35m	●	30 dives
	284	Abu Galawa	Reef	* 30m	●	20 dives
	285	Abu Mansi	Reef	* 40m	●	20 dives
	286	Testes	Reef	* 30m	●	20 dives
	289	The *Iona*	Wreck	32m	●	20 dives

ACCESS	CURRENT	MUST SEE
Liveaboard & support boat	Moderate – Powerful	The engine room; the wheels if you can find them; the bridge area with its soft coral
Liveaboard & support boat	Powerful	The engine room; soft coral and reef fish on the following dive
Liveaboard & support boat	Slight – Moderate	Oceanic thresher sharks, schooling snapper and bigeye trevally, great barracuda
Liveaboard & support boat	Powerful	Hammerhead and grey reef sharks; the reef wall
Liveaboard & support boat	Moderate	The hawksbill turtle; the gorgonian fan coral forest
Liveaboard	Moderate	Scalloped hammerhead sharks; the anemone city
Liveaboard	Moderate – Powerful	Pelagic fish of all sizes
Liveaboard	Slight – None	Spanish dancers, crocodilefish, cuttlefish
Liveaboard	None	The ship's picturesque bow and mysterious holds
Dayboat	Slight – None	Green turtles; the dugong; the seagrass meadow
Dayboat	Slight – None	The small engine room
Dayboat	Slight – None	The yacht wreck; the garden of hard coral
Dayboat	Slight	The skeleton of the shipwreck; the anemone pinnacles; Spanish dancers at night
Liveaboard	Slight	Lionfish hovering around the winches; the dark holds inside the ship
Liveaboard	Slight – None	The ghostly outline of the wreck from the deepest point of the dive
Dayboat	None	Spinner dolphins moving in large groups
Dayboat	None	Shafts of light falling from the cavern roof to the sandy bottom
Dayboat or liveaboard	Moderate – Powerful	Grey reef sharks and pelagic fish in the deeper part of the dive
Dayboat or liveaboard	Moderate	Snapper, trevally and barracuda; sea turtles; dolphins
Dayboat	Slight – None	The wreck itself; disgruntled damselfish
Liveaboard	Moderate	Hammerheads and grey reef sharks
Liveaboard	Moderate	The thin pinnacle; hammerhead sharks
Liveaboard	Moderate	Manta rays from July until September; the 'cathedral' cavern
Liveaboard	None	The coral pinnacles and their associated life; bumphead parrotfish
Liveaboard	Slight – None	The coral labyrinth of caverns and tunnels
Liveaboard & support boat or dayboat	Slight	Grey reef sharks; bumphead parrotfish; great barracuda
Liveaboard or dayboat	None	The 'garage'; the 'toolshed'; the collapsed shark cage; the remains of the fish farm experiment
Liveaboard & support boat or dayboat	Moderate	Longnosed hawkfish; schooling bigeye trevally and barracuda
Liveaboard or dayboat	Slight – Moderate	Soft coral pinnacles; grey reef sharks; hammerhead sharks; hawkfish; gorgonian fan coral
Liveaboard & support boat	Powerful	Napoleon wrasse; schooling jacks; wide diversity of soft and hard corals
Liveaboard	Slight – Moderate	Manta rays
Liveaboard	Moderate	Toyota cars; giant table corals on the nearby reef
Liveaboard & support boat	Moderate	Schooling barracuda; silvertip sharks
Liveaboard & support boat	Slight – Moderate	Resident spinner dolphins; giant groupers on the reef
Liveaboard or dayboat	Slight – None	The huge propeller; Fiat Lunga cars; bombs; the engine room
Liveaboard or private charter	Slight – Moderate	Pelagic fish, jacks and tuna
Liveaboard	None	Dugong, seahorses, pipefish
Liveaboard or private charter	Slight – None	The dry dock's cranes, coated in soft coral
Liveaboard or private charter	Moderate	Eagle rays, soft coral, green and hawksbill turtles
Liveaboard or dayboat	Slight	White-tip and black-tip reef sharks
Liveaboard or dayboat	Moderate – Powerful	Moray eels on the reef, swirling sardines and trevally
Liveaboard	Moderate – Powerful	The crack itself and the black coral that grows around it
Dayboat	Slight	Big groupers under the bow
Liveaboard	Powerful	Mobula rays, schooling snappers, soft coral and sweetlips
Liveaboard	Powerful	Dogtooth tuna, jacks
Liveaboard	Moderate – Powerful	The stern section of the *Alma*, zebra sharks, potato cod
Liveaboard	Slight – Moderate	Schooling snapper, grey reef sharks
Liveaboard	Moderate – Powerful	Schooling tuna and manta rays
Liveaboard	Moderate – Powerful	Scalloped hammerhead sharks; bumphead parrotfish
Liveaboard	Slight – Moderate	Oceanic white-tip sharks; scalloped hammerheads; forest of gorgonian fans
Liveaboard	Moderate	Scalloped hammerheads; dogtooth tuna; bonito; potato cod
Liveaboard	Slight – Moderate	The hanging garden, with its sponges and black coral; the wall
Liveaboard	Slight – Moderate	Grey reef sharks, coral pinnacles, fusiliers
Liveaboard	Slight – Moderate	Aggregating fish; manta rays; caverns and eagle rays
Liveaboard	Moderate	Grey reef sharks resting on the sandy bottom
Liveaboard or private charter	None	The stern section; masses of reef fish

Vision

Aladin TEC 2G Wrist Computer

The Aladin TEC 2G is an easy to use
two-gas computer, offering decompression
calculations that adjust to your actions.

PMG predictive multi-gas algorithm,
fully adjustable settings, and the compact
size and accessibility of the Aladin line.
The truly accurate Aladin TEC 2G from UWATEC.

Foresight is key.
Unlock the adventure.

Passion

MK17/S555 System

If you are looking for smooth airflow in any water condition, ease of operation and captivating design, this is your regulator.

Balanced diaphragm first stage, dry ambient chamber, balanced second stage with diver adjustable VIVA. The powerful MK17/S555 from SCUBAPRO UWATEC.

Follow your passion. Anywhere.

INTRODUCTION

WHENEVER I VISIT THE JORDANIAN TOWN OF AQABA, I ENJOY WALKING ALONG THE SEAFRONT AT DUSK. IT'S A TRANQUIL VANTAGE POINT FROM WHICH TO CONTEMPLATE THE IMMENSITY OF THE RED SEA, STRETCHING 2,100KM SOUTH TO THE STRAIT OF BAB EL MANDAB – THE GATE OF LAMENTATIONS. I STROLL TO THE EDGE OF A PONTOON AND LOOK OVER THE SIDE. LIONFISH HAVE EMERGED FROM DAYTIME SLUMBER AND ARE PATROLLING THE SHADOWS BENEATH MY FEET, EDGING CLOSER TO A SCHOOL OF TINY GLASSFISH. EVEN HERE AT ITS BOUNDARY, THE SEA IS ALIVE.

I look up to see the sun setting behind the mountains of the Sinai Peninsula, and the Red Sea unfolding before me. It is a sea of extraordinary possibilities, where pods of dolphins sweep through lagoons, hammerhead sharks swarm up from the abyss and fields of coral flourish on wartime shipwrecks. There is nowhere else in the world to compare with the Red Sea.

Still, this corridor of marvels is defined by its boundaries. In the strictest geological sense it is actually an ocean (albeit the world's youngest), because it separates the continent of Africa from the Arabian Peninsula. In fact, the precise origins of the Red Sea remain a subject of debate in the scientific world. For years, geologists believed that a small tear in the African continental crust gradually spread northward, slowly unzipping Arabia from Africa. However, a new school of thought holds that the Red Sea opened suddenly and violently across its entire length 34 million years ago. A great rift threw up steep cliffs on either side of a fissure that became the sea, at the same time setting off an upwelling of molten rock near the southern end. The theory has found credibility with the study of rocks from Egypt and Saudi Arabia: using a technique called fission-track analysis, scientists have determined the precise times when the cliffs on either side and along the length of the Red Sea were uplifted.

Believe it or not, the first thing divers notice about the Red Sea is its taste. No permanent rivers enter the Red Sea, since desert conditions prevail along the shore for practically its entire length, and the high level of evaporation has resulted in abnormally high salinity. You feel this on your lips as soon as you enter the water, and it is sufficiently high to make people slightly more buoyant: divers find they have to add an extra kilogram or two to their weightbelt when they first dive here.

The next thing divers notice is the clarity of the water. Although visibility differs as you journey from areas surrounded by deep water to shallow shelves, the region's low rainfall means a lower rate of runoff from the land, which is normally a major cause of low visibility. Scientists generally characterise warm water as being nutrient-poor, but the clear water of the Red Sea is ideal for the development of coral reefs.

There is something unmistakable about a Red Sea reef. Whereas so many tropical reefs suffered damage through the climactic changes that accompanied the El Niño event of 1997/98, the Red Sea's reefs were largely unaffected. The hard coral gardens of St John's Reef in southern Egypt are held to be among the richest in the world. To swim through one of this area's trademark mazes of table and staghorn coral is to explore an underwater Eden, one of the most diverse and beautiful environments on the planet.

Visit any Red Sea reef, and one of the first things you will notice are schools of anthias flitting back and forth from the protection of the reef. When you see these bright orange fish highlighted against the royal blue of the sea, you know you can only be in one place: it is a visual archetype of Red Sea diving. But the sea is so much more than one fish.

If you were to travel its length, starting from the Gulf of Aqaba and heading south towards Aden, you would notice a series of environmental changes, often subtle, sometimes profound. Contrast the current-fuelled adrenaline ride of Sanganeb Atoll in Sudan with the tranquil waters off Taba in northern Egypt. Grey reef sharks rule the roost in Sudan, while the latter is the domain of the endearingly hideous frogfish. You could be forgiven for thinking the two were in totally different seas!

This variety is the Red Sea's great strength: wherever your interest may lie, you will find it. Those in search of sharks can head to the offshore islands of Egypt, Sudan or Djibouti; divers with a penchant for small animals will be delighted with the bizarre invertebrate life of Eritrea's remote Hanish Islands. The Red Sea has scores of shipwrecks waiting to be explored, such as the stately *Cedar Pride* in Jordan, or the underwater museum of the *Thistlegorm* in Egypt, possibly the world's most popular dive site. As the great Jacques Yves Cousteau once said: 'The Red Sea is a corridor of marvels – the happiest hours of my diving life have been spent there.'

Divers love this desert sea for its richness and variety, but its popularity must also be due in some measure to its sheer convenience. You can step onto a plane anywhere in Europe in the sure knowledge that, five hours later, you will arrive at an affordable destination with reliable weather, warm water and world-class diving.

Of the eight nations with Red Sea coastlines, Egypt has attracted the greatest number of diving visitors, and continues to do so. This guide will offer fresh insights into the classic Egyptian dives, as well as exploring a few spots that have only recently been discovered. But we will also delve far beyond the shores of package tourism, unlocking the secrets waiting to be enjoyed in the Red Sea's new frontiers: destinations such as Sudan, Eritrea and Djibouti.

While tourism has stalled or even been banned from some Red Sea coastlines, a new generation of divers has emerged for whom the inconvenience of travel to a 'difficult' country such as Sudan is all part of a greater challenge. Few divers are likely to visit Yemen in the near future, but it nevertheless represents a significant element in the Red Sea story. This book thus aims to celebrate the diversity of the Red Sea in its entirety.

Along the way, we will swim with sharks, explore shipwrecks and venture to wild, uninhabited islands. Each dive site will be explored in detail, as we paint a comprehensive picture of what this enchanting place has in store for the fortunate few who can peer through the magic window of the sea. So check your gauges, take a deep breath and prepare to plunge in!

Simon Rogerson

▶▶ A classic scene from the Red Sea; anemonefish hiding among soft coral.
(Simon Rogerson)

▼ A diver swims in front of the funnel on the Giannis D wreck.

Alexander Mustard

FORMATION AND HISTORY OF THE RED SEA

THE RED SEA BEGAN ITS FORMATION SOME 42 MILLION YEARS AGO IN THE EOCENE PERIOD, WHEN ARABIA BEGAN GRADUALLY SPLITTING FROM AFRICA, THOUGH THERE WASN'T A RECOGNISABLE SEA UNTIL ABOUT 25 MILLION YEARS AGO.

WHAT'S IN A NAME

Any diver will know that far from being red, the waters of the sea are normally a clear royal blue. There are several explanations to account for the name, the most likely being a reference to the surrounding mineral-rich red mountains, though it is equally possible that it could refer to seasonal blooms of the reddish bacteria *Trichodesmium erythraeum* collecting close to the surface, or in bays. Some suggest the name came from a mistranslation of what should have been the 'Reed Sea' in the book of Exodus, while others have ascribed it to the Himarites, a local group of people whose own name means 'red'. Further debate has taken place around the idea that 'red' somehow stands for 'south', the theory holding that some Asiatic languages used colour to denote directions. Whatever the truth, the name has stuck, and generations have gazed across the sea's cobalt blue water, wondering at its mysterious name.

▶ Seen from space, the Red Sea appears as a blue scar separating Africa from the Arabian Peninsula

The widening continues today, at a rate of about 1-2cm per year. The world's northernmost tropical sea, its surface water temperatures vary between 21ºC and 31ºC. A high rate of evaporation, coupled with a lack of rainfall and rivers, has caused the Red Sea to have a relatively high salinity of about four per cent. During the ice ages, the strait at Bab El Mandeb closed when sea levels fell globally, and much of the sea would have evaporated into a salty basin.

The dynasties of ancient Egypt were the first to set out to explore the Red Sea, but it was the Greek explorer Hippalus who opened the sea up as a major trade route between Asia and Europe. From the Gulf of Aqaba and Suez in the north to the strait of Bab el Mandeb to the south, the sea is approximately 1,900km long and 300km wide at the widest point between Sudan and Saudi Arabia. In the abyssal zone of the Central Median Trench, it drops away to depths of 2,500m, while the coastal fringes are noted for their prolific marine life and corals, with more than 1,000 invertebrate and 200 coral species recorded thus far.

Human activity in the Red Sea dates back to before the 15th century BC, when Hatshepsut, a female Pharaoh, built her temple to the west of Luxor. While the temple itself was not on the sea, its reliefs tell of Hatshepsut's trade expeditions to the land of Punt, a mysterious place thought to be located in what is now Somalia. The carvings feature the first ever depictions of Red Sea fish life, including recognisable wrasse, parrotfish, sharks and dolphins. At the time, the principal Pharaonic harbour was at Gawasis Bay, 23km to the south of modern day Safaga.

By the 12th century BC, the Phoenicians had established a base at what is now Jeddah in Saudi Arabia. Later, in the sixth century BC, the Red Sea was one of the routes used by Cyrus the Great of Persia as he and his successors set about claiming the most extensive empire of the ancient world. Persian domination gave way to Greek, and the Red Sea became a vital route from the Indian Ocean to Suez, then Alexandria. The trade route between Egypt and Punt came to an end after the 12th century BC, possibly because of rival trade routes and the likely break-up of the Punt federation.

There is little record of Red Sea activity in the years of Roman domination, but recent excavations at the ancient port at Quseir have revealed botanical evidence of the Roman and Islamic spice trade between Egypt and India. In medieval times, it was the port from which the Karimi merchants organised trade with Yemen, Saudi Arabia and India.

From the 15th century onwards, Europe began to have greater interests in the Red Sea, although Egyptian control limited direct European access to ports. Local vessels had priority, and were used to bring exotic wares into Egyptian markets serving as redistribution markets for the Mediterranean. Although there have been precious few archaeological excavations of shipwrecks from this period, at least one has been carried out (on a merchant ship that sank about 1765), yielding evidence of Chinese porcelain, aromatic resin and one all-important commodity – coffee.

The consumption of coffee has had a significant effect on Red Sea trade. Although coffee first appeared in Europe in the 17th century, it had already been through a long history in the Orient, beginning in the Red Sea around the 13th century. Wild coffee berries were consumed originally in Ethiopia, and the habit spread north along the Red Sea, reaching Yemen, Arabia and Egypt, where the drink's stimulative qualities were greatly appreciated.

The strategic importance of the Red Sea lead to French attempts to invade Egypt in 1798, under General Bonaparte. Although he failed, plans for a canal joining the Red Sea with the Mediterranean became a reality in 1869, when the Suez Canal finally opened. Trading posts along the canal were at first shared by British, French and Italians, later joined by Americans and Soviets. The canal was effectively closed from 1967 to 1975 as a result of the Six Day War, and some commentators say it has never recovered supremacy over the Cape route. Today, Britain, France and the USA maintain a strong military presence at the mouth of the Red Sea, in Djibouti.

NATURAL HISTORY OF THE RED SEA

'DON'T TOUCH THE CORAL' EVERYONE SAYS. AND, FOR THE MOST PART, THIS IS SOUND ADVICE. ASIDE FROM THE FACT THAT THERE IS A GOOD CHANCE OF BEING SCRAPED OR STUNG, THE CREATURES THAT LIVE WITHIN THE STONY SKELETON ARE EXTREMELY DELICATE.

THE CORAL WORLD

Evolution may have equipped coral for dealing with the small animals that use it for shelter, but a flailing fin or a misguided hand will invariably cause damage.

When people first started diving in the Red Sea, the rules were not so strict. Divers used table corals as, well, tables. Or chairs. If a fish swam into the shelter of branching coral, a photographer would pull away the stony branches to get a clearer shot of the retreating animal. Even the man regarded as the first Red Sea conservationist, Jacques Yves Cousteau, used dynamite to blast channels into the lagoons where he wanted to moor his boats. Today most people appreciate that coral is fragile. Nonetheless, the importance of its role in the Red Sea shall not be underestimated.

Coral, it might surprise some people to know, is an animal, not a plant. In the Red Sea, most species of coral are colonial. They build their communities by secreting limestone, which eventually forms an exo-skeleton to protect the soft-bodied polyps inside – the animals themselves. These polyps exemplify the success of a simple design: their bodies comprise tentacles, a mouth, a simple digestive space and tissues that secrete the limestone shell. In the Red Sea, the polyps generally stay inside their limestone casing during the day and emerge to feed on plankton at night.

Coral grows at just a few centimetres a year. When a polyp dies, its skeleton stays attached to the reef and eventually becomes part of the limestone bedrock, serving as a foundation for more living coral. When a shipwreck attracts corals, they build so heavily on its surface that the whole structure is slowly subsumed into a self-perpetuating reef system. Hard coral takes many different forms in the Red Sea, all dictated by local factors such as current and depth.

Most corals feed by catching and eating plankton and other nutrients in the water, but they also derive

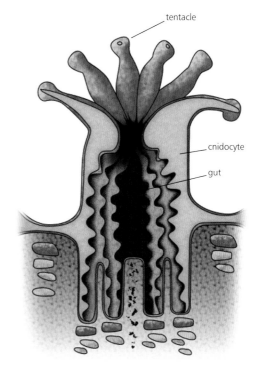

▲ A cross section of a coral polyp, one of the planet's simplest but most successful animals.

energy from a sort of in-built garden. Red Sea corals live in symbiosis with microscopic plant cells known as zooxanthellae, which speed up the coral's ability to extract calcium from seawater and so continue to maintain its skeleton. Corals can also feed on the waste products of the zooxanthellae's photosynthesis, to the extent that some species derive most of their food and oxygen from these tiny plants.

Coral can survive storms and – over the long term – predation by fish and invertebrates. However, it is also an extremely sensitive animal that requires certain conditions in order to thrive. Clear waters are essential for the zooxanthellae to develop, and corals generally need a water temperature of 23–30ºC. The Red Sea has some of the northernmost reefs in the world, and the corals

Alexander Mustard

◄ A wide variety of hard coral species flourish in the shallows in this typical reef scene from northern Egypt.

▼ Cross section of a typical Red Sea wall reef, with the stony corals of the surface giving way to fan corals at depth.

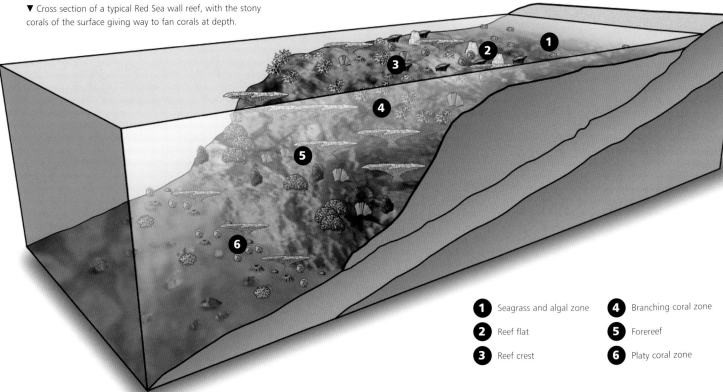

1 Seagrass and algal zone
2 Reef flat
3 Reef crest
4 Branching coral zone
5 Forereef
6 Platy coral zone

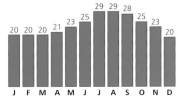

RED SEA STATISTICS

Area: 450,000sq km (175,000sq mi)
Length: 1,900km (1,200mi)
Widest point: 300km (190mi)
Maximum depth: 3,040m (9,975ft)
Average depth: 500m (1,640ft)

Average air temperature
Summer: 40°C
Winter: 21°C

Average water temperature:
Summer: 29°C
Winter: 20°C

Salinity: 36–38%

Species:
over 1000 invertebrate species
200 soft corals
1,167 fish species

AVERAGE WATER TEMPERATURE (°C)

J	F	M	A	M	J	J	A	S	O	N	D
20	20	20	21	23	25	29	29	28	25	23	20

AVERAGE AIR TEMPERATURE (°C)

J	F	M	A	M	J	J	A	S	O	N	D
21	21	24	28	32	35	38	40	34	31	27	21

have adapted to cope with temperatures that may drop to 21°C at the height of winter. Coral diversity falls away significantly as you travel up the Gulf of Suez, where conditions are simply too cold and silty.

For the most part, the Red Sea has impressive coral, in terms of both diversity and cover. The key factors are in place: shallow, dynamic currents to deliver food and warm, clean seawater. Yet the coral remains under threat: shoreline development has created run-off that smothers and eventually kills coral. Ironically, this has taken place around hotels and resorts that have been built as a direct result of the Red Sea's coral riches.

When coral becomes stressed due to a sudden rise or fall in water temperature or some other environmental threat, it expels its symbiotic zooxanthellae. Under such circumstances, the coral turns a deathly white and can only survive for a matter of weeks. The phenomenon is known as coral bleaching, and it is a widespread problem throughout the world's oceans. The most infamous example was the death of approximately 80 per cent of the Maldives' hard coral during the extreme El Niño event of 1997–98, when water temperatures rose across the Indian Ocean, unbalancing delicate ecosystems.

The Red Sea escaped the worst of the bleaching event, and the area around southern Egypt and northern Sudan subsequently became known as one of the world's richest areas for hard coral. The southern Egyptian reef systems known as the Fury Shoal and St Johns are the places to go if you want to see hard coral at its most impressive.

THE REEF AS BATTLEFIELD

Despite their apparent serenity, coral reefs are actually battlefields, with many of the inhabitants locked in a never-ending struggle for survival. Spend long enough on a reef and you will witness almost every link in the food chain. The plankton is eaten by anthias and other small reef fish, which in turn are targeted by larger reef fish such as grouper or trumpetfish. These become prey for larger fish, such as jacks or barracuda, which themselves live in fear of apex predators such as sharks. Even the Red Sea's reef sharks have to be wary of super-predators, including tiger sharks, shortfin makos and great hammerheads.

Divers understandably think of tropical seas as rich environments, but the actual biomass of fish and other life is relatively low compared to that found in the temperate seas, where oxygen-rich cold water generates more plankton. The clear water that attracts divers to the Red Sea owes its clarity to the relative dearth of food suspended in it. In the Red Sea, the coral reefs that fringe the deep waters are the exception rather than the law. The open sea is more like a desert, so the coastal band of coral is really just an oasis between two different deserts. Of course, the advantage of having such an environment on the margins of an oceanic desert is that every inch of space is fought over by encrusting sponges and corals. Similarly, the resident fish tend to occur in great numbers, creating a riotous, visually stunning environment. Coral reefs display nature unfettered, showing just how colourful and vibrant the undersea world can be.

FISH BEHAVIOUR

So, how do we make sense of what we see on a reef? The fish seem to be milling around in a thousand different directions, and at first it all looks like chaos. But there is actually a very specific reason why every fish is swimming in a particular direction at any given time. To get to grips with this complex world, the diver has to slow down, keep quiet and observe.

One of the first examples of fish activity to look out for is cleaning behaviour. Keep an eye on the reef and look for an area where, from time to time, an individual fish seems to stop for no apparent reason in mid-water, opening its mouth, angling its body and quivering in expectation. Look closer and you may be able to see a tiny fish darting around the larger one. This is a cleaner fish – usually a small wrasse or goby. It occupies its own portion of reef and provides a service for other visiting fish, removing parasites from their flesh. Under this mutual arrangement, the client fish gets rid of its irritating parasites, while the cleaner fish gets a free meal for its troubles. The deal involves a temporary suspension in the predator-prey relationship that exists between fish of different size, but for the most part it seems to work well enough. Many cleaner fish will even venture right inside a predator's mouth in order to locate a suitable morsel. Cleaner wrasse also feed on dead skin and fungus, so they may play an important role in inhibiting the spread of disease among reef fish.

Just as a barber's shop must have a pole, so the cleaner fish need a means of advertising its services. Look for a small fish with an electric blue stripe running along the length of its body, the universal mark of the cleaner. Some species of shrimp also act as cleaners in the Red Sea, though they are less common than elsewhere in the Indo-Pacific.

There are other notable examples of symbiosis across a typical Red Sea reef. The best known is probably that of the anemone and the anemonefish. Under this arrangement, the fish receives shelter among the stinging tentacles of the anemone (it is immune to the sting), while the anemone benefits from a feisty tenant who will chase away some of its potential predators. In fact, some anemonefish will challenge intruders far larger than themselves – you only need to approach an anemone to find out how far they will go. It is a favourite trick of divers to waggle their fingers in front of an anemone, as the anemonefish cannot resist making its characteristic darting attacks. Be careful, though: larger ones can draw blood.

Amicable as the rules of reef symbiosis may seem, some animals will break the treaty for the sake of an easy meal. Cleaner wrasse sometimes seem nervous around barracuda – and they have good reason: there

are many documented cases of ungrateful barracuda biting down on a trusting cleaner wrasse and abruptly shattering the truce of the cleaning station. But it can cut both ways: sometimes you will see a large fish flinch violently while being cleaned, as though it has been stung. In fact, it has fallen victim to a little villain of the reef, the false cleaner wrasse, which instead of eating parasites, simply bites a chunk out of its 'client'. (It has been unkindly suggested that the false cleaner should be renamed 'the lawyerfish'.)

Alexander Mustard

▲ A parrotfish hovers patiently as a cleaner wrasse pecks the parasites from its scales.

► A male adult yellow boxfish, completely different from the juvenile and female forms of the same species.

RHYTHMS OF THE REEF

During the day, the Red Sea reef is buzzing with activity: fish are busy feeding, fleeing, schooling and separating; territories are constantly being defended and intruded; every inhabitant has to fight to maintain its place in the order of things. There is a theory that the reason coral dwelling fish are so colourful is that, amid all this activity, they use colour to communicate important facts about themselves and their position within the reef hierarchy. Angelfish use their dazzling colours as part of courtship rituals, while bigeye soldierfish blush a deeper red when they feel threatened. Lionfish can hover in mid-water, fins outstretched in full defensive posture, confident in the knowledge that any predator trying to rush them will be speared on one of their poisonous spines. Equally, nudibranchs may not be able to sting or bite, but their coloration sends out a strong message: any fish that tries to eat them will suffer the mother of all stomach-aches.

The onset of dusk raises the stakes, as the time just before sunset is a period of transition. The fish that were active during the day return to the reef, while predators such as jacks, snappers and sharks take advantage of the parade. Their eyes are better suited to the low-light levels, and for a short while they have an advantage over the daytime fish, whose vision is more attuned to brightness. It is at this time of day that you are likely to see predatory jacks surrounding schools of smaller fish, herding them into a corner and then sweeping through the silver column at high speed to pick off stragglers.

▼ Fish activity normally intensifies in the build-up to dusk.

Lionfish emerge from their daytime shelter around this time. These ornate predators have a completely different approach to the jacks, slowly insinuating themselves closer to the target, then striking with a speed that takes the target (often glassfish, anthias or cardinalfish) completely by surprise.

Meanwhile, on the reef, that master of camouflage, the frogfish, waits for a returning fish to stray too close to its capacious maw. Frogfish cannot hover elegantly in mid water in the manner of the lionfish. Instead, they sit on the reef, occasionally moving around with fins that have been modified into legs. As an unsuspecting fish draws close, the frogfish lunges forward, rapidly extending its jaw so that both water and prey are sucked inside. Then it settles down again as though nothing had happened. All this takes place so quickly that you literally cannot see it: the frogfish gives a little jolt, then sits there looking quietly smug. Watch the process on normal video, and you will see a frogfish and its prospective prey, then the picture will jump slightly and suddenly only the frogfish is there. Only with special high-speed cameras can you see the terrible beauty of the strike, which is recognised as one of the fastest movements in the animal kingdom.

For divers, the period of dusk is the 'magic hour', a time when reef activity builds into a crescendo. There is certainly a sense of climax, as it is also the time when diurnal fish choose to spawn. At first, the mating rituals can be hard to spot, but they gradually become more overt, typically culminating in the pair of fish rising up through the water column and dispatching eggs and

Alexander Mustard

▲ Night sees no respite from predation on the reef – here, a white-tip reef shark is seen hunting small fish at night, hounding them across the moonlit coral.

sperm at the conclusion of their dance. There are still a few fish around to feed on the protein-packed discharge, but most of the reef dwellers are by now tucking themselves away. The eggs will join the mass of microscopic zooplankton floating away from the reef into the open sea, and will benefit from the 12-hour head start before their principal predators become active again.

A word about sharks and dusk: this is the time when several Red Sea shark species lose their natural wariness, as the instinct to feed becomes overpowering. There have been many documented cases of oceanic white-tips and silky sharks buzzing and bumping into divers after hours of innocuous behaviour. This time of day, with its bouts of frenzied fish activity, has a way of shifting shark behaviour up a gear. Author Simon Rogerson was on a dusk dive at Big Brother Island in Egypt when he came across a group of silky and grey reef sharks that

were excited by the presence of a school of unicornfish. By day the sharks had drifted lazily by the school, sizing them up and looking for stragglers, but the onset of darkness had raised the stakes, and the sharks drove through the fish at high speed, hurtling after their prey. Several times, the sharks' streaming runs took them right up to the divers, and they only changed direction at the very last moment, eyes blazing in the torchlight. It was an awe-inspiring display of predatory prowess, but Rogerson now believes he and the other divers should have left the water.

Similarly, beware of swimming with dolphins over deep water, especially in the late afternoon. In the Red Sea, dolphins are often stalked from below by tiger sharks, and there is a chance that an accompanying human swimmer could be mistaken for an injured dolphin. There is one extraordinary case on record, in which

Alexander Mustard

a great deal more active by night, when their huge eyes equip them with night vision for hunting shrimps. On some reefs, you may be lucky enough to see white-tip reef sharks ghosting over the coral, looking to provoke a fish into breaking cover. As with most sharks, the white-tip is armed with a battery of sensory equipment that gives it an edge over many reef fish when it comes to the chase. In the first instance, it can locate the fish hiding under the sand by sensing the tiny discharges of electricity given off by all living things. These electrical impulses are detected via pores in the shark's nose known as the ampullae of Lorenzini. Then, when the fish tries to flee into the darkness, the shark pursues it using its highly developed night vision and a tough body that protects it from any battering against the reef.

During the hours of darkness, you will see many of the familiar creatures from daytime in a phase of rest that we recognise as sleep. Most are aware of their vulnerability during this time, and have adopted tactics to remain safe while they rest. Some fish seek shelter under the sand. Triggerfish swim into narrow cavities and then extend their defensive dorsal spines, effectively locking themselves into position. Hiding is not an option for the larger parrotfish: instead it cocoons itself in a barely visible bubble of mucus, which prevents 'smell predators' such as moray eels from tracking it down. If an intruder does breach the bubble, the parrotfish will immediately be roused from its rest and another moonlit chase will begin. But it will at least have a fighting chance.

Dawn offers another opportunity to see the reef in a state of spectacular transition, although this does involve being ready to dive at 6–6.30am. As the pale light of morning suffuses the reef, the same fish that were targeted the previous evening again find themselves under attack as the barracuda and jacks prepare for another day of hunting. Many believe this is the best time to view deep-dwelling shark species such as scalloped hammerheads, which return to patrol warmer waters after a night of hunting squid and stingrays at depths below 100m.

The first dive of the day should always be the deepest: it is a pleasurable prospect for the experienced diver to 'freefall' down to 30–40m, there to be greeted by the unearthly forms of hammerheads warming up after a night of hunting in the twilight zone. It is a magical meeting between two very different animals: the divers at the edge of their depth limits; the sharks at the shallowest phase of their patrols. Then there is the gradual ascent, as the gorgonian fans first give way to soft coral, then to the fields of stony coral that dominate the shallows. The morning sun feeds the reef, bringing the energy that will fuel it and its colourful inhabitants through another day of survival in this most beautiful of seas.

a pod of bottlenose dolphins kept a large, unidentified shark at bay after it had severely injured a man who had been swimming with them. The adult dolphins reportedly drove the shark away by ramming its soft underbelly with their hard beaks.

The scene is transformed by darkness. Small fish such as the anthias retreat to the protection of the coral, where they tremble slightly in response to the torch-lit advances of night divers. Calm descends on the reef, which moves into a different phase as the nocturnal creatures begin to stir. Feather stars and the giant basket stars unfurl their slender arms to trap plankton, coral polyps extend out from the skeleton to do the same and a chorus of strange clicking sounds can be heard as a million tiny crustaceans begin the night shift.

Fishes that you see sleeping in caves by day – in particular the bigeye soldierfish and the squirrelfish – seem

▶▶ Bohar snapper stream across an Egyptian reef during the summer spawning season, providing a spectacle for divers. (Alexander Mustard)

▼ Like many animals squid are more active and easier to approach at night.

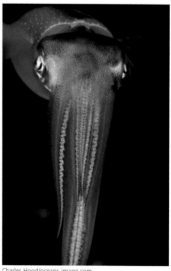

Charles Hood/oceans-image.com

THE NEW
explorer

The world's largest unexplored playground.
What will you discover?

Introducing the new Explorer BCD incorporating our unique
re::flex comfort-fit technology - fully padded, anatomically
contoured harness and backpack system with all-round
adjustment. A simple one-time setup allows you to tailor
the BCD precisely to your individual body shape – including
100mm adjustment in the backpack length – offering supreme
comfort, both on-land and in-water.

Other innovations include: easy-find dump-pulls that sink at
the shoulder and float at the kidney, a third dump integrated
into the inflator assembly allowing one-handed buoyancy
control if you need it, a mechanical release system with the
option of integrated weight pouches or cargo clips,
encapsulated reflective piping and our unique new
high-traction cylinder cradle with multiple curves which
not only caters for different diameter singles but will
also support twin cylinders with absolute security.

Configure your new BCD at **apvalves.com**

Built in the UK by A.P.Valves

AQABA

JORDAN MAY HAVE ONLY A SHORT STRETCH OF COASTLINE, BUT THERE ARE GOOD REASONS TO CONSIDER IT AS AN ALTERNATIVE TO THE CROWDED EGYPTIAN DESTINATIONS OF SHARM EL SHEIKH AND HURGHADA. THIS COMPARATIVELY TINY SLICE OF THE RED SEA OFFERS MORE THAN 20 GOOD DIVE SITES IN JUST 27KM.

And although Aqaba diving is generally easy, this does not mean – as some might imagine – that it is of a lower quality. The abundance and variety of marine life here is enough to occupy any diver, especially novices, photographers and technical divers. Furthermore, the dive sites tend not to suffer from the 'lemonade' effect of other crowded Red Sea destinations, in which the water is so full of bubbles it can sometimes be hard to concentrate on the reef.

With the advent of digital stills and video cameras, the number of divers capturing their own undersea mementos has grown inexorably. Aqaba is well worth a visit for this reason alone. Commonly seen subjects for newly equipped digi-divers include pepper moray eels, scorpionfish and the normally impossible-to-find stonefish, while toadfish can sometimes be found lurking grumpily under a few of the coral outcrops. Many dive guides offer a cautious promise of tracing the gorgeous giant red nudibranch commonly known as the Spanish dancer, which is usually only found on night dives. Lionfish are also a dominant presence in the shallower waters of Aqaba: it is not uncommon to discover veritable 'lions' dens', where a dozen or more may congregate. From June to August there is even an outside chance of bumping into the biggest fish of all, the whale shark, which has been known to roam these very northernmost reaches of the Red Sea. Add to this a healthy and colourful bounty of anthias and other schooling fish, and you have enough picture opportunities for a very satisfying portfolio.

For many divers, however, the prospect of shore diving is enough to make them think twice about choosing this destination. Humping heavy dive gear a few hundred metres across the beach or to the end of a jetty can be a bit of a chore, especially in the hotter months. This is compounded by the additional burden of a pick-up from hotel to dive site before kitting up. Still, for many divers, such experiences are

◀ The picturesque bow of the *Cedar Pride* has become an icon of Jordanian diving.

Jane Morgan

► Sandstone mountains known as Seven Pillars of Wisdom rise vertically from the desert at Wadi Rum, where Sir David Lean shot key scenes of Lawrence of Arabia.

►► A dusk scene looking across the Gulf of Aqaba towards Eilat. (Jane Morgan)

all part and parcel of the sport. A few centres offer daily boat excursions to the majority of the sites, so it is worth investigating what is on offer before deciding what kind of diving you want to do.

Aqaba also has three popular and contrasting wreck sites. One is an old American M40 tank, which sits regally at a depth of just 6m. Not only does this have an obvious novelty value, but it is so different from other Red Sea wrecks that in less than a decade underwater it has become a symbol of Jordan's unique place in Red Sea diving and tourism. Nearby is a sizeable cargo ship called the *Cedar Pride*, which has become Aqaba's pride and joy. For the ever-growing army of technical divers and lovers of all things deep, there is also the recently discovered wreck of a large Korean barge, the *Taiyong*, whose once towering crane now extends down the reef to a depth of over 60m. While the *Taiyong* lies at the very limits for air diving, a few local dive centres have embraced it as the perfect site to train people in the art of trimix diving.

In short, Aqaba has enough different dive sites to warrant a varied itinerary, especially as it is so easy to combine diving with some world-class topside attractions. Just a few hours from Aqaba are the celebrated ancient monuments of Petra, the most famous of which is the stunning red sandstone tomb carved into the rock-

Jordan Tourist Board

face in a small opening in the Shara mountains. This was the setting for the final scenes of the Hollywood blockbuster *Indiana Jones and the Last Crusade*. Breathtaking scenery is also to be found a 90-minute drive from Aqaba in the protected national park known as Wadi Rum, where the spectacular rock formations and haunting desert wilderness provided the perfect backdrop for the David Lean classic, *Lawrence of Arabia*.

For a complete holiday, Jordan and Aqaba provide plenty of above water activities for both divers and those who prefer to stay dry. Certainly, it is a destination for those who prefer to do more than read a book on non-diving days.

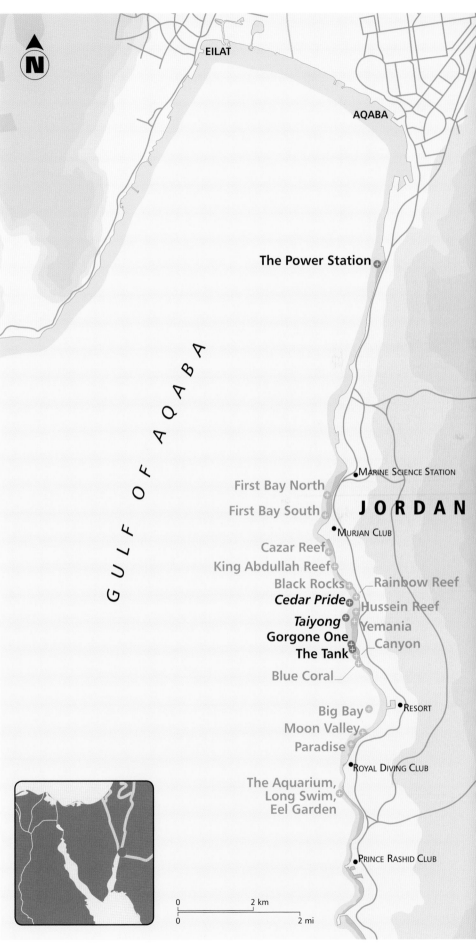

EILAT

AQABA

The Power Station

GULF OF AQABA

MARINE SCIENCE STATION

First Bay North

First Bay South

JORDAN

MURJAN CLUB

Cazar Reef

King Abdullah Reef

Black Rocks

Cedar Pride

Rainbow Reef

Hussein Reef

Taiyong

Yemania

Gorgone One

Canyon

The Tank

Blue Coral

Big Bay

RESORT

Moon Valley

Paradise

ROYAL DIVING CLUB

The Aquarium,
Long Swim,
Eel Garden

PRINCE RASHID CLUB

0   2 km

0   2 mi

GORGONE ONE

Max depth: 15m

Skill level: novice

Access: shore dive or dayboat

Current: small to none

Must see: lionfish in their den; stonefish atop the reef

Gorgone One gets its name from a big gorgonian fan coral that signposts the reef. But this is actually not the main attraction of the dive. That accolade goes to the three coral pinnacles that punctuate a gently sloping, eye-pleasing seabed. The central of these pinnacles is especially beautiful, and surrounded by fish. Divers with patience and an interest in the dynamics of a small ecosystem can easily spend an entire dive meandering the various wildlife hotspots of this bustling undersea habitat. It is perhaps the best location in Aqaba to guarantee lionfish by the dozen, which congregate like so many oriental dancers in an overhang at the foot of the pinnacle. Glassy sweepers and hatchet fish sweep from one side to another in tight, swirling schools, ensuring an endless supply of food for the pride of lionfish occupying this den. As the fairly gentle currents usually – but not always – move from north to south, the more shaded aspect of the cylindrical reef struc-

ture is alive with the Red Sea's most visible resident, the golden anthias. Other reliable occupants include small grey peppered morays, bottom-dwelling toadfish, scorpionfish (both the bearded and devil varieties) and their more deadly cousin, the common stonefish. Atop the pinnacle's honeycomb coral dome there often sits a well-camouflaged and sizeable stonefish, as though cast in the role of reef guru.

Even the dive guides struggle when it comes to picking out the delicate seahorses that live in the many patches of seagrass. The combination of vibrant colour, eager prey and healthy soft and hard corals, especially during an afternoon sunburst, make this an ideal location to take good set-piece photographs.

Gorgone One is extremely popular as a dive from the shore. Away from the pinnacles – the other two are also worth visiting but are not quite as grand – it is common to see schooling fish such as juvenile barracuda and snapper. The occasional hawksbill turtle simply adds to the charm of this gorgeous site. There is also the adjacent Gorgone Two, which culminates in a reef dropoff. It can be dived separately and offers a similarly thriving reef system. Thanks to the predictability of the marine life and the location of certain territorial creatures, night diving is good here, though it is only done from the shore.

 VISIBILITY

Generally good to exceptional, at around 20–45m. This tends to fall to 10–15m during the plankton blooms in April/May. In summer, when air temperatures can be roasting, local dive operators say visibility can be a gin-clear 45–50m.

 WATER TEMPERATURE

Water temperatures vary from a chilly 20–21ºC in January/February to a warm-bath 28ºC in August. Some dive guides actually wear drysuits in the winter months, while a shorty 3mm wetsuit is more than adequate when temperatures are 26ºC or more.

 SEASONALITY

Much of Aqaba's marine life – such as hawksbill turtles, frogfish and stonefish – is present year round, but certain species are more prevalent seasonally. Napoleon wrasse, for example, tend to be out in force from December to April. This is also the time when manta rays visit the gulf. Lucky divers may see whale sharks from the middle of June through to August, while other pelagics such as tuna and, very rarely, ocean sunfish can be spotted in autumn.

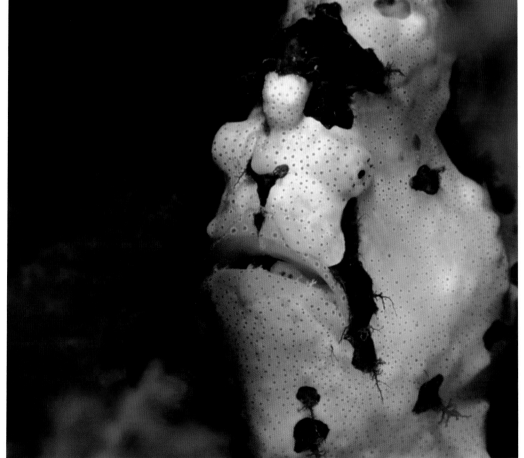

Alexander Mustard

OTHER DIVE SITES

Big Bay
Black Rocks
Blue Coral
Canyon
Cazar Reef
Eel Garden
First Bay North
First Bay South
Hussein Reef
King Abdullah Reef
Long Swim
Moon Valley
Paradise
Rainbow Reef
The Aquarium
Yemania

◄ Though rare and extremely hard to find, the ugly/beautiful frogfish is one of Jordan's most exotic residents.

◄◄ Lionfish are one of Jordan's specialities – their spines can inject a powerful toxin, and it is best to allow them space.

► The *Cedar Pride's* crow's nest has provided a foothold for soft and hard corals.

WRECK OF THE *CEDAR PRIDE*

Max depth: 28m

Skill level: medium; 20+ plus dives

Access: shore dive or dayboat

Current: small or none

Must see: large grouper below the wreck

The *Cedar Pride* has royal blood coursing through her holds and walkways. She is important to Aqaba as a sort of diving kingpin that helps bolster the local itinerary: without her, the resort would have to rely primarily on its reefs and pretty fish. At 80m in length, she is a sizeable wreck and has easy access from the shore, a mere 150m away. This is also one of the main sites for the few dayboats that make the daily (*enshala!*) one-hour journey from the Aqaba marina. The royal connection dates back to 1983, when King Hussein was inspired to create a living artificial reef programme with the help of his son, now King Abdullah II. With such credentials, the *Cedar Pride* was naturally given every priority. The Spanish-built ship received her name in 1982 after being bought by a Lebanese company, but was abandoned by her owners after a fire gutted her, killing two crew members. The then-prince took a leading hand in ensuring that the vessel was made safe for divers, and personally dived many of the sites along Aqaba's 27km coastline to find the ideal spot to site the wreck.

It was the Prince's decision to scuttle the ship between the two popular sites known as Rainbow Reef and the Japanese Gardens. All went fairly well to plan, with the explosives finally sending this 1960s Lebanese-registered cargo ship to the seabed in November 1985. A permanent buoy now marks the spot.

The wreck now rests with a slight list to port, nestling over two reefs at about 28m, where divers can swim

▼ Squirrelfish occupy coral ledges and overhangs.

JP Trenque

Jane Morgan

Jane Morgan

▲ Anthias fish are tended by shrimp at a cleaning station.

▼ Tyres still hang from the stern of Jordan's deep wreck, *Taiyong*.

right under the hull. Here, they may be lucky enough to bump into large grouper that have made the *Cedar Pride* their home. Squirrelfish are fairly abundant, as are sergeant majors, glassfish and lionfish. Coral colonisation has been comprehensive and is especially luxuriant in and around the crow's nest, making for dazzling pictures. As a deliberately sunken wreck, *Cedar Pride* is largely intact and has all the accoutrements of a working ship, from the many deck winches and gears, to the hefty propeller.

Ultimately, the *Cedar Pride* lives up to her billing as one of the Red Sea's most important wrecks. It is easy to spend up to an hour diving Aqaba's star attraction, and most divers come back for more. As with any wreck, once you have got your bearings and an understanding of the story behind her, subsequent dives can be much more enjoyable. A number of the dive operators in Aqaba offer nitrox fills, so this is an ideal site at which to take advantage of the benefits of an increased bottom time.

WRECK OF THE *TAIYONG*

Max depth: 60m

Skill level: advanced or technical; 50+ dives

Access: shore dive or dayboat

Current: usually light to medium strength

Must see: inner workings of the crane where it's joined to the barge

This is a heavyweight wreck in more than one sense. Not only is the *Taiyong* an imposing superstructure, but at nearly 60m at her deepest, she is also an extremely challenging dive. Technical knowledge of the conditions and good planning are important: the wreck lies right at the limits of air diving, and a long decompression stop – perhaps in the order of 20 minutes – should be taken into consideration when planning the dive.

The *Taiyong*, which is of Korean origin, was discovered by a team of technical divers carrying out work for the Aqaba Marine Park in 2004, having been scuttled at the turn of the century. She is quite unlike any other wreck in the Red Sea, and lies on her starboard side with her spectacular A-frame crane derrick stretching out some 30m down the sloping sandy seabed.

The derrick is the section to aim for at the start of the dive. You should be aware of the danger of nitrogen narcosis, which can be fairly pronounced at these depths. The view through the maze of metal supports towards the barge is impressive. Moving further along, the huge crane is fixed to the stern section, which is bedecked with impressive winches, gears and cables. These were the workhorse of the *Taiyong* when part of the Aqaba Port Authority shipping muscle during the 1970s, used to load and unload vessels anchored away from the jetties.

The wreck has a surprising level of coral growth, including a number of healthy gorgonians and black corals, the latter more often found in deeper waters. There is also a burgeoning sponge population. Fish life can be sparse, but schooling pelagics have been seen by divers at various times of year. At its shallowest, the wreck levels out at 37m. Diving on open circuit equipment, divers tend to spend no more than ten minutes on the wreck itself before leaving its shadowy structure to head for the reef wall, which lies almost straight ahead if you are following the line of the bow. With a lengthy decompression stop pending, there is the distraction of another of Aqaba's popular reefs, the Japanese Gardens, whose name derives from the pretty coral formations, inhabited by a wide variety of colourful fish.

Jane Morgan

▶ A diver inspects the A-frame derrick crane, the dominant feature of the *Taiyong* shipwreck.

Jane Morgan

THE TANK

Max depth: 6m

Skill level: novice

Access: shore dive or dayboat

Current: usually little or none

Must see: speckled grey morays under the tank tracks

The Tank is simply a must-do dive if you are in Jordan. To be honest, it is about as challenging as taking a bath, but it does present a unique Red Sea experience. Dive operators often schedule it at the start or end of the second dive of the day. Despite the fact that this American M40 anti-aircraft tank (not Russian, as was initially thought by some) has only been in the water since 1999, it has become heavily associated with diving in Aqaba. It rests at a depth of just 6m and is easily diveable from the shore, falling between the dive sites Oliver's Canyon and Seven Sisters.

Since the tank was sunk by the Jordanian Royal Ecological Diving Society, a number of Aqaba's fairly common species have taken up residence. Small grey peppered morays seem to enjoy the protection of the tank's armoury, as do the lionfish that now stand guard

Jane Morgan

▲ This anti-aircraft tank was sunk deliberately and has proven a popular novelty dive.

◀ Lined butterflyfish feed by pecking at coral polyps.

◀◀ Peppered moray eels can be seen hunting for small fish and crustaceans along the seagrass flats.

▶ A grouper pauses in its reef territory, where glassfish and soft coral mingle in a living kaleidoscope.

▶▶ A lyretail angelfish swims above a hard coral reef. (Alexander Mustard)

▼ A Mozambique host goby rests on hard coral.

in and around the guns – once part of the Jordanian military. If you are taking pictures it is worth trying to persuade others in the party to give you a head start, since the sandy seabed can soon whip up into a cloudy fog. This is not a difficult dive and some people even snorkel to enjoy the site. It is wonderfully quirky and great fun.

THE POWER STATION

Max depth:	40m plus
Skill level:	medium; 20+ dives
Access:	shore dive or dayboat
Current:	usually small or none
Must see:	goldies among the black coral

The Power Station is Aqaba's most notable wall dive. In the summer months, this vertical, 200m wall is excellent for encounters with schooling fish, big and small. Jacks and barracuda patrol the wall in dense schools, revealing another dimension to Jordan's tranquil diving experiences. You enter the site itself from a point about 5km from the town – either a short drive for shore diving, or a gently chugging boat journey of about half an hour from the marina. If shooting video, it is worth taking lights with you.

The site, which is named because of its proximity to an old power station, is best known for its overhangs

and large fan corals. Dive guides will easily be able to locate one particular place to find the more exotic black corals that seem to thrive in 30m-plus depths, and beautiful sea goldies, close cousins of the bright orange anthias, can be found sheltering from the currents here. Sharks are rare in this part of the Red Sea, but there are occasional summer sightings of the biggest fish of them all, the breathtaking whale shark. Encounters take place annually but, as is so often the case, the big stuff is hard to find. The months of June to August are your best bet, but there have been rare sightings in January, which, incidentally, is the best time to look out for the big rays, including graceful eagles and even giant mantas.

Other impressive pelagics include sunfish and the big, fast-swimming dogtooth tuna. Napoleon wrasse, thankfully no longer indulged by egg feeders, often sneak up behind divers.

After drifting along the wall, you have a good chance of tracking down some of the more elusive critters of the fringing reef system. High on everyone's list is the frogfish: Aqaba seems blessed with more than its fair share of these tropical oddballs, noted for their ability to disguise themselves as corals or sponges. Bright red painted frogfish – similar in colour to the Spanish dancer – are hard to find, but local guides have a good idea of where they are. And as they tend to spend long periods waiting for food, a photographer can easily return to the same spot to get those all-important pictures.

Jane Morgan

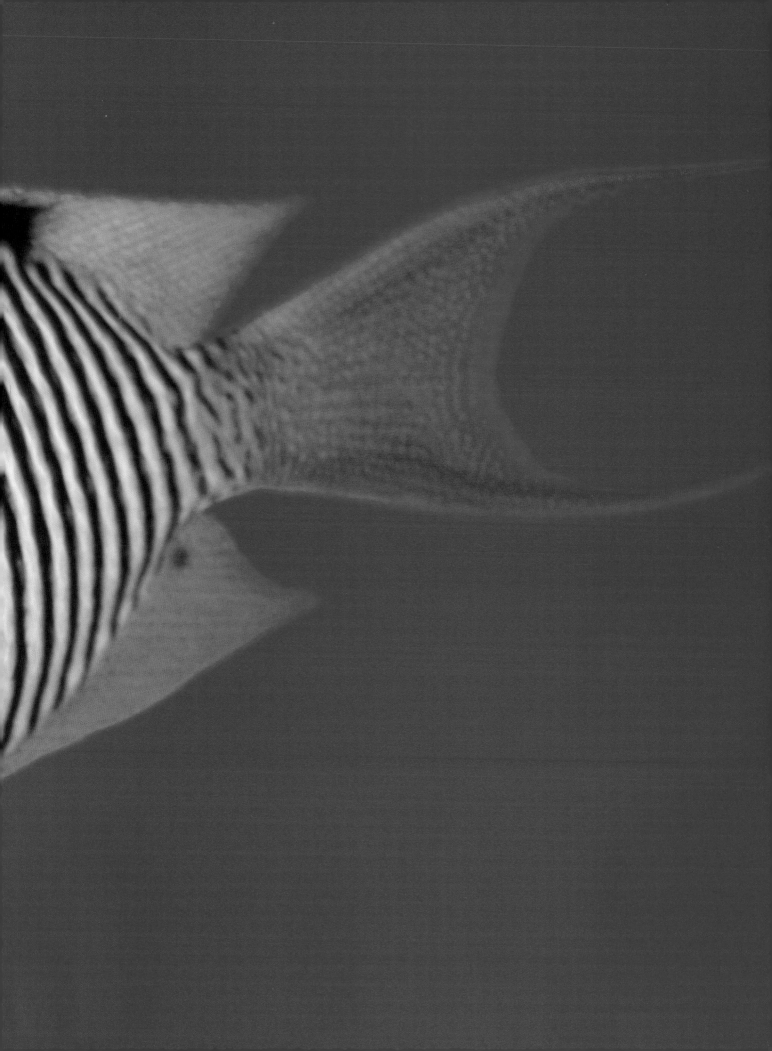

EILAT

THERE IS SOMETHING BOTH PROFOUND AND LASTING ABOUT A TRAINEE DIVER'S FIRST EXPERIENCE ON A TROPICAL REEF. THOSE DAZZLING COLOURS AND FEELINGS OF EUPHORIA REMAIN FIRMLY EMBEDDED IN YOUR PSYCHE.

Perhaps this is why Eilat has managed to impart its image as the world's underwater classroom – even though today more divers are trained in countries such as Australia and Egypt.

In the days when flying was still the preserve of the rich and famous, Eilat's luxury beachfront hotels epitomised the swagger and decadence of the jet set. Today, while these hotels continue to attract holidaymakers in their droves, low cost air travel has made Israel as accessible to the ordinary visitor as any destination in this region. Long before the rest of the Red Sea was catapulted into the diving stratosphere, Israel's tiny corner of the Gulf of Aqaba had established itself as a diving wonderland.

As the Red Sea began to open up further south, Eilat faced increasing competition, not just from Egyptian dive centres, but also from the popularizing – in the mid-Nineties – of liveaboard safaris. Yet the prolific fish life and safe, easy access from the pebble shores have ensured Eilat's survival as a place of open water learning. Ask anyone who has trained to dive in Eilat and they will wax lyrical about its most famous dive site, Moses Rock. It is true, however, that the once pristine coral reefs have suffered from too many careless divers over the years. Still, the good year-round weather and absence of dangerous currents has kept the local diving trade fairly buoyant.

In 1990, Eilat added Dolphin Reef to the equation. This has become a major attraction in Israel's southernmost city. According to the management's philosophy, the dolphins here are not captive, and only approach divers or snorkellers of their own volition. There is a fee for entering the enclosure, whether on scuba or snorkel.

Eilat also lies conveniently close to several other regional attractions. Aqaba, in neighbouring Jordan, is but a short taxi or bus ride away: visitors to Eilat often combine a trip over the border to visit the stupendous attractions at Petra and Wadi Rum. There is also the heavily salt-laden Dead Sea, where you can test the theory that it is possible to read a newspaper while floating unaided. Another option is to spend a day on one of the large sailing schooners that head for the Egyptian dive destination at Coral Island, where you get a better idea of the Red Sea's characteristic wall dives.

◄ A group of divers follow their guide, as Eilat's waters see a new generation of underwater explorers baptised.

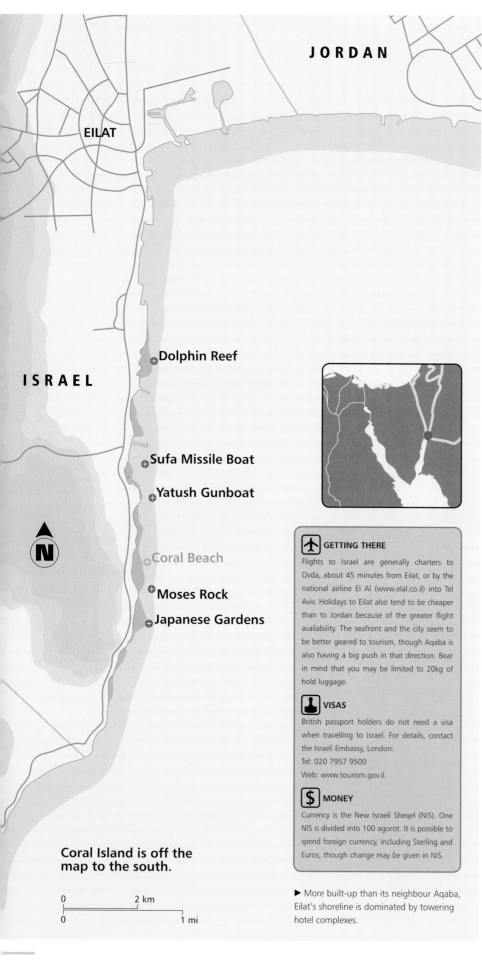

JORDAN

EILAT

ISRAEL

Dolphin Reef

Sufa Missile Boat

Yatush Gunboat

Coral Beach

Moses Rock

Japanese Gardens

N

Coral Island is off the
map to the south.

0   2 km

0   1 mi

GETTING THERE

Flights to Israel are generally charters to
Ovda, about 45 minutes from Eilat, or by the
national airline El Al (www.elal.co.il) into Tel
Aviv. Holidays to Eilat also tend to be cheaper
than to Jordan because of the greater flight
availability. The seafront and the city seem to
be better geared to tourism, though Aqaba is
also having a big push in that direction. Bear
in mind that you may be limited to 20kg of
hold luggage.

VISAS

British passport holders do not need a visa
when travelling to Israel. For details, contact
the Israeli Embassy, London:
Tel: 020 7957 9500
Web: www.tourism.gov.il.

$ MONEY

Currency is the New Israeli Sheqel (NIS). One
NIS is divided into 100 agorot. It is possible to
spend foreign currency, including Sterling and
Euros, though change may be given in NIS.

▶ More built-up than its neighbour Aqaba,
Eilat's shoreline is dominated by towering
hotel complexes.

Malcolm Nobbs

Jane Morgan

▲ Emperor angelfish are found around coral ledges.

▶ An intimate portrait of a striped butterflyfish, though the species is more often seen in pairs.

OTHER DIVE SITES

Coral Beach

 VISIBILITY

Ranges from quite poor, especially during the plankton blooms and after howling northerlies have blown through, to beautiful, clean 30m. Visibility is especially affected in the extensive shallow areas after poor weather.

WATER TEMPERATURE

This almost mirrors Aqaba, with the thermometer sliding from a 7mm wetsuit 21ºC in January, to a swimsuit-warm 28–29ºC in August.

 SEASONALITY

The most noticeable changes in Eilat are more to do with the climate. While the winter months provide a pleasant 21ºC surface temperature, the summer can be blisteringly hot. In June, July and August, when rainfall is unlikely, the mercury nudges the 40ºC mark. Much of the marine life in Eilat is present year-round, though some of the larger creatures are more often seen during the cooler months.

MOSES ROCK

Max depth: ±10 metres
Skill level: novice
Access: shore dive
Current: slight to none
Must see: glassfish, garden eels

Moses Rock, which falls within the protected area of the Eilat Marine Nature Reserve, has achieved an almost mythical status, thanks largely to the years of novice divers who have celebrated their moment of qualification with a photograph taken alongside this bustling coral outcrop. In fact, Moses Rock is probably one of the single most photographed reefs in the entire 2,000km-length of the Red Sea. The sandy seabed surrounding the pinnacle is dotted with a wide variety of hard and soft corals, and the fish population is lively and varied. Glassfish are ever present, which means their most common predator – the lionfish – are constantly on the prowl. Other usual suspects are also here, including anemonefish, morays, scorpionfish and sergeant majors.

The dive site is approached from the shore, and it takes no more than four or five minutes to swim or fin the 100m or so directly from Coral Beach. This makes Moses Rock an excellent and reasonably effortless introduction to the aquarium-like world of clear-visibility diving.

It has to be said, though, that this site is a victim of its own popularity, with the countless visiting divers having left their scars. It may have survived reasonably well

in the face of the daily onslaught, but it has certainly seen better days. Nearby is a well-populated garden eel community, which is well worth a visit. The trick with garden eels is to lie down gently on the seabed five to ten metres away and wait for them to emerge from the sand, waving in the current while picking off their tiny plankton prey. They always seem canny enough to realise when a diver is getting too close.

JAPANESE GARDENS

Max depth: 40m optimum
Skill level: novice
Access: shore dive and dayboat
Current: slight to none
Must see: table corals, blue-spotted stingrays

There is a vaguely Disneyesque quality to the Japanese Gardens dive site, for it is dominated by the spectacle of the Underwater Observatory Marine Park. This is basically a large aquarium offering a window on the Red Sea. Divers may also come across a yellow tourist submarine or glass bottom boat, both of which ply the vicinity. Having progressed from Moses Rock, this site offers a chance to explore further among the table corals and deeper reef wall. The shape of the table corals inspired the name Japanese Gardens, since they resemble oriental buildings. The site is mostly dived from the shore, but it is also visited by dayboats and can become very busy. Fish life is not dramatic, but it is possible to find small schools of barracuda and jacks. Ferret around on the sandy patches and you may also discover the

Jane Morgan

blue-spotted stingrays that are common throughout the Red Sea. Diver training is popular here, especially as the site offers easy depth changes to test buoyancy control, navigation and rescue skills.

DOLPHIN REEF

Max depth: ±18m

Skill level: novice

Access: shore dive

Current: slight to none

Must see: bottlenose dolphins – if they choose to seek you out

The commercial diving enclosure known as Dolphin Reef opened in 1990, giving holidaymakers the chance to mingle with these smiling cetaceans in a more natural environment. It covers an area of about 10km^2, and the owners insist the bottlenose dolphins are free to return to the wild as and when they choose. Dolphin interaction is also at the will of the animals. Some seem to be more curious and playful than others and over the years the level of human contact has inevitably grown. The reef also offers a programme to help children with a range of physical and mental ailments and disabilities. Children experience the dolphins either from the safety of a pontoon or in the water. Such encounters are well publicised around the world and it is claimed that they benefit the youngsters' wellbeing.

Visibility can be an issue for divers, and it is luck of the draw whether the dolphins actually make a close pass. Those who wish to experience Dolphin Reef should book in advance.

EILAT WRECKS (SUFA MISSILE BOAT AND YATUSH GUNBOAT)

Depth range: 20–30m

Skill level: intermediate/advanced

Access: shore dive

Current: small or none

Must see: the wrecks, with their developing coral growth

These two wrecks lie fairly close to each other and make an ideal introduction to the attractions of manmade dive sites. Both were deliberately sunk to add to Eilat's reputation as an underwater playground. The easiest of the two is the Sufa Missile Boat, which was scuttled in the mid-1990s to create an artificial reef. Much to the delight of the dive team, this 45-metre wreck settled upright on the seabed. Marine life slowly but surely took a hold on the wreck, and it has now firmly established itself on the Eilat dive circuit. This has, to a certain

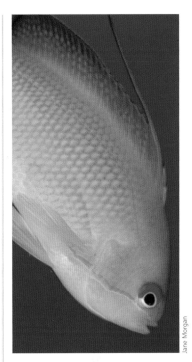

Jane Morgan

▲ Viewed up close, the familiar anthias of the Red Sea is even more beautiful.

◄ A Christmas tree worm extends its spiralling, delicate fronds to gather plankton.

extent, relieved some of the pressure on the resort's limited number of dive sites. In slightly deeper water is the Yatush Gunboat, providing cover for a few impressive grouper. Pelagics can also be seen swimming past.

CORAL ISLAND

Depth range: exceeds 30m on the eastern wall

Skill level: intermediate/advanced

Access: shore dive or cruise boat

Current: occasionally strong

Must see: eagle rays, turtles, anthias schools

Coral Island warrants a mention in this chapter because cruise boats from Eilat offer excursions to this small, historic island. Not all the tourists who take advantage of the trip are divers. Nonetheless, it is a leisurely day out, with one or two dives in Egyptian waters to add to your logbook. The diving is not difficult as such, but the walls on the eastern and southern sides are deeper than divers are used to in Eilat. This can therefore be a good way for beginners to broaden their experience. While the corals are hardly the most vibrant there is a reasonable variety and colour. Visibility also tends to be very good. Look out for solitary great barracuda, some of which grow to nearly 2m in length. Eagle rays and turtles are other notable inhabitants of this reef. The island is extremely close to the mainland, just a short distance south of the Egyptian village of Taba. It used to be under Israeli control, but is now part of Egypt, where it is called Pharaoh Island. The site is best known for its Moorish castle, built during the 12th century Crusades. A walk around the island followed by a lazy barbecue lunch is the norm. People taking the cruise from Eilat are often asked to submit their passports, but as it is a return day trip, no Egyptian visa is officially required.

◀ Set against the blue, clouds of anthias create the archetypal Red Sea scene.

▼ Blotched hawkfish rest on fire coral, seemingly unaffected by its stinging cells.

Alexander Mustard

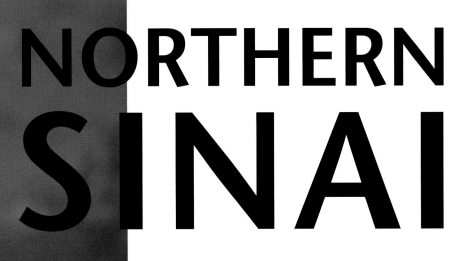

NORTHERN SINAI

TABA, NUWEIBA AND DAHAB ARE THREE MODEST DESTINATIONS THAT HAVE COME TO EXEMPLIFY THE 'RIVIERA' THEME OF THE HIGHLY SUCCESSFUL RED SEA TOURIST CAMPAIGN IN THE NORTHERN REACHES OF THE EGYPTIAN PENINSULA.

They are far less manic than the bustling resort of Na'ama Bay. This is where Egypt nudges the border of Israel at the upper most parts of the Gulf of Aqaba. Modern hotels and well-run diving centres reflect the more laid-back character of this part of Egypt, perhaps better known among veterans in its previous 'hippie' incarnation. The more benign diving conditions belie the quality of marine life to be found so close to shore – in some cases just a few metres from the water's edge adjacent the hotels. Perhaps the most famous, even infamous, of the dive sites is the 'Blue Hole' at Dahab. Divers who conquer the archway at 55 metres – exiting onto the 'reef wall proper' – feel they have notched a challenging ambition. It is however also one of the most hazardous dive sites, having claimed a number of lives over the years.

Further north, Nuweiba and Taba have flourished as more upmarket retreats where visitors find their holiday focussed on life in and around their hotel, from dining to diving. The growth of tourism here is aided considerably by the proximity of a local international airport which is served from the UK by both Gatwick and Manchester. Though much of the diving is shored-based, there is a real bounty of marine life, from the more unusual and clumsy-looking frogfish to the abundant populations of lionfish and small moray eels including the peppered variety. Such concentrations of easily accessible wildlife coupled with healthy coral gardens make this part of the Red Sea especially rewarding for photographers and videographers who are happy to park up on a sandy seabed and take pictures to their heart's content without the hassles of strong currents.

Both Israel and Jordan are easily accessed from here, either by road or ferry to Aqaba (this takes about 90 minutes).

These northern resorts of Sinai are offered very much as an alternative to the crowds of Sharm el Sheikh.

◀ Long considered a rarity in the Red Sea, frogfish are being found in greater numbers as new sites open up in Taba and Nuweiba.

Jane Morgan

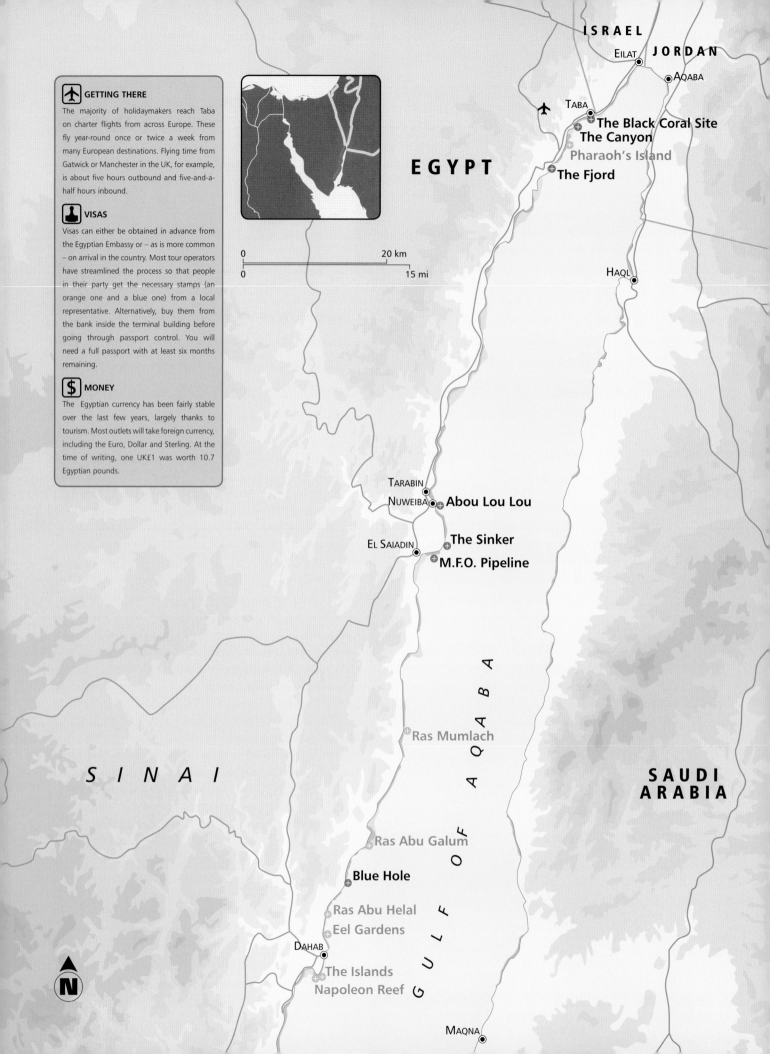

ISRAEL

JORDAN

EILAT

AQABA

TABA

The Black Coral Site
The Canyon
Pharaoh's Island

The Fjord

EGYPT

HAQL

✈ **GETTING THERE**

The majority of holidaymakers reach Taba on charter flights from across Europe. These fly year-round once or twice a week from many European destinations. Flying time from Gatwick or Manchester in the UK, for example, is about five hours outbound and five-and-a-half hours inbound.

👤 **VISAS**

Visas can either be obtained in advance from the Egyptian Embassy or – as is more common – on arrival in the country. Most tour operators have streamlined the process so that people in their party get the necessary stamps (an orange one and a blue one) from a local representative. Alternatively, buy them from the bank inside the terminal building before going through passport control. You will need a full passport with at least six months remaining.

💲 **MONEY**

The Egyptian currency has been fairly stable over the last few years, largely thanks to tourism. Most outlets will take foreign currency, including the Euro, Dollar and Sterling. At the time of writing, one UK£1 was worth 10.7 Egyptian pounds.

0 _____ 20 km
0 _____ 15 mi

TARABIN
NUWEIBA **Abou Lou Lou**

The Sinker
EL SAIADIN
M.F.O. Pipeline

Ras Mumlach

G U L F   O F   A Q A B A

S I N A I

SAUDI
ARABIA

Ras Abu Galum

Blue Hole

Ras Abu Helal
Eel Gardens

DAHAB

The Islands
Napoleon Reef

MAQNA

N

BLUE HOLE, DAHAB

Max depth: 100m in the hole

Skill level: experience with trimix if you want to navigate the arch

Access: shore dive

Currents: none

Must see: yourself – safely back to the surface

Diving the legendary Blue Hole in Dahab is risky but exhilarating. It's not a dive for the faint-hearted. Over the years, it has been associated with a wide range of approaches and attitudes, ranging from the highly professional to the downright reckless. People have lost their lives here, drawn by the lure of the deep and perhaps that trite maxim in the world of adventure: 'because it's there'. On the rugged shore parallel to the Blue Hole's opening, divers of all levels perspire in the Egyptian sun as they don their wetsuits and lug their tanks to the water's edge in readiness for one of the most challenging of dives. In the winter months drysuits are popular, as temperatures can fall to near 20ºC. This, especially at depth, can have a significant effect on how nitrogen narcosis creeps up on a diver. If you are planning to negotiate the arch at 55m, the choice is either pushing at the limits of air or using a mixed gas that reduces nitrogen narcosis and the threat of oxygen toxicity. Our advice is to venture no deeper than 50m on air (and even then only if you have built up the necessary experience), and to undergo trimix training if you want

to carry out this sort of dive. There are plenty of training agencies in the area.

Visibility in the Blue Hole can vary enormously, sometimes decreasing so much that the large arch is not obvious until you get within ten metres. But to many people the point of the dive seems to be making it through to the other side, to the outer reef wall. Since the arch is on the opposite side of this remarkable, giant coral chimney it is best to snorkel or at least swim on the surface until you find a suitable place to descend.

You should not take too long with the descent once you have got your bearings. The alien-like glow of the arch looms into view at 55m and, even allowing for the soporific effects of the inevitable narcosis, the experience is like arriving at the entrance of a cathedral. It is possible to make it through to the outer wall in just a few minutes. Keep a check on your depth gauge and buoyancy, as it is all too easy to drop quickly without noticing. This dive is less about the marine life and more about the experience and conquering the challenge, but once you're on the outer wall and moving back towards the surface the corals become increasingly more colourful and luxuriant.

Of course, there are people who come to the Blue Hole who don't dive the arch. Others, meanwhile, enjoy the safety of snorkelling without the worries of a current. Whatever your approach, there is always the option afterwards to enjoy a local tea and *shisha* pipe (or hubbly bubbly) on an Arabic carpet in the tranquil surrounds of Dahab's Blue Hole lagoon.

VISIBILITY

Northern Sinai is famous for the reliable clarity of its water, though currents, plankton blooms and sand storms can affect it from time to time. Generally later in the year is clearest. Visibility is usually around 20–30m. Plankton blooms are less predictable but are more frequent in the summer months.

WATER TEMPERATURE

Sea temperatures vary from a chilly 20–21ºC from January to April, to 28ºC in the summer. The hottest months are July, August and September. In the winter you will need a 5mm wetsuit with a neoprene or lycra hood when diving.

SEASONALITY

May, June, July and August are often regarded as the best months to dive in the Red Sea as the fish life seems much more abundant. The end of May through to the start of July is often regarded as the prime time for shark activity.

▼ Longnose hawkfish are skittish, but much prized by visiting photographers.

Jane Morgan

▶ The Sinker provides a basis for coral, and a playground for divers.

NUWEIBA

Nuweiba combines the charm of Bedouin Egypt with the demands of a modern-day resort. It also has an important port from which ferries travel daily to Aqaba. It may not be a large, bustling resort, but access to the less-touristy attractions in the Sinai mountains and the not-so-crowded Red Sea dive sites make Nuweiba more of an escapist destination than most. Perhaps the best way to decide if this is the place for you is to think award-winning pictures. This is just the location to fill up gigabytes of space on your memory stick with the sort of images that often adorn diving magazines and guide books.

The diving is not over-challenging but there are some unusual sites. The house reef, known as Abou Lou Lou, is a lion-sized delight; then there's the 'MFO Pipeline' and another strange but compelling dive known as 'The Sinker'. Access to the house reef tends to be from the sandy shore, alongside a jetty that has featured in many a professional photograph. With a good wide-angle or fisheye lens, the jetty and its white sandy seascape provide an excellent underwater canvas. A large cloud of small silver fish is a regular feature of this part of the dive, adding to its photogenic qualities.

ABOU LOU LOU

Max depth: 20m

Skill level: 1–5 dives

Access: shore dive

Currents: small

Must see: lionfish galore

Moving north from the entry point, where the sandy bottom slopes gently to around 20m, there is an expanse of seagrass that provides a habitat for creatures including crocodile snake eels and several species of shrimp. Finding them is reward enough for an entire dive, but 'Abou Lou Lou' is full of surprises and there are more in store. Strange-looking stargazers are just as likely to

have a beady eye on you, as is the rare mimic octopus, whose cunning ability to adopt different shapes, colours and patterns makes it a true survival expert. Beyond the seagrass area and over a small gully lies a thriving coral garden, where good-sized grouper are among the many clients that use the reef's shrimp cleaning services.

THE SINKER

Max depth: 35m

Skill level: 15-plus dives

Access: shore dive

Currents: small to medium

Must see: boxer shrimps and glassy sweepers

So to 'The Sinker', which is either a good walk or, more usually, a 4x4 trip from the dive centre. On the face of it, this doesn't sound like much of an offering: it is little more than a mooring chain and buoy anchored on the seabed, albeit in the wrong place and therefore of no use to surface traffic. The traffic underwater, however, is exquisite. This discarded human contraption has been transformed from a long, narrow mooring line into a delightful habitat packed with Red Sea characters: a wizened frogfish sits atop the buoy; angelfish, glassfish and bright orange anthias all dart about; and soft corals flow from top to bottom as though in a fashion parade. Divers usually approach this dive from shore, swimming for about five to ten minutes before descending to the deepest section. Then it's a case of slowly perusing the exotic marine oasis on the way back to the surface.

M.F.O. PIPELINE

Max depth: 20m

Skill level: 5 dives

Access: shore dive

Currents: small

Must see: look out for colourful frogfish

Another dive site worth a mention is the 'M.F.O. (Multiple Forces and Observers) Pipeline', where some of the larger animals can be found. These include turtles, barracuda and – most exciting – rare guitar sharks that lurk on the bottom. The pipeline itself is a dramatic sight, looking more like a modern sculpture that's been laid out on the seabed as a divers' playground. The pipes are smothered in coral, and it's a regular haunt for our old friend the frogfish.

Because of the variety of fish life around Nuweiba, the sites have been likened to the 'muck diving' of Lembeh Straits in Indonesia. It is certainly a place to get up close and personal with a range of the Red Sea's more unusual critters.

▼ A stargazer looks up in search of prey – he'd eat you if he could!

JP Trenque

Jane Morgan

▲ During research for this book, a rare sighting of the mimic octopus was made in Taba – the species was not thought to live so far north.

OTHER DIVE SITES

Eel Gardens
Napoleon Reef
Pharaoh's Island
Ras Mumlach
Ras Abu Galum
Ras Abu Helal
The Islands

TABA

Taba is as near as you can get to Israel without actually setting foot in the country. It comprises a small village and the resort hotels. Taba Heights, about 20 minutes by road further south, is exclusively made up of resort hotels, with a golf course and a good-sized, reputable dive centre. Regular charter flights ensure a steady, year-round traffic of holidaymakers into Taba's own international airport, which lies a cool 800m above sea level and is some 45 minutes from the hotels or an additional one hour's drive from Nuweiba, further south. Being so close to Israel, and therefore Jordan, day trip options include the marvels of Petra and the vast desert wilderness of Wadi Rum. Alternatively, there's the lively nightlife of Eilat.

Taba's diving sites are akin to that of the fish-rich sites of Aqaba. The best of the bunch is within easy reach of the Taba Hilton Hotel, whose own dive centre boasts three distinctive sites in close proximity: the excellent house reef; neighbouring Black Coral site; and an impressive spot known as the Canyon. There are others, too, but these three demonstrate the qualities that make this area especially appealing to photographers. No real currents also makes this an ideal training area.

Taba has an abundance of marine oddities that are hard to find elsewhere in the Red Sea. A gentle amble from the sandy beaches to the House Reef reveals a veritable smorgasbord of danger and delight. Big stonefish, looking like prehistoric rocks, seem determined not to be driven from their shallow hunting grounds by the recently arrived resort divers. If anything, it is the clumsy, unobservant visitor who needs to be wary. The humble frogfish is also at home in these northernmost reaches of the Red Sea: the dive centres here claim even greater numbers per dive site than at Aqaba.

THE BLACK CORAL SITE

Max depth: 25m

Skill level: 5 dives

Access: shore dive

Currents: small

Must see: peppered morays by the handful

The Black Coral site, which dips down below 25m, does not actually possess forests of black corals but is teeming with fish. Such is the density of peppered morays that they sometimes bunch together, weaving their multiple heads in unison like a medusa. Another impressive feature of this reef is the amount of symbiotic cleaning, with grouper and the like queuing for their daily manicure.

THE CANYON

Max depth: 32m

Skill level: 15 dives

Access: shore dive

Currents: small

Must see: keep eyes peeled for gorgeous pyjama nudibranch

Further south still there is the Canyon, which is, strictly speaking, half a canyon – the coral forming a ledge on one side that gives way to a sandy-bottomed gully. The stonefish, frogfish and octopus have decided that this is the best real estate in town: they occupy the best ledges, overhangs and pinnacles, in keeping with the adjacent Hilton's reputation for top accommodation. Of course, the diving does get deeper if you negotiate the length of the Canyon, which drops well past 40m. With so many distractions, it's easy to end up with a decompression stop.

THE FJORD

Max depth: 24m

Skill level: 5 dives

Access: dayboat

Currents: small

Must see: the hole or undersea well-like formation

As for the Fjord, this site is accessible only by boat and is on the regular run from the Taba Heights. The site itself is a natural hole – not quite on the scale of the infamous Blue Hole of Dahab, but an interesting site nevertheless. The hole appears at about 16–18m and among other things has some very beautiful red anemones.

▶ A dive isn't a dive without a nudibranch, and this species, a pyjama nudibranch, is a regular sighting on Taba's reefs.

Charles Hood/oceans-image.com

SOUTHERN SINAI

WHEN THE SUN GOES DOWN BEHIND THE JAGGED PEAKS OF THE SINAI PENINSULA, THE SEA BECOMES AN OIL PAINTING OF SCORCHED RED AND OCEAN BLUE, REFLECTING A GOLDEN TRIANGLE THAT IS VISIBLE FROM OUTER SPACE.

Little wonder that this extraordinary stretch of water became known as the Red Sea. It is indeed a unique natural environment, where a biological paradise beneath the surface meets a desert wilderness above. It is also a place of great significance to religions around the globe: Ras Mohammed, whose name is believed to derive from wind-carved cliffs that resemble the prophet, is a potent symbol of the peninsula's place in Arabic history; and it is in the Straits of Tiran that Moses is said to have parted the Red Sea.

The Peninsula has a long and turbulent history. In the late 19th century, when Britain was still a naval super power, the Ottomans relinquished the Sinai and a British governor was installed. Then there was the famous Six-Day War in 1967, which resulted in Israel gaining control of the peninsula. In a region burdened by political upheaval, 12 years passed before a peace deal was signed giving Sinai back to the Egyptians.

The real story of Sinai, however, dates back some 30 million years to when two continents began pulling apart, tearing at the earth's mantle to leave behind land and seascapes of profound natural beauty. Today the peninsula straddles the Arabian and African tectonic plates like a giant wedge facing southwards. It comprises some 98,000 square kilometres of granite, sandstone and desert, rising to the highest peaks of Gebel Katrina at 2,641m. On either side, the Sinai is flanked by important shipping routes: to the east, the Gulf of Aqaba; to the west, the Gulf of Suez.

Famous diving pioneers Jacques Yves Cousteau and the glamorous couple Hans and Lotte Hass were among the first few to explore this virgin undersea territory. Cousteau's lyrical French narrative in

Alexander Mustard

◄ Golden anthias fish billow from a typical south Sinai reef, providing visitors with one of diving's most iconic scenes.

Alexander Mustard

▲ Dive boats at Ras Katy, Sharm el Sheikh.

the compelling film *Silent World* opened the public's eyes to the Red Sea's natural treasures. It would be many years, however, before new and affordable scuba technology paved the way for the masses. In the 1970s and 80s, this barren desert wilderness saw only a few adventuring pioneers prepared to rough it with the Bedouins under the stars. Their reward was some of the best tropical diving in the world, unhindered by crowds of subaqua tourists. Slowly, however, the hotels and dive centres took centre stage in Na'ama Bay. At first, facilities were basic, but the advent of Sharm el Sheikh International Airport changed everything. Soon tourists were flocking in on charter flights from all over Europe to take advantage of low-cost holidays. Not only did Sharm become a focus for the trained diver: it also developed quickly as a place to learn. The fringing reef around the peninsula offered a vast array of dive sites to suit every level of experience.

Dozens of dive centres were soon competing for the hugely expanded market of novices and veterans clambering to see the best the northern Red Sea has to offer. Such was the scale of boat traffic, the authorities built the nearby Sharm Marina to cope with the ever growing fleet of vessels. Further north, the less crowded resorts of Taba, Nuweiba and Dahab attracted a more laidback style of diver. But even these resorts have now given in to the commercial demands of the mainstream travel trade, with luxury hotels, restaurants and even golf courses sprouting on these desert shores.

Topographically, diving on the Sinai varies considerably from one site to another. There are sloping sandy shelves, gaping crevasses, deep blue holes, dramatic walls, vertical dropoffs and imposing pinnacles that provide homes and anchorage to a wealth of marine life.

The Straits of Tiran, at the mouth of the Gulf of Aqaba, have four remarkable reef systems, which have proved hazardous to shipping over the years. An armada of dayboats converges on these reefs, but the power of the currents sweeping over the lush coral walls keeps them in relatively good health. Big animals can be seen here, everything from grey reef sharks to giant manta rays, scalloped hammerheads and even an occasional whale shark or tiger shark. By contrast, the 'Gardens' on the northern shores of Na'ama Bay provide the perfect haven for the beginner to learn and see. Once you've won your spurs, though, there is one destination on the Sinai Peninsula that is impossible to ignore: at the world-renowned Shark and Yolanda reefs you can experience true high-voltage diving during the summer months, with numerous varieties of shark and large schools of jacks, barracuda and snapper all converging in the abyssal waters.

 GETTING THERE

The majority of holidaymakers reach Sharm el Sheikh on charter flights from across Europe. These fly year-round once or twice a week from many European destinations. Flying time from Gatwick or Manchester in the UK, for example, is about five hours outbound and five-and-a-half hours inbound. If you fancy combining a trip to Cairo with your holiday there are daily flights to the capital on many airlines. Egypt Air (www.egyptair.com) offers connecting flights from Cairo to Sharm and also to and from Luxor. A more long-winded way of getting to Sharm is by flying to Hurghada and then catching the catamaran/ferry service. This usually runs on time, but bad weather can cause cancellations.

 VISAS

Visas are easy to obtain. You can either get them in advance from the Egyptian Embassy or – as is more common – on arrival in the country. Most tour operators have streamlined the process so that people in their party get the necessary stamps (an orange one and a blue one) from a local representative. Alternatively, buy them from the bank inside the terminal building before going through passport control. You will need a full passport with at least six months remaining. The fee is waived for people entering Egypt by land at Taba, if they are staying in the Gulf of Aqaba or visiting St. Catherine's Monastery in the Sinai. When filling in the visa entry form, use clear block capitals; if you fail to do this, the immigration official will simply rewrite it and the whole process will take longer.

 MONEY

Egyptian cash is adorned with images of its glorious past: from the legendary Pharaoh Ramses to the boy king Tutankhamun. The currency has been fairly stable over the years, largely thanks to tourism. Most outlets will take foreign currency, including the Euro, Dollar and Sterling. At the time of writing, one UK£1 was worth 10.86 Egyptian pounds.

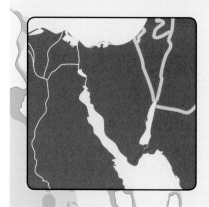

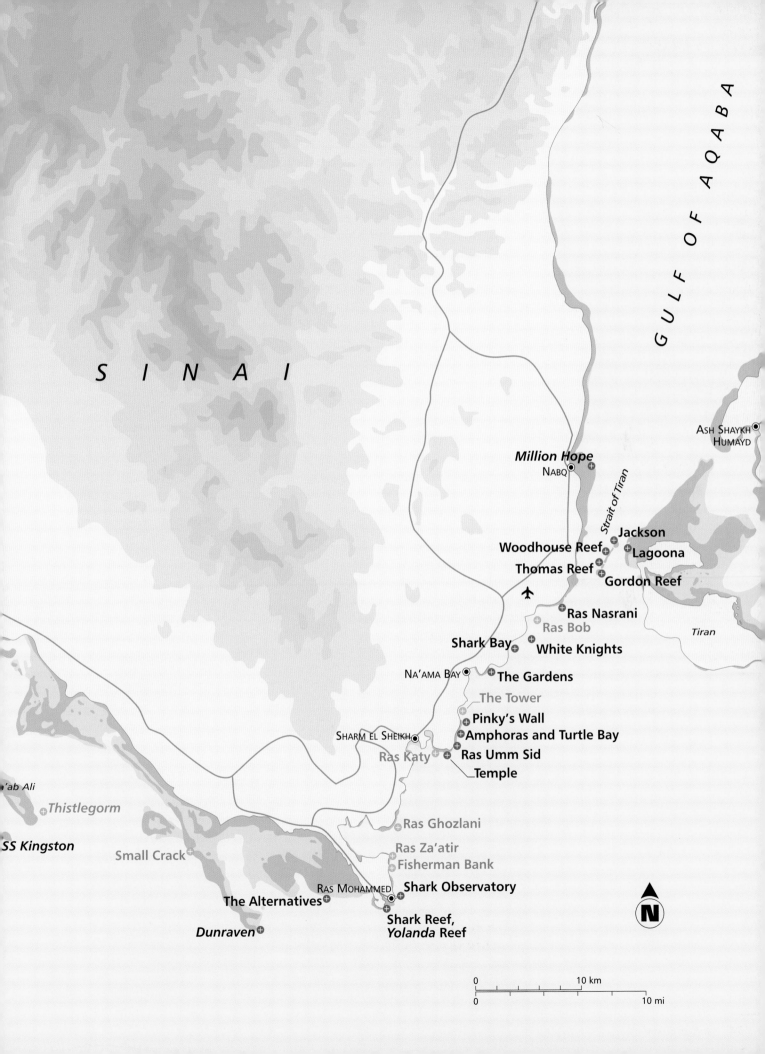

GULF OF AQABA

SINAI

ASH SHAYKH HUMAYD

Strait of Tiran

Million Hope
NABQ

Jackson

Woodhouse Reef

Lagoona

Thomas Reef

Gordon Reef

Ras Nasrani

Tiran

Ras Bob

Shark Bay

White Knights

NAʻAMA BAY

The Gardens

The Tower

Pinky's Wall

Amphoras and Turtle Bay

SHARM EL SHEIKH

Ras Katy

Ras Umm Sid

Temple

ʻab Ali

Thistlegorm

Ras Ghozlani

Ras Zaʻatir

Fisherman Bank

SS Kingston

Small Crack

Shark Observatory

The Alternatives

RAS MOHAMMED

Dunraven

Shark Reef,
Yolanda Reef

N

0   10 km

0   10 mi

VISIBILITY

The northern Red Sea is famous for the reliable clarity of its water, though currents, plankton blooms and sand storms can affect it. There is no hard and fast rule dictating when the visibility is at its best, but generally later in the year is clearest. Exceptional visibility can exceed 40m, though 20–30m is more usual. Plankton blooms are less predictable but are more frequent in the summer months in the northern Red Sea, while the reverse is often true in the Deep South.

WATER TEMPERATURE

Sea temperatures vary by anything up to 10°C over the year, from a chilly 20–21°C from January to April, to a swimming pool 28°C in the summer. The hottest months are July, August and September. As a rule, you will need a minimum 5mm wetsuit with a neoprene or lycra hood when diving in the winter months. When it's hot, a 3mm shorty may suffice, but a 5mm may still be preferable if you are diving three times a day.

SEASONALITY

May, June, July and August are often regarded as the best months to dive in the Red Sea. The colours are more vibrant, the sun is high in the sky and the fish life seems much more abundant. The end of May through to the start of July is often regarded as the prime time for shark activity, especially at the Ras Mohammed sites. The large schools of snapper, barracuda and jacks tend to appear at sites such as Shark and *Yolanda* Reefs in June, July and August, tailing off as the year goes by. Tiger shark activity here also tends to occur in June and July, while May and June is the season for hammerheads at Tiran.

OTHER DIVE SITES

Fisherman Bank
Ras Bob
Ras Ghozlani
Ras Katy
Ras Za'atir
Small Crack
Thistlegorm (see also p123)
The Tower

▶▶ In the peak months of summer, Shark Reef comes alive with schooling fish, from the visiting snapper to the reef's most colourful inhabitants.

▶ A photographer displays the requisite buoyancy control as he captures a hard coral scene at Ras Mohammed.

SHARK REEF / *YOLANDA* REEF (RAS MOHAMMED)

Depth: 800m wall; maximum depth 40m

Skill level: 20 dives

Access: early morning departure from Sharm el Sheikh or liveaboard

Currents: can be strong and unpredictable, some down-currents

Must see: Shark Reef's vertical wall; schooling barracuda and snapper in summer; *Yolanda's* toilets

Ras Mohammed is a part of diving folklore. At the head of the Sinai peninsula, two pinnacles breach the surface like giant coral jewels: these are known as Shark Reef and *Yolanda* Reef. When Shark Reef is at its best, the sheer vertical face of the wall looms into view like an undersea mountain waiting to be scaled. It is the reef of a thousand stories, told over and over by dive guides and their guests. Sure, it can appear dull and almost lifeless on a cold winter's day. But from May to August, and even occasionally in December, Ras Mohammed can equal the best dive sites anywhere. The world-famous marine biologist Dr Eugenie Clark called it, simply: 'my favourite place on Earth'.

The appeal of Shark Reef is its delightful unpredictability. Most divers enter the water near the sloping gulley to the east. Dive boats usually prepare their divers so that everyone is ready to hit the water when they get about 20m from the reef. This is when you should take time to orient yourself: you need to be able to swim in the direction of the reef, and it is easy to lose your sense of direction once the descent has begun. Almost immediately – and this is most pronounced during the summer months – the swirling schools of jacks and snapper appear and the magic of this reef becomes evident.

Ultimately, your entry will depend on the currents, which can be very powerful – especially around the time of the full moon – even when surface conditions appear calm. Once at the wall, try to resist the urge to fly past the reef without savouring the moment or the marine life. Dive guides often try to keep up a steady pace to ensure the party has enough air to make it to the broken remnants of the *Yolanda* wreck. If you are frugal with your air, this should not be a problem.

The trick is to establish where the fish activity is taking place and to get in there! At the head of the wall, at depths of 10–30m, you should find a 'sweet spot' where schooling fish congregate in great numbers. The wall itself is just as intoxicating: in places, it seems

Alexander Mustard

Charles Hood/oceans-image.com

▲ The spilled cargo of toilets provides one of the sea's most unusual sights at Yolanda Reef, where the main wreck has plummeted far below the range of sport divers.

to slope inwards, beckoning the diver to drop deeper and deeper. It is alarmingly easy to find yourself below 40m while innocently enjoying the spectacle: Napoleon wrasse travel back and forth, happily checking out nearby divers; jacks and flutemouths sometimes hitch a ride, hovering in the diver's bubbles; and batfish congregate here in greater numbers than on almost any other Red Sea reef.

Then, fingers crossed, it's time to find out first-hand why Shark Reef gets its name. A number of the big boys can turn up here: grey reef sharks are completely at home in the rich waters of the wall; black-tip reef sharks are frequently seen; on one balmy July morning, the author even witnessed a pair of sinewy silky sharks bursting through the massed ranks of jacks. But there can be no more daunting and exhilarating experience than meeting a four-metre tiger shark surging up the wall, looking mean and hungry. At times, divers have encountered up to three or four tigers approaching them at close quarters, unperturbed by the bubbles.

Keep a constant eye out, both above and below, as it's impossible to judge where the action will come from next. Sometimes, in fact, it has shifted to *Yolanda* Reef. A deep valley lies between the corner of Shark Reef and *Yolanda*, where currents sometimes drain downward

like a waterfall. There are a few sizeable sea fans and clumps of fire coral growth at this point, and you should stick close to these to avoid the currents.

You will then reach the most famous toilets in the diving world. These are the porcelain remnants from the sinking of the *Yolanda* freighter in the early 1980s, and they are where most dives tend to conclude. For a while after the ship sank, the majority of the wreck lay in the channel for all to see. But eventually she succumbed to stormy weather and broke up. A substantial part tumbled down the reef wall, leaving behind the now famous collection of bathroom ceramics.

With the advent of technical diving came ever deeper adventures, and so it was that in May 2005 the British divers Leigh Cunningham and Mark Andrews found the rest of the ship on a shelf at a depth of more than 145m. In the process, they went even deeper, reaching an incredible 160m.

It's a lot less deep, but diving around the broken toilet zone is still a lot of fun. Currents here can flush through at a fair speed, which means plenty of wildlife – the unusual cargo providing hiding places for a variety of fish, corals and invertebrates. This is the place to carry out decompression stops and enjoy the reef before surfacing. Be wary of the zodiacs racing around trying to pick out their dive party. It's especially hazardous if the sea state is choppy, and delayed surface marker buoys are strongly recommended. Depending on the currents, dive guides will usually advise you to surface close to the reef wall and then move out, so that the zodiacs are at less risk of being swept onto the corals when they pick you up.

Back on the boat, it's time to tell your ultimate Ras Mohammed story.

SS *KINGSTON*

Depth: 19m

Skill level: 10 dives

Access: dayboat & liveaboard

Currents: none to medium

Must see: swim-throughs on the aft section; twin boilers; vertical struts buzzing with surgeonfish

The *Kingston* is a captivating wreck dive. She is located next to the reef at Shag Rock, a short distance from the mighty *Thistlegorm*, and an easy dive with which to end the day. The dive is only feasible in flat calm seas, as the wreck breaches the surface and is subject to strong swells at times. Still, it can be a gem of a dive. The cargo of coal may have been far from glamorous, but today the decking and remaining skeletal structure is awash with beautiful soft corals and teeming with fishlife.

One issue should be cleared up. This vessel is not the 'Sarah H', even though this name has been associated with it for a number of years. The confusion started when the pioneering liveaboard skipper David Hillel jokingly named the wreck after his wife, Sarah. Spread by word of mouth and an unfortunate inclusion in an early guidebook, the name stuck until the wreck was properly researched.

The story of the *Kingston* dates back to 1871 in Sunderland, where she was launched as one of the new generation of steam-driven cargo ships. She came to grief a decade later, when she failed to navigate the treacherous reefs in this area. Today dive boats tend to tie up at the stern, which is still mostly intact. As you progress towards the bow section, the wreck becomes increasingly broken-up, but marine life is prolific throughout the structure. When the sea is calm, the bustling schools of anthias reflect a gorgeous orange on the surface. Emperor angelfish and bannerfish provide a more regal atmosphere and help disguise the ordinariness of the Kingston's former life.

Inside the wreck, a canopy of beams and cross supports makes for a delightful swim-through, with the sunlight streaming down from above. Two coral-encrusted boilers can be found amidships, straddling a dense collection of finger and pulse corals. Off the starboard

WORLD RECORD DIVE AT *YOLANDA* REEF

In December 2005 two British technical divers carried out an extraordinary world record dive at Ras Mohammed when they descended the dark blue depths of the reef to locate the remains of the *Yolanda*. The technical diving duo Mark Andrews and Leigh Cunningham made it to the stern of the wreck at a staggering depth of 205m, during a marathon dive that lasted three hours, 40 minutes. In May of that year Andrews and Cunningham had already found the forward section of the *Yolanda* at 145m, and they could not resist the prospect of going all the way.

A major training programme, combined with endless hours of preparation and the support of a 12-man team made the dive possible. Despite all the planning, there were last minute hitches and a few nervous moments trying to track down the necessary equipment. Sharm el Sheikh's hyperbaric chamber and the local search and rescue team were put on standby. A number of 'shallower' dives were made, to depths of 150m. Everything was in place. Finally, on 9 December 2005, in excellent conditions, they reached the stern of the *Yolanda*. Andrews recalls: 'As we levelled, we could see that we were just under the stern of the wreck and that the ship was perched on a ledge roughly 40m wide. Beyond this, a vertical wall descended into the abyss. The wreck had slid down the reef walls and slammed into this small ledge stern first, the rest of the wreck had crumpled under the force and there she rests today, slowly filling with sand.'

The pair had made history, and in the process had helped solve the mystery of what had happened to the *Yolanda* wreck when she slid down the wall all those years ago. With technical diving becoming an increasing feature of the Red Sea, doubtless more will be discovered and new records broken in the future.

side lie her two masts, both fairly well decayed and smothered in marine life. Another distinctive feature of the bow section is the upright frames that jut out from the seabed at 8–9m, like a monstrous ribcage. Sohal surgeonfish behave in a brave territorial fashion when divers dare to encroach on their piece of the wreck, offering easy photo opportunities. With such a generous quota of schooling fish, don't be surprised if, late in the afternoon, you hear the squeals and clicks of bottlenose dolphins. Though, as is so often the case, you are more likely to see them once you are back on the boat.

▶▶ A school of chevron barracuda forms a spectacular defensive spiral formation at Shark Reef, Ras Mohammed. (JP Trenque)

▼ A regal angelfish shelters in the reef.

Alexander Mustard

DUNRAVEN

Depth: 32m at stern

Skill level: 10+ dives

Access: dayboat and liveaboard

Currents: none to medium

Must see: propeller at 32m; glassfish around the boilers; crocodilefish on the sand

The *Dunraven* is a Red Sea classic: a hugely enjoyable wreck with a fascinating history. Despite the fact that the ageing hulk lies upside down, its depth and accessibility provide more than enough interest for an entire dive. The vessel's story takes us back to the heady days of ship engineering in the late 19th century, when she was built in Newcastle, England: an iron screw steamer capable of a steady eight knots.

However, these facts were obscured when the wreck was discovered in the 1970s. A certain dive operator keen to promote this new attraction suggested that the *Dunraven* was a legacy of the days of Lawrence of Arabia, and laden with treasure. Doubtless the story was concocted to attract tourists and the media, and it did the trick. Not even the BBC could resist this charming deception and made a television programme about it. The simple truth is that the *Dunraven* was on a return journey from Bombay to England in 1876 when she struck a reef at Sha'ab Mahmud. The legendary TE Lawrence was not involved!

Today the wreck is mostly favoured by liveaboards, though day boats from Hurghada do stray in this direction, mostly to dive the *Thislegorm* and the *Rosalie Moller*. Divers tend to be dropped in either at the stern or the bow, then make their way down the upturned hull, following the keel to the propeller. There is a dense growth of hard coral encrusting the ship, complemented by a healthy smattering of fishlife.

The *Dunraven* bottoms out at 32m, though the bow section is much shallower. It's a good opportunity to learn the art of wreck penetration, as the interior is spacious and ambient light filters through cracks in the hull. There are large gaping holes on her starboard side, along with the two rusting masts lying perpendicular to the wreck. Once inside there is plenty of room to explore and, though light penetration is good, a torch will enhance the experience. In and around the wreck, you should find lionfish, pipefish and squirrelfish, while on the sandy seabed crocodilefish lurk expectantly, blending seamlessly into their surroundings. For photographers, the more interesting features are nearer the bow, where the large boilers provide something to focus on. At the opening, just past the engine gear, groupers and their swarms of glassfish play out a daily game of cat and mouse.

Alexander Mustard

This is an easy wreck dive, with plenty of scope to shelter from the current washing over her. The reef is not spectacular and most people tend to end the dive on the wreck – another relic of British empire languishing at the bottom of the Red Sea.

THE ALTERNATIVES (STINGRAY STATION)

Depth: 30m

Skill level: 10 dives

Access: mostly liveaboard

Currents: light to strong

Must see: gorgonian fans; coral pinnacles; blue-spotted stingrays

Some dive site names leave little to the imagination. The Alternatives are so-called because they offer shelter and are regarded as an 'alternative' to the likes of Shark and *Yolanda* Reefs when the weather is rough. Their location is a short boat ride to the west and offers an ideal place for liveaboards to moor up at night when diving around the head of the Sinai Peninsula. It is an easy option for the conclusion of the day's diving.

The site is essentially a series of seven ergs and the adjoining pinnacle known as 'Stingray Station', a solitary coral outcrop known for its population of blue-spotted stingrays. Perhaps because of its second-best reputation, the site seems to attract fewer divers and therefore bears fewer battle scars than those around the big resorts. In fact, some of the pinnacles are positively glowing in the summer. Large gorgonian fans and whip corals abound, as do some of the prettier Red Sea fish such as masked butterflies and glassfish.

◀ The Dunraven wreck offers an easy penetration at its base.

▼ Soft coral thrives in the moderate currents that prevail around the Alternatives.

The expanse of sandy seabed at 18m reflects the light from above and is a good environment for bottom dwellers. These include crocodilefish and the occasional sleeping white-tip reef shark. A smidgen further west lies 'Stingray Station', which is busiest with its eponymous critters between March and June. It's easy to get close to stingrays while they are feeding, and they make particularly good photographic subjects for both video and stills. Certain other members of the elasmobranch or shark family also seem to prefer the habitat of the Alternatives, including the beautiful zebra or variegated shark, a relative of the nurse shark. Both of these sites also present good night diving opportunities, with the chance to find sleeping turtles and the elusive Spanish dancer.

SHARK OBSERVATORY

Depth: 70m; 40m optimum

Skill level: 30 dives

Access: mostly liveaboard

Currents: fair to strong

Must see: pelagic action in May and June; caves and overhangs; the reef wall

▼ A grey reef shark patrols the depths at Shark Observatory.

Shark Observatory is a sheer underwater cliff face. It drops like a skyscraper hundreds of floors to the seabed, to depths beyond the reach of mainstream divers. Scientists and tourists used to make the hour-long trek by road to watch from an overhanging cliff as sharks patrolled the reef below, and the spot subsequently became popular with adventurous divers. The sharks that drew the tourists were probably black-tip and grey reef sharks, though in recent years some of the biggest fish have made an appearance here, including tigers and oceanic white-tips.

In common with Shark Reef, the wall is almost perfectly vertical, to the extent that some divers complain of vertigo when visibility is good. A drift along the wall is loaded with potential: jacks and barracuda are almost always seen, but sharks are a matter of luck. About halfway along the wall, there is a lovely overhanging cavern at about 18m, followed by another overhang much nearer the surface and just ahead of the jump-in point for Shark Reef.

When sea conditions are rough, or when there is too much boat traffic, it is sometimes possible to dive here rather than at Shark Reef. Ask your dive guide to radio other boats in the area, to find out about what people are seeing and also who is diving which site. When word of the visiting tiger sharks gets out, the news spreads like wildfire, and this is one species of shark that does not become afraid when there are plenty of divers in the water.

JP Trenque

Alexander Mustard

JP Trenque

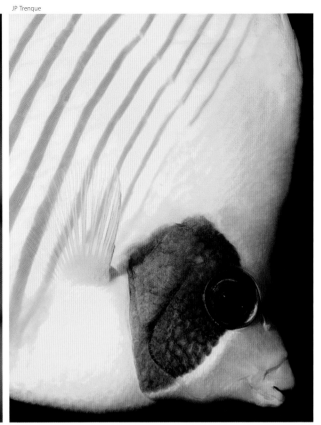

THE GARDENS (NEAR GARDEN, MIDDLE GARDEN, FAR GARDEN)

Max depth: range 10–40m

Skill level: five dives

Access: shore, dayboat or liveaboard

Current: usually light, though at Far Garden things can hot up

Must see: anemonefish at Near Garden; eagle rays at Middle Garden; black corals at Far Garden

A favourite story from the Gardens involves a veteran dive guide who was eagerly chivvying up her party for a night time plunge at Near Garden, just a stone's throw from Na'ama Bay, Sharm el Sheikh. The dive guide in question is no waif. Seconds after jumping from the dive deck, she let out a loud yelp. She had in fact just landed on top of a whale shark, which had been idling below the boat. To this day, no one is certain who was the more shaken by the incident, the dive guide or the shark!

The Gardens comprises three distinct sites: Near Garden, Middle Garden and Far Garden. They are best known as the first staging posts in a newbie diver's road to qualification. To this end, they are subject to thousands of dives every year. Near and Far Gardens benefit from little or no current while still providing a sumptuous introduction to the joys of reef diving. This is very much the domain of the day boat, though some liveaboard clients do ask to come here.

Near Garden is the closest of the three to Na'ama Bay and boasts a veritable playground of coral pinnacles, sandy slopes and fish life. It is often the place where divers see their first blue-spotted stingray or Napoleon wrasse. To the uninitiated, the latter can seem huge and unnerving, particularly as these fish often show no obvious fear of divers. The average depth of 15m makes this a suitable setting for learning buoyancy control, while the sandy bottom ensures the corals don't get too much of a bashing from the classroom mob. The sand also makes it easier to settle down and get right in close to the corals to enjoy the smaller marine life such as glassfish and anemonefish. Try to remember the topography: the site is popular for night dives, and when you come back for more after dark, you'll have a better idea of where you are.

Middle Garden is composed largely of bushy clumps of lettuce corals, with a few generous patches of sand. Though there is little current, visibility tends to be good and often exceeds 20m. The reef starts in the shallows at 6m and gradually falls away to a steeper wall. Look out for eagle rays, turtles and the occasional white-tip reef shark. Middle Garden's sheltered location means it is usually diveable, even when the weather turns bad.

Far Garden, at the northern corner of Na'ama Bay, serves as a gentle introduction to the world of walls and currents, usually by way of a drift dive. It comprises a coral garden and a dropoff, complete with a series of small caves and overhangs. On the deeper walls, you

▲ Masked butterflyfish, conspicuous by their colouration, are often found sheltering at the base of coral heads.

▲◄ A Red Sea anemonefish defends its home with typical vigour.

Alexander Mustard

▲ A gorgonian fan coral stands out against the subdued light of the late afternoon.

RAS UMM SID

Max depth: 30m optimum

Skill level: 15 dives

Access: dayboat or liveaboard

Currents: slight to medium

Must see: gorgonian fan coral forest starting at 15m; hunting octopus by night

Ras Umm Sid may not have the most inspiring of names, but for those who've just consigned their diving L-plates to the bottom of the Red Sea, this is a real treat. It has all the hallmarks of the big dive sites found further south. The presence of a large, current-swept plateau creates the perfect environment for coral growth which, in turn, establishes a rich food chain from top to bottom. Another compelling feature of Ras Umm Sid is the lush forest of gorgonian fans set against a plunging reef wall at 15–30m. This deeper section is usually dived first while heading towards the plateau. Here the evenly spaced pinnacles and good-sized table corals make for an ornamental garden, with many fish to distract the diver, including beautiful angelfish, parrotfish, anemonefish, grouper and glassfish. Octopus, moray eels and the stunning Spanish dancer are among the many creatures more easily spotted on a night dive.

The impact of development on the future of Ras Umm Sid is a cause for concern. Once this was simply a gorgeous dive site in the shadow of the local lighthouse. Nowadays, like so much of the Sinai Peninsula around Sharm el Sheikh, the hotel trade is almost on top of the reefs.

RAS NASRANI

Depth: 40m optimum

Skill level: 15 dives

Access: shore, dayboat or liveaboard

Currents: none to medium

Must see: moray eels hiding in the coral, eagle rays, Napoleon wrasse

Back when Sharm el Sheikh was a fledgling dive destination, Ras Nasrani was among the shore-based dives guaranteed to wow divers. It offers a delightful mishmash of wall, small caves, overhangs, coral heads and large gorgonian fans. Author John McIntyre dived here in the late 1980s and was mesmerised by the experience of gliding over the reef precipice. Today this is one of the furthest of the mainland sites visited by the Sharm dayboat brigade.

Divers often approach this as a drift: currents can be strong and tend to push you south, with the reef to your right. As with the majority of drifts, the optimum

may find the supposedly rare black coral trees. It is always worth keeping half an eye on the blue, as pelagic traffic can range from dogtooth tuna and rainbow runners to small sharks and rays. On rare occasions the real giants turn up, including graceful giant mantas and that other awesome plankton feeder, the whale shark.

Ultimately, the Gardens are a rite of passage: most divers who graduate from the 'University of Sharm' will have these among the earliest entries in their logbooks.

depth tends to be around 25–30m, gradually ascending while looking out into the blue for the first ten minutes. Small schools of bullet-shaped tuna are commonly seen, plus large numbers of blue fusiliers and surgeonfish, and there is a fifty-fifty chance of bumping into our old friend, the Napoleon wrasse. Other signature animals to look out for are large moray eels poking their toothy, swaying heads from their coral hideaways.

Ras Nasrani's sea floor topography varies from sand-covered plateau to steepish walls along the fringing reef. The plateau can be good for finding scorpionfish and camouflaged stonefish, while the wall enjoys the sort of flowing currents that attract jacks and barracuda. This is one of the northern Red Sea's prettiest dive sites and remains a firm favourite with many old hands who have been diving Sharm el Sheikh since the Eighties and before.

WHITE KNIGHTS

Depth: 40m

Skill level: 15 dives

Access: shore, dayboat or liveaboard

Currents: small to fair

Must see: the canyon; small wooden wreck of dive boat

White Knights is effectively a part of the Ras Nasrani stretch of coast, overlooked by luxury hotels. It is best known for its impressive canyon formation, apparently the geological result of a 'blue hole' system whose outer wall eroded and collapsed. For the most part this is not a deep dive, though like many of the fringing reef sites in the Red Sea, it is nearly always possible to find deep water without difficulty. The canyon drops down to 35–40 metres, punctuated by swim-throughs, over-hangs and mini caves. A sandy bottom slopes down the middle of the canyon like a large slide in a theme park. Well, sort of.

It is worth spending a good ten minutes or more exploring the canyon, though it can feel a little crowded if too many visitors all try to dive it at once. When the sun is at its apex, the effect of the light dappling through the canyon makes the scene very agreeable indeed. If the current is weak – and often it is – you can head in either direction afterwards. If your fancy is to head off with the reef on your left (in the direction of Ras Bob), you will come across the *Noos 1*, a small wooden wreck that was a dive boat in a former life. This has been on the seabed at 15m since the mid 1990s, when it sank after catching fire. Head off in the opposite direction and the main attraction is an eel garden nestling among the coral topography. This is an excellent site for people learning to dive.

AMPHORAS AND TURTLE BAY

Depth: 30m optimum

Skill level: 10 dives

Access: dayboat and liveaboard

Currents: none to medium

Must see: the old anchor from the Turkish shipwreck; tiny globules of mercury from the broken amphoras

Very few of the Red Sea's really old wrecks can be seen, as they are steadily eaten away by worms, and there is little sign of the 17th century Turkish shipwreck whose cargo can still be found here. In the case of 'Amphoras' you should be able to find the odd remnant of the ship's cargo of Greek-Roman containers, but little more than that. For maritime historians, however, such artefacts can be precious discoveries, providing clues about how people lived and died in a bygone age.

The amphorae carried by this old vessel were used to transport mercury. At around the 25m mark, there are still tiny, puddle-like globules of this highly toxic element (which remains in liquid form) among the corals and in the sand. Just a few metres deeper, the old vessel's anchor still survives. This and the amphorae

▼ Slingjaw wrasse are among the reef's most colourful fish.

Alexander Mustard

JP Trenque

▲ A crinoid or feather star unfolds its fronds as it emerges to feed at dusk.

▶ Only the keenest of eyes can see tiny host gobies when they rest on soft coral branches.

▶▶ A familiar sight on the sandy seabed of the Alternatives, the blue-spotted stingray often seeks shelter under table coral. (Jane Morgan)

are found near the edge of the dropoff, where the wall starts to drop sharply into the blue. Depending on the direction of the current, dives tend to start ahead of the amphorae, with the reef on the right. There are a few good-sized coral outcrops or pinnacles along the way, as well as some brightly coloured soft corals.

The mellow drift should lead you along to Turtle Bay, another site whose name suggests its historical background. This was once an excellent place to find hawksbill turtles, though today you'd be as likely to find them anywhere else along the Egyptian Red Sea coast. A coral garden stretches out over a sloping, sandy seabed peppered with pinnacles and gorgonians. As with many of the dive sites close to Na'ama Bay, there is some evidence of minimal diver-inflicted damage on the coral.

PINKY'S WALL

Depth: 30m optimum

Skill level: 10 dives

Access: shore, dayboat or liveaboard

Currents: none to medium

Must see: colonies of *Alcyonaria* and *Dendronephthya* corals; moray eels and octopus

Next along from the Amphoras site is this extremely pretty dive, which comes into its own during the warmer months of June to October, when the reefs of the northern Red Sea are at their most vibrant. At Pinky's Wall

the colours are the reason for diving, and the dominant colour here is indeed a vivid pink. Gorgeous *Alcyonaria* and *Dendronephthya* corals (sometimes known more commonly as cauliflower corals) dominate the sloping wall, leading to the largest vertical gorge of this series at the 'Tower' (see Temple).

The greatest congregation of soft corals, or hydrozoans, occurs at 10–15m, mostly on the exposed parts of the reef. These bushy, brightly coloured corals are among 120 or so soft corals occurring throughout the Red Sea. They look especially pretty close-up in strong sunlight, and have become understandably popular with photographers.

To get the best from this dive, either take the narrow entrance from the shore near to 'Amphorae', or make a return circuit or a drift dive from either end, maintaining a constant depth of around 20m. Currents can sometimes be strong but the dive guide will probably test the direction and strength before the rest of the party enters the water.

On such a dramatic wall with plenty of hiding places, you should be prepared to encounter all manner of creatures, especially moray eels and octopus. But also don't forget to keep one eye on the blue for passing tuna. For more adventurous and advanced divers this is an excellent wall to enjoy the sense of the Red Sea's depths. Descend to 30m and you should find some enchanting scenery, even if the diversity of reef life starts to thin out.

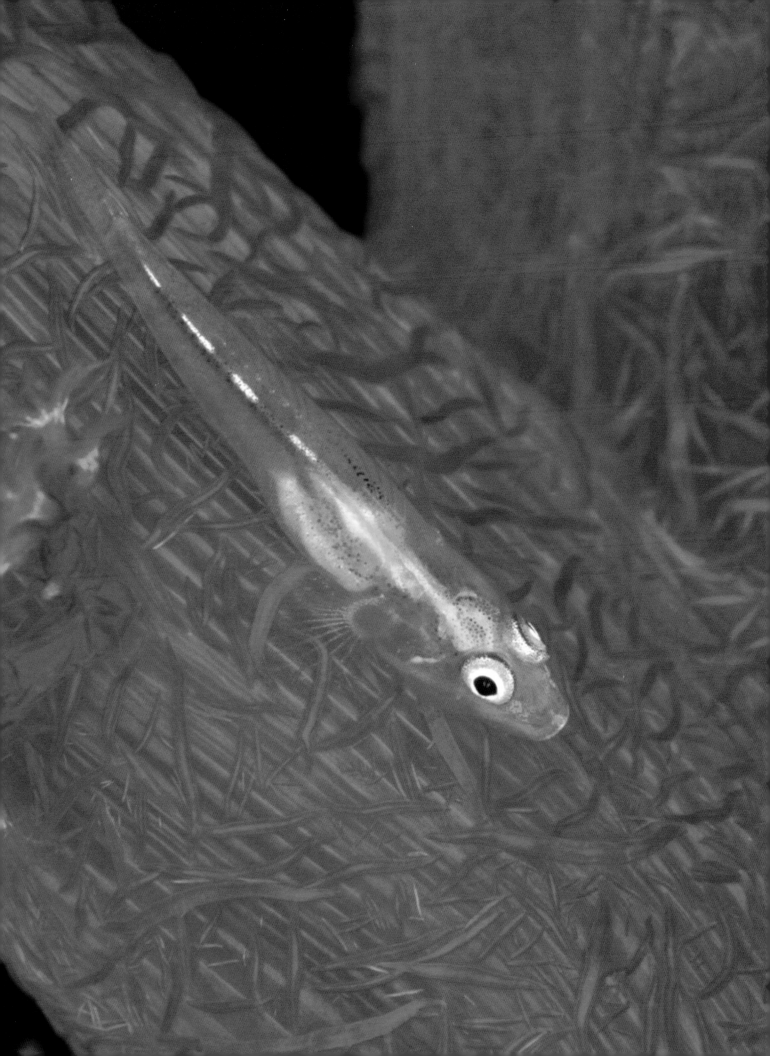

SHARK BAY

Depth: 30m optimum

Skill level: 10 dives

Access: shore, dayboat or liveaboard

Currents: none to medium

Must see: whale sharks and mantas if you're feeling lucky; otherwise, stingrays are common

Before Sharm el Sheikh became one of the world's most popular holiday destinations, Shark Bay epitomised the pioneering spirit of Red Sea diving. Back in those days, Bedouins provided a starlit feast, cooked to the grunt of camels and the rustle of scorpions ferreting in the sand. A tasty meal of grouper or snapper was prepared and baked in a covering in the ground. This formed the sustenance for the next day's shore dive at Shark Bay, where a morning dash to the water's edge was the form if you wanted to escape the dawn invasion of sand flies.

Today, we have luxury hotels, cappuccinos on demand and a range of Italian ice cream to choose from, but Shark Bay remains popular with many of the pioneering operators. Do not be fooled by the name, though: Shark Bay is so called because local fishermen once used to sell their day's catch nearby. If you do happen to see a shark, it will be purely by luck.

With so many tourists staying in Shark Bay resort, the reef is perhaps too popular. It is ideal for snorkellers and a good choice for a checkout dive. There is a sloping sandy bottom with a fairly impressive canyon on the southern side of the site, so swim to the right if entering from the shore. The slope starts at 15m and continues to more than 50m. Being a natural trap for plankton in the summer months, the site can occasionally attract manta rays, but sightings are now fairly rare. Coral cover is mediocre, but keen-eyed divers will find scorpionfish and crocodilefish lurking in the vicinity.

TEMPLE

Max depth: 20m optimum

Skill level: 10 dives

Access: dayboat or liveaboard

Currents: slight

Must see: the larger of the coral pinnacles; moray eels

Temple is a great introduction to the world of the coral pinnacle or erg, the reef's equivalent to high-rise apartment blocks. Here, the position and size of these coral 'skyscrapers' has made them ideal hosts for vibrant soft corals, invertebrates and a wide range of Red Sea fishlife. Their position close to Na'ama Bay has also made this one of the oldest and most popular of all the local dive sites. It comprises one smaller system of pinnacles clumped together in about six or seven metres and rising to a snorkel's length from the surface; then the larger system of one main pinnacle complete with its limestone branches.

It's fair to say that these ergs are over-dived by both divers and snorkellers. Some of them have suffered a Leaning Tower of Pisa effect, as a result of an earthquake in the mid 1990s. Divers tend to drop in at the site of the smaller, shallower corals. Between the pinnacles, the sandy seabed slopes down well past the dive site's advertised 20m, but there's no real reason to push deeper. The big attraction is the larger block, which some call the 'Tower' – not to be confused with the dive site of the same name on the Sharm el Sheikh beat. Here there is an attractive swim-through surrounded by some bedraggled gorgonian fans. A smaller opening in the coral is best left alone to help prevent further damage. Of course, there is never any shortage of the ubiquitous glassfish in the coral fissures and overhangs, and their presence attracts lionfish in impressive numbers. The pinnacles also provide a home for moray eels, which weave their sinewy forms through the coral architecture. With such easy, protected diving conditions, Temple is the ideal setting for night dives out of Sharm.

▼ A mass of large anemones provides a 'high-rise' environment for anemonefish and other species of damselfish.

Alexander Mustard

David Lloyd

STRAITS OF TIRAN

The island of Tiran benefits from a powerful flow through the Gulf of Aqaba, and its four large reefs are awash with nutrient-rich northerly currents. In effect, these form one enormous reef system, which is perched on a volcanic ridge overlooking abyssal depths. The area of sea between the island and the mainland reefs is barely 1,000m across, resulting in a bottleneck effect that has sometimes proved a disaster for local shipping. Divers can see only too clearly the giant vessels that have come to grief, as their remnants litter the reef tops.

Travelling from Sharm el Sheikh, the first reef you encounter is Gordon Reef, followed by Thomas, then Woodhouse and finally Jackson. The boat ride takes about an hour and a half. Liveaboards usually moor up at Gordon overnight, so divers are ready to beat the rush hour at first light. The four reefs get their names from British cartographers. Each has its own distinctive qualities and attractions. Some of the sites are truly spectacular, with vertical walls plunging 200m into the Red Sea abyss. On the eastern flank of Thomas reef is a stunning, narrow canyon, which has the power to draw divers into a narcosis stupor. Big animals are regularly sighted, among them one of the most dangerous of the Red Sea's predators, the tiger shark. For just a few months, and only in certain years, tigers exceeding 4m in length have provided heart-pounding encounters for divers fortunate enough to meet this veritable dustbin of the world's tropical oceans. Schooling scalloped hammerheads and, very rarely, solitary great hammerheads have been seen around Jackson and Woodhouse. The number of dive boats converging on Tiran can at times seem like an armada, but at its best, the reefs here are capable of producing fantastic diving experiences.

GORDON REEF

Max depth: 30m optimum

Skill level: 15+ dives

Access: dayboat from Sharm el Sheikh or liveaboard

Current: can be strong at corners and along walls, from north to south

Must see: Napoleon wrasse circling below dive boats; schooling surgeonfish on the southern wall

Many of Sharm's day boats indulge in a daily ritual of vying for the best moorings on the southern part of Gordon. Long before arriving at the reef, however, Gordon is easily identified by the presence of a rusting wreck perched on the northern tip. This is the wreck of the *Louilla*, an old cargo ship that rotted from the lower hull before crumbling onto the reef. In calm conditions, it is possible to get close to the wreck and scour for oil drums and other remnants littering the wall.

▲ While massed ranks of day boats are a common sight in southern Sinai, the operators are adept at working together.

The majority of dives are from the back of the boat, keeping the reef on the left or right depending on currents, and then returning after reaching either corner. Another option is to take a rib ride, usually to the eastern wall for a drift dive heading south back towards the boats.

Even with the levels of boat traffic experienced here, the fish life can still be prolific. Schooling surgeonfish and good-sized Napoleon wrasse appear to tolerate the large numbers of divers without much concern. In the shallows, there are coral inlets where crocodile-fish and scorpionfish lurk on rocks and sandy patches below buzzing schools of anthias. Anemones, with their attendant anemonefish, thrive at various depths down to 30m.

Another option is to take an inflatable boat ride, usually to the eastern wall, for a drift dive heading back towards the boats. Gorgonian fans thrive in the currents along the wall. Bright red soft thistle corals and hazardous fire corals are among the many other varieties found here. As with all the drift dives in the Straits of Tiran, there are clear dangers to watch out for, in the form of choppy seas and zodiacs racing along the surface. Strong winds can whip up without warning and so a delayed SMB (surface marker buoy) is a necessity. Apart from keeping one eye on the blue for passing pelagic animals, such as sharks and rays, a safety stop in the shallows can be equally rewarding, as the top ten metres are usually the most diverse.

THOMAS REEF

Max depth: 40m optimum
Skill level: 30 dives, if considering the canyon
Access: dayboat from Sharm el Sheikh or liveaboard
Current: usually manageable, but can be very strong and the direction is unpredictable
Must see: with appropriate experience, the canyon

Thomas may be the smallest of the Tiran reefs but it can also be the most dramatic. If you are planning to dive the canyon, it's a good idea to agree an approach and to have a real grasp of the topography. Equally, the dive guide should check the current first, as the direction can switch. Under normal conditions, divers enter the water and drift down to the shallower entrance to a deep gorge at about 33–35m, which looms into view, beckoning divers into the unknown.

This is a superb dive, but it is not one for novices. If you enter the canyon, there are two arches that appear fairly close together (there is actually a third near the end). It is possible for one diver at a time to negotiate these, but the depths and the narrow spaces can trigger nitrogen narcosis.

A few minutes are all that you need in the gorge before emerging on to a sloping, sandy plateau circled by hard corals. White-tip reef sharks can be found resting here. Feisty triggerfish seem to like this part of the reef, too. Out in the blue, grey reef sharks and the occasional scalloped hammerhead may swim past. Hawksbill turtles are usually spotted munching on soft corals, unconcerned by the presence of divers.

WOODHOUSE REEF

Max depth: 40m optimum
Skill level: 25 dives
Access: dayboat from Sharm el Sheikh or liveaboard
Current: varies from reasonable, directional drift to chaotic, 'washing-machine' currents in the channel with Jackson reef
Must see: reef sharks on the wall; see if you can find the coral wall running to Jackson

Woodhouse is a long, cigar-shaped reef, and can be dived on either flank. There is a connecting reef at about 6–10m, which eventually merges with Jackson, but be careful, as you may become confused and lose your bearings if you try to follow this. The dive often begins at the northern end, following the reef on the left if diving the steeper western edge. Co-author John McIntyre has seen a three-metre great hammerhead at this very point, easily identifiable by its unusually tall, sickle-shaped dorsal fin.

Day boats tend to summon all divers to the dive platform so that everyone can enter the water at the same time. Those diving from liveaboards can take a rib ride

◀ Soft coral against a blue background makes for an irresistible photo-subject.

▼ A pufferfish engages in a standoff with the cameraman.

JP Trenque

Simon Rogerson

▲ The formidable tiger shark is an occasional visitor to the reefs of Tiran and Ras Mohammed.

from a sheltered mooring to the drop zone. This site is rarely as busy as Gordon Reef, so there's less likelihood of diver congestion. The western wall is more barren, while the eastern flank benefits from more sunlight and is richer in coral diversity, including fans and tree corals.

JACKSON

Max depth: 40m optimum

Skill level: 30 dives

Access: dayboat from Sharm el Sheikh or liveaboard

Current: northern flank and corners can experience wicked swirling currents

Must see: schooling hammerheads, hawksbill turtles

When surface conditions are flat calm, the best place to start the dive is close to the fragmented remains of the rusting freighter *Lara*, perched on the northern point. Descend to 20–30m and move away from the wall, still keeping it well in sight. This is the best point of the reef to look for scalloped hammerheads from May to September. These mysterious sharks sometimes make long, sweeping circles around the reef, appearing and

disappearing without warning. It can be worth waiting for as long as decompression concerns permit in the hope of catching a glimpse of these amazing beasts, but do not leave it too long: have a plan that matches your ability and stick to it.

When you leave this spot, head east, keeping the reef on your right. Towards the corner, the currents can become intense, but if you persevere and keep finning, you should get around it with no problems. Here, the large fan corals and flourishing soft corals are exposed to constantly flowing waters and are suitably luxuriant. Many of the dayboat divers do not venture this far north on the Tiran system, so you may have the reef to yourself. If the sea is breaking over the north of Jackson, divers tend to be dropped in on the eastern wall for a drift south with the reef on the right, back towards the mooring point on the leeward side.

The reef is at its peak from June to September, with fantastic colours and, of course, millions of those stars of the Red Sea, the orange anthias fish. There is perhaps a 40 per cent chance of seeing shark action: white-tip reef sharks, greys and black-tips can all be seen here, and tiger sharks have been known to move through the area, putting a dent in the local turtle population.

LAGOONA

Max depth: 40m optimum

Skill level: 20 dives

Access: dayboat or liveaboard

Currents: fair to strong

Must see: liner-inflicted reef scars; night dive inside the lagoon

Lagoona is worth considering for a number of reasons. It is not over-dived, as are so many of the reefs around Tiran, and it presents a fair to strong drift dive. It is also a good place to see how coral reefs can recover after suffering a man-made disaster.

In 1996, the Cunard liner *Royal Viking Sun* was steaming north through this bottleneck channel between the Island of Tiran and the four reefs. Despite having nearly a kilometre of grace, she smashed into Lagoona Reef with a crunch. The ship, packed with passengers, lost power and started to list. She scraped off the reef and drifted into the Tiran reef system before a large dive boat acted as a tug and held her steady. The Egyptian authorities impounded the ship until Cunard coughed up a multi-million dollar fine.

Author John McIntyre was the first journalist to witness the level of destruction to the reef, covering some 2,000 square metres. He reported on the incident for the BBC's flagship news programmes. Large, black scrape marks scarred the reef, looking like the work of some giant chisel. Egyptian authorities treat any damage by vessels in exactly the same way: a formula based on the area of destruction determines the level of the fine, whether the culprit is a diveboat, fishing vessel or cruise liner. Cunard could not dispute the scale of the damage and dutifully paid up.

Interestingly – though this is not a strictly scientific observation – the reef at Lagoona has made a good recovery. For months afterwards, the fish seemed to have vanished along with the coral. But now, a few years down the line, nature's healing ability is evident. Among the first to make a comeback were the anemones, complete with their attendant anemonefish.

Liveaboards use the sheltered bay inside Lagoona Reef to moor up at night, and it is a suitable area for night diving. Inside the lagoon, the seabed is no deeper than 10–15m and a night dive should yield crabs, lionfish and scorpionfish.

THE WRECK OF THE *MILLION HOPE*

Max depth: 24m

Skill level: 15 dives

Access: liveaboard

Currents: fair to strong often with significant swell

Must see: giant propeller and rudder system; vast holds; port hull so giant it looks like a reef wall

It is often said of wrecks that shipping's loss is diving's gain. This is certainly true of the *Million Hope*, a cavernous monster of a wreck that was once overlooked by many liveaboard itineraries but is now very much in demand. This Japanese-built bulk carrier lies along the reef wall on the Egyptian coast of the Tiran Straits. It is prone to terrible swells and choppy seas around the upper decks and bridge, which breaches the surface, so can only be dived safely when the sea is relatively calm.

In 1996 the *Million Hope* became yet another victim of this unforgiving sea when she struck a reef while heading south. She was carrying around 2,500 tons of fertiliser raw materials at the time, which were later salvaged, leaving the five enormous holds empty. Astonishingly, the stricken vessel actually came to rest right on top of another wreck – that of the *Hey Daroma*, a cargo vessel that sank a quarter of a century earlier. You have to look hard to work out that the crumpled metal beneath belongs to another ship.

▶▶ As sunlight fades, a lionfish emerges from daytime slumber to hunt small fry along the reef. (Alexander Mustard)

COUSTEAU AND THE CORRIDOR

Jacques Yves Cousteau first captured the magic of the Red Sea in glorious colour in the 1950s, and his influence over diving has been nothing short of monumental. It is impossible to estimate how many people have been inspired to take up the sport of diving as a result of the wonderful images brought to our screens by this lyrical man. Today we take the aqualung for granted, but it took Cousteau and his engineer friend Emile Gagnan to visualise and then create the apparatus that would set generations of underwater explorers free.

Cousteau first ventured into the Red Sea in the early 1950s aboard the legendary Calypso. He described the Red Sea as 'a corridor of marvels', adding that the happiest hours of his diving experience had been spent there. People were glued to their television sets with his epic tales and never-before seen images of a beautiful 'Silent World'. These images are still available today, and it is a treat of extraordinary nostalgia to follow one famous journey: viewed from a small glass dome under the ship, the form of a large wreck comes into view, and the slightly grainy pictures reveal what is arguably today the most dived wreck in the world, the *Thistlegorm* (see Chapter 6). Cousteau provides little narrative for this major discovery. Instead the pictures are powerful enough to do the talking. Perhaps Cousteau did the world of diving a favour by not revealing the whereabouts of this giant British casualty of the Second World War.

The *Thistlegorm* is not the only survivor of the Cousteau era. In Sudan, his experimental Conshelf at Sha'ab Rumi is still there for divers to enjoy (see Chapter 8). This mushroom-shaped undersea home tested man's ability to live under the sea for days at a time. The divers, known as 'Oceanauts', ventured out from the confines of their pressurised pod to survey the coral gardens and to feed reef sharks.

Cousteau died in 1997 at the age of 87. For decades, the Frenchman had entertained millions with his poetic insight into this watery world. His enduring legacy lies in our profound sense of wonder at the marvels of the world's oceans. The Cousteau odyssey continues in spirit every time a diver enters the sea. In the great man's words: 'From birth, man carries the weight of gravity on his shoulders. He is bolted to earth. But man has only to sink beneath the surface and he is free.'

Peter Collings

▲ A diver examines the wreck of the Million Hope.

On a day of flat calm, diving the *Million Hope* is a real treat. At close to 175m in length, she is one of the biggest wrecks you can dive in the Red Sea. Dropping down to the bow, the profile of the wreck is truly enormous. Move around to the starboard, now pockmarked with colourful hard corals, and the hull seems so big that you lose any sense of it being a wreck: it just seems like a reef wall.

There is a big crack in the side of the hull, where it is easy to gain access to one of the large holds. Fish life is still sparse here, with little more than the odd lionfish dwarfed by this hulking piece of metal. Head to the stern and there is an equally massive propeller and rudder system, slightly the worse for wear after the crash. A picture with a diver in shot taken at this point helps convey the scale of this vessel.

Perhaps the more interesting features are to be found on and around the deck, where the funnel and bridge area are subject to a daily battering by the waves. If the sea is calm, it is possible to surface here – though if you're not careful, the swell can force you against the wreck, possibly causing an injury. Photographers and videographers will find that a good wide-angle lens helps capture those fantastic split-level shots above and below the waterline.

Plenty of soft corals, anemones and some hard corals have taken hold along the railings, jibs and heavy-duty cabling, where anemonefish, glassfish and surgeonfish are among the new residents. Schools of hatchet fish are also usually present around the bridge area. But ultimately, the *Million Hope's* status as a star attraction is justified by its size alone: there certainly is a lot of ship to cover!

▶ Chevron barracuda are found in great schools along the Sinai Peninsula.

Alexander Mustard

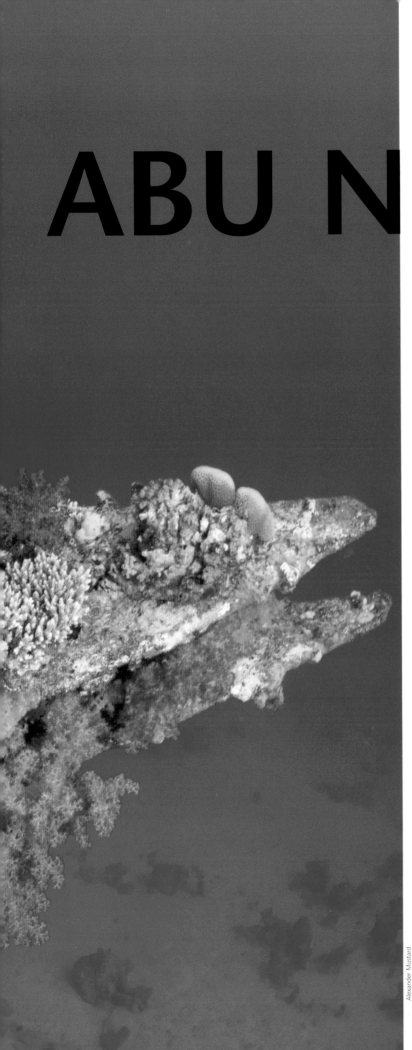

SHA'AB ABU NUHAS

SHA'AB ABU NUHAS IS FAMOUS IN THE NORTHERN RED SEA AS THE 'CURSE TO SHIPPING'. THIS SIZE-ABLE REEF IS LOCATED OMINOUSLY IN THE GUBAL STRAIT, WHERE THE RED SEA CHANNELS INTO THE GULF OF SUEZ, AND BARELY BREAKS THE SUR-FACE IN PLACES.

Anyone who has suffered the rolling, heaving seas of this tropical maritime highway understands its brutal and unforgiving nature. But a curse for sailors has in turn been a blessing for armies of divers, who regard this hazardous reef system as a must-do destination.

Depending on whom you talk to, there are somewhere between four and seven wrecks here. With divers converging on Abu Nuhas from all corners of Europe and beyond, eagerly devouring the per-suasive briefings of dive guides of varying experience and knowledge, the ensuing confusion comes as little surprise. Whoever dares to offer a definitive version may fall foul of the same curse that has caused so much grief to the shipping industry, as wreck historians seldom agree with each other. For the purposes of this book, how-ever, there are four important dive sites. They range from the highly photogenic old-timer the *Carnatic*, which was the first of the known Abu Nuhas casualties, to more recent wrecks. Perhaps the next most dived is the bulky Greek freighter *Giannis D*. The histories of these first two wrecks have never really been in doubt, but the identities of immediate neighbours *Chrisoula K* and *Kimon M* have had Red Sea experts getting their high-pressure hoses in a twist for years.

The best way to enjoy this undersea graveyard is by liveaboard, though the dayboat traffic is fairly heavy, especially from Hurghada. Liveaboards will often try to dive at least two of the wrecks as part of their itinerary, depending on the highly changeable weather. Conditions can vary from glassy calm to surging swells, which can be felt even at 30m. At dusk, divers sometimes enjoy the rare treat of being accompanied by a small pod of bottlenose dolphins that scour the reef for food. They probably know the wrecks better than any diver.

Alexander Mustard

◀ Soft and hard corals smother the carcass of the steam sailing vessel the Carnatic, one of the four classic casualties of the 'curse of Abu Nuhas'.

Qaysum Island

Bluff Point

Gubal Island

Tawila Island

Ras Mohammed

Carnatic

Giannis D

Kimon M

Chrisoula K

Sha'ab Abu Nuhas

Sha'ab Abu Nuhas

Shadwan Island

R E D
S E A

GOUNA

Sha'ab el Fanadir

Careless Reef

ABU SHA'R

E G Y P T

Giftun Kebir

HURGHADA

Giftun Seghir

Giftun Seghir

N

Erg Abu Ramada

UMM AJAWISH

✈ GETTING THERE

Direct flights to Hurghada and Marsa Alam depart from several major European airports, including Gatwick in the UK. However, charter companies dominate these routes, and it often works out cheaper to buy your accommodation and flights together rather than separately.

▮ VISAS

Visitors can either get them in advance from the Egyptian Embassy or – as is more common – on arrival in the country. You will need a full passport with at least six months remaining.

$ MONEY

Egyptian currency has been fairly stable over the years, largely thanks to tourism. Most outlets will take foreign currency, including the Euro, Dollar and Sterling.

```
0                    10 km
0                    8 m
```

Jane Morgan

CARNATIC

Max depth: 27m to the stern

Skill level: medium, 20+ dives

Access: liveaboard or dayboat

Current: usually light or none

Must see: by far the most attractive part of the Carnatic is from within the wreck behind the metal structure – more of a rib cage in appearance. Great for pictures, and works especially well if you co-ordinate a diver to swim past

This skeletal old iron wreck is a feast for photographers and videographers. She slopes down the reef from the coral shallows to 27m, where the terrain is an expanse of sandy seabed. Visibility in the Red Sea can vary considerably, but when conditions are reasonable the entire wreck looms into view. Essentially, she is divided in two: her coral encrusted bow resting atop the reef; her stern section luring divers into deeper water.

What distinguishes the *Carnatic* from the other Abu Nuhas wrecks is her rich history and design. With her layered ribs of rusting iron, she represents the fine workmanship of a bygone era. Finning in between these cross members and supports, it is possible to conjure an image of passengers in their hand-woven finery on deck enjoying the Arabian landscape in the shadow of the ship's vast, square-rigged sails. But this London-built P&O mail/passenger steamer also enjoyed the power of a lumbering four-cylinder engine.

At the time of her sinking, the *Carnatic* was carrying a valuable cargo of copper and bullion destined for the Indian Mint. Her journey to Bombay in 1869 was cut dramatically and tragically short when stormy seas caused her to break in two and sink adjacent to the reef, with the loss of more than 30 lives – mostly crew. After the subsequent salvage operation, it was claimed that the cargo had all been recovered. But a part of this dive's great charm is the remote prospect that a small part of the bullion remains undisturbed somewhere in the vicinity.

The obvious place to start the dive is at the stern, where a large propeller rests on the seabed, caked in more than a century of hard and soft coral growth. Keen-eyed divers may spot some of the marine residents here. The mottled markings of the impressive crocodilefish can sometimes be spotted on the sandy bottom next to the wreck. In the many nooks and crannies of the old ship lurk numerous lionfish, which are often attracted to wrecks as ideal lairs for hunting their favourite prey – glassfish.

The *Carnatic* is frequently the easiest of the Abu Nuhas dives because of her position, nestling into the northern part of the reef between the wrecks of *Giannis D* and *Chrisoula K* (see later in this chapter). Still strong northerly winds can make surfacing a bumpy experience, to say the least. Since many of the Red Sea's wrecks are from the 20th century, the *Carnatic* ranks highly as an historical treat. Don't dive this wreck without a camera!

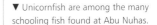
▲ The classic build of the Carnatic evident at the stern resting at 27m.

▼ Unicornfish are among the many schooling fish found at Abu Nuhas.

Alexander Mustard

CARNATIC

In her day, the *Carnatic* would have cut an impressive dash on the seascape. She was built in the 1860s under the old P&O banner, with the combined qualities of steam and sail craftsmanship. As well as carrying a relatively valuable cargo of unminted coins, she was also modestly furnished for carrying passengers. Her demise came towards the end of the same decade in 1869. She was travelling through the Red Sea en route from Liverpool to Bombay when she struck the large reef of Sha'ab Abu Nuhas in the early hours. Had the captain abandoned ship the following day it's likely there would have been no loss of life. As it was they remained on board, and when the boat split in two the following night, more than 30 passengers and crew lost their lives. Today this photogenic wreck is among the Red Sea's favourites, not only as a reasonably easy dive for all levels, but also as a skeletal reminder of the engineering of the day.

1. Missing bowsprit
2. Bow
3. Latticed iron framework
4. Masts lying on seabed
5. Mid-section wreckage
6. Lifeboat davits
7. Poop deck
8. Three-bladed prop and rudder

▲ Most dives end towards the bow where the hole for the missing bowsprit can be seen.

(Charles Hood/oceans-image.com)

sea level

top of wreck 20m

lowest point 27m

▲ Carnatic bow resting in shallower water.
(Peter Collings)

▲ Classic features of Carnatic build.
(Peter Collings)

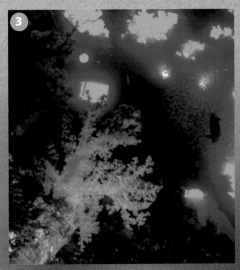

▲ Carnatic 'ribs' provide photogenic lighting.
(Peter Collings)

▲ The mid-section of the wreck.
(Charles Hood/oceans-image.com)

▲ Gorgeous soft red corals of the *Dendronephthya* family.
(Alexander Mustard)

▲ Diving inside skeletal remains.
(Alexander Mustard)

▲ A diver swims through a school of glassfish which frequent the wreck. (Alexander Mustard)

▶ Alex Mustard's picture shows off the Giannis D to great effect.

▶▶ The vast pock-marked starboard hull of the Giannis D makes for impressive pictures. (Jane Morgan)

▼ A juvenile grouper yawns while lying in wait for its prey.

GIANNIS D

Max depth: 27m stern

Skill level: medium, 20 dives

Access: liveaboard or dayboat

Current: possible current and/or strong surges

Must see: Try diving at sunset when there is good chance of seeing bottlenose dolphins actually swimming close to the wreck

This impressive hulk of a Japanese-built Greek freighter is both haunting and fun to dive. She is the first in line from the usual mooring points on the south-western edge of Abu Nuhas. So a rib ride of no more than three to four minutes drops you right on top of the wreck. Since her demise in the 1980s, Giannis D has become a tangled mass of metal from midships to bow, while the bridge and imposing stern section has developed into an undersea playground favourite. It is impossible

not to be awestruck by the vast area of hull inclined at 45º degrees skyward. But the most dominant features are the giant 'A-frame' and bridge, which dwarf the boatloads of divers who converge on the wreck almost every day of the year.

It is best to concentrate your diving in and around the stern section, and remember to take a torch. But be warned: when penetrating the narrow corridors of the this tilting giant, even experienced divers can feel disorientated by the ship's 45º-degree list to port. Pictures of divers negotiating the starboard companionway demonstrate this to good effect.

As a 1960s vessel, the Giannis D is adorned with interesting features, but given half a chance, most divers make straight for the engine room. This is comparatively easy to enter on the Giannis D, whose Japanese six-cylinder diesel engine was capable of an industrial-strength 12 knots.

Perhaps the greatest surprise about the ship is that she sank at all. She had excellent navigation equipment and a skipper who knew these treacherous waters well. His only mistake was to relinquish the bridge to someone less experienced so he could catch some sleep. The mistake cost him the ship. The fact that there was no loss of life makes it easier for divers to enjoy the wreck – though there is, of course, the usual need to respect the marine environment.

Built in 1969, the Giannis D was a 3,000-tonne cargo vessel a fraction less than 100m in length. As a large wreck with a maze of cabins and corridors, she has nurtured a steady growth in marine inhabitants. Inside, the countless hiding places suit a number of moray eel species, the most attractive of which is the honeycomb moray. Parrotfish graze on the slowly growing coral clumps that adorn the expansive hull. Scorpionfish camouflage themselves in the varying shades of ageing metal and rust as they lie in wait, especially in the debris field forward of the bridge. And hawksbill turtles are not uncommon visitors; they are usually unconcerned by the presence of divers, so long as they are not harassed.

Most divers focus their entire dive on the more dramatic stern. However, if the seas are relatively calm, it is well worth a look at the bow section, where the shallower, brighter waters have encouraged a more luxuriant coral growth.

The Giannis D can be an extremely busy dive site. It is worth finding out from other dive boats the order in which they are diving, in order to avoid a logjam. Some of the inflatables tie off above the wreck, but when there is a swell this isn't always possible. If a number of groups are on the wreck simultaneously, look out for other ribs racing around the surface. Accidents have happened in the Red Sea. A surface marker buoy is obligatory in such conditions.

Alexander Mustard

GIANNIS D

1. Bow section
2. Mast
3. Crumpled midships
4. Mid-section wreckage
5. Crane gantry
6. Bridge
7. Ventilation system
8. Large funnel with letter 'D' of shipping line

This is perhaps the most imposing of the Sha'ab Abu Nuhas famous four. It's certainly one of the most popular. Divers are greeted by a vast expanse of hull as they descend on to the wreck, often in something of a disorientating swell – especially around the walkways, which, like the wreck, lean heavily to port. *Giannis D* was a Japanese-built, Greek-owned general cargo ship, which was launched in 1969. Fourteen years later, the 'curse of Abu Nuhas' claimed another victim, as a skipper's tiredness cost him his ship. Today the wreck rests in 24–25m at its deepest and is relatively easy to penetrate. The best area to concentrate your dive is around the distinctive, large A-frame bridge. On the funnel, you can still make out the large letter D. There is a reasonable level of marine life, though the dive site can be fairly busy.

sea level

top of wreck 10m

lowest point 27m

▲ Disintegrating bow section. (Alexander Mustard)

▲ Tilting walkways can disorientate. (Alexander Mustard)

▲ Wreck penetration easy in many places. (Alexander Mustard)

▲ Debris between stern and bow sections. (Alexander Mustard)

▲ A bridge with a view. (Alexander Mustard)

▲ The bridge looms out of the darkness. (Charles Hood/oceans-image.com)

▲ Mushroom-like ventilation system. (Alexander Mustard)

CHRISOULA K

Max depth: 30m to the stern

Skill level: medium, 20 dives

Access: liveaboard or dayboat

Current: usually light or none

Must see: best seen from inside, where you will find the stacks of tiles for which the wreck is best known

As with the other wrecks at Abu Nuhas, the *Chrisoula K* has merged and blended with the reef over the years. By the far the most enjoyable features of this German-built, Greek-registered cargo ship are the tile-filled interior and the engine room. As the cargo of Italian floor tiles (which had been bound for Jeddah) was not worthy of salvage, it remains stacked and scattered inside the holds like some chaotic DIY store. These are not your average bathroom tiles. They are small, heavy-duty slabs of granite littering the inside of the wreck. It is not surprising, therefore, that many divers simply refer to her as the 'Tile Wreck'. Visually, this cargo would merit little attention, were it not for the fact that cracks in the ship's hulls create an undersea light show, with the sun beaming down in rhythmic pulses.

As for the story of the *Chrisoula K*, disputes over the truth of this ship's identity continue to fuel claims and counter claims within the wreck-diving community: some claim it to be the *'Seastar'*; other experts argue that there was no such vessel. Either way, divers should be aware that the tears in the hull can easily shred a BCD or wetsuit – or worse still, slice through an air hose.

Manoeuvring into the silt-laden engine room is best done with the help of a guide. If pipes, valves and gauges are your thing, the *Chrisoula K* does not disappoint. The workshop area, in which a rusting but largely undamaged bench drill stands upright, gives a sepia-tinged impression of German engineering standing still from the day she sank in August, 1981.

At the wreck's deepest point, around 28m, is the ship's large propeller, which had been running at full pelt when she smashed into Abu Nuhas. Fortunately there was no loss of life and once again it seems human error was at the heart of the sinking.

All the usual suspects are here when it comes to reef marine life. Lionfish are fairly common – a natural control on the sizeable population of glassy sweepers and hatchet fish. Hunting grouper are never far from view, either.

No doubt the wrangles over her precise identity will rumble on, but as a similar-sized wreck to her neighbour the *Giannis D*, the *Chrisoula K* is a worthy addition to any diver's logbook.

◄ The *Chrisoula K* stern section with its intact deck and railings.

▼ Predatory lionfish especially love wrecks as excellent places to hunt for food.

Alexander Mustard

CHRISOULA K

Before ending her days at the bottom of the Red Sea, the *Chrisoula K* had undergone numerous name changes. This German-built cargo ship was originally known as the *Dora Oldendorff* (a name used by many ships before and since) when she was launched in 1954. She was a typical freighter vessel, a shade under 100m in length, and chugged the seas for decades before coming to grief in 1981. Thankfully, though she smashed into the coral reef at full speed, there was no loss of life. Today she lies in around 26m at her deepest and offers a mangled collection of metal and broken holds to the diver, with some fairly good access points. It is fairly easy to find the massive collection of Italian floor tiles, her final cargo, which remain stacked inside under layers of silt. The tool room is also good to find, and the marine life includes most of the usual suspects.

▲ Propeller at deepest part – 30m. (Charles Hood/oceans-image.com)

▲ Stern of *Chrisoula K* leaning to starboard.

(Charles Hood/oceans-image.com)

1. Four-bladed propeller
2. Stern
3. Air vents
4. Wreckage midships
5. Tiles in hold
6. Mast
7. Bridge
8. Funnel
9. Lifeboat davit
10. Forward hold
11. Bow section

- sea level
- top of wreck 18m
- lowest point 30m

▲ Tangled mass of damaged midships. (Alexander Mustard)

▲ Stacks of tiles inside the wreck. (Peter Collings)

▲ *Chrisoula K*'s workshop with drill still intact. (Alexander Mustard)

▲ Diver highlighting lifeboat davit. (Charles Hood/oceans-image.com)

▲ Interior of one of the *Chrisoula K*'s holds. (Charles Hood/oceans-image.com)

▲ The sharp features of the coral encrusted bow pointing skyward. (Alexander Mustard)

▲ The sleek lines of the Kimon M stern look more like a bow; her ribbed rudder and propeller still intact.

▶ Wrecks make ideal anchors for a variety of corals; which provide shelter and camouflage for many species including this forster's hawkfish.

KIMON M

Max depth: 32m to the stern

Skill level: medium; 20+ dives

Access: liveaboard or dayboat

Current: usually light or none

Must see: investigate the hardened sacks of inedible lentils which are evidence that she really is the *Kimon M* and not some other wreck

Sea conditions have to be fairly stable for dive boats to venture this far round the exposed northern flanks of Abu Nuhas, where white water can make it pretty heavy going. But *Kimon M*, which like its neighbours, has for years been the subject of debate over its identity, completes the famous four. This German-built ship met its fate in 1978. Like a badge of honour, adding the wreck to your logbook is a must.

There are major similarities with *Chrisoula K* and *Giannis D*, in that all these wrecks are roughly 100m in length, with their sterns resting on the deepest part of the sloping reef wall while their bow sections take a constant battering in the shallows. So it comes as little surprise that the diving experience is also similar. Again, diving tends to be concentrated in the stern, which dips to just over 30m. Here, divers will find a more intact propeller and rudder system. *Kimon M*'s stern actually gives the appearance of a bow and has even been mistaken for such. But the only value of her cargo would have been nutritional, as she was carrying a load of lentils.

The story of Kimon M's demise is familiar: a vessel making good speed from the Gulf of Suez into the

Charles Hood/oceans-image.com   Jane Morgan

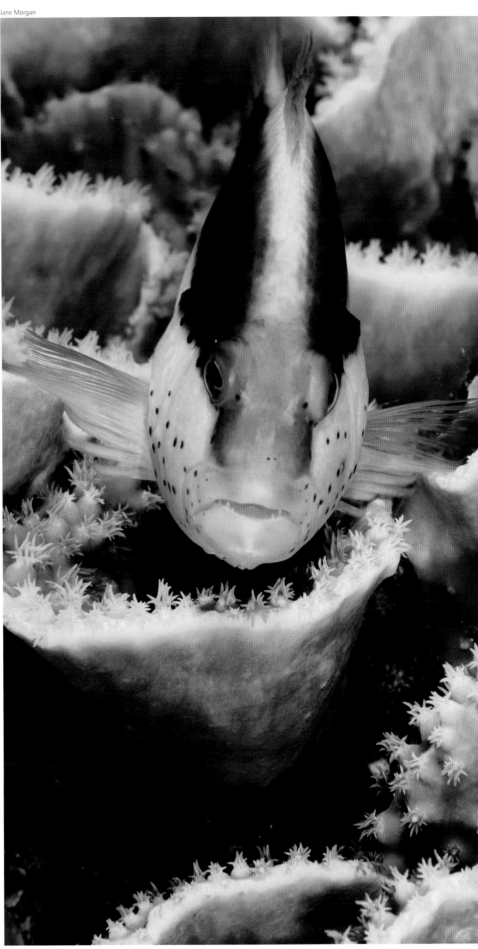

Egyptian Red Sea, when all of a sudden the curse of Abu Nuhas struck with deadly force. The sacks full of lentils were hardly going to inspire a full-blown salvage operation, so they now enjoy a healthy coating of marine life, their sell-by-date having well and truly expired.

Kimon M is a highly satisfying dive. Not only does she posses an interesting maze of corridors, spacious holds and overhangs, but the engine room offers a pleasing mish-mash of rusting pipes and valves to satisfy hard-core wreck divers.

Dusk is an especially good time to enjoy this wreck, when predator and prey begin in earnest their nightly battle for survival. Listen out for the squeals of the bottlenose dolphins, which are seldom far away at this time of the day: you may just be lucky enough to see them making a quick detour onto the wreck.

KIMON M

As a wreck story, that of the *Kimon M* could not be less romantic than that of the *Carnatic*. This 1950s vessel was simply an average-sized cargo ship that, at the time of her demise, was carrying hundreds of tons of lentils. She had been following the heavily trafficked route through the Gulf of Suez into the Red Sea proper, when human error yet again cost a skipper his ship and reputation. As the wreck lies at the furthest point from where dive boats tend to moor up, she is probably the least dived of the four, and conditions often prevent diving entirely. She lies on her starboard at a deepest point of 32m. The stern is the most diveable part while the bow section is fairly broken up. One of the best places to aim for is the engine room. Although much of the engine was salvaged, there is still plenty to see. She also has a fairly distinctive stern. Like all the wrecks of Abu Nuhas, the *Kimon M* is visited by both dayboats and liveaboards almost every day of the year.

▲ A diver navigates the stern section of the *Kimon M*.
(Charles Hood/oceans-image.com)

1. Stern
2. Four-bladed propeller
3. Mast
4. Funnel
5. Access to Captain's cabin
6. Bridge and engine room
7. Bow section

— sea level
— top of wreck 6m

— lowest point 32m

▲ She lies on her starboard having sunk carrying a few thousand tons of lentils.

(Charles Hood/oceans-image.com)

▲ Anthias swim among the brightly coloured soft coral growing on parts of the wreck.

(Peter Collings)

▲ Glassfish swirl through the interior of the *Kimon M.* (Peter Collings)

▲ Coral growth can be found in small patches over the wreck. (Peter Collings)

THISTLEGORM & ROSALIE MOLLER

QUITE SIMPLY, THESE TWO MAGNIFICENT SHIP-WRECKS ALONE JUSTIFY A VISIT TO THE RED SEA. THEIR FATE BECAME INTERTWINED FROM THE MOMENT A GERMAN AIRCRAFT'S BOMBS STRUCK THE *THISTLEGORM* IN OCTOBER 1941.

The explosion lit up the night sky, exposing the whereabouts of the *Rosalie Moller*, who then suffered the same fate exactly 48 hours later. Between them, the two ships lost eleven lives. Today these two very different wrecks offer a sense of the pioneering days of scuba, as well as the chance to savour their lingering historical presence and character.

The *Thistlegorm* is among the top wreck dives in the world. The *Rosalie Moller* has less to capture the imagination, but is more of a challenging dive. Wreck aficionados, especially lovers of all things Red Sea, cannot call themselves true wreck divers until they have logged both of these undersea marvels.

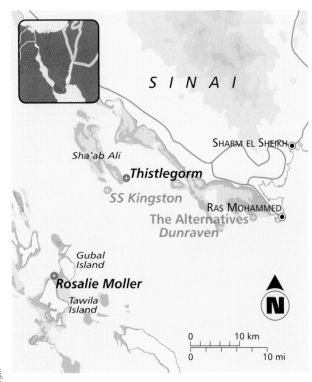

Jane Morgan

◄ The Thistlegorm's stern-mounted machine guns provide excellent photographic opportunities.

Alexander Mustard

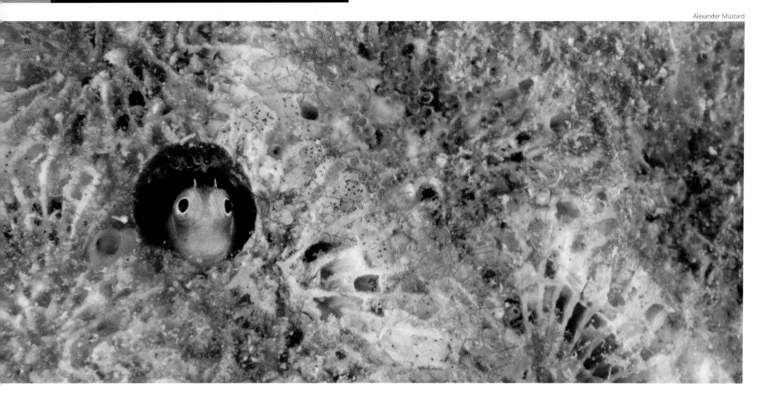

▲ Marine life of all sizes is to be found in the nooks and crannies of the *Thistlegorm*.

▶ Caked in decades of rust and detritus, the rows of BSA motorcycles are among the star attractions in the holds.

✈ GETTING THERE

The best way to enjoy either of these two wrecks is, without doubt, from the comfort of one of the many liveaboards plying their trade in the northern Red Sea. If wrecks are your reason for diving, it's possible to choose operators offering exclusively wrecks for the duration of your stay. Since the location lies more or less in between Sharm el Sheikh and Hurghada, it matters little which of these is your port of entry into Egypt. This is more likely to be determined by the operator's preference of charter. Some liveaboards have itineraries that include the wrecks of the *Numidia* and *Aida* at The Brothers. If this is your chosen trip, the likelihood is that your diveboat will sail from Hurghada. Dayboat trips range from the crack-of-dawn starts from Sharm and Hurghada to one- or two-night safaris. The big advantage of liveaboards is avoiding the mad rush. The journey takes about three-and-a-half hours from Hurghada and a couple of hours from Sharm. A liveaboard also offers the chance to go night diving on the *Thistlegorm*. Mostly it is still the liveaboards that take on the *Rosalie Moller*, as she's considered too difficult for novice divers.

THE *THISTLEGORM*

Depth: 30m

Skill level: 20 dives

Access: liveaboard or dayboat from Sharm el Sheikh or Hurghada

Current: varies from mild to strong

Must see: the motorbikes and trucks; guns on the stern section; the dramatic bow viewed from the seabed; the Lee Enfield rifles and wellington boots

Much has been said and written over the years about this mighty British war ship. Almost every nut, bolt, rusty motorbike wheel, cracked windscreen, torn wellington boot, rotten rifle butt and crumbling round of live ammunition has been pored over by the armies of divers who converge on the *Thistlegorm* from morning till night almost every day of the year. The reason is simple: this is an awesome wreck. It inspires divers, perhaps more than any other, to follow in the finprints of the great masters like Cousteau, who first discovered the site in the 1950s back in the pioneering days of the aqualung. On a clear, baking hot day when the sea is mirror-calm, the stricken vessel's shimmering form can be seen from the upper decks of a liveaboard. In stark contrast, when the cold, howling northerlies are blowing, the Red Sea becomes ferocity incarnate. On days such as this, only the hardiest of vessels can be found moored to creaking metal struts of the wreck.

It is a measure of the wreck's allure that she is still dived in such extreme conditions. Over the decades, this haunting 130m-long supply ship has endured the ravages of an unforgiving sea and countless trophy hunters. But the spirit of the *Thistlegorm* remains undimmed. With her unrivalled museum of military cargo stacked in every hold, she still has the power to evoke the so-called glory days of a bygone age.

The *Thistlegorm's* short life began in 1940, when she was launched by Joseph Thompson and Sons in Sunderland – a town once regarded as the very birthplace of ships, where whole communities lived and breathed the daily grind of a centuries-old industry. It ended in the Gubal Straits just over a year later. Re-assigned as an armed freighter, the *Thistlegorm* was carrying vital supplies for British forces at Tobruk, having travelled the long way round via the Cape of Good Hope, and was forced to wait at anchor for two agonising weeks. On the night of October 6, 1941, German bombers, believing they were about to attack a large troop ship rumoured to be the Queen Mary, chanced upon her. The *Thistlegorm* was a sitting duck: her meagre weaponry could do little against a squadron of Heinkels. The bombs struck one of the rear holds, killing four crew members and nine sailors. Fires broke out on the deck and there were acts of heroism as the remaining crew managed to make it to safety. With the Egyptian night sky lit up by the blazing ship, all 4,900 tonnes of her sank quickly to the seabed.

The demise of the *Thistlegorm* soon led to the downfall of another British ship, whose position was revealed to the German bombers by the brightness of the ensuing explosions. The ship in question was the *Rosalie Moller*. Today this wreck, though not that far away, offers an altogether different dive in deeper, murkier water.

THISTLEGORM

1. Anchor windlass
2. Railway tender
3. No.1 Hold
4. Railway wagon
5. No.2 hold
6. Bridge
7. No.3 hold
8. Sheet metal roof
9. Funnel
10. No.4 hold
11. Locomotive
12. Bren carrier
13. Heavy machine gun
14. Anti-aircraft gun
15. Propeller

sea level

top of wreck 10m

lowest point 30m

▲ Windlass bedecked in life.
(Charles Hood/oceans-image.com)

▲ Railway tender.
(Charles Hood/oceans-image.com)

▲ A diver enters one of the many holds.
(Peter Collings)

▲ Buffers of railway wagon.
(Charles Hood/oceans-image.com)

▲ Railway wagon perched on
starboard. (Charles Hood/oceans-image.com)

▲ Crumbling armoured car.
(Charles Hood/oceans-image.com)

▲ Upturned Bren carrier.
(Charles Hood/oceans-image.com)

▲ Heavily listing stern section.
(Charles Hood/oceans-image.com)

▲ 4.7 inch light anti-aircraft gun.
(Charles Hood/oceans-image.com)

▲ Parked side by side, this Bedford truck is one of many WWII military vehicles the Thistlegorm was carrying.

THE DIVE

The *Thistlegorm* sits proudly on the seabed in the middle of the Gubal Straits, unprotected by reefs or land. Depending on conditions, there may be as many as 20 boats vying for space above the wreck. The more impatient are kitted up and in the water by the crack of dawn. This can be as early as 6am, when light levels are extremely low. But since many aim for three to four dives in a day to get the most out of the wreck, early starts are often a good idea. This dive is also an excellent candidate for nitrox diving, with either a 32 per cent or 36 per cent mix to maximise bottom time.

Mooring lines are usually attached to the bow, midships or the separated stern section. If you're not familiar with the wreck, study our diagram (page 126-127) to get an idea of where the holds are located and decide in advance which of the artefacts you most want to see. A typical dive plan involves dropping down a shotline just to one side of an expanse of crumpled metal decking around the funnel.

It is possible, with very good visibility, to make out the shadowy form of the stern section. There is a large area of shattered remains where the ship was broken in two; from here, you pass hold number three and will very quickly see the bridge. Deck level sits at about

Jane Morgan

SHIPWRECKS OF SUEZ

As the Red Sea narrows at its northernmost extreme, a long thin arm of water stretches up towards the Mediterranean. Flanked to the east by the Sinai Peninsula and to the west by the Egyptian mainland, the entrance to the Gulf of Suez is marked by a treacherous finger of reef known as Sha'ab Ali. A narrow but important seaway dating back to before the opening of the Suez Canal, this forms a vital link between east and west trade routes. It is also a hive of industry, with oilfields dotted along its length and refineries along its banks.

Very little diving takes place here: the coral reefs die away as the water becomes shallower and less clear due to the presence of sand and silt. Water temperature also plays a part in the ecology, with temperatures as low as 16°C in winter. But while this may not be a viable tourist area, it might just be the Red Sea's greatest repository of unexplored shipwrecks, and has the added bonus of some unusual marine life.

Heading north past Sha'ab Ali, the headland of Ras Dib heralds an area rich in shipwrecks. First are the *Attiki* and the *Muhansia*, both of which are visible from the surface, well salvaged and quite broken-up. Lying at a depth of only 12m, they are home to schooling fish and some very large specimens of the endemic nudibranchs found elsewhere in the Red Sea.

Rounding the headland, the wreck of the *Elliot* is embedded in the reef, her headlong grounding evident from the attitude of her rudder. This wreck's superstructure still protrudes above the water – divers can enter the hull, swim through into the engine room and take a walk around. Half a mile offshore, in deeper, clearer water, lie three unidentified modern merchant ships in less than 50m of water. Discovered during an expedition in 2004, their identities remain a mystery.

At Ras Shuckier, the hustle and bustle of the oil industry becomes very evident. Close to shore are two shallow wrecks, while again offshore there are several deeper ones. *Birchwood 11*, or the 'Plastics Wreck', lies to the north of the port in a large bay that has three wrecks within its confines. The Birchwood is a small, 50m-long cargo ship. It lies on its starboard side at a depth of 12m, completely intact and with the light of the shallows streaming down into its hold. A school of juvenile barracuda circles the mast, which still has its radar array and aerials.

Just forward of the superstructure at the aft of the vessel is an intact crane, almost certainly once used to service the hold. The criss-cross framework of the jib is covered in encrusting life. There are some superb swim-throughs from the weather deck into the holds, where cargo bags of polythene granules float hard against the port hull. The fo'c'sle is easy to access and explore, and the winch gear is covered in sponges and encrusting corals. The bow appears intact and a deep scour runs along the keel, becoming circular towards her propeller and rudder.

Hundreds of nudibranchs smother the red sponge fingers found throughout the wreck. Snowflake morays, a rare sight elsewhere in the Red Sea, are commonplace here. Almost every surface of the wreck is alive with anemones, sponges and small crustaceans.

Not far from the Plastics Wreck sits a 40m-long vessel with its bridge out of the water. This is the *Laura Security*, also known as the 'Eagle Wreck', after the osprey that has made a roost on the upper levels, which protrude from the water. Many of the hull plates have fallen to the seabed, allowing sunlight to stream through the vertical supports, highlighting shoals of fish. With the hull intact, the bow and stern are very photogenic and the resident fish life is quite prolific. Due to its location, the wreck is blessed by the afternoon sunlight, long arcs of which shine through many holes in its structure.

The headland of Ras Gharib is a terminal for the oil industry and marks the limit of diving exploration in the Gulf of Suez. There is evidence to suggest that at least 20 wrecks lie in the vicinity, some in shallow water, others at an appreciable depth. The *Aboudy* was a small, aluminium-hulled cargo ship 76m long, which sank on 7 May 1988. She was carrying a cargo of cattle, aluminium extrusion and thousands of 300ml bottles of cough medicine. Today she lies on her port side, totally intact and with masts lying horizontal towards the shore. Remnants of the cargo lie in her holds, spilling out onto the seabed. Divers can swim from the fo'c'sle through these holds to the bridge section at the stern, where the engine room is located. Marine life here includes chevron barracuda, fusiliers, emperor angelfish, crocodilefish, torpedo rays and encrusting corals and sponges. Visibility is subject to swell, as the seabed consists of fine sand that is easily stirred up.

Other wrecks in the Ras Garib area include the Bahr, a Russian-built motor survey vessel. This was in service for the United Arab Republic General Petroleum Company when Israeli missiles sank it in 1973, during the *Yom Kippur* War. Today the 45m-long wreck lies in just 14m of water. There is also the wreck of the *Scalaria*, an allied steam tanker attacked by aircraft during the Second World War. One of the ship's officers was awarded the George Cross for saving the lives of men who were left struggling for survival in a sea of burning oil. This wreck has been partially dismantled and only the lower hull remains, lying in shallow water.

17m. Then the larger opening of hold two looms into view. This is a good point to descend into the bowels of the ship, where you'll find an amazing treasure trove of Bedford trucks and BSA motorcycles. It is like a watery Aladdin's Cave, where time has stood still since the Second World War. You've seen the pictures and you've seen the videos, but this is it: you are finally seeing the *Thistlegorm* for real.

There is plenty of room to move around inside, so even with a fair few divers about, you are still able to avoid the crowds. Inside the holds you are protected from currents, but it's worth being aware that by the time you decide to emerge, these can become fairly strong – sometimes flowing across the beam, and at other times from bow to stern. Hold number two has a fascinating array of vehicles that were carefully loaded to maximise the cargo. Inside the rusting Bedford trucks are row upon row of now yellow-greenish BSA motorbikes, whose headlights and petrol tanks have either been eaten away by rust or damaged by the daily onslaught of divers.

You can just imagine the pristine condition of the wreck when Cousteau's team of pioneers first discovered her back in the 1950s during the making of the seminal *Silent World*. Cousteau never revealed her location, and it once again passed into obscurity until its rediscovery

Charles Hood/oceans-image.com

Charles Hood/oceans-image.com

▲ Divers entering holds should always remember to take a torch.

▲► Many of the shells littering the wreck are still live.

► A well camouflaged crocodile fish lurks on the deck of the *Thistlegorm*.

►► A turtle forages on the coral growth that grows on the top deck of the *Thistlegorm*. (Alexander Mustard)

by a team of divers in the early 1990s. The rest, as they say, is history. The *Thistlegorm* is now regarded as one of the greatest wreck dives in the world. The sheer numbers who visit her time and again is testament to her enduring charm and irresistible pulling power. Inevitably the souvenir hunters have taken their toll. In the first few years after she was rediscovered, some of the trucks and motorbikes still had keys in the ignition, windscreens were unbroken and foot pedals still had their rubber covers. No longer. Even live rounds of ammunition found scattered on the deck were unwisely slipped into BCD pockets. One diver who could not resist temptation brought a live round to the surface and was busily sanding off the years of grime when suddenly it went off in his hands, fizzing across the deck of the boat. Fortunately no one was injured, but it just went to prove that even after more than half a century at the bottom of the sea, explosives still pack a punch.

Moving through to hold number one, you will come across more and more vehicles, including Morris cars. The silt-laden tread on the unworn tyres gives the vehicles a timeless quality, making them wonderful photographic subjects. Less obvious are the rusting remains of

the Lee-Enfield rifles, whose wooden boxes have long since been eaten away, exposing the fused barrels of the guns caked in decades of iron oxides and silt. Then there are the wellies: dozens and dozens of long black rubber wellington boots, which troops required for crossing muddy, flooded terrain. These are piled high in the backs of trucks and appear in excellent condition, if a little torn.

Rising from the holds, the engine tenders appear on the decks on either side of the wreck. A sure sign of the wreck's decay is the precarious position of the tender on the port side adjacent to hold number one: the entire deck area and tender have been collapsing inward for some time. Another option for a first dive is to aim for the bow. From a vantage point on the seabed some ten metres away, the hefty anchor chain and sharp lines of the bow make for a dramatic photograph when set against the midday sun.

Back on the deck, the winch gear on the raised bow section is largely undamaged. Among the marine characters occupying this section are striped sergeant majors and golden anthias. Wildlife on the *Thistlegorm* can be quite breathtaking. This is much more the case when

▶ Vast swathes of glassfish swarm around the decks of the Rosalie Moller in numbers like few other ships.

▼ Blades of the giant propeller and intact rudder resting on seabed at about 30 metres.

the currents are running, since the wreck provides the only sanctuary for miles around. There is most activity at dusk, when you're likely to see frenzied jacks hunting the length and breadth of the ship. Schooling barracuda also move in, targeting the smaller schools of bait fish and chasing them around the decks in tightly knit balls. Batfish congregate in large numbers, too, often wavering stoically in the vicinity of the bridge. There are also giant barracuda, very occasionally sharks, hungry tuna and on lucky dives a pod of bottlenose dolphins may join the party. A good-sized hawksbill turtle has long been a resident of the *Thistlegorm* and is usually found dozing near the bridge.

You will usually need a separate dive to take in the stern section. Descending again down the midships mooring line, you may first wish to head past the debris of mines and other explosive devices just off the port side. About 20m further out from here is one of the locomotives that was blown off the decks during the bomb attack. In the debris between the two sections of

the wreck is an easily identifiable Mark Two Bren carrier, along with various types of ammunition.

The stern itself is characterised by a large torn hull, whose railings have been further damaged by the many anchors and shotlines tied to her over the years. While swimming along the seabed, aim for the large propeller, which was once capable of pushing this 4,900-tonne ship through the water at a comfortable ten knots. As the stern section bore the brunt of the attack, it is inclined at a steep angle. Here you will find the only real firepower available to the armed freighter: a heavy fixed-position machine gun and a 4.7in (120mm) anti-aircraft gun.

As a giant of the Red Sea, the *Thistlegorm* is without doubt one of the true greats. Her fascinating history and sense of nostalgia enrich the diving experience tenfold. More than half a century after Cousteau's discovery, the old ship may be slightly the worse for wear, but she is likely to continue giving pleasure to divers from all over the world for many decades to come.

Charles Hood/oceans-image.com

THE *ROSALIE MOLLER*

Depth: 25m to deck; 50m to seafloor

Skill level: 25+ dives

Access: liveaboard from Sharm el Sheikh or Hurghada

Current: mild to strong, often with poor visibility

Must see: countless glassfish swarming over her decks; damage caused by German bombers; the workshop and engine room (experienced divers only)

This wreck is sometimes seen as a poor relation of the *Thistlegorm*, with none of the more famous ship's glamour and no treasure trove of historical gems from a bygone military era. But the *Rosalie Moller*, a workhorse cargo ship carrying coal supplies for the British Navy, has charms that are all her own. Her fate was sealed when the explosions from the *Thistlegorm* lit up the night sky and gave away her position. Just 48 hours later, at 1am on October 8, the same German pilots sunk her with a deadly strike on one of the holds. It took little more than an hour for her to go down, with the loss of two lives.

It was nearly the end of the 20th century before divers found the *Rosalie Moller* and her story could be told to a new generation. The wreck sits upright on the seabed in the deeper, murkier waters off Gubal Island, just south-west of the mouth of the Gulf of Suez. Many dive operators ignored her for a while because of the difficulties of diving in this spot, not least the poor visibility and occasional ripping currents. Increasingly, however, diving the *Rosalie Moller* has become something of a cherished ambition among wreck devotees old and new. This has been boosted by tour companies eager to offer exclusively wreck itineraries. So the 'Rosy', as she is affectionately known to regulars, has gained rapidly in status as a premium log entry. This wreck will never have the pulling power of the *Thistlegorm*, but the direct historical links make her a compelling and serious diversion for divers wanting more of a challenge.

As a dive, there are few comparisons between the two. For starters, the *Rosy* rarely enjoys the luxury of clear blue water. If anything, it is almost ghostlike, permanently blurred by varying shades of green. If it were not for the temperature of the water, divers could be forgiven for thinking this was Scapa Flow instead of the Red Sea. After reaching the wreck via the shotline, the first glimpses have a more eerie feel than those of her distinguished fellow bombing victim. At around 25m to the deck, there is an acute awareness of depth. This tempers the desire to wander too far afield, which is why it is a good idea to pre-plan the dive's objectives. A first encounter is enough to get a sense of her size, which at a shade under 110m is just short of the length of the *Thistlegorm*. The fact that her masts remain vertical, despite their frequent use as anchorage for dive boats,

Charles Hood/oceans-image.com

makes her all the more impressive. The *Rosy's* railings have also suffered at the hands of dive boats, but the rest of the deck superstructure and machinery is well preserved. Perhaps the most unforgettable and dominating feature of the deck area is the sheer numbers of glassfish. They swarm from bow to stern in greater density than you will find on any other wreck. It is quite a spectacle.

Of course, such a nutritious bounty does not go unnoticed. At almost every turn, there are predators picking off tasty morsels at leisure. Among the most common are the squadrons of lionfish that prefer to bide their time until nightfall. Jacks, meanwhile, prowl with increasing enthusiasm and determination at dusk. Like many wrecks, the *Rosy* has developed its own frenetic eco-system, but the sheer size of the fish population can take any diver by surprise.

At exactly 50m, the greying seabed is almost lifeless and offers little more than the chance to explore either the large propeller and rudder system or the narrow form of the bow. It is well worth a look at the blast area – a gaping hole that appears, for all the world, to be the work of a giant can opener. The sheets of metal have peeled outward, exposing the hold that suffered the fatal damage.

As you move amidships, you will see the large signature letter *M* of the *Moller Line*. When she was launched in Glasgow in 1910, the *Rosalie Moller* actually sailed under the name of the *Francis*, but this was changed when she was later sold.

Even more clues about the vessel's build and role are to be discovered deep in the bowels of the ship. But be warned: this is challenging diving and a very tight squeeze. At these sorts of depths, beyond the open circuit capabilities of nitrox, it takes little time to acquire decompression penalties, so it is vital to monitor air supplies.

If you manage to navigate down the narrow, railed stairs to the engine room and workshop area at about 45m, you will experience a strong sense of time standing still. Here you can marvel at the engineering of the old ship. When the author first made it into the workshop, a rusting old oil lamp lay undisturbed on the bench, presumably in the very spot where it fell after the bomb attack. Even more surprising was the sight of a domestic tungsten bulb still dangling in its socket from the ceiling, unbroken after decades.

When beginning the ascent, usually up one of the masts (the forward mast has a crow's nest, providing a more interesting diversion for decompression stops), spare a thought for the *Rosy's* ebullient Australian skipper, Captain James Byrne, who stood on the bridge and shook a defiant fist at the German pilots as they released their deadly cargo. What he would have made of the armies of divers now converging on his old ship is something we can only imagine.

◄ The bow of the *Rosalie Moller* rises sharply from the murky dephs.

◄▼ Sitting upright, the stern section reveals three of the four remaining blades and rudder.

▼ Access in and around the 'Rosy' is fairly easy though great caution is needed if entering the engine room.

Charles Hood/oceans-image.com

Charles Hood/oceans-image.com

ROSALIE MOLLER

1. Propeller and rudder
2. Railings
3. Engine room
4. Bomb damage
5. Workshop
6. Bridge
7. Winch gear
8. Mast
9. Crow's nest
10. Main deck
11. Bow
12. Anchor

▲ Railings – some damaged by anchors – at the stern.
(Peter Collings)

▲ Amazing workings of the intact engine room. (Peter Collings)

sea level

top of wreck 25m

lowest point 50m

▲ Stairway to the depths of 'Rosy'.
(Peter Collings)

▲ A work bench inside the wreck.
(Peter Collings)

▲ Winch gear in the gloomy shadow of the
main mast. (Charles Hood/oceans-image.com)

▲ Heavily populated crow's nest.
(Peter Collings)

▲ One of the many bits of machinery
on the main deck. (Peter Collings)

▲ A hungry grouper lies in wait on
the bow. (Peter Collings)

▲ Anchor ready for deployment.
(Peter Collings)

Divers explore the heavily encrusted stern of the *Rosalie Moller,* where boat anchors have caused some damage to railings over the years. (Charles Hood/oceans-image.com)

HURGHADA
TO EL QUSEIR

THE DIVING IN THIS CHAPTER IS CHARACTERISED BY SHALLOWER SITES AND PATCH REEFS. THERE ARE MANY EXCELLENT SITES FOR THOSE WHO ARE NEW TO DIVING, BUT THERE IS MUCH TO ENTHUSE THE MORE EXPERIENCED, NOT LEAST THE SHEER VOLUME OF FISH LIFE IN EVIDENCE.

The reefs also prove two different but related points: first, what can happen if dive boats are left to operate without control and legislation; and second, how the reefs can be preserved if the boats are given a system of mooring buoys and a code of conduct to abide by.

So, we progress southwards down the Egyptian coast and reach the ever-expanding resort strip of Hurghada. A sleepy fishing village back in the early 1980s, Hurghada mushroomed with the construction of its own airport and now sprawls along 30km of coastline, offering everything from the most basic 'bucket and spade' hotels to five star luxury resorts where the design and opulence rival any in the world. As with Sharm, there are countless options for nightlife and dining (we visited a nightclub in a massive tent, with a kebab shop inside!), but it could be said that the town lacks the character that comes with having a definable centre. All the same, it is a lot of fun: a cultural and linguistic melting pot where you can enjoy a *shisha* pipe and watch the neon night unfold.

Most of the diving is centred on the offshore islands of Giftun and Abu Ramada, with their satellite patch reefs. By the mid-Nineties, though, it was evident that Hurghada was becoming the victim of its own rapid success, with the anchoring of boats on the offshore reefs and islands causing great damage to the corals. Some of the more responsible dive centres came together to form the non-governmental organisation HEPCA – the Hurghada Environmental Protection and Conservation Association – which began installing mooring buoys on the most popular sites.

Today, there is little doubt that the proliferation of divers and boats has adversely affected some of this area's best sites. Still, thanks to the work of HEPCA in training more than 250 boat

Charles Hood/oceans-image.com

◄ Dive boats moor on the sheltered side of a Hurghada reef system, where permanent moorings now mean that no one should anchor on the coral.

skippers in environmental awareness and proper use of moorings, the area has a bright future. The Marine Conservation Society has been monitoring the condition of the reefs here since 1996 and its records show that the decline has been halted.

The port of Safaga lies about 65km south of Hurghada and has blossomed as a tourist destination since the mid-Nineties. Its significance goes back a lot further as an embarkation point for pilgrims on their way to Mecca, and it remains an important industrial port. The focal point for tourism here is Soma Bay, to the north of the city, where a cluster of resorts, golf courses and water sports centres has been established. The surrounding desert and mountains provide an inspiring backdrop to a town where the nightlife may not be as wild as Hurghada or Sharm, but there is still much to do. As we shall see, Safaga's diving is varied and of extremely high quality, though Panorama Reef is no longer the beacon of excellence it once was.

Journey south another 95km from Safaga, and you arrive at El Quseir. This ancient settlement dates back to the Ptolemaic period, when it was a strategically important port for the trading ships that criss-crossed the Red Sea. It fell into abandonment for 700 years after the Roman period, but was revived when trade with Asia resumed in the Middle Ages.

You can still get a taste of the old Red Sea by visiting El Quseir's Historic Quarter, where many of the buildings

► The sun sets behind the Eastern Desert, casting a reddish hue across the sea. Could this be the reason behind its name?

Charles Hood/oceans-image.com

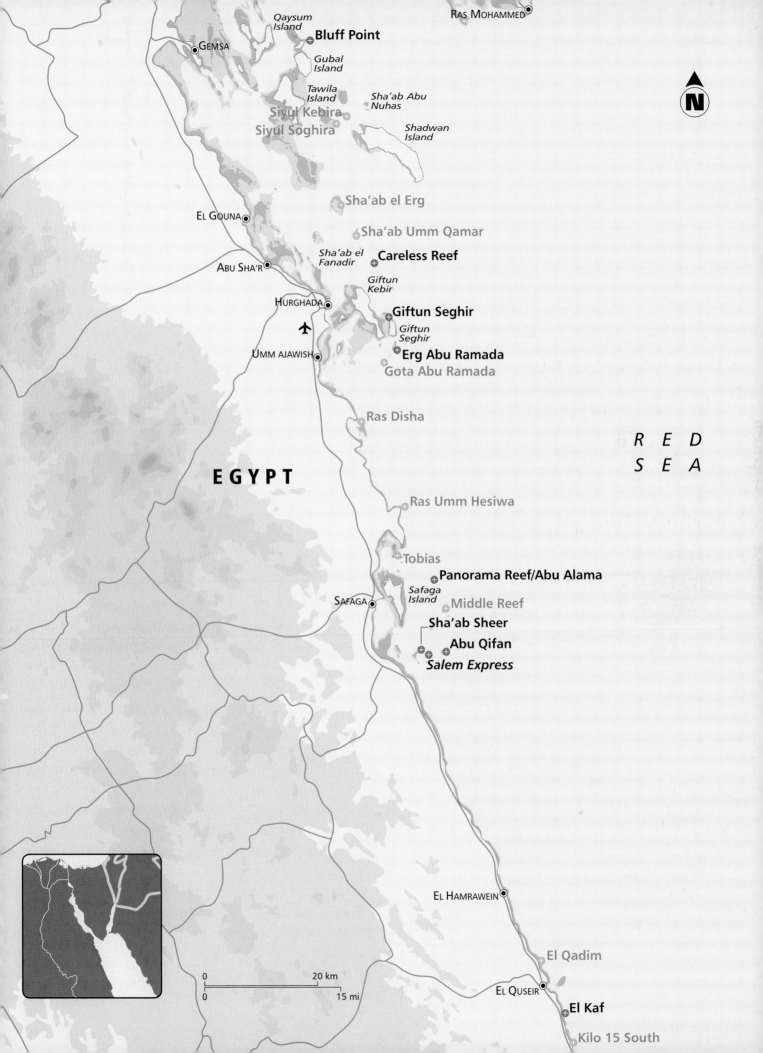

Qaysum Island

Bluff Point

GEMSA

Gubal Island

Tawila Island

Sha'ab Abu Nuhas

Siyul Kebira

Siyul Soghira

Shadwan Island

RAS MOHAMMED

N

Sha'ab el Erg

Sha'ab Umm Qamar

Sha'ab el Fanadir

Careless Reef

EL GOUNA

Giftun Kebir

ABU SHA'R

HURGHADA

Giftun Seghir

Giftun Seghir

UMM AJAWISH

Erg Abu Ramada

Gota Abu Ramada

Ras Disha

E G Y P T

*R E D
S E A*

Ras Umm Hesiwa

Tobias

Panorama Reef/Abu Alama

Safaga Island

Middle Reef

SAFAGA

Sha'ab Sheer

Abu Qifan

Salem Express

EL HAMRAWEIN

El Qadim

EL QUSEIR

El Kaf

Kilo 15 South

0   20 km

0   15 mi

are made of coral limestone. The old fort, founded in 1571, has been adapted into an engaging visitors' centre, with displays on pearl diving, the local phosphate industry and Bedouin trade, among other aspects of desert life. Its proximity to some of the area's best dive sites, not to mention the new Marsa Alam airport, has ensured El Quseir's continuing importance as part of Egypt's Red Sea Riviera.

◀ Hurghada's coastal strip has been the subject of intense development, a sign of Egypt's growing popularity but for some, a step too far.

EL GOUNA

To the north of Hurghada, you will find the sprawling, purpose-built tourist enclave of El Gouna. Constructed across a series of islands and linked by bridges and canals, it constitutes a mini-city in itself, comprising 15 hotels, two shopping centres and a brewery. Facilities include golf courses, a cheese factory and a shopping mall with a cinema and a strip of bars. Utterly bizarre, it is neither Egyptian, nor European, nor American, but exists as a sort of international hotel state. It has proven especially popular with divers because it offers relatively good departure points for the sites of Abu Nuhas. There are several excellent dive operations here, and while it hardly offers a true taste of Egypt, you will find all the comforts of home in the Neverland that is El Gouna.

www.elgouna.com

Charles Hood/oceans-image.com

VISIBILITY

Most sites in this region can guarantee 20-metre visibility for most of the year, though some sites may become silted out after exceptionally violent storms.

WATER TEMPERATURE

Air temperature: 35°C in summer; 24°C in winter. Water temperature: 29°C in summer; 22°C in winter.

SEASONALITY

You can usually rely on water clarity of 25–30m for most of the sites here during the summer months, though the *Salem Express* lies in a relatively silty area where it's typically a slightly milky 20m or less. During winter, the area can be subject to rough periods when sediment is blasted off the reef tops and hangs suspended in the water for several days, or until it is moved on by the current.

OTHER DIVE SITES

El Qadim
Gota Abu Ramada
Kilo 15 South
Middle Reef
Ras Disha
Ras Umm Hesiwa
Sha'ab el Erg
Sha'ab Umm Qamar
Siyul Kebira
Siyul Soghira
Tobias

▶ This gorgonian fan coral shelters a sleeping lionfish. Can you spot it?

▼ A devil scorpionfish lurks in the coral.

BLUFF POINT

Max depth: 42m (optimum 28m)

Skill level: 20 dives

Access: dayboat from Hurghada or liveaboard

Current: moderate to brisk

Must see: anthias schools; moray eels out in the open; caverns from 22m; green and hawksbill turtles

Bluff Point is a long promontory that extends from the north-eastern point of Gobal Seghira island. It can be identified from the sea by its small lighthouse, part of the system for guiding ships into the Gulf of Suez. The reef is defined by a colourful wall that descends to 40m, providing a catwalk of Red Sea fauna. As this spot is quite exposed, your dive here will be dictated by the prevailing conditions, especially the swell.

Often, your boat will moor southeast of the point. It is then a simple case of jumping in and keeping the wall to your right. If you want simply to enjoy the best of the reef, stay at 15–20m, where there is an excellent mixture of table corals and soft corals, with the area's trademark clouds of anthias fish billowing backwards and forwards from the reef. Ideally, you should visit this site in the mid-morning, when the soft light from the east suffuses the reef with colour and clarity. Visibility is generally fine, though it can become quite milky with sand particles if the wind is blowing strong from a northerly direction.

There is an opportunity for a deeper dive here, as the wall leads down to a sandy seabed at about 40–42m. It is possible to see white-tip reef sharks here, but they tend to be skittish and seldom allow divers to get close. Instead, keep an eye out for the many large morays, which are numerous in this area. You can dive some of the Red Sea's southern sites for days without seeing a good moray, so relish their natural abundance here, but don't venture too close with your camera, as they have been known to bite intrusive divers.

At 28–22m you should come across a set of pretty caverns, which can be worth exploring. The atmosphere inside is decidedly moody, but you should find plenty of animals, including disciplined schools of glassfish, which form captivating patterns as they shift and turn in perfect unison. There are also plenty of cleaning stations here, so if the current allows you to stay in one place and observe the rituals of fish cleaning, it can be rewarding to pair off from those divers who feel the need to cover the reef at high speed.

As with many other sites in this strait, there is always a chance of running into some of the resident bottlenose dolphins, which are big enough not to feel scared of divers – though they only approach people if they are feeling playful and unthreatened. We recommend you switch off your camera flashes, as these seem to deter the dolphins from sticking around. You can usually rely on sightings of both the Red Sea's turtle species here, green and hawksbill, as the island is a nesting site and the reef's many sponges provide an abundant food source.

As you turn around the western point and head up the reef, you may come across the wreck of a supply barge at a depth of around 14m. Some liveaboards offer this as a night dive, as it is home to many shrimps and scorpionfish. We have heard reports of large stonefish on this wreck. In addition to being potentially lethal, these are also extremely difficult to spot. You could spend a minute or more admiring what you think is a lump of coral, before a slight movement gives away the fact that it is, in fact, the most venomous fish in the sea! Suffice it to say that good buoyancy skills are essential here.

Charles Hood/oceans-image.com

Alexander Mustard

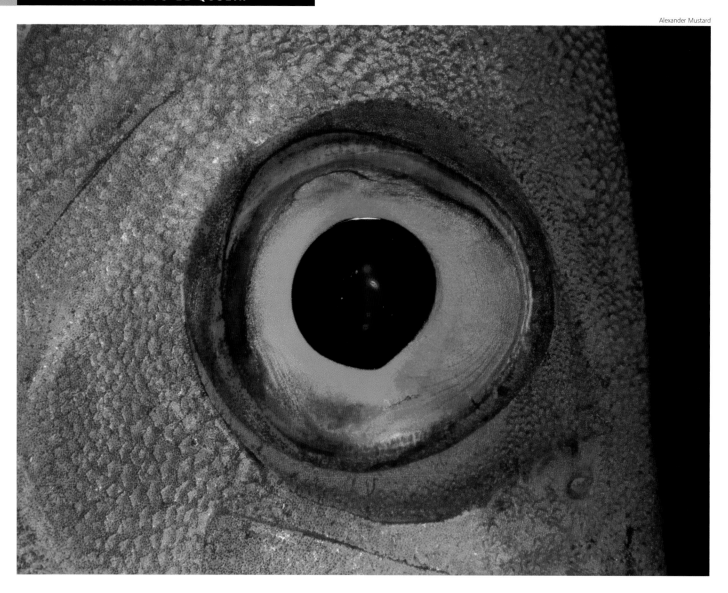

▲ Bigeye soldierfish lurk in caverns and coral overhangs, where they allow divers to approach quite closely.

GIFTUN SEGHIR

Max depth: 50m (25m optimum)

Skill level: 20 dives

Access: dayboat from Hurghada

Current: slight to moderate

Must see: gorgonian fans on the wall; longnose hawkfish; black coral at depth

Currents sweeping up towards the Gulf of Suez, coupled with rich upwellings from nearby deep water, enrich the Straits of Gobal, creating the perfect conditions for coral reef development. One of the best dives in this intense area is this beautiful coral wall, found on the southern side of Giftun Seghir island.

This is not a sheer wall of the type you would find in the offshore sites to the south. It is pocked with cracks, ledges, overhangs and swim-throughs, creating a more complex environment that in turn is host to a greater variety of reef life than you would expect even at the Brother Islands.

There is excellent shelter for overnight mooring here, so many divers find themselves exploring this site on the earliest dive of the day, which often takes place around 7–7.30am. That said, dayboat divers should not feel they have been beaten to the best of this reef, as it truly comes into its own in the mid-morning, when the gathering sunlight shines across it. The sun's energy even reaches an impressive colony of gorgonian fan corals, marking the deepest extreme of the dive at about 45m. In the deeper areas, you will also see a great deal of black coral, which acts as shelter for a various reef fish, including filefish, soldierfish and longnose hawkfish. Also at this depth, you should be able to find a beautiful cave filled with yellow fan corals.

Dives typically begin from an inlet, from where you can drift onto the most impressive part of the reef, keeping the wall on your right. While on the deeper section of the dive, look out for pelagics such as dogfish tuna and giant trevally. There have been reports of scalloped hammerheads being seen here, but sightings tend to be confined to early spring, when the conditions are ideal.

As you ascend, the reef becomes even more beautiful as the wall separates into two sections, offering plenty of shelter for pufferfish, blue-spotted stingrays and other creatures that enjoy the cover of table corals. Watch out for the schools of yellowtail goatfish and friendly Napoleon wrasse, as well as various camouflaged sand-dwellers such as the crocodilefish. The dive ends in an area where mooring buoys have been provided; there are liable to be quite a few boats here, so make a point of remembering what your own vessel looks like from underwater. Sending up a surface marker buoy is also advisable if inflatable boats are zooming around at the surface.

CARELESS REEF

Max depth: 25m

Skill level: 20 dives

Access: dayboat from Hurghada or liveaboard

Current: moderate

Must see: moray eels everywhere; glassy sweepers in cracks and ledges; jacks and visiting pelagics

Despite its relative proximity to Hurghada, Careless Reef sits in a particularly exposed area, and diving is often impossible due to heavy swells from the north. The site is centred on two pinnacles that sit in the middle of a plateau where a very comprehensive array of Red Sea species can be observed. It's a rich hunting ground for trevallies and other blue water predators, but the most famous residents here are the various species of moray eel, which seem to occupy every conceivable crack in the reef.

If you want to take photographs of big eels, this is the best place in the Red Sea. For a start, there's a good mixture of species, including the giant moray. But what really helps is that the eels appear to be semi-tame, possibly as a result of feeding sessions back in the Eighties and Nineties. Many of the older eels here have virtually no fear of divers, so do not be alarmed if they swim up to you (though we would advise you hold your hands close to your chest, lest the eels assume you have something to offer them!).

If you're looking for a deeper dive, head to the eastern section of the reef and you will find a steep wall that drops away to 50m, with numerous caves and ledges. White-tip reef sharks are occasionally seen here and in the shallower area of the plateau, but tend to be more active towards the end of the day. There is enough coral cover here to keep most divers happy, although a series of crown-of-thorns starfish infestations has taken its toll on the variety and quantity.

Still, the pinnacles are spectacular, and act as home for coral grouper, anthias, glassfish and grunts. Most boats choose to moor up to buoys attached to the southern pinnacle, so you can ascend slowly along the rising reef, then complete your safety stops while admiring the sunlit shallows. Suitable for those relatively new to the sport, yet with enough complexity to engage seasoned divers, this is one of the truly great reef dives of the north. In terms of its variety and atmosphere, we rate it alongside Ras Mohammed.

▼ Within the vastness of the gorgonian coral, tiny fish such as this longnose hawkfish gain shelter and a habitat for hunting even smaller fry.

Alexander Mustard

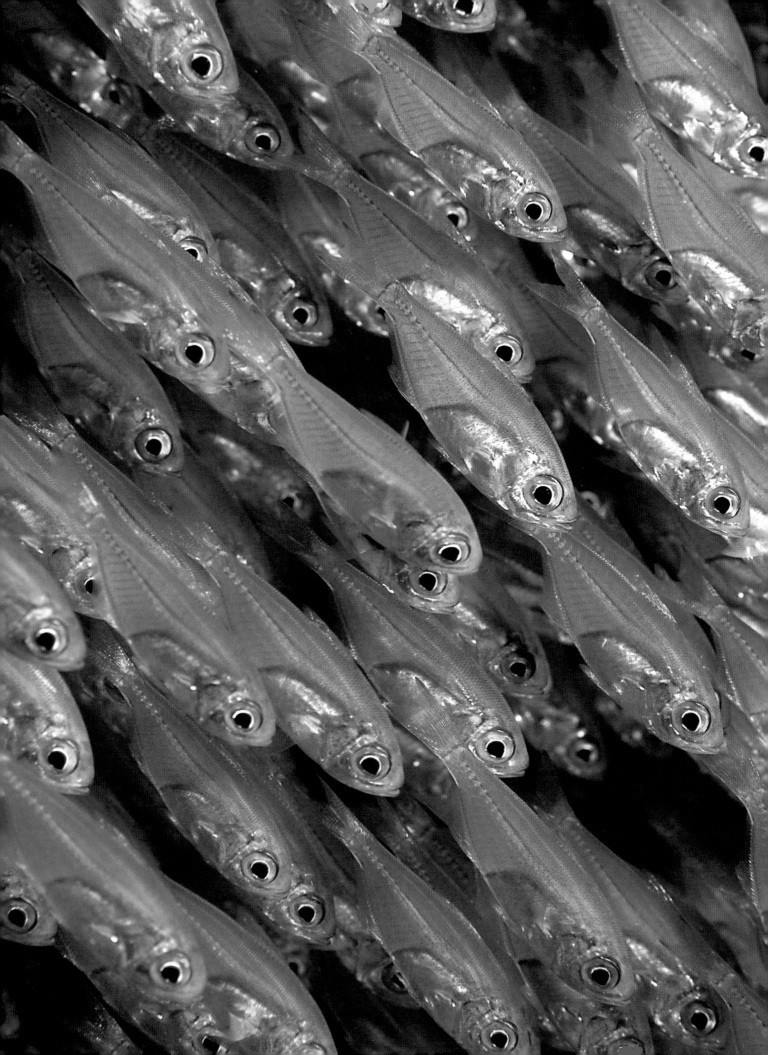

ERG ABU RAMADA

Max depth: 22m

Skill level: 15 dives

Access: dayboat from Hurghada or liveaboard

Current: moderate to strong

Must see: the biggest erg and its resident fish life

If you subscribe to the notion that third dives are necessarily dull, this is the one to prove you wrong! It may be shallow, but this dive pulses with fish action at the beginning and end of the day. The site comprises a series of three ergs, or pinnacles, located just off Abu Ramada island. It's quite a compact area, but fish and coral occur in great concentration around these pinnacles.

When you arrive at the site, your first job will be to determine the direction of the current, then enter the water in an place where you can quickly descend and shelter behind one of the coral towers. Most of the time, it's very simple and the current is easy to cope with. Sometimes, though, you find yourself having to alternate between bouts of frenzied finning and moments of serenity in the lee of the ergs.

Each of the ergs has its own specialities, though these seem to change from season to season. One is much larger than the other two, and merits a good amount of attention as it is swathed in soft coral and patrolled by grouper and glassfish. During one visit while researching this book, we found 23 lionfish scattered around the base of the middle erg, though there was no sign of them the following week. This is a dynamic site where conditions and aggregations are dictated by the whims of the current.

Look carefully along the base of the large erg and you will find an attractive cave that is brimming with fish and soft corals. As well as sheltering local wildlife, these caves can provide welcome respite from the strong current; experienced divers tend to use the topography of the reef to avoid any prolonged bouts of exertion. It is meant to be a holiday, after all! Most divers ascend along the walls of the big erg, pausing to admire the dense schools of anthias that dominate the shallow sections.

PANORAMA REEF/ABU ALAMA

Max depth: 40m (optimum 30m)

Skill level: 15 dives

Access: dayboat from Safaga or Hurghada

Current: light

Must see: the mixture of soft and hard corals on the reef; anemone city on the southern wall

This famous site is one of those favoured by liveaboards when rough weather prevents their passage to the Brother Islands. Conventional wisdom has it that the sheer number of divers, together with the legacy of the Eighties, when boats moored on the coral, has left this site a shadow of its former self. Conventional wisdom, in this case, has a fair point, but to write off Panorama would be doing visiting divers a disservice. There is still much to admire here, and the reef has a way of unlocking its secrets just when you think you've seen all it has to offer.

Panorama is essentially a big chunk of coral in the middle of open sea. The shallow, rounded reef top lies

◄ Glassy sweepers form tight, disciplined schools as a defence to confuse predators.

Alexander Mustard

◄ A lemon goby swims over *Acropora* coral.

Alexander Mustard

▲ A blue triggerfish defends its nest.

just a few metres below the surface, dropping away to two level areas at about 23m on its eastern and western sides. The classic dive starts on the north point and continues on a drift along the eastern section of the reef. The wall is picture-perfect, with a healthy smattering of soft corals and gorgonians. In summer months you should encounter a lot of schooling fish here, including bigeye trevally and snapper. The deeper sides of the wall are said to be patrolled by grey reef and white-tip sharks, but the authors have never seen any such sharks here – bad luck, perhaps, or yet more evidence of the worldwide population collapse caused by the brutal shark fin trade.

If you want to keep your dive shallow, you can swim slowly along the first wall, which has impressive fish life and enough coral to make it pretty. Take a close look at the dappled water at the surface: quite often, this border between two different worlds is patrolled by large packs of needlefish, streamlined predators that appear to have been designed as biological darts. They are almost invisible against the azure water of the shallows, but once you've got an eye for spotting them, you realise they are relentless observers of the reef.

It is possible to swim all the way around Panorama, but we do not recommend this. It is far more civilised to enjoy a leisurely, multi-level dive on the eastern section, which culminates in a visit to the anemone colony on the

southern point. Watch out for friendly Napoleon wrasse throughout your dive, but especially at the mooring area on the southern side of the reef.

Panorama can only be said to be truly spectacular on a few weeks in the year when conditions are fine and visiting fish numerous, but it's still a very enjoyable dive that is held in high esteem by the thousands who visit it each year.

THE WRECK OF THE *SALEM EXPRESS*

Max depth: 31m
Skill level: 15 dives
Access: dayboat from Safaga or Hurghada
Current: normally turbid, occasional current
Must see: the propellers; the area under the wreck; resident frogfish

On the night of 15 December 1991, tragedy struck the seas off Safaga. Returning from Jeddah with pilgrims who had completed the *Hajj*, the ferry *Salem Express* struck Hyndman Reef. The impact ripped open a hole in the hull's forward section, and the stern doors were flung open by the weight of the water. The ferry sank in just ten minutes, giving passengers little opportunity to escape. The exact number of people on board is still a subject of debate: the official figure was 690, but it is now commonly believed that the ferry was overloaded, and that there may have been as many as 1,600 onboard. Only 180 survived.

If your crew offers to take you to this wreck, it will be on the understanding that you do not go inside. It isn't like any other wreck dive in the Red Sea: you simply do not treat it like an underwater playground. This was a recent tragedy, and evidence of the final desperate minutes can be seen all around in the debris surrounding the wreck. To dive the *Salem Express* is a sombre experience, like visiting a monument or a cemetery.

The wreck lies on its starboard side close to the reef that claimed it, with a maximum depth of about 31m. With the exception of the tear in the hull, it is still intact, and there is some vestigial coral growth on the hull and superstructure. The top of the port side is just 10m below the surface, so it is suitable for a range of diving abilities. Thanks to the shelter of the reef, even a big liveaboard can moor up above the wreck, and – if visibility is good – divers will see the grey vastness of the hull as soon as they enter the water. (Unless the sea has been very rough, you can usually rely on visibility of about 20m.)

Start your tour around the large, four-bladed propellers at 26m, then you can swim under the wreck, as there is a spacious swim-through between the structure and the seabed where you may find schools of snapper,

THE *SALEM EXPRESS* AND THE *AL-SALAM BOCCACCIO '98*

On 3 February 2006, the *al-Salam Boccaccio '98* ferry sank after a fire broke out as it was sailing from Duba in Saudi Arabia to Safaga in Egypt with 1,310 passengers and 96 Egyptian crew. Most of the passengers were Egyptians working in Saudi Arabia, but some were pilgrims returning from Mecca.

The surviving third officer on the ship told the Arabic news channel al-Arabiya that the ferry sank because of 'firefighting operations'. He said that water flooded the car deck and pooled on one side, the water level increasing until the ship listed sharply. At the time, the ship was sailing in extremely rough conditions, which, coupled with 5–8cm of water on the car deck, would have been enough to set in motion a deadly phenomenon known as 'free surface effect'. According to this theory, the water inside the vessel starts slopping from side to side, making the ship rock. As the water moves, it gathers momentum, increasing the rocking and causing cargo to shift. The ship becomes unstable and can quickly capsize.

The *al-Salam Boccaccio '98* went down about 50 miles off the Egyptian coast in near-abyssal depths, so it is highly unlikely that divers will ever be able to visit the wreck. However, the sheer intensity of feeling around this tragedy can be compared to the sinking of the *Salem Express* fifteen years earlier. There are dive guides working in Egypt today who actually helped in the recovery of bodies from the *Salem Express*, and some crews may be reluctant to take you to the wreck.

Author Simon Rogerson had decided not to dive the *Salem Express*, but was persuaded to do so by a dive guide, Waleed El Sawy, who had been one of those that carried out dives inside the wreck as part of the official recovery operation. The harrowing experience had left Waleed unable to sleep for three weeks afterward; he never joined the dives, but if he felt that the divers were capable of following his brief and showing the appropriate respect, he let them go down. 'We don't go there often, but if you have the right people on board, it can be done,' said Waleed. 'In my mind, it is no different to walking through a graveyard. As long as you behave in a respectful way, you will not cause offence.'

No single shipwreck epitomizes the moral dilemmas of wreck diving more fully than the *Salem Express*. At present, divers rightly treat it like a monument to those who died, but as time passes and the superstructure is colonised by coral, it will very slowly take on a different identity. There are other wrecks in the Red Sea in which people have lost their lives, but after a while the pain of a tragedy dims and, at some indefinable point in time, the wreck ceases to exist as a tomb.

Eventually, hundreds of years after the sinking, all signs of the *Salem Express* will be subsumed by nature. The life of a coral reef will have sprung from the death of the ship. Yet, such is the emotive power attached to shipwrecks such as the *Salem Express* and the *al-Salam Boccaccio '98*, that many generations will have passed before they complete their final journey as underwater monuments.

Some advice: if your crew express disquiet at the prospect of diving the *Salem Express*, drop the idea and enjoy some of the other great dives in this chapter. But if you do find yourself descending to this sombre scene, be aware of where you are and do not treat the experience lightly, for you will be swimming around the grave of pilgrims.

Simon Rogerson

white-tip reef sharks and stingrays. It can be unsettling to think that a 1,100-tonne shipwreck is lying above you, so by all means swim around from the propellers if you want to avoid the darkness under the wreck.

As darkness gives way to dim light, you will see piles of sheet metal roofing that was somehow dislodged during the sinking. It is this part of the dive that brings home the full calamity of the *Salem Express* and its sinking: the seabed around the poop deck is littered with personal effects – suitcases flung open, tape recorders dusted with silt, shoes lying pitifully in the sand. As a reminder of the terrible speed of the sinking, no image is as potent as that of the lifeboats, still attached to their davits and waiting for passengers who never managed to escape.

For all its tragedy, the structure of the *Salem Express* is still imposing. Without venturing inside, you can still admire the two big smokestacks, which bear the letter 'S' and a laurel wreath which seems all the more appropriate now that the vessel has become a tomb. It is still very easy to find features such as the radar near the quarterdeck. Those in search of an atmospheric wide-angle photograph should swim to the bow and photograph its ghostly outline from the blue water beyond.

SHA'AB SHEER: EASTERN POINT

Max depth: 20m

Skill level: 10–15 dives

Access: dayboat from Safaga

Current: slight

Must see: the diversity of reef fish in the shallows

This reef is a Red Sea classic, brimming with fish life, corals and caverns. It's a 90-minute sail from Safaga, but the tranquillity and richness of the area make it more than worth your while. The riot of life serves as a perfect contrast to the nearby *Salem Express* wreck, and we recommend it as a second dive.

It's possible to do drift dives along this reef's north wall to the western tip, but the best dive is around a series of coral pinnacles that lie off the eastern side. If currents permit, you jump in on the northern wall and then swim with the reef on your left until you reach the point. The little wall is studded with small gorgonian fans and soft coral, and you should see plenty of coral grouper and soldierfish along the way.

When you see a collection of ergs dominated by brain coral, you'll know you've reached the point. As

▲ A propeller on the wreck of the *Salem Express*, Egypt's most poignant dive.

Alexander Mustard

▲ Take time to look into holes in the coral and you may be rewarded by sightings of shy fish such as this mimic blenny.

▶ Normally found under table corals, a pair of masked butterflyfish takes a daring move into open water.

▶▶ Fast-growing acropora corals proliferate on a shallow reef top, where super-heated water also promotes algal growth for grazing fish. (Alexander Mustard)

well as the impressive patches of soft and hard corals, this is a great place for fish spotting. This area is likely to yield blue-striped snapper, giant moray eels, lizardfish and several species of parrotfish, among others. If you're lucky, you may see a white-tip reef shark here, but the sandy seabed is more often home to crocodilefish and blue-spotted stingrays.

During the later stages of the day, this reef does not benefit from the best light, but you may see activity among some of the more elusive animals, such as octopus and scorpionfish. Author Simon Rogerson saw bearded scorpionfish going about their mating ritual here, the male performing what looked like a clumsy dance before both fish rose up into the water column in an amorous frenzy.

You should allow about 15 minutes to swim back to your boat, although many will be prepared to come and collect you (by prior arrangement) if you send up a surface marker buoy. Otherwise, just follow the wall back, keeping it on your right shoulder as you swim back along the north wall, enjoying the flitting anthias and surgeonfish in the shallows. We have heard that some

divers prefer to dive the dropoff beyond the reef in order to look for hammerhead sharks, but the real pleasure here is the diversity of smaller fish and corals.

ABU QIFAN

Max depth: 40m
Skill level: 40 dives
Access: dayboat from Safaga
Current: moderate to strong
Must see: barracuda, sweetlips and bottlenose dolphins, if you're lucky

Safaga has an undeserved reputation for offering only low energy dive sites. While it is true to say that there are plenty of leisurely coastal sites, there are equally a few current-fuelled reefs that have been known to attract their share of pelagics over the course of a year. 'Abu Qifan' translates enigmatically as 'father of the deep', a reference to the 200m dropoffs around this speck of a reef, two hours sail from Port Safaga. You need good weather to get here, as the narrow, 300m-long reef has little shelter and is subject to strong currents.

Anchoring points have been located at the southwest point, where there is a modicum of shelter. If the current permits, the best way to approach this site is to drop in on the north plateau and carry out a drift dive along the east wall, which is covered in gorgonian fans and black coral. Fish life is profuse here: expect to see bannerfish, barracuda and plenty of sweetlips. Your dive will be dictated by the current: simply enter the water on the side where it is running and swim around the reef to be picked up on the lee side.

Head down to about 30m to enjoy the best of the branching coral, and don't forget to look out for white-tip reef sharks, a familiar sight on the deeper zones of this reef. Further up, at about 25m, you should find a flat area studded by coral growth and frequented by hunting trevally (the local wrasse have a decidedly nervous look!). There seem to be a few resident eagle rays here, and mantas have been regularly sighted during plankton blooms in winter.

There have been quite a few reports of solitary hammerhead sharks visiting this reef during winter months, when the cool surface water encourages them to ascend to mainstream diving depths. It is likely the sharks come close to the reef to be cleaned by angelfish, but no one has ever seen it happen here.

A healthy mixture of hard and soft corals dominates the shallower portions of the reef, with plenty of parrotfish, wrasse and lyretail grouper to keep you amused. As with Panorama Reef, you can often see packs of needlefish hunting at the surface. Dolphins occasionally visit divers on this reef.

EL KAF

Max depth: 40m (optimum 18m)

Skill level: novices and above

Access: dayboat from Safaga or as a shore dive

Current: very slight

Must see: the coral tunnels, where getting lost is a good idea

There are times when you want to battle with raging currents and dive deep to find pelagics. Then there are times for a more contemplative dive, a dive that gives you the opportunity to savour its intricacy and subtlety. That dive is El Kaf.

Of course, you can do this dive from the comfort of a boat, but it is one of Egypt's most satisfying shore dives, and your dive operator can take you to the beach about 11km south of El Quseir. The entry point is just a couple of hundred metres off the coastal road. You stroll into the water and swim across the lagoon towards a cut in the reef that is just big enough to allow divers through comfortably.

After swimming through the cut, follow the wall to your right and you will soon come to an erg dominated by hard coral and a smattering of reef fish. From here, head in a southerly direction (with the reef on your right) and you will enter a labyrinth of caves, tunnels, openings and dead ends. This is a magical topography, a living maze of coral and colour in which you can dive to whatever depth you like.

The magic of this site lies in not knowing what may be waiting for you around the next corner. Although its overriding attraction is its topography, there's also plenty of scope for fish spotting: you are certain to find blue-spotted stingrays, batfish and spotted pufferfish among scores of Red Sea regulars. On the sand, look out for lurking crocodilefish, plus countless blenny and shrimp partnerships, which disappear as divers approach. In the late afternoon, shafts of sunlight cut through the water, lending the site a romantic atmosphere.

Finding your way back is not as complicated as you may fear. Keep the contours of the main reef on your left and just keep picking your way through the various tunnels and pinnacles until they lead you back to the cut or canyon through which you entered the coral maze. Plan your dive time in advance: if you're good on air, you can easily while away at least 90 minutes here, but make sure your surface cover or instructor knows what you're up to during that time. Alternatively, if the prospect of an underwater maze does not appeal to you, ask for a guide to accompany you. We promise that you will want to return and explore this site on your own, as it has an appeal that lingers in the mind long after you return home.

Alexander Mustard

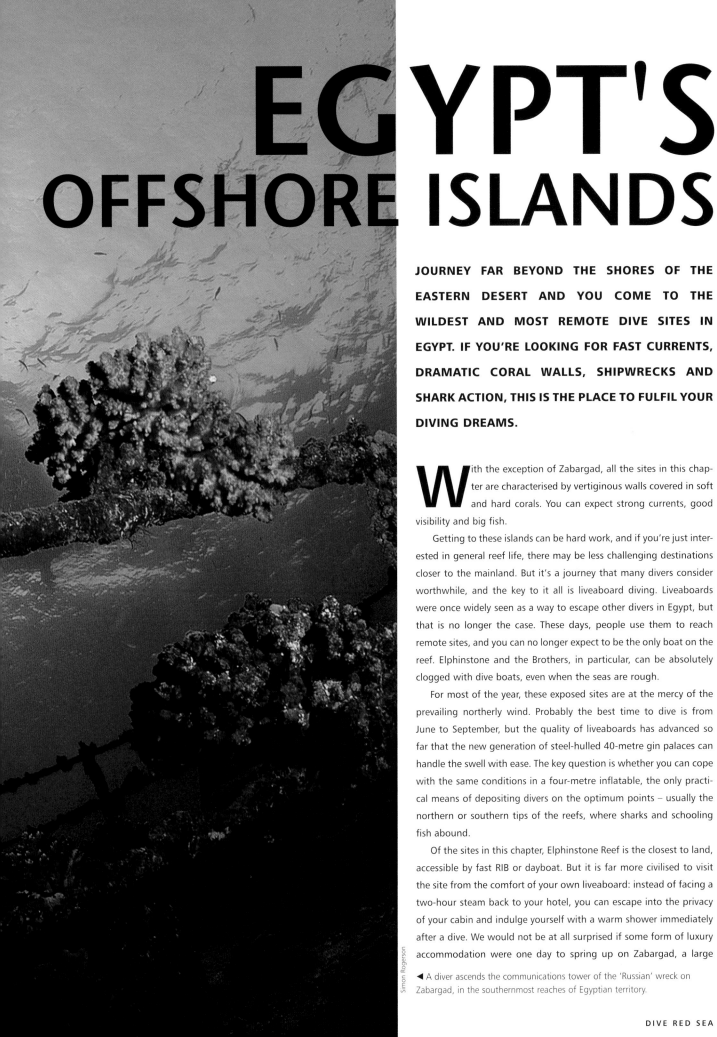

EGYPT'S OFFSHORE ISLANDS

JOURNEY FAR BEYOND THE SHORES OF THE EASTERN DESERT AND YOU COME TO THE WILDEST AND MOST REMOTE DIVE SITES IN EGYPT. IF YOU'RE LOOKING FOR FAST CURRENTS, DRAMATIC CORAL WALLS, SHIPWRECKS AND SHARK ACTION, THIS IS THE PLACE TO FULFIL YOUR DIVING DREAMS.

With the exception of Zabargad, all the sites in this chapter are characterised by vertiginous walls covered in soft and hard corals. You can expect strong currents, good visibility and big fish.

Getting to these islands can be hard work, and if you're just interested in general reef life, there may be less challenging destinations closer to the mainland. But it's a journey that many divers consider worthwhile, and the key to it all is liveaboard diving. Liveaboards were once widely seen as a way to escape other divers in Egypt, but that is no longer the case. These days, people use them to reach remote sites, and you can no longer expect to be the only boat on the reef. Elphinstone and the Brothers, in particular, can be absolutely clogged with dive boats, even when the seas are rough.

For most of the year, these exposed sites are at the mercy of the prevailing northerly wind. Probably the best time to dive is from June to September, but the quality of liveaboards has advanced so far that the new generation of steel-hulled 40-metre gin palaces can handle the swell with ease. The key question is whether you can cope with the same conditions in a four-metre inflatable, the only practical means of depositing divers on the optimum points – usually the northern or southern tips of the reefs, where sharks and schooling fish abound.

Of the sites in this chapter, Elphinstone Reef is the closest to land, accessible by fast RIB or dayboat. But it is far more civilised to visit the site from the comfort of your own liveaboard: instead of facing a two-hour steam back to your hotel, you can escape into the privacy of your cabin and indulge yourself with a warm shower immediately after a dive. We would not be at all surprised if some form of luxury accommodation were one day to spring up on Zabargad, a large

Simon Rogerson

◀ A diver ascends the communications tower of the 'Russian' wreck on Zabargad, in the southernmost reaches of Egyptian territory.

GETTING THERE

Although you can dive Elphinstone from a land base at Port Galib or Marsa Alam, the other sites in this chapter all require liveaboards. Tour operators offer liveaboards out of various little bays, but we recommend Port Galib if you are diving the more southerly sites here. Port Galib is also a fine point of embarkation for the Brother Islands, but Hurghada will serve just as well. Some operators like to bus their divers from the airport at Hurghada down to Quseir or Safaga for a quicker sea journey to the Brothers. It depends on your tastes, but we think it's preferable to get straight onto the comfort of your liveaboard after landing. Accordingly, the two airports of choice are Hurghada or Marsa Alam, both of which have regular charter flights from major European cities.

 VISAS

Visitors can either get them in advance from the Egyptian Embassy or – as is more common – on arrival in the country. You will need a full passport with at least six months remaining. There are three types of visa: the tourist visa lasting three months; entry visas for people working in Egypt; and transit visas.

$ MONEY

Egyptian currency has been fairly stable over the years, largely thanks to tourism. Most outlets will take foreign currency, including the Euro, Dollar and Sterling. It's always worth having single Egyptian pound notes, even the smaller denominations called piastres. Coins are rarely used.

island that represents a sort of final outpost before the Sudan border. For now, though, liveaboards out of Hurghada, Port Galib or Marsa Alam are the way to go.

Many of these reefs are designated as national parks and are subject to certain rules. Divers are supposed to have at least 50 dives under their belt, gloves are banned (to dissuade you from touching the coral) and vessels are required to have both underwater and boat-based safety support for all diving activity. During the mid-Nineties, divers were barred from visiting the Brothers Islands for several years after someone suffered a serious bend there and foreign flags were planted on Zabargad Island. There is always a chance that such a ban could again be imposed if the authorities reach the conclusion that divers are more trouble than they are worth.

For now, the offshore islands represent a playground for anyone in search of the Red Sea at its wildest. It may not be the place to visit if you're after tranquil lagoons or benthic fish, but for sharks, shipwrecks and schooling pelagics, it's unbeatable.

► The shallow reef top at Daedalus, as seen from the top of the lighthouse.

►► The view from the top of the lighthouse on Big Brother, with liveaboards moored on the sheltered south-west side and Little Brother just visible on the horizon. (Simon Rogerson)

Simon Rogerson

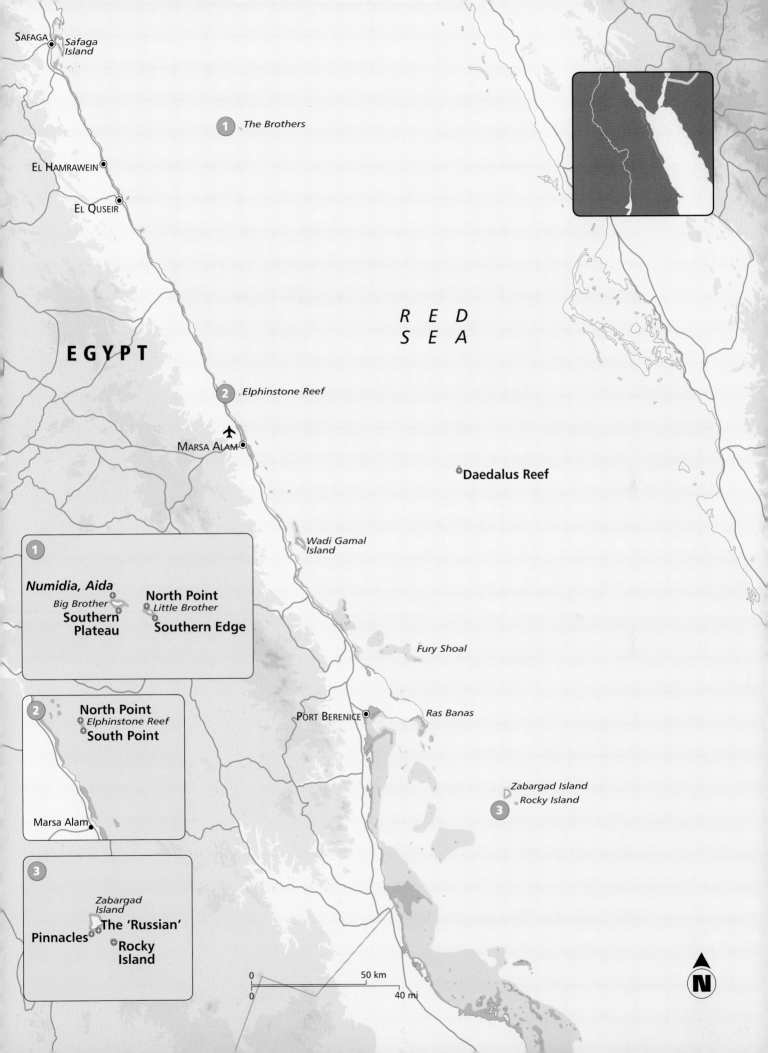

SAFAGA
Safaga Island

1 The Brothers

EL HAMRAWEIN

EL QUSEIR

EGYPT

2 Elphinstone Reef

MARSA ALAM

R E D
S E A

Daedalus Reef

Wadi Gamal Island

1

Numidia, Aida
Big Brother
North Point
Little Brother
Southern Plateau
Southern Edge

Fury Shoal

2
North Point
Elphinstone Reef
South Point

PORT BERENICE

Ras Banas

Marsa Alam

Zabargad Island
Rocky Island

3

3

Zabargad Island
The 'Russian'
Pinnacles
Rocky Island

0   50 km

0   40 mi

N

VISIBILITY

Water clarity is excellent year-round, though it can be milky after rough weather, and plankton blooms can affect light and surface visibility in the summer. Generally, you should think of 25m as the average working visibility, but it can be much more.

WATER TEMPERATURE

23ºC in winter; 28ºC in summer.

SEASONALITY

For reef sharks and hammerheads, March to May is probably the best time to visit, as the seas are not too rough and the thermocline is shallow enough for experienced divers to enjoy a reasonable amount of time. For oceanic white-tips, the best time is from October to the end of November.

▶ Grey reef sharks cruise along the northern points of the Brothers, at the points where the current is strongest.

THE ARCH AND THE HOLE

A large underwater arch can be found in the deep sections of Elphinstone south at 50–60m. Undoubtedly, it lies beyond the range of most sport divers, but a colourful story (some would say modern myth) has sprung up around this famous feature.

The story has it that the sarcophagus of an early pharaoh lies at the foot of the arch, and indeed at a depth of 60m there is the unmistakable form of what just might be a sarcophagus, encrusted with sponges and whip corals. There are several notions about the origins of the rock, which does have a certain man-made symmetry to it. Certain historians have seized on it as evidence that local culture dates back much further than mainstream Egyptologists believe, and that the sarcophagus was placed there at a time in ancient history when the level of the Red Sea was shallower.

Most professional dive guides in Egypt (inevitably, they are the ones who have seen the 'sarcophagus' on the most occasions) believe the structure to be natural. They claim it is even possible to see a hole in the underside of the arch, from where the block fell.

The debate will rage on, but we will leave you with one last piece of advice: if you really want to examine this structure, go as a qualified trimix diver and carry out the dive responsibly with an appropriate gas mix and plan. If you go there just using air, there is a good chance of running into difficulties due to nitrogen narcosis or oxygen toxicity. Let's face it: who wants to get decompression sickness, or worse, for the sake of a lump of rock?

Steve Jones

ELPHINSTONE REEF (ABU HAMRA): SOUTH POINT

Max depth: 40m optimum

Skill level: 50 dives

Access: liveaboard and dayboat

Current: medium to strong

Must see: grey reef sharks, soft coral, hunting trumpetfish, oceanic white-tip sharks in season

Are you looking for one reef that encapsulates all that is good about wall diving in southern Egypt? Look no further than Elphinstone, a 450m-long finger that runs north to south in the open sea, about 11km off Marsa Abu Dabab on the Egyptian mainland. Although it is much closer to land than many of the other sites in this chapter, don't be fooled into thinking of it as an easy site. Even when the surface waters are placid, the north and south tips of this reef usually have a good current pushing over them.

Named after Lord Elphinstone (a famous 19th century British general and Viceroy of India) during the British Admiralty's original survey of the Red Sea, the reef is defined by steep walls along its eastern and western sides. These are always worth exploring, especially for those who relish steep dropoffs, but the most rewarding portions of Elphinstone are its northern and southern extremities.

The southern plateau is arguably the superior dive. If your boatman puts you in right above the tip, you should descend as soon as possible to escape the swell and ensure that you reach the site without being pulled away by the current. As you descend, you will notice that the coral cover is both diverse and comprehensive. Small schools of yellow snapper flit around close to the coral, while giant morays view the theatre of the reef from the shelter of their lairs.

Initially, a small dropoff leads you from the top of the reef near the surface down to about 17m. Then you need to fin out along a long tongue of reef that gradually slopes away into deeper water. This is the place to look for sharks. But, as you descend, do not neglect the reef itself: in the shallower sections, the soft coral is a uniform pastel green, but below 22m the same species occurs in vivid reds and purples. Reef life is very intense in this zone, and it is a superb place to photograph those little standard-bearers of the Red Sea, the bright orange fish we know as anthias.

Anywhere from 30m downwards, there's a good chance of running into some of the resident grey reef or scalloped hammerhead sharks. If you get lucky, it can be worth continuing to a theoretical maximum of 40m, from which point the reef drops away sharply. As a shark site, Elphinstone tends to blow hot and cold: sometimes it can be hard to drag yourself away from the action; the next dive can be uneventful.

There are rumours of a resident great hammerhead on this reef. Both of this book's authors are well acquainted with the species, the largest and most impressive of the hammerhead family, but in more than 80 dives at Elphinstone, we have never seen one at or around the reef.

The ascent is always a pleasure, as the gathering light imbues the reef with energy. In the shallower section of the tip, you will find butterflyfish, coral groupers and the ubiquitous trumpetfish. The latter have perfected a hunting technique which, while not peculiar to this part of the Red Sea, is something of a local speciality. As divers make their way along the reef wall, the trumpetfish tuck in close behind, using the diver as cover from which to launch swift, darting attacks on unsuspecting reef fish. The reef fish know that divers themselves present little threat, so this hunting strategy allows the trumpetfish to approach within striking range.

Simon Rogerson

ELPHINSTONE REEF: NORTH POINT

Max depth: 40m optimum

Skill level: 50 dives

Access: liveaboard and dayboat

Current: strong

Must see: Napoleon wrasse, grey reef sharks, oceanic white-tip sharks

Depending on which end of the reef your skipper has been able to moor the liveaboard, it is sometimes possible to swim back to it. The trick is not just remembering the position of your own vessel, but being able to recognise it while you are underwater; after all, hulls and ladders tend to look much the same from below.

The north point offers a very similar dive to the south, but drops in steps from 8m to 25m and then onto 40m. If anything, the current is usually stronger at the north point, which makes for hard work, but there are often more sharks here than on the easier southern plateau. Again, the reef is draped in a variety of colourful soft corals, and the shallower levels are home to a family of Napoleon wrasse, one of the most popular fish on the Red Sea's reefs. It can be very hard to get close to these fish elsewhere in the world, since they are often targeted by spearfishermen, and their flesh is much prized in Southeast Asia.

Egypt's offshore reefs enjoy the protection that comes with being highly profitable tourist resources. Indirectly, these fish make the local economy a lot of money, so it is hoped that Egyptians will continue to cherish them as living symbols of the sea's vitality. In the past, they may have been fed hard-boiled eggs, but try to discourage this practice if you come across it today, as the poor fish can suffer from constipation and cholesterol problems. They tend to inspect some divers at close quarters, so by all means swim up to them, but resist the temptation to chase them, as this will ruin everyone's chances of a face-to-face encounter.

From September through to early December, there's a high chance of seeing oceanic white-tip sharks all over Elphinstone. Encounters on the north point are often excellent, with up to ten sharks cruising around from 30m right up to the surface. Otherwise, lookout for the oceanic's homelier cousin, the white-tip reef shark, and perhaps even a scalloped hammerhead or two.

Back in the shallows, keep a good eye on the blue. We have often seen manta rays and other pelagics here, and there is a tiny chance that you may see a thresher shark somewhere down in the darkness. Some believe that there is a thresher shark cleaning station somewhere on Elphinstone, but the cleaning behaviour (famously recorded at Malapascua in the Philippines) has not been recorded here – yet!

OCEANIC WHITE-TIPS

One of the most exciting times to visit Elphinstone is from late October through to early December, when anyone spending a day or more there has a very good chance of seeing oceanic white tips, one of the most distinctive sharks of the open sea.

This opportunistic and powerful predator has something of a grim reputation, having been implicated in the infamous feeding frenzy that ensued after the *USS Indianapolis* sank in the Pacific at the end of the Second World War. As a result, it has been listed as the fourth 'villain', after the three other most dangerous species – the great white, tiger and bull shark. Whether the oceanic deserves to be classified as a man-eater is not clear: while there are a notable amount of attacks attributed to it, it is probably no more dangerous than lemon sharks, silky sharks and a host of other predators. However, it was co-star (with the great white) of the pioneering shark documentary, *Blue Water White Death*, in which Peter Gimbel and Stan Waterman filmed large numbers of oceanics tearing into the body of a dead whale.

Certainly, this fish demands respect. It grows to nearly four metres, though most of the sharks seen on Elphinstone seem to be between 1.5 and 2.5m long. Some divers mistake it for the white-tip reef shark or even the silvertip; the way to identify an oceanic white-tip is the rounded first dorsal fin, which also has that distinctive white tip. It has been suggested that this prominent marking helps the sharks to identify each other in the open sea, possibly even preventing them from preying on each other.

At Elphinstone, the sharks swim lazily under the moored liveaboards, perhaps hoping for a meal to be thrown overboard. If you want to dive with them, you can simply jump off the back of the boat and hang out at 5m. It may sound easy, but there's nearly always a current pushing through. You can relax by holding onto a chain or decompression line, but when you let go of that line and venture out into the blue, it can be very hard work swimming back to the security of your boat.

Also, you need to be mentally prepared for some very close encounters. Oceanic sharks are not like the timid reef sharks or hammerheads. If for some reason you interest them, they will inspect you from a few feet, sometimes just a few inches away. Some may even bump you with their snouts to see what you're made of. Sharks cannot feel or touch with hands, so this is their way of checking you out. It is also a sign that the shark has overcome what little timidity it had. Veteran shark photographers Ron and Val Taylor recommend giving the shark a return thump to show that you're no pushover.

We recommend getting out of the water if things get physical: oceanic sharks are known to build up aggressive behaviour as the prelude to an attack. As afternoon gives way to evening, a shark's mind turns to feeding, and sudden shifts in behaviour are well documented during that time of day. The good news is that the oceanic white-tips of Elphinstone are generally curious rather than dangerous. If divers respect them for what they are, both can continue to visit this splendid reef unharmed.

Simon Rogerson

THE BROTHER ISLANDS: DIVING PERFECTION?

They may appear to be barren rocks from the surface, but the twin towers of coral known as the Brother Islands – El Akhawein in Arabic – rank among the world's most vibrant dive sites. These tiny, dust-bitten islands are the peaks of two pillars that rise up from a depth of 300m and are surrounded by a narrow reef. It's a textbook scenario for high-octane diving action: two lonely reef systems provide oases of life in a desert of blue, while the surrounding deep water ensures nutrient-rich upwellings to provide the foundation of the ecosystem.

The Brothers' natural isolation means that only committed divers tend to visit, so the coral is generally in better condition than at many coastal sites. For much of the year, strong winds bring rough seas and heavy swells. The optimum season is the June to September period, although these days tour operators offer the Brothers on a year-round basis. Egyptian liveaboards are getting better every year, but you should still be prepared for some bumpy rides in the winter months.

Big Brother, the more northerly of the two, covers an area of 300m² and is topped by a lighthouse built by the British in 1880. The original searchlight mechanism has been replaced with a modern, fully automatic alternative, but the sweaty climb up the spiral stairs is

◀ Blue-lined snapper swim along the vertical wall on Elphinstone's west side.

▶▶ An oceanic white-tip shark patrols under the dive boats moored at Elphinstone, possibly attracted by food thrown overboard. (Simon Rogerson)

Simon Rogerson

▲ The lighthouse at Big Brother, 150 hot and dusty steps to a hot and dusty view.

BIG BROTHER: THE WRECK OF THE *NUMIDIA*

Wreck depth: 10–90m

Skill level: 50 dives

Access: liveaboard support boat

Current: frequent, moderate to very powerful

Must see: the engine room; the bridge area with its soft coral; the wheels if you can find them

The Red Sea has well and truly claimed the wreck of the *Numidia*. In a way, it is remarkable that so much of the structure has survived after being immersed for more than a century in such an exposed area. Many of the wreck's features are still easily recognisable – the bridge, foremast, lifeboat davits, stern mast – swathed in soft and hard corals.

This is not simply one of the best wrecks in the Red Sea: it is one of the most beautiful dives in the entire world. The *Numidia* may have been built in Glasgow, but its defining features today are the result of sinking in one of the most biologically diverse areas on the planet. Though the ship itself has died, its structure supports a riot of invertebrate life and is patrolled by snapper, jacks and barracuda.

One of the advantages of diving such a well-established wreck is that the wooden decking and floors have rotted away, allowing light to invade much of the interior. Even in gloomy areas such as the engine room, enough light filters down for divers to find their way. Some of the interior features here are still intact, though your time inside the wreck will be limited by decompression concerns.

The top of the wreck proper starts at a relatively shallow 10m, where a set of rolling stock wheels used to lie until they were removed by persons unknown. A strong current often runs across from east to west, so our advice is to use the structure to protect yourself. You can enter some of the companionways via the starboard side of the wreck and progress downwards until you reach a set of holds at about 40m. Grey reef sharks visit the deeper portions of the *Numidia*, so it's always worth keeping an eye on the blue.

Thereafter, this wreck is strictly for trimix divers. Those with the training and equipment to descend to depths of 90m may be able to locate the propeller and rudder, but the shallower portions of this wreck are so beautiful that it is just as rewarding to retrace your way back up toward the open sections of the bridge, the foremast and the rolling stock wheels in the shallows.

An alternative approach to this dive – especially useful if the current is running fast – is to spend less time on the wreck and then go for a drift along the west side of Big Brother, with its signature coral walls and over-

worthwhile just to admire the view from the top. The lighthouse keepers don't always welcome visitors; it seems to depend upon who is on duty and how friendly they happen to be with your crew. They sometimes offer a few curios and T-shirts, so it could be worth bringing some cash.

You will hear that the Brothers are the islands to visit if you want to see sharks, and this is true: they are home to resident grey reefs and white-tips, in addition to attracting visiting oceanic species. It is illegal to lay bait for sharks here, so encounters tend to be more natural – and for 'natural', read 'fleeting', though bold individuals may sometimes check out divers briefly before swimming away. What we do know is that shark sightings here tend to be seasonal, with grey reef shark and hammerheads prevalent during the cooler months of December to May, while oceanic white-tips often appear during the warmer period from July to October. Other visiting pelagics such as manta rays, thresher sharks and silky sharks can turn up at any time of the year.

hangs. In this sense, the *Numidia* is one of the Red Sea's most complete diving experiences, offering high quality wreck, reef and shark dives, all in one dive.

BIG BROTHER: THE WRECK OF THE *AIDA*

Wreck depth: 30–60m

Skill level: 50 dives

Access: liveaboard/inflatable

Current: frequent/powerful

Must see: the engine room; soft coral and reef fish on the following dive

When the *Aida* sank, its bow section caught on the reef and soon broke off. The stern landed on an extremely steep portion of the reef wall, with the propeller lying below 60m. There's still some wreckage on the reef top, but the real dive here is the stern section, in particular the engine room.

It's a quite different experience from diving the *Numidia*. Instead of a decompression-friendly, multilevel dive, the shallowest substantial point of this wreck starts at 30m. It is a testament to the skill of the Egyptian boatmen that they can (*enshallah!*) put divers in at exactly the right point, taking into account the prevailing current so that you descend onto the wreck after 'free-falling' through layers of cobalt-blue water.

If you've timed it right, you should land right on top of the engine room. It is easy to get inside: the ship was ripped apart at the fo'c'sle, leaving a gaping hole through which several divers can enter. The inte-rior is darkly beautiful, with pale light streaming down through skylights and a resident school of glassy sweepers pulsing in the darkness. Take a torch if you want to see the remaining pipes and gauges along the walls.

This is one of the most visually appealing places in the Red Sea, but it's not easy to take photographs here. Your time is limited, the natural light is subdued and those pesky glassfish stay still for nobody! If you want to emerge from the engine room with some decent snaps, plan the dive in exhaustive detail with your buddy. Determine how long you're going to stay in there, and stick rigidly to your plan (remember, depths inside the engine room vary from 30–36m). One of you should take a powerful torch and shine it at the glassfish, then the photographer should meter for the skylight, over-expose a tad, then try a few different manual settings, using a wide angle and different intensities of flash. Easy it is not!

You'll need an advanced camera set-up to get anything from this wreck interior – at least a good external flash and a wide-angle lens. But is it possible to get eerily impressive photographs here. The outside of the wreck is coated in even more soft coral than the *Numidia*, in deep purples, reds and pinks. While on the outside, it's worth briefly seeking out the accommodation block and bridge, where the colours are especially riotous. Watch out for some beautiful anemones along the structure.

Your time on this wreck will be brief, but intense. The remainder of the dive will take you along the beautiful western walls of the island, a distracting backdrop for decompression time.

▼ A diver swims over the winch gear on the deck of the *Aida*.

Simon Rogerson

NUMIDIA

You have to be unlucky to run into the one of the few islands in the very centre of the Red Sea, but that's how it was for this cargo ship, which ploughed into the north point of Big Brother in July 1901. When the island was sighted off the port bow, the captain altered course, planning to pass a mile to its west. Showing a misplaced confidence in his crew, he left the bridge, ordering them to call him when the lighthouse was close.

In the early hours of the morning the Numidia ran aground on Big Brother. The crew tried to force her off the rocks, but the hull had been breached, water was streaming in and the pumps were fighting a losing battle. The crew abandoned ship and began a sun-scorched vigil on the island. Over the coming weeks, most of the 7,000 tonnes of general cargo was salvaged, but the vessel itself began a gradual descent down the coral wall, which gathered pace as more water flooded in.

The bow section broke off and was gradually broken up by decades of storms and current. Some wreckage still remains at the top of the reef, but there's no longer any recognisable bow structure.

1. Rolling stock wheels (only two sets remain)
2. Fore mast
3. Cargo hold
4. Life boat davits
5. Wreckage on seafloor
6. Engine room
7. Hold No.3
8. Hold No.4
9. Rudder and propeller

sea level
top of wreck 10m

lowest point 90m

Copyright © 2006 Ultimate Sports Dive Co Ltd

▲ A diver penetrates the wreck in one of the shallower holds.
(Peter Collings)

AIDA

▲ These wheels have recently been removed from the site. (Peter Collings)

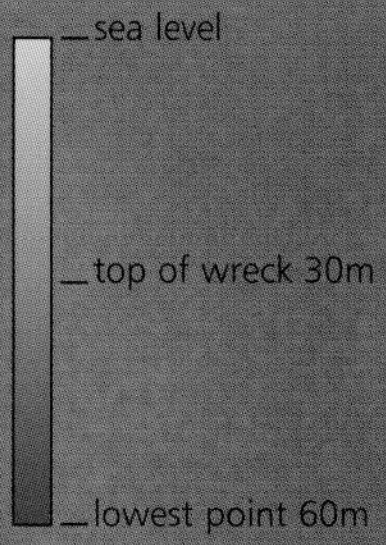

sea level

top of wreck 30m

lowest point 60m

At first, the Aida was commissioned to function as a general supply ship for Egypt's lighthouses and ports, but with the outbreak of the Second World War she served as a ferry for troops. Bizarrely, she was actually KO'd twice: the first time came when she was bombed while at anchor and beached.

With the damage patched up, she returned to service but came to grief at Big Brother while helping with a change of personnel in 1957. Her demise was due to the very same danger that dive guides must guard against when visiting these islands today: rough seas. As the crew tried to unload at a jetty, she was smashed against the rocks and began to sink. The crew was evacuated and the stricken vessel drifted for a while before finally disappearing below the waves.

10 Engine room

11 Lifeboat davits

12 Hold

13 Windlass

14 Emergency steering

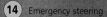

▲ Light streams down into a cargo hold, but torches are still essential. (Peter Collings)

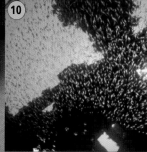

▲ Glassfish flit in and out of the engine room, where divers can easily enter.

(Charles Hood/oceans-image.com)

▲ Soft coral grows profusely on the wreck's superstructure.

(Charles Hood/oceans-image.com)

▲ The Aida's davits and railings stand proud despite decades of immersion.

(Simon Rogerson)

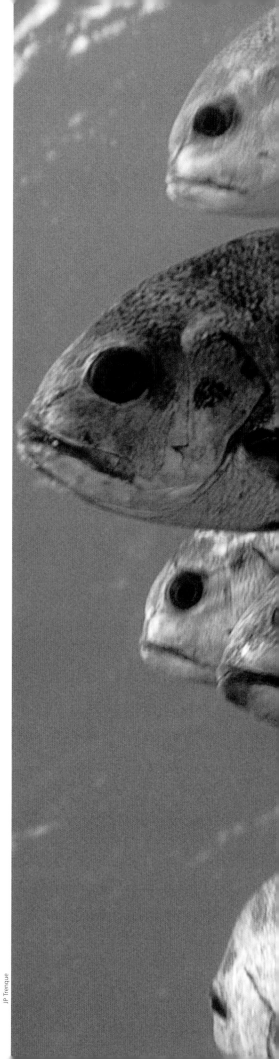

BIG BROTHER: SOUTHERN PLATEAU

Max depth: 34m

Skill level: 30 dives

Access: liveaboard/support boat

Current: mostly sheltered, moderate to light

Must see: oceanic thresher sharks, schooling snapper and bigeye trevally, great barracuda

This is the sheltered side of Big Brother, the area where liveaboards tend to moor up. It is less spectacular than diving on the northern side, but provides a good alternative when strong winds make the northern section too dangerous to tackle. On the southern tip, you descend straight down until you reach a plateau at 30–35m, stretching out into the blue. Bathed in light, it's a colourful stage for the Red Sea's stars: you will see lots of anemones and anemonefish, lumps of *Acropora* coral and plenty of coral grouper.

Some very special visitors are drawn to this oft-ignored arm of the Brothers: oceanic thresher sharks, which rise from the abyss to be cleaned by tiny wrasse on the reef. These are skittish sharks, very hard to find and evidently scared by divers' bubbles. If you are lucky enough to see one, it will be unmistakable: the enormously elongated tail accounts for two-thirds of its total body length. The shark is thought to use this whip-like appendage to stun schools of fish when they hunt in deep feeding grounds. It also has unusually large eyes, a common adaptation among deep-water predators.

If you do come across a thresher, stay still and close to the reef. Chances are it is in the process of being cleaned, so it may tolerate your presence. But if you steam straight towards it with camera raised and flashing, it will speed off into the blue with one flick of that extraordinary tail, leaving you to face the wrath of your fellow divers. Remember: an encounter with a thresher is one of diving's rarest experiences, more exceptional even than a meeting with a whale shark. So if you do find yourself getting lucky, make the most of every second. We have had reports of divers seeing these sharks elsewhere on the Brothers, but the cleaning stations of the southern plateau have yielded the most sightings in recent years.

▶ Black snapper patrol offshore reefs in schools of up to 200 fish.

▼ A lizardfish perches on hard coral.

Charles Hood/oceans-image.com

JP Trenque

LITTLE BROTHER: NORTH POINT

Max depth: 40m optimum

Skill level: 50 dives

Access: liveaboard/support

Current: often very powerful

Must see: hammerhead and grey reef sharks; the main reef wall

In common with its larger sibling, Little Brother Island is famed for its vertical fields of soft corals and big fish. If anything, it's probably the better of the two when it comes to shark encounters.

When conditions permit, the northern side offers the most exciting diving, with a prevailing current running north to west over the ridge. Here, a plateau at 40m provides a useful platform to spy on passing sharks riding the thermoclines. Hammerheads, grey reefs and white-tips are common sightings, and there have also been many sightings of the chunky-yet-elegant silvertip on this promontory.

Conditions may seem relatively calm when you first step into your support boat or inflatable, but do not be fooled. As you near the northern corner, you head into exposed waters and your driver may have to negotiate some hefty swells as he and the dive guide judge the best spot to drop you. Hold on tight and make sure that any cameras are stored safely either in your BCD pocket or in a part of the boat where they will not shift around and be damaged.

Every dive in this frenetic place is loaded with possibility: you simply don't know what you're going to find when you make it to that sweet spot where the current streams past the reef. The downside is that, quite often, you will find yourself finning madly against the running water to make it to the corner. Streamline your posture, hug any cameras or torches close to your body and fin like an enraged pufferfish. But don't be ashamed to give up if it is simply too much effort: you don't want to waste all your breathing gas flailing against the powerful current when the ascent back along the western wall is so beautiful.

If you do make it to the north point, find a place to gaze up and along the reef wall. If there's any sign of shark activity, stay still and they may come closer. Sometimes, when currents are weak, it can be worthwhile swimming away from the protection of the reef, where scalloped hammerheads may emerge from the blue to investigate you. Be careful not to go too far: there is a danger you will be caught by one of the eddies swirling around the island.

◀ Little Brother's southern tip has a forest of giant gorgonian fans from 20–45m.

DRIFTER DANGER

The Brother Islands are probably the most talked about dive sites in the Egyptian Red Sea. Back in the Eighties, a collective of divers set up a campsite on Big Brother, brought over a compressor and started inviting tourists to dive with them from the shore. All was well until one of them suffered a serious bout of decompression sickness after carrying out the sort of dive you wouldn't want to tell your mother about.

Not long after, the Egyptian Navy banned tourists from visiting the Brothers; the islands – possibly the finest dive sites in all of Egypt – did not see a diver for another four years. Diving was only re-introduced in 2000, by which time attitudes to tourism among the Egyptian ruling class had softened.

These seemingly insignificant islands hit the headlines again in 2004, when a group of European divers was swept off the reef by powerful currents and found themselves floating in the water for nine hours. Thankfully, they were found before anyone died of hypothermia, but the episode was an instructive drama that taught dive professionals several key lessons for operating in Egypt's offshore islands.

First, the current caught the divers in question because they ventured too far from the protection of the reef. Powerful eddies swirl around the Red Sea's islands, and while it is tempting to swim into the blue in the hope of seeing a shark, the trick is not to venture too far, and never to lose sight of the reef. If you feel a current starting to take hold, fin back towards the coral wall.

Second, some of the group suffered sunburn while they waited at the surface, and not every one of them had surface visibility devices such as a marker buoy or a flag. Every diver visiting the Brothers should have at least one such device, and more people are now packing back-up gadgets such as vials of marker ink (they create an area of brightly discoloured sea that is easy to spot from the air) or even an emergency position indicating radio beacon, or EPIRB. Some of the drifters had spare hoods in their BCD pockets, a blessing that shielded them from the sun during the day and kept them warm at night.

Finally, the group was only located at night because some of them had torches, with which they signalled to a passing boat. Most of the group agreed that the torches saved their lives, and soon afterwards the Red Sea Association announced a new set of rules requiring every diver visiting offshore sites to have a surface marker buoy and an emergency light. To be fair, the Brothers are not inherently dangerous dive sites, but it pays to be properly equipped.

Charles Hood/oceans-image.com

▼ Close-up of a masked butterlyfish.

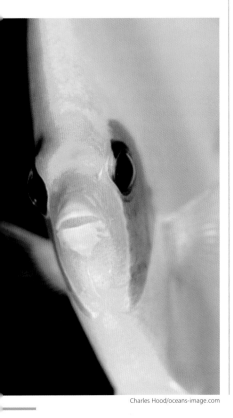

If currents permit, it is possible to circumnavigate the entire island on a single dive. The shallows on the western wall provide an entertaining latticework of caves, crannies and overhangs. Once you've passed the adrenaline rush of the north point, you should have more time to spend exploring the walls themselves, which are rich in sponges, anemones and black corals.

If there's one tip to bear in mind when diving Little Brother, it's to expect the unexpected. You are, in effect, diving on an ocean oasis, and there's no telling which Red Sea wanderers may choose to pay a visit. We have seen visiting pods of bottlenose dolphins, solitary manta rays and huge schools of unicornfish here, while in March and April you can find dense aggregations of moon jellyfish close to the reef wall – the dappled light of the dying sun playing eerily across them.

LITTLE BROTHER: SOUTHERN EDGE

Max depth: 40m optimum

Skill level: 30 dives

Access: liveaboard/support

Current: moderate, though unpredictable

Must see: the hawksbill turtle; the impressive gorgonian fan coral forest

You're at Little Brother and everyone wants to dive the northern tip. And so they should – it's a classic dive and one of your best chances to see sharks in Egypt. But let's face it, the dive can be tiring, and some of us like to have a more sedate option. You can of course view the southern reef at the conclusion of a round-the-island dive, but to get the best out of it you need to start deep, descending to 30–35m to take in the beauty of the gorgonian forest.

Gorgonians are among the most impressive of the non reef-forming corals. Instead of building themselves up on top of previous generations of hard coral, they billow out from the reef in giant, golden fans, which act as a net to snag passing nutrients. When you see dense groupings of gorgonian fans on a reef, you know two things: that it is a high-energy site, and that the coral is in especially healthy condition.

Swimming among the deeper sections of Little Brother's gorgonian forest is one of diving's most chilled-out experiences: few places have such a delicate, ethereal beauty. Take a good look around the folds of the fan structures, and you will see plenty of little animals, including the longnose hawkfish. These are skittish little creatures, but with a little patience and controlled breathing you can approach to within a few feet. Under a diver's torch, they appear deep crimson and offer a real challenge for photographers; get too close and they speed away behind the coral, leaving you wondering where your subject disappeared to.

There's also a good chance of finding free-swimming lionfish and moray eels here, especially late in the afternoon when a Red Sea predator starts to think of supper. Sometimes, the lionfish use divers as cover while hunting tiny glassfish on the reef. It can be unnerving to have those poisonous spines so close to you, so our advice is to move on swiftly if you find yourself with one buddy too many!

At the 30-minute mark, or halfway through your projected dive time, make a 180° turn and retrace your route back to the boat. In the mid-depth range of 15–10m, you'll find lots of anemones and a very healthy array of Red Sea reef life. There is a resident hawksbill turtle here, which has a particular obsession with the dome ports of underwater camera housings – possibly because they look similar to jellyfish, a favourite snack of this myopic reptile. Whatever the reason, it has been known to approach photographers head-on and may even take an exploratory peck at your camera.

Your liveaboard should offer an inflatable to pick you up in case you don't make the return trip, but those who want to complete the swim under their own steam should ask their dive guides to leave a recognisable symbol on the correct mooring line leading back to the vessel. There's nothing more embarrassing than following the wrong line and being greeted by a dive deck full of strangers.

DAEDALUS REEF (ABU KIZAN)

Max depth: 40m optimum

Skill level: 50 dives

Access: liveaboard only

Current: moderate

Must see: scalloped hammerhead sharks; the lively anemone city

If you're looking for offshore excitement, Daedalus Reef is the most remote dive site in all of Egypt. Fifty miles east of Marsa Alam, this speck of reef sits almost in the middle of the Red Sea, halfway between Egypt and Saudi Arabia. About 600m long, the reef rises almost to the surface and is marked by a lighthouse.

The north, south and east sides of the reef are defined by sheer walls, which plunge vertically from the shallows to more than 70m. Hard and soft coral cover is superb along the walls, but the real attraction is the chance of seeing big fish. Daedalus is probably the most productive site for the illusive scalloped hammerhead sharks in Egyptian waters.

As is often the case, the northern tip of the reef is the best for finding sharks, as it is here that the current flows in fast from open water. This is the place to find

Alexander Mustard

◄ A hawksbill turtle pauses from feeding, ready to head to the surface to breathe.

hammerheads, those mysterious sharks that represent the Holy Grail of Red Sea diving. Grey reef sharks are also regularly seen here, alongside occasional visits from various oceanic sharks, which can – at least in theory – turn up anywhere on the reef.

When you move off that northern tip, head down the eastern wall towards the south-eastern promontory. In the past, this has been a spot favoured by the rarely seen thresher shark, and there is always a good chance of coming across a hammerhead.

Impressive though the sharks may be, the reef has its own merits. A wide range of Red Sea coral thrives on the sheer walls, and several species of schooling fish can be found from 20m to the surface, including snapper and longnose unicornfish. On the western side of the reef, the dropoff features a concentration of anemones and some attractive soft coral in shades of blue.

When sea conditions are rough, the southern side is well worth a dive. Most of the liveaboards moor here, so you may find you can swim to the reef by diving off the back of your vessel, rather than using an inflatable tender. Thresher sharks have been seen on this side

of the island. If you have time between dives, try to persuade your guides to take you to the lighthouse, where you can enjoy a panoramic view over the entire reef. The lighthouse keepers are a friendly lot, and a present of biscuits, sweets or cigarettes will be more than welcome.

ROCKY ISLAND

Max depth: 40m optimum

Skill level: 50 dives

Access: liveaboard only

Current: moderate to strong

Must see: keep watching the blue for pelagic fish of all sizes

The southernmost of Egypt's classic offshore dive sites, Rocky Island sits close to the Sudanese border and offers little shelter for mooring liveaboards. If you want to see big fish, the northern tip is a good option, though its exposure to the prevailing north wind makes the approach to the dive site an exhausting journey. If you

►► Scalloped hammerheads are difficult to get close to, but for many divers, they represent the ultimate Red Sea encounter.

(Charles Hood/oceans-image.com)

HAMMERHEAD TIME!

Throughout the Red Sea, divers speak of hammerhead sharks in tones of hushed reverence. There may be rarer shark encounters (the thresher, the guitar shark) and bigger ones (the whale shark), but the mystique of the hammerhead, coupled with its shy nature, make this the fish everyone wants to see.

When Red Sea divers speak of hammerhead sharks, they generally mean the scalloped hammerhead, *Sphyrna lewini*, a sociable species that feeds primarily on squid, rays and fish. Scalloped hammerheads purportedly grow to four metres in length, but it is rare to find individuals of that size anywhere. In the Red Sea, they generally measure between two and three metres long.

Scalloped hammerheads tend to favour offshore reef pinnacles surrounded by deep water. There is evidence that they hunt in deeper water during the night and then return to circle the reef by day, warming up in shallower water. That said, they seldom occupy the first 20 metres, but favour the thermocline where warm surface water meets cool upwellings. In Egypt, this can be anywhere from 90m in the summer to 20m during the winter months.

Although they are shy, these sharks cannot help their curious nature and often make a single close approach. In such circumstances, they have been observed shaking their extraordinary heads from side to side, perhaps in order to fix a diver with those side-mounted eyes. One explanation for the long, flat head is that it has evolved to extend the shark's sensory apparatus, and certainly hammerheads are unusually sensitive animals. Indeed, they seem to recoil at the sound of scuba bubbles.

Schooling hammerheads provide one of nature's greatest wildlife spectacles. You have to be lucky to see it, but Daedalus is probably the best place in Egypt. Other proven hammerhead reefs in the Red Sea include Little Brother, Jackson Reef and Habili Ali in Egypt, and Sha'ab Rumi and Sanganeb in Sudan.

Why do hammerheads come together in these impressive aggregations? Biologists are still torn: some suggest that the schools are indicative of mating behaviour (the schools tend to be exclusively female); others believe the sharks are following invisible magnetic paths on the seabed. Whatever the explanation, to swim with a school of hammerhead sharks is the ultimate Red Sea experience. You shouldn't try to enter the school, but stay low on the reef and with a bit of luck the sharks will come closer. When there's no current, you can try swimming out into the blue to look for sharks, but don't venture too far, as you could be caught by one of the currents coursing beyond the protection of the reef.

Finally, there is another species of hammerhead shark, and one that is seldom seen in the Red Sea: the great hammerhead, *Sphyrna mokarran*. This impressive fish grows to six metres and is an aggressive predator, feeding on eagle rays and grey reef sharks. If you see a very large, solitary hammerhead: look at its first dorsal fin – if it appears unusually tall and sickle-shaped, chances are you are diving with a great hammerhead. They do not pose an immediate threat to divers, but they are much bolder than scalloped hammerheads and may approach you for a close-up look. As with any large shark, keep your distance and leave the water if it shows signs of overt agitation or aggression.

do manage to enter the water here, you will find sheer walls and a powerful swell. Stony and soft coral abound, and there are some diver-friendly Napoleon wrasse.

A good alternative is to dive the south-east corner, where a plateau at 40m is washed by strong currents and visited by a healthy selection of big fish, including jacks, barracuda and grey reef sharks. Scalloped hammerheads are also seen here, especially during April and May.

Spend as long as you can on the corner, then slowly ascend along the wall of the southwest side, which is broken by caves, overhangs and ledges. Dive guides are fond of describing Rocky as 'the Red Sea in miniature', as soft and hard corals are all well represented here, and the broken topography of the wall provides an environment for small reef fish. Watch out for various species of moray eel, glassfish, lionfish, scorpionfish and stonefish, as well as occasional pelagic visitors. On the sandy patches at 35m, sleeping white-tip reef sharks and blue-spotted rays are common.

► An anthias, one of billions in the Red Sea, swims into the blue to feed on plankton.

▼ The gills of a Spanish dancer nudibranch, usually seen on night dives.

Simon Rogerson

ZABARGAD ISLAND: PINNACLES

Max depth: 25m

Skill level: 25 dives

Access: liveaboard only

Current: slight to none

Must see: Spanish dancers, crocodilefish, cuttlefish

Zabargad is the only large island in the extreme south of offshore Egypt. A useful overnight mooring site for liveaboards, this triangular island offers handy protection as well as some intriguing dives. Unlike the other islands in this chapter, its topography is characterised by shallow waters and a gently sloping bottom, making it ideal for an afternoon dive after a day at nearby Rocky Island.

On its southern margins, a sandy slope stretches towards the drop off at 40m and is scattered with coral pinnacles or ergs. It's a great place for fish spotting, home to cuttlefish, octopus and nudibranchs. Don't neglect the sandy areas between the pinnacles, where you may also find blue-spotted stingrays, lionfish and crocodilefish.

As the area is subject only to minimal current, it serves as an ideal spot for night dives. Once darkness has fallen, you can hear the clicking of a thousand crustaceans feeding and flexing their limbs as the evening's foraging unfolds. Watch out for anything red under the glare of your torch beam, as it is quite common to find Spanish dancer *Hexabranchus* (a large, colourful relative of the nudibranchs) here.

Though visibility is more variable and pelagic fish are not as plentiful, Zabargad offers a welcome contrast to the sheer-wall extravaganza of Rocky and the other offshore sites. You benefit from a rewarding dive in benign conditions, and there's often a chance of a manta ray sighting during the day.

ZABARGAD ISLAND: THE 'RUSSIAN' WRECK

Max depth: 24m

Skill level: 15 dives

Access: liveaboard only

Current: none

Must see: the ship's picturesque bow and mysterious holds

Here's an unexpected gem at the uttermost limits of Egyptian diving: a mysterious shipwreck that sits at a depth where you can take your time to explore the structure at your leisure. The 70m-long freighter lies upright on the western side of Zabargad's southern bay, where visibility can be reduced by silt in rough conditions. Most of the time you can rely on average visibility of 20m.

▲ Bathed in afternoon light, the stern section of the 'Russian' wreck still has most of its deck features in place.

▶ The 'Russian' wreck's communications mast makes an ideal ascent route, leading almost to the surface.

The extent and size of the encrusting coral reveal that this vessel went down in the late Seventies. The bow and small hold have broken from the rest of the ship and now list to starboard, with the bow embedded firmly in the reef.

The stern section is especially photogenic, as all the original deck features are still in place, including lifeboat davits, stern winches, cable drums and ventilator tops. Beyond this area are the bridge, navigation room and stairs leading down to the accommodation and galley. As all the doors are open, it is very easy to enter this wreck, but be careful while moving around inside, as space is limited and there is a great deal of rusty silt.

You can reach the engine room from doors situated on the rear deck.

For those who don't relish the claustrophobic delights of wreck penetration, the outside of the vessel is also well worth exploring. Its dominant feature is the communications mast, which rises almost to the surface, providing a useful visual reference for decompressing divers. At the foot of the mast, a small school of glass-fish billows in shifting patterns while lionfish lurk in the shadows, waiting for darkness to herald the evening hunt. During the day, sunlight usually shines brightly on this shallow wreck, so torches are only really necessary for exploring the interior. The ship doesn't appear

Simon Rogerson   Simon Rogerson

to have any cargo, except for some coils of corrugated hoses that lie in the hold and a pile of unopened boxes in a cramped room inside the bow.

This wreck can offer either a relaxed dive or a challenge for budding undersea detectives, as the reason for the ship being in the Red Sea is still something of a mystery (see page 188). Whatever the truth behind the 'Russian's sinking, this little-known wreck is one of the most enjoyable dives in southern Egypt, and well worth a visit. Marine life is sparse on the wreck itself, but the surrounding reef warrants a diversion away from the wreckage; look out for a pretty cavern in the area opposite the ship's mast.

THE 'RUSSIAN'

The identity of the 'Russian' has been the subject of enthusiastic debate among Red Sea wreck detectives. While this book was being researched, author Simon Rogerson joined the English wreck expert Peter Collings on a trip to survey the wreck and try to make some educated guesses about its origins.

For years, received wisdom had it that the wreck was that of a simple trawler, but Collings's suspicions were raised by several factors: the presence of a large and complex battery room; the apparent removal of several watertight doors; several bakelite panels with Russian lettering; and a series of leads running to shore. Was this ship at anchor when it sank? A hole ripped into the stern appears to have come from inside the vessel – does this reveal the event that sank the ship, or was the hole created when the ship was salvaged soon after the sinking?

After much research, Collings concluded that the vessel was a Russian 'Moma' class surveillance ship, probably constructed in 1974. The exact circumstances surrounding its sinking and salvage remain a mystery, and we can only guess why such a vessel would be in southern Egypt. What we do know is that the Russians were operating out of Eritrea during the Cold War, and that they also had good relations with Egypt. Perhaps the innocent 'container ship' was watching shipping for Russia and Egypt during this time of international tension.

If this hypothesis is correct, it might explain the mysterious umbilical lines. If the ship had been communicating with a very distant base, then it would probably have been using high frequency transmission. And if so, then it would have make sense to mount an antenna on land to reduce the dangers of non-ionising radiation. Whatever the case, the ship was salvaged and someone went to the trouble of removing its watertight doors, ensuring it could not easily be refloated by pumping the vessel with air.

1	Bow section	4	Mushroom vents	7	Mast
2	Winch gear	5	Entry to	8	Funnel
3	Holds	6	Bridge	9	

| 10 | Winches |
| 11 | Hole in stern |

sea level

top of wreck 10m

lowest point 24m

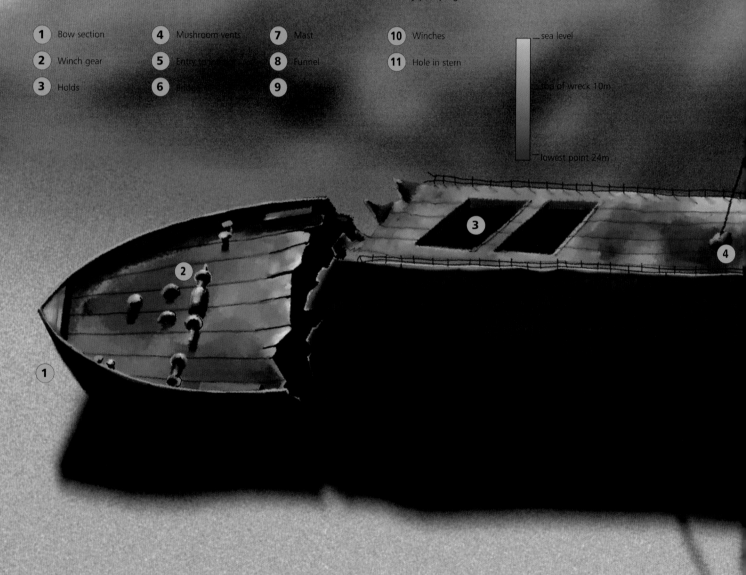

▲ At the bow, the winch gear can be found in fine condition.
(Simon Rogerson)

▲ The debris covered interior of one of the ships holds. (Simon Rogerson)

▲ Mushroom air vents cover the upper decks. (Simon Rogerson)

▲ The interior of the wreck is rusty and space is confined. (Peter Collings)

▲ A school of glassfish lives at the base of the communications mast.
(Simon Rogerson)

▲ These deck steps are still pristine, with minimal coral cover.
(Peter Collings)

Think Red Sea liveaboards, Think blue o two...

EL QUSEIR TO SUDAN

EGYPT'S SOUTHERNMOST SHORES ARE CHANGING FASTER THAN ANY OTHER PART OF THE RED SEA. FOR CENTURIES, THIS REGION WAS ONE OF THE MOST OBSCURE CORNERS OF THE MIDDLE EAST, BUT THE RECENT OPENING OF A PRIVATE AIRPORT TO THE NORTH OF MARSA ALAM IS HAVING A PROFOUND EFFECT.

Diving pioneers dubbed this area 'The Deep South' back in the 1980s, reflecting its frontier reputation. The term refers loosely to the 180-mile stretch of coastline between the town of El Quseir and the border with Sudan, and incorporates several offshore reefs. While the coast is defined by a long fringing reef, the best diving takes place on reef systems that lie further out from the barrier.

The Fury Shoal is a series of reefs noted for its excellent hard coral and varied diving options. Those in search of a soothing experience can enjoy long dives in peaceful lagoons studded with hard coral, while adventure-seeking divers have the choice of exposed reefs with deep drop-offs, where pelagic fish can be seen most of the year. This same system has some of the Red Sea's lesser-known shipwrecks, and there is a general consensus that more await discovery.

On land, there are a few towns, but the resorts start to thin out as you head further south towards Sudan. One of the region's lesser-known attractions is the rock art of the Eastern Desert – timeless patterns and figures carved into the sandstone, dating back as far as 7,000BC. Also along the southernmost extremes of this coast are the abandoned emerald mines of Wadi Sakait and the jagged rock spires of Jebel Farayid and the Berenice Bodkin, both representing serious challenges for extreme climbers.

Yet there is little doubt that the Deep South is finally being tamed. With growing pressure on northern Egypt's dive sites, things began to develop around Marsa Alam in the late 1990s. Where previously the only land-based diving operations had been desert camps with fast inflatable boats, there are now smart new resorts. As well as the new airport to the north of Marsa Alam, a big marine development,

◄ A diver swims around one of the ancient pore corals that typify the Fury Shoal area.

Simon Rogerson

Simon Rogerson

▶ Glassfish swirl through the interior of the yacht wreck at Abu Galawa Soraya.

▶▶ Offshore diving in the Deep South does not mean you get the reef to yourself. Here, dayboats jostle for mooring space on an offshore reef. (Simon Rogerson)

Port Galib, was built to service the liveaboard industry, creating a new hub for hotels and resorts. As a result, the region has suddenly become accessible.

Many have expressed concern at the scale of shore-side development. As already mentioned, much of the coast is protected by a barrier reef, which has only a few natural openings. Already, one resort has bulldozed its way through the reef to open sea in order to provide easy access for its watersports clients. Its owner was fined a sizeable sum, but there is now fear that other resort owners will follow suit, simply factoring in the fine as part of development costs. There is no telling what may happen to this fragile environment if it is altered on a massive scale, purely to suit holidaymakers who come to this part of the world to experience what they believe to be a pristine environment.

For now, though, the scattered reefs of the Deep South can be enjoyed in all their glory, either from land-based centres or by liveaboard. And there are still natural wonders to be discovered: south of the Fury Shoal and Ras Banas lies St John's Reef, a remote smattering of habilis, ergs and drop offs, which *aficionados* say is like diving Ras Mohammed when it was a virgin site. There are sharks, huge tracts of pristine coral and schools of rarely-seen creatures such as the spectacular bumphead parrotfish. It could be that we are only beginning to understand the complexity of this richest of environments.

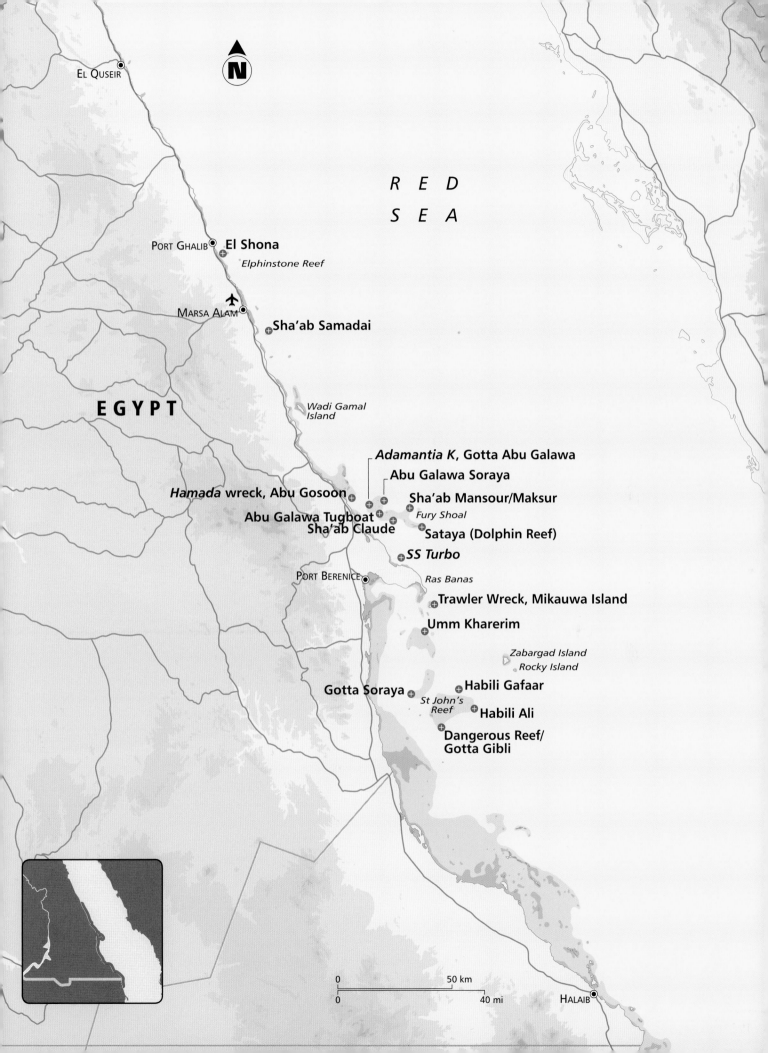

RED
SEA

EL QUSEIR

PORT GHALIB **El Shona**
Elphinstone Reef

✈ MARSA ALAM

Sha'ab Samadai

EGYPT

*Wadi Gamal
Island*

Adamantia K, Gotta Abu Galawa
Abu Galawa Soraya

Hamada **wreck, Abu Gosoon**   **Sha'ab Mansour/Maksur**
Abu Galawa Tugboat   *Fury Shoal*
Sha'ab Claude   **Sataya (Dolphin Reef)**

SS Turbo

PORT BERENICE   *Ras Banas*

Trawler Wreck, Mikauwa Island

Umm Kharerim

Zabargad Island
Rocky Island

Gotta Soraya   **Habili Gafaar**
*St John's
Reef*   **Habili Ali**

**Dangerous Reef/
Gotta Gibli**

0		50 km
0		40 mi

HALAIB

VISIBILITY

Most sites in this region can guarantee 20-metre visibility for most of the year, though some sites may become silted out after exceptionally violent storms. For most of the sites listed here, 30m visibility is the norm and 40m is not unusual from June to October.

 WATER TEMPERATURE

24°C in winter; 29°C in summer.

SEASONALITY

While it can be stiflingly hot in the summer months, the heat is quite bearable from October until April. It can even be decidedly chilly! Schooling fish are more plentiful during the summer months, but the best time for sharks is from March to June, when the water is cool enough to draw them from the depths. During winter, visitors should be prepared for bigger seas and the possibility of violent storms. Some boats head for dry dock in January and February, but the best ones stick it out and their guests have some of the best reefs in the world to themselves.

▼ Large green turtles inhabit the seagrass meadows close to the mainland south of Quseir.

EL SHONA

Max depth: 28m

Skill level: five dives

Access: dayboat from Port Galib

Current: slight to none

Must see: green turtles; the dugong; the seagrass meadow

This picturesque but busy bay is where most of the southern liveaboards moor up for the night before returning to Port Galib. The bay is only about 500m across, but presents good opportunities for hard coral dives and night dives. We carried out several night dives here while researching this book and found stonefish every time.

The southern portion of the bay has an outer wall that is well worth diving, but only the section closest to the mouth of the bay has good coral cover. Further back, the reef wall is drab and choked with algae. Look out for various species of nudibranch, bigeye soldierfish and schools of batfish along the healthy section of the wall.

Chances are you'll be visiting this site towards the end of your trip, so you may be looking for a different sort of dive. If so, one option is to ignore the coral dives on either side of the bay and concentrate instead on the expanse of sea grass that grows within it, at depths of 4–18m. This appears, at first, to be a rather dull environment, but you need to look at it with different eyes.

The seagrass does not generate a biodiversity to rival that of a coral reef, but it harbours creatures that are not easily found on the mainstream dives in this chapter. In the mid-water zone, you may see marauding packs of Bloch's pompano, giant trevally and juvenile goldbody trevally, while closer to the grass you will see various species of boxfish and parrotfish. If you get lucky, you may find tiny frogfish and perhaps even a seahorse.

The stars of the show here – at least at the time of writing – are a giant green turtle and a large dugong that can sometimes be found grazing on the sea grass, using its powerful lower jaw to drag up the nutritious root systems beneath. The dugong is a very rare sea mammal, with only a few thousand in the whole of the Red Sea. By reputation they are very skittish, but the individual at El Shona seems to be tolerant of divers and simply goes about his vegetarian business, taking occasional breaks to swim to the surface and breathe. He already has some propeller scars on his head, so how long he chooses to remain in the bay is anyone's guess.

Most of the time, the dugong is hard to find, but the turtle usually puts in an appearance and the dive provides a welcome contrast to the coral walls that tend to feature in most of the liveaboard itineraries. To maximise your chances, bring a compass and carry out underwater search techniques. There are a lot of boats here, so send up a delayed surface marker buoy prior to your own ascent. How long these large animals choose to remain here is anyone's guess, as the sheer volume of

Simon Rogerson

Simon Rogerson

boat traffic is such that they may be fatally injured by a propeller while at the surface, or may simply choose to move on somewhere quieter.

ABU GALAWA TUGBOAT

Max depth: 17m

Skill level: suitable for novices

Access: dayboat from Marsa Wadi Lahami

Current: slight to none

Must see: the small engine room

There is ongoing speculation as to the identity of this tugboat, which sank in a picturesque corner of the reef system known as the Fury Shoal. Abu Galawa translates as 'father of the pools', a reference to the azure lagoons protected by the reefs that make up this portion of the shoal. What exactly a harbour tugboat was doing on this offshore site has never been explained, but it certainly created a lovely dive site. It obviously collided bow-first with the reef and quickly sank, coming to rest on the sloping reef wall so that the stern hull can be explored along the white sand seabed at 17m. Some researchers have claimed that this wreck is the Tienstin, an English naval tug that disappeared in this area in 1945. They

may be correct, but no maker's plates have been found to confirm the boat's identity; the tyres found in the hold date from 1964 and the vessel's engine appears to be oil-fired, suggesting a later date.

The bow is still ground firmly into the shallows on the south side of the reef, and, with a slight list to the starboard side, it is every inch the picture-perfect shipwreck. There is a two-level engine room, which can be accessed through a door on the starboard side. It's a tight fit for a diver, but the engine room's interior really is quite pretty, with a school of yellow sweepers that pulse and billow in the half-light. It seems a little eerie, but do take the trouble to descend into the lower level of the engine room, where there are several intact features.

Unless you have a specific interest in wrecks, you may find that this one only takes 15 minutes or so to cover. By the time everyone has taken the classic photograph looking up the wreck from the vantage point of the rounded stern, most divers feel it is time to move on and circumnavigate the reef, which has plenty of fish and a beautiful garden of hard corals on the north side. Almost everyone who visits this reef seems to miss two atmospheric caves, which can be entered at about 5–8m on an area of reef close to the wreck.

▲ The Abu Galawa tugboat is shallow enough for beginner divers to enjoy their first wreck.

▶ The yacht wreck may not be big, but it is one of the prettiest shipwrecks in the world.

In the late afternoon, the wreck takes on a different atmosphere as dappled light cuts through from the surface and lionfish emerge to feed. With so many fish around, it's a great place to arrange a dusk dive, during which you can enjoy the setting sun from underwater and watch the subtle changes in fish behaviour as light gradually gives way to darkness. Whatever the time of day, it's always worth taking a good torch on this dive.

ABU GALAWA SORAYA

Max depth: 18m

Skill level: suitable for novices

Access: dayboat from Marsa Alam

Current: slight to none

Must see: the yacht wreck; the garden of hard coral

This delightful dive on the northern edge of the Fury Shoal is a firm favourite with visitors. Essentially, you get two dives for the price of one: a descent onto the small, coral covered wreck of a pleasure yacht, followed by a leisurely tour of some of the best hard coral scenery you will find anywhere in the world.

The yacht is unnamed, but local rumour holds that it was owned by an American sailor who somehow managed to sink it during the Eighties. Today it lies on its starboard side in water that is normally clear, yet shel-

tered from major currents and swell. The fibreglass hull has had time to attract life, and now acts as the foundation for some table corals, as well as impressive clusters of soft coral. It's quite entertaining to swim around, but avowed wreck divers may feel short-changed by such a small (it is 15m long) and relatively featureless craft.

Still, many visitors rate this as one of the most picturesque and enjoyable dives in the Fury Shoal. It is possible to venture inside the wreck, though space is so limited that only two divers should enter at the same time. There are a few dials left among the yacht's decaying innards, but the real motivation for going inside is to admire the resident school of yellow sweepers, which have made this wreck their home. They tend to shift around inside, but seem to be especially fond of a space inside the bow, where they mass over a red sponge which has grown over some old wiring.

A note to photographers: if you want the wreck to yourself, just be patient. Most groups only stay on it for 15 minutes, so you can take photographs of your friends and then settle down to the more 'purist' wreck photography when the group has moved off. In fact, there's a very good motivation for leaving the wreck, as the second half of the dive takes you to a coral garden that seldom fails to touch a diver's heart-strings.

Let's say you leave the yacht wreck from the bow: simply keep the reef to your left and swim along its contours for about 80m. After a while the reef starts to lead off sharply to the left; keep following it and you will see a shallow pass (about 5m deep) where you can swim into a well-lit area dominated by *Acropora* stony corals in their many forms. There are tables, ridges, clumps, boulders – all featuring healthy coral of the sort that these days is increasingly rare.

If you follow the obvious route between the coral formations, you should come to a cut that brings you down into deeper water, still framed by that gorgeous hard coral. This passageway leads to a lagoon of pure white sand interspersed with coral pinnacles. Visibility is usually excellent, creating an impression of vistas of sand that seems to change colour as different light falls on it across the course of a day: in the morning it sometimes appears stark and monochromatic; the overhead light of midday brings out yellows, blues and greens; then, as the sun heads to the east, flickering shadows from the reef cast it in a pale bronze.

On a shallow dive such as this, your air should last for some time. Unless you have plans to race off to another site, negotiate with your dive guide for more than the standard 45-minute or hour-long dive. We recommend a good 90 minutes, if your gas consumption allows. You can head outside the lagoon, or return to the yacht; just remember to bring your delayed surface marker buoy in case you become lost.

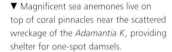

▼ Magnificent sea anemones live on top of coral pinnacles near the scattered wreckage of the *Adamantia K*, providing shelter for one-spot damsels.

Simon Rogerson

▲ Battered by 50 years of storms and consumed by the reef, it is nevertheless possible to make out the *Adamantia K's* propeller shaft.

ADAMANTIA K, GOTTA ABU GALAWA

Max depth: 18m

Skill level: 10 dives

Access: dayboat from Marsa Alam

Current: slight

Must see: the skeleton of the shipwreck; the anemone pinnacles; Spanish dancers at night

This old German freighter went down in 1958 and was not discovered by divers until the late Nineties. You are likely to find yourself on this dive on specialist wreck itineraries, or possibly if easterly winds prevent you from diving other sites in the area. The wreckage is now so broken up that it only really holds appeal for a certain sort of wreck diver. But, while this site is very much a third dive, it is by no means a bad one, as the surrounding reef is worth a visit on its own merits.

The *Adamantia K* struck the reef while travelling up from Port Sudan, initially settling at a depth of about 12m. The site was too shallow and too exposed for the wreck to stay in one piece, and the years have taken

Simon Rogerson

nacles that resemble ornate pagodas. These are topped with magnificent sea anemones, each with a family of anemonefish and hordes of three spot damsels. In the late afternoon, the anemones start to close, exposing the bright scarlet of their bodies. While this isn't exactly a rare sight, their positioning on raised areas makes the anemones easy to view or photograph from below, with the white sand reflecting the soft light of the afternoon.

The same site is sometimes offered as a night dive. Once darkness has fallen, you can see Spanish dancers, cuttlefish and squid in this area, alongside an army of crinoid feather stars.

SS TURBO

Max depth: 28m

Skill level: 25 dives

Access: liveaboard

Current: slight

Must see: lionfish hovering around the winches; the dark holds inside the ship

The British tanker, *SS Turbo*, was attacked by German aircraft on 20 August 1941 during World War 2, while travelling from Haifa to Alexandria with a cargo of fuel. The damaged vessel was then towed towards Aden the following year, but was overtaken by heavy weather, broke in half and was set adrift. The bow section was sunk as it was deemed a hazard to navigation, while the stern section was presumed to have foundered about 11km offshore.

Today, that stern section lies on its port side off Ras Banas, at a maximum depth of about 27m. It can be quite tricky getting divers onto the wreck, as it lies close to the headland and winds coming from the east tend to push moored boats towards the coast. In extreme circumstances, a liveaboard captain may agree to maintain position without setting anchor, but calm weather is the ideal.

The wreckage has a good population of fish, notably lionfish and hawkfish, but it is the scope for exploration and the presence of original ship features that lures wreck *aficionados* here. Be warned that some of the interior rooms are completely dark and prone to silting, so carry a torch and be sure of buoyancy before venturing inside.

If wreck penetration isn't your thing, the exterior has a few excellent features worth checking out, including some large deck winches and a huge funnel which is almost big enough to swim inside. There is a good coverage of encrusting sponges and colourful coral, but the wreck lies so close to land that visibility can sometimes be poor.

their toll. Today, the remains are best described as the anatomy of a shipwreck, with much of the structure having been subsumed by the reef. But many key features remain visible: the boilers still lie close together and the propeller shaft is intact, running between clumps of coral and leading to the steering gear. The engine block is the only substantial part of the wreck still standing proud of the seabed, and is now home to glassy sweepers and various tiny blennies.

Below the wreckage at about 15m is an area of white sand interspersed with some pretty coral pin-

▼ This funnel on the Turbo is almost big enough to swim inside.

Simon Rogerson

Simon Rogerson

TRAWLER WRECK, MIKAUWA ISLAND

Max depth: 52m

Skill level: 50 dives, plus experience at depth

Access: liveaboard

Current: slight to none

Must see: the ghostly outline of the wreck from the deepest point of the dive

Liveaboards sometimes use the shelter of this little island to moor up overnight on the journey back to Marsa Alam from the southernmost sites. In the morning, most of them chug off towards the Fury Shoal or Port Galib. Only a few guides seem to know about this interesting little wreck, which presents a challenging first dive. To locate the wreck, your guide has to find a mass of debris starting at a depth of about 10m. You drop in at this point, and follow the debris trail down until you come to the stern of the wreck at a depth of about 34m.

It isn't a dive for everyone. In the morning, surface conditions can be choppy, and the wreck is too deep to be well illuminated by the soft light at this time of day. Even the wreck itself is nothing special, an unnamed local trawler that went down at some point in the late Eighties. It has no historical significance, few features and no guns. But that doesn't matter, because this dive isn't about looking for obscure artefacts or rare creatures: it's all about atmosphere.

To get the best perspective, follow the hull and swim down to the deepest point – the seabed just in front of the bow. The wreck lies upright on a slope, so when you find yourself hovering in the blue, look up and you will see the structure rising above you in the gathering light. The morning sun beautifully illuminates a magnificent sight: the simple form of the trawler, its gantries and deck dusted with a fine layer of white silt. It would be churlish to deny that nitrogen narcosis plays some part in a diver's appreciation of this scene, but if you are happy diving to 50m, it is a great way to start the day.

The wreck is home to a few batfish, but is otherwise devoid of life and will only take about 10–15 minutes to cover adequately. The rest of your dive should be an easy, gradual ascent along the reef and its satellite pinnacles. It's a pleasant hard coral environment, with quite a few resident moray eels. Simply keep the reef to your left and swim along at your leisure until your decompression and safety stops are all complete. After this dive, you will really enjoy your breakfast!

▲ A rare view of the trawler wreck at Mikauwa Island, taken from 51m.

◄ A golden cardinalfish shows the ultimate in childcare, nursing a clutch of eggs in its mouth.

Simon Rogerson

▲ A blue-spotted stingray hunts the sand flats at Sha'ab Samadai.

SHA'AB SAMADAI

Max depth: 15m

Skill level: suitable for novices and snorkellers

Access: dayboat from Marsa Alam

Current: none

Must see: spinner dolphins moving in large groups

There are a few locations in the Egyptian Red Sea where you might encounter dolphins, but this one is the best. A reef shaped like a horseshoe provides shelter for a large resident pod of spinner dolphins, famed for their acrobatic stunts and often friendly towards divers. For a while, the lagoon was a free-for-all, but HEPCA instituted a system of issuing daily tickets. With a cap now placed on the number of people who can visit the lagoon each day, it is hoped the dolphins will continue to delight visitors to this site.

So, how does it work? An approved boat drops you off near a series of buoys that marks the entrance to the lagoon. You then snorkel in for 100 metres or so, until you reach an area where the dolphins are likely to swim past. The key to a good encounter is to avoid the big groups of day-trippers who flail around in the water, and find a good space of your own. Such large groups tend to charge around after the dolphins, so keep away from the pack. There are plenty of dolphins inside the

lagoon, and many are all too willing to show off in front of an appreciative snorkeller who knows better than to chase or touch. One school of thought holds that dolphins are attracted by people singing and playing in the water. Well, this can't do any harm, though there's no hard evidence for the theory. Above all, be patient and let the dolphins come to you.

Visibility is usually excellent, and light is reflected up from the white sand bottom. If you want to try snorkelling down to interact with the dolphins, it helps to wear a little lead, perhaps half the amount you would wear for scuba diving. There are a few little ergs scattered around, as well as some rope, which photographers use to stabilise themselves when they dive down to take a photo from below.

Over the course of a day, you will notice the character of the place seems to change. Dolphins come and go, mothers shield their calves from strangers and adolescents often give in to temptation and make close passes to show off their bravado. Timing can be important: there seem to be more dolphins from first light until 10am, but it's worth visiting at any time of the day. You will need at least an hour in the water, so wear a wetsuit and lash on the sunscreen. If you are prone to sunburn on your neck, consider wearing a Lycra hood, which covers you up without making you feel too hot or constricted.

SHA'AB CLAUDE/CLAUDIA

Max depth: 18m

Skill level: 5–10 dives

Access: dayboat from Marsa Alam

Current: none

Must see: shafts of light falling from the cavern roof to the sandy bottom

Feeling tired, listless, fed up with modern life? Well here's a cure. Whether you've come to Egypt in search of inspiration, relaxation or exploration, there's a little bit of magic in this site to please everybody. Supposedly named after a guide who found it especially agreeable, Sha'ab Claude (or Claudia, depending on your guide) is a patchwork of pinnacles, caves and swim-throughs that shows the Fury Shoal at its most enticing.

Your boat will drop you off in an area outside the cavern system, so you will most likely drop in on a sandy seabed dominated by ergs. Swim towards the main reef and you will find an entrance on your right that leads into the coral labyrinth. *Acropora* hard corals grow profusely in this area, but it is the tunnels between the open sections that make the dive. Before you leave the open reef, or perhaps on your return to the boat, you should watch out for the school of bannerfish that favours this area. A typical dive should also bring Napoleon wrasse, as well as – at the time of writing – a slightly deranged moray eel that seems to prefer open water to the shelter of the coral.

The coral tunnels could have been created as a diver's playground. They are just the right size for a buddy pair to swim along without fear of bumping into the sides. Just as a tunnel seems to darken, you reach a wide chamber where columns of light cut through the water from above. Black coral and sponges grow on the walls, while groupers and blue-spotted stingrays patrol the white-sand bottom. It's easy to get lost, but that's precisely the point. There's little danger, because whatever route you take, you will end up in open water quite soon as long as you keep swimming. There are a few sections in which caverns lead into full caves – environments that are completely enclosed overhead, allowing no light to penetrate – but these areas are relatively small and take some effort to find.

The contrasting light and space of the coral maze, coupled with the heady vista of the open reef, makes this one of the Red Sea's most memorable dives. It can have a surprisingly profound effect on a diver's mood, perhaps burning itself so deeply into the memory that you remain imbued with a sense of Sha'ab Claude's tranquillity even when boarding the plane home. Such musings may be fanciful, but then Sha'ab Claude brings out the fanciful in the most jaded of divers. It has a quiet sort of magic that lives on long after your dive kit is back in the bag.

▼ Divers find black coral growing at a depth of 12m inside the cavern system at Sha'ab Claude.

Simon Rogerson

SHA'AB MANSOUR/MAKSUR

Max depth: 30m optimum

Skill level: 25 dives

Access: dayboat or liveaboard

Current: moderate to strong

Must see: grey reef sharks and pelagic fish in the deeper part of the dive

This is one of the most exciting sites in the Fury Shoal, with sheer walls and reef tips that are similar to those found at Elphinstone to the north. In contrast to the mellow hard coral sites that typify this area, Sha'ab Mansour is surrounded by deep water and subject to powerful currents.

Unless conditions are friendly, you will probably be diving the southern plateau, where fish aggregate on the sloping coral walls. Expect to see schools of snapper, barracuda and trevally, as well as bigger fish such as Napoleon wrasse and grey reef sharks on the deeper section. After exploring the deeper portions of the reef, you can either return to the main wall or use one of three ergs that rise to within a few metres of the surface. Coral and fish life is prolific on these pinnacles, but you will need a delayed surface marker buoy to mark your place as you ascend, as there may well be several dive groups on the site and inflatable tenders are likely to be zipping around.

If conditions permit, the long plateau on the northern side should be your priority. Just as with Elphinstone, the tongue of reef is covered in soft corals, and grey reef sharks – occasionally even scalloped hammerheads – may patrol the deeper sections. Above all, the proximity of deep water seems to ensure a steady stream of pelagics, so watch out for tuna, dolphins and even manta rays. The coral in the shallow section is home to blennies, cleaner wrasse and juvenile sweetlips.

SATAYA (DOLPHIN REEF)

Max depth: 30m optimum

Skill level: 25 dives

Access: dayboat or liveaboard

Current: moderate

Must see: snapper, trevally and barracuda; sea turtles; pods of dolphins

Located about 11km south of Sha'ab Mansour, this oval reef surrounds a big lagoon frequented by bottlenose dolphins. Most dives take place on the south and east outer sides of the reef, where the wall is thick with soft corals and gorgonian fans and where fish tend to aggregate. Great barracuda are common here, and large schools of bigeye trevally can be seen throughout the warmer months. The only downside is the amount of boat traffic that such diving attracts: Sataya is a very

◄ There are several entrances from the open reef into the semi-closed cavern system at Sha'ab Claude.

►► A pod of spinner dolphins plays in the protected waters around Sha'ab Samadai, where visiting divers have to obtain a permit to snorkel. (Jane Morgan)

▼ The great barracuda is as imposing as any shark, and shows no fear of divers.

Simon Rogerson

popular site, but when it gets busy the fish life tends to move away, possibly towards some habilis north of the reef.

Most divers treat the outer walls as drift dives: try to enter the water at the leading edge, then drift along the wall watching the massed ranks of fish feeding (and being fed on) in the current. White-tip reef sharks are common here, either snaking into the current or dozing under the protection of coral. On the reef itself, you can find turtles feeding on soft coral or sponges.

The entrance to the lagoon is marked by seven ergs, which make for a decent and easier alternative dive. These pinnacles are suitable for night dives, but dusk is the ideal time to visit, as the resident snappers and other reef fish seem to be especially active during this time. Whether or not you actually see dolphins here is a matter of luck; if you really want to see dolphins in the Red Sea, your best bet is probably around the Sha'ab Samadai reef, up towards Marsa Alam, where they are permanently resident.

HAMADA WRECK, ABU GOSOON

Max depth: 15m
Skill level: suitable for novices
Access: dayboat from Marsa Alam or Marsa Wadi Lahami
Current: slight to none
Must see: the wreck itself; disgruntled damselfish

This easy wreck dive is a bonus for shore-based divers in the nearby Marsa Wadi Lahami area. The *Hamada* was on its way from Saudi Arabia to Suez with a cargo of plastic granules when she sank on 5 August 1993. According to the official report, the vessel caught fire and went down in deep water after the crew abandoned her. When a group of British divers first discovered the wreck, they found that all the crew's personal effects and tools had been taken, and there was some evidence of a fire in the wheelhouse.

Today the wreck lies on its starboard side, presenting a well-lit shallow dive for shipwreck enthusiasts. It has broken in two, with the forward holds just a few metres away from the stern superstructure. When the wreck was first discovered, there were many original features still in place around the bridge, but these have gradually been pocketed by divers and the only remaining items of note are packets of plastic granules. Both masts now lie on the seabed.

The best way to enjoy this dive is a leisurely swim around the superstructure, where clumps of raspberry coral and other fast-growing varieties of *Acropora* are now taking hold. Most of the coral growth is concentrated on the rails and the hull, its smooth surface

interspersed by coral clumps. There seem to be quite a few pipefish hiding around the growing coral, and the familiar anthias fish have already staked a claim on the wreck, as have various species of damsel, which tend patches of algae and chirp with discontent whenever a diver strays into their patch. All in all, an eminently enjoyable second or third dive.

ST JOHN'S: HABILI ALI

Max depth: 40m optimum
Skill level: 30 dives
Access: liveaboard
Current: moderate
Must see: hammerheads and grey reef sharks

This is one of the best dives in the St John's area, so perhaps it is unsurprising that any local dive guides called 'Ali' will all tell you it was named in their honour. Habili Ali is the easternmost of the St John's group, and its isolation and proximity to the open water perhaps explains why it is such a high-yield reef for pelagic fish. It's also a convenient reef to visit if you are sailing in from the offshore sites of Rocky Island or Zabargad.

The dive takes place on a big coral pinnacle, which is classified as a habili because it stops around 5m shy of the surface. It takes around 40–50 minutes to swim around the whole pinnacle, but the idea is to drop in and descend to about 40m as the deepest point of a multi-level dive. Visibility here is particularly clear, averaging 30–40m for most of the year.

Habili Ali is a magnet for pelagics. From March to June, the water is the ideal temperature for scalloped hammerheads, which can be seen here singly or in small schools. Then, from July to September, manta rays visit the reef to socialise, feed and be cleaned by wrasse on the reef. Grey and white-tip reef sharks can be seen on the deeper sections throughout the year.

Whether or not the big fish put in an appearance, this is a blue chip wall dive with excellent coral cover and plenty of fish – expect to see black snapper and barracuda swimming close to the wall. The current generally comes in from the north, but this site is not especially renowned for its flowing water. In fact, if you have been frustrated by the violent currents at places such as the northern side of Little Brother, this spectacular habili could provide a workable alternative.

St John's is also one of the northernmost points of the Red Sea where bumphead parrotfish can be found. Their famous stronghold is in super-warm Sudanese waters to the south, but a few hardy ones have adapted to the slightly cooler waters of southern Egypt. In Sudan, they often occur in big schools, but here you will usually see them singly or in pairs.

▼ Wary of the photographer, a damselfish edges closer to the protection of the coral.

Alexander Mustard

Simon Rogerson

ST JOHN'S: HABILI GAFAAR

Max depth: 40m optimum

Skill level: 30 dives

Access: liveaboard

Current: moderate

Must see: the thin pinnacle; hammerhead sharks

This extraordinary pinnacle dive is about 11km due west of Habili Ali, and so makes a popular second dive for those moving towards the coast from the direction of Zabargad and Rocky Island. Its name is something of a mystery, but is thought to derive from the safari skipper who first popularised the site in the 1990s. As a dive, it is similar to Habili Ali, attracting hammerheads and manta rays at different times of the year. However, the pinnacle itself is much smaller – perhaps just 20m by 15m at the surface, widening only gradually as it plunges into the blue. Viewed from the surface, it is shaped rather like an elongated egg.

Even at a depth of 35–40m, the pinnacle is so small that you can easily swim all the way around it, as though it were a massive pillar. In fact, this is exactly the way you should approach this dive: there's no saying where the big fish are going to be, so you should descend to your agreed maximum depth and then gradually ascend, making a full circumnavigation of the pinnacle at (for instance), depths of 35m, 20m and 15m. There is a small plateau deep on the northern side of the reef, but in general the site is defined by sheer walls that plunge down as far as you can see. It makes for a unique dive, but the limited size of the reef is such that there should only really be two boats on it at any given time.

Local dive guides say this site has the greatest concentration of fish in southern Egypt. On a typical summer dive, you can expect to see big schools of snapper and bigeye trevally, to the extent that it can sometimes be hard to see past all the fish. It's a great place to get photographs of massing fish, but you will need a wide-angle lens or attachment to capture the scene in all its glory. All the same, the fish are not the sole attraction on this dive: the reef walls and overhangs have excellent coral growth and support a wide range of marine life including blennies, moray eels and crustaceans.

▲ A magical moment as an adult scalloped hammerhead approaches a diver in St John's, while fellow divers survey the scene from above.

Simon Rogerson

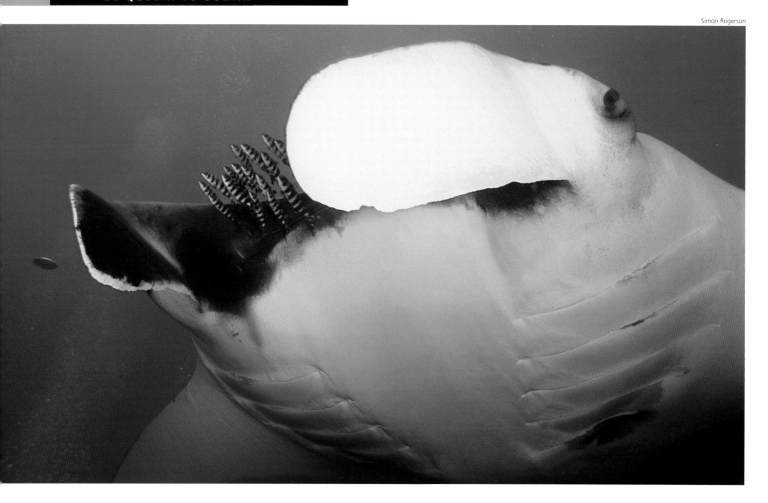

▲ If you see a manta ray, play it cool, stay still and it may swim up to you – swim at the ray and you get nothing but a swiftly disappearing tail.

ST JOHN'S: GOTTA SORAYA (SMALL SON OF)

Max depth: 30m optimum

Skill level: 25 dives

Access: liveboard

Current: moderate

Must see: manta rays from July until September; the 'cathedral' cavern

Although similar to the St John's Reef habilis, this structure qualifies as a reef or 'gotta' because its top just breaks the surface at low tide. From the surface it looks circular rather than oval. The texture of the reef wall also differs, offering a craggier environment, with more ledges for the sort of animals and corals that prefer shelter. The north side bears the brunt of the prevailing currents, but there is no definite point, just a reef slope where hammerheads are sometimes seen.

The wall is thick with gorgonian fans, and large bushes of black coral that look brown-red under torchlight. It provides a protective environment for small fish such as anthias, blennies and hawkfish, so do have a close look at that intricate lattice of coral branches. You do not need to charge around to see all it has to offer, but it is possible to circumnavigate it in about 40–50 minutes, as it is roughly the same size as Habili Ali. At first, the walls are steep until you reach a reef at 30m, then the reef drops away down to 50m. At 12m, there is an opening that leads to a cathedral-like cavern where you can look up and see cardinalfish and squirrelfish darting around in the shafts of light. It's a pleasing distraction, but do not be tempted to spend too much time in here, because there's plenty of action outside.

If Gotta Soraya has a specialty, it is the manta rays that visit the wall to have their parasites pecked off by cleaner wrasse. It is sometimes possible to see two or three mantas, making this probably the best manta site in Egypt. There is one fundamental rule of manta diving: do not swim directly at the rays, or they will swim away at high speed. Ironically, while researching for this book, one of the authors was the unwitting beneficiary of another diver's lack of self-control. The offending diver in question swam right at a cruising manta, which predictably spun away into the blue. The great ray then executed another turn and returned toward the rest of the group, who had only seconds earlier been denied a close encounter. It soared up along the reef wall, over their heads and straight towards the final straggler in the group – your author – who photographed the ray as it passed by just inches from his wide-angle lens. Thus justice was ultimately served!

ST JOHN'S: DANGEROUS REEF OR GOTTA GIBLI

Max depth: 24m

Skill level: 15 dives

Access: liveaboard

Current: none

Must see: the coral pinnacles and their associated life; bumphead parrotfish

This is the southernmost reef of note in the St John's system, and certainly the most inappropriately named. The reef forms a rough horseshoe shape that rises to the surface and offers good shelter for liveaboards. In contrast to some of the others in this area, it doesn't offer dropoff dives. Instead, you get a white sand bottom at 23–24m, with various ergs and pinnacles rising from the seabed with their own communities of fish and invertebrates.

Amid this relaxing environment, you will find a little cave system that starts at 7–8m. It's not as extensive as the system at Sha'ab Claude, but it does add an extra facet to the dive. Elsewhere, the reef is dominated by giant *Acropora* corals that are hundreds of years old. In the summer, bumphead parrotfish swim up from Sudanese waters, while there's usually a good chance of finding scorpionfish and blue-spotted stingrays.

The closed section of the reef faces north, so most liveaboards naturally choose to moor up in the south. Thanks to the level of protection, the lagoon is ideal for night dives, giving divers a chance to appreciate the changes that happen when darkness falls across a coral community. Watch out for Spanish dancers and, if you're very lucky, a guitar shark – a strange animal that shares characteristics of both the shark and ray families.

In general, this reef offers a pleasant spot to moor up and enjoy one of the most isolated spots in the Deep South. Its ambience is welcoming and tranquil. Anything, in fact, but dangerous.

ST JOHN'S: UMM KHARERIM

Max depth: 20m

Skill level: 15 dives

Access: liveaboard

Current: slight to none

Must see: the coral labyrinth of caverns and tunnels

As liveaboards prepare to depart the St John's area, this is one of the last reefs they pass in the northern section before moving on towards the Fury Shoal. It first became popular with groups of divers who wanted something different after all the wall dives of the Deep South and the offshore islands. Umm Kharerim translates as 'mother of the tunnels', and that's exactly what you get, as this is a very extensive system of coral caves – a real playground for divers who enjoy complex scenery.

The reef is very similar to parts of Sha'ab Claude, but the network of caverns is larger, and much of it is shallow enough to treat as a challenging snorkel (the entrance to the tunnels is at about 4–6m). Swimming from chamber to chamber is very relaxing on scuba, but the whole experience becomes a lot more adventurous if you attempt it under your own steam, free-diving through the tunnels that connect the many open sections. Be warned that this is not for everybody: you need to be a fit and confident swimmer and you must take care not to bump your head as you dive through the tunnels. Semi-enclosed environments such as this do not support large amounts of fish life, but you may happen across a sleeping white-tip reef shark, and there are some good-sized groupers in the caverns.

Most divers will be content to spend the entire duration inside the caverns, but there are also pinnacles on the site, where you will find anthias, lionfish and pufferfish. There's also a beautiful sandy lagoon in the middle of it all, which is frequented by a family of Napoleon wrasse. Do not worry about getting lost in the caves, as that is part of Umm Kharerim's appeal. It's not a particularly dangerous place and most guides are quite happy to stay dry and let capable divers go off to explore on their own. From the vantage point of the boat, they can keep an eye on the reef, watching as the divers periodically surface in order to try and work out how to get back to the boat.

▼ Sneaking close to sleeping white-tip reef sharks is a good test of a diver's stealth skills, as these fish tend to swim off when approached.

Malcolm Nobbs

OONASDIVERS
Picture of the Day

ESTABLISHED 1985   FOR DIVERS, FROM DIVERS

Every day we put a picture from an Oonas tour taken by one of our guests on our web site - see www.oonasdivers.co.uk/potd/
This advert uses just a small selection of these fantastic pictures.

Ralph Mortimore

Keith Green

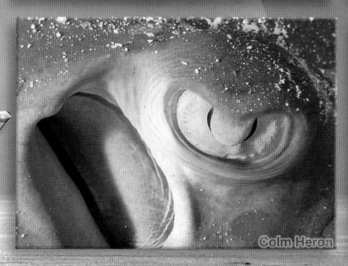
Colm Heron

Phil Clifford

www.oonasdivers.com

SUDAN

SUDAN, WITH ITS POLITICAL INSTABILITY AND BYZANTINE BUREAUCRACY, DOES NOT IMMEDIATELY SPRING TO MIND AS A HOLIDAY DESTINATION. THAT SAID, THIS MASSIVE, COMPLEX NATION IS STILL REGARDED BY MANY AS THE SPIRITUAL HOME OF RED SEA DIVING. IT WAS HERE THAT COUSTEAU AND HASS CARRIED OUT THEIR BOLDEST EXPERIMENTS, AND SUDANESE WATERS ARE STILL FAVOURED BY SEASONED DIVERS IN SEARCH OF THE WILD AND EXOTIC. SUDAN MAY NOT HAVE THE ESTABLISHED TOURISM INFRASTRUCTURE OF EGYPT, BUT FOR THOSE WHO MAKE THE EFFORT, IT CAN BE UNIQUELY REWARDING.

The Sudanese coast is blissfully free of the dive boat congestion that plagues Egypt during peak season. It has been estimated that there are more than 500 different dive vessels working the Egyptian Red Sea, while in Sudan there are never more than about 15 (and at the time of writing, just three). If you want a reef to yourself, it's not going to be a problem.

So why are there so few boats? Could it be because the quality of diving here is substandard? The answer is an emphatic 'no'. In fact, there are many who will tell you that, taken as a whole, Sudan offers the best diving in the entire Red Sea. Underwater visibility is not quite as reliable as in Egypt, but the corals are as healthy as you will find anywhere in the world. And Sudan is certainly the place to visit if you want to see sharks: most offshore reefs have a good population of resident grey reef and blacktip sharks, not to mention the schools of hammerheads found in the deeper waters off reef systems such as Sanganeb or Sha'ab Rumi. In fact, Sudan is probably the best place outside of the Eastern Pacific to dive with scalloped hammerheads.

The Austrian adventurer Hans Hass first dived in Sudan in the 1940s, and Jacques Cousteau visited in the Sixties to carry out his

Simon Rogerson

◄ A view of Sanganeb Reef – the Red Sea's only true atoll – from the top of the lighthouse. Access to the lagoon was created by Jacques Cousteau, whose team deepened the entrance with dynamite.

GETTING THERE

All dive operations are based in Port Sudan, an important, if grimy, industrial harbour. It is possible to fly into Port Sudan from the Sudanese capital, Khartoum, but the liveaboards generally operate in harmony with a Sudan Airways flight that goes to and from Cairo on Saturdays. It's a good opportunity to combine your Sudan adventure with a day of sightseeing in Cairo, where dozens of tour companies offer museum and pyramid tours to fill your spare time.

Sudan Airways (London office tel: 020 7631 3373, www.sudanair.com, email: lonmgr@sudanair.com) is the only carrier that will get you to Port Sudan. While it generally restricts operations to North Africa and the Middle East, there are two weekly flights between Khartoum and London. Most major European airports offer direct flights to Cairo, so the Cairo-Port Sudan connection remains the most popular option for divers, and it is the one we recommend. There are no direct flights between Sudan and North America.

In early 2007 an Egyptian liveaboard was due to begin charters to Sudan out of Port Ghalib.

VISAS

All visitors to Sudan require a visa, which must be applied for in advance or through your tour operator. Tourist visas are normally given for a one-month stay, but the actual charge can vary. The official fee in London was £56 at the time of writing, but the amount is subject to periodical changes, and additional charges are usually levied for various taxes. These days, most divers visit Sudan as part of a package in which their tour operator appoints a local fixer to buy the visas in advance on your behalf and affix them to your passport when you arrive. It may seem unusual to use such a fixer (you may have to entrust your passport to him for a prolonged period), but if you only have a limited time, and with liveaboard and flight schedules to meet, it's more than worth the extra 'fees' to ensure that the processing runs smoothly. We've seen people try to get past immigration at Port Sudan without local aid; it isn't pretty. You need to bring along about US$250 in new notes to cover the various charges, but consult your tour operator for a precise figure.

MONEY

The Sudanese Dinar (often confusingly referred to as the 'pound') is the official currency and should be used for small transactions. Payments for visas and large bills are usually made in US Dollars, though Euros and Pounds Sterling are often welcome. At the time of writing, the exchange rate was 276SD to the Euro, 230SD to the US Dollar and 409SD to the UK Pound.

▶ A local market in a Sudanese town is full of unusual sights.

famous Conshelf II experiment in underwater habitation. So why did it all dry up? The truth is that Sudanese governments since the early Eighties have placed a very low priority on tourism (and there are elements in the establishment who would rather no westerners visit Sudan at all), so little effort has been made to make life easy for visitors. Visas are costly and awkward to arrange; flights are unreliable and the immigration procedures inside the sweltering airport complex appear designed to test the visitor's endurance.

Sudan is also a 'difficult' destination from the operator's point of view. Fuel costs can be surprisingly high, supply lines for food and other essentials are unreliable, and dive boats are seen as an irrelevance in the international transportation hub of Port Sudan. The people running dive boats here are adventurers, often veterans of Egyptian diving who grew weary of the crowds. But it is hard work running a dive operation in Sudan, and with the exception of a few who seem addicted to the place, it has a way of burning out dive professionals.

So what does this mean for the visitor? In the first instance, prices tend to be higher than in Egypt and you have to resign yourself to spending four days of your holiday travelling instead of two. Also, you may find even the superior boats in Port Sudan fall well below the standards of the luxurious vessels now accepted as commonplace in Egypt. On the other hand, once you're in the country and on your boat, you can leave the sweat and grime of the port behind you. You are now in Sudan, an adventure destination with some of the most colourful reefs in the world. You will swim with sharks and manta rays. You will experience the Red Sea at its wildest and most beautiful, and you will have it all to yourself.

Charles Hood/oceans-image.com

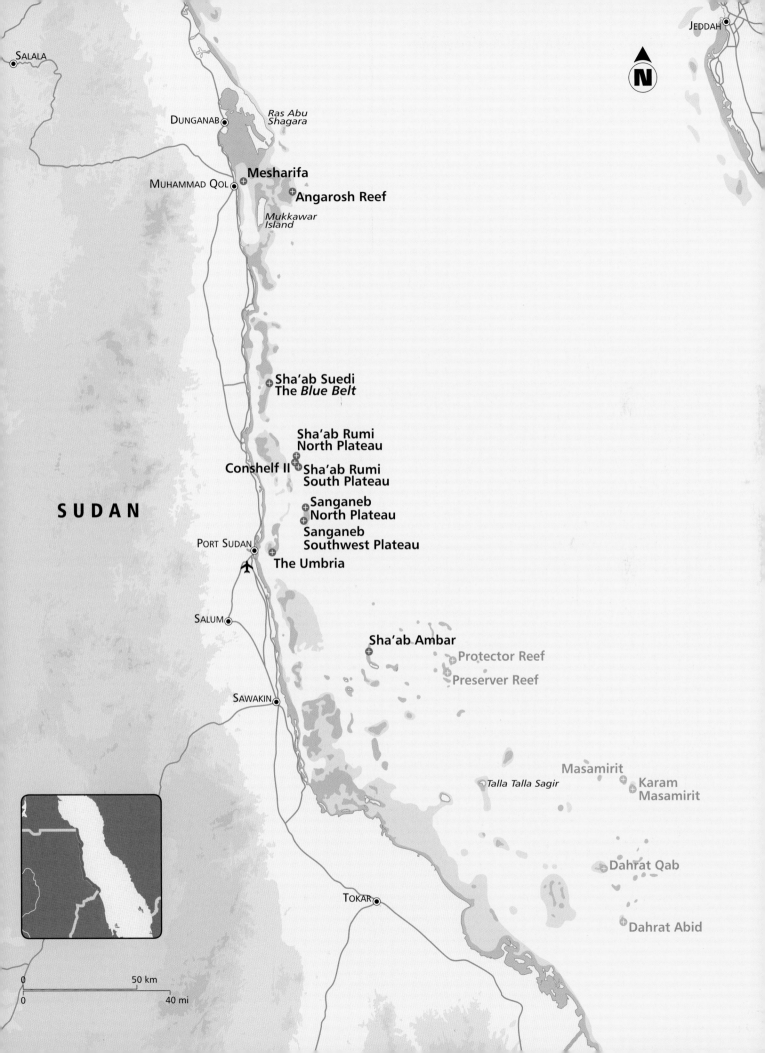

SALALA

JEDDAH

DUNGANAB

*Ras Abu
Shagara*

Mesharifa

MUHAMMAD QOL

⊕ **Angarosh Reef**

*Mukkawar
Island*

⊕ Sha'ab Suedi
The *Blue Belt*

⊕ **Sha'ab Rumi
North Plateau**

Conshelf II ⊕ ⊕ **Sha'ab Rumi
South Plateau**

S U D A N

⊕ **Sanganeb
North Plateau**

⊕ **Sanganeb
Southwest Plateau**

PORT SUDAN

✈ **The Umbria**

SALUM

Sha'ab Ambar

⊕ Protector Reef

Preserver Reef

SAWAKIN

Masamirit

Talla Talla Sagir ⊕ Karam
Masamirit

⊕ Dahrat Qab

TOKAR

⊕ Dahrat Abid

| 0 | | 50 km |
| 0 | | 40 mi |

Charles Hood/oceans-image.com

HANS HASS:
RED SEA PIONEER

Born in Vienna in January 1919, Hans Hass is one of history's greatest underwater explorers. He first started swimming underwater in 1937 during a holiday in the South of France and soon recognised the Red Sea's potential for diving. But it was in Sudan rather than Egypt or Israel that he began his first serious exploratory dives.

After the Second World War, Hass embarked on the journey from Vienna to Sudan, stopping off in Rome and Cairo before arriving in Port Sudan. He went diving on his own using a primitive oxygen rebreather. Locals warned that he was risking an attack by sharks, but he remained undaunted. He emerged with pioneering footage and photographs of sharks, manta rays and the wreck of the *Umbria*, all of which appeared in his 1947 documentary, *Men Among Sharks*.

Hass subsequently returned with his wife, Lottie Baierl, to film a feature-length documentary, *Adventures in the Red Sea* (1951), which included worthy scientific experiments in which human-generated noises were aimed at barracuda and groupers. By way of light relief, there was also plenty of footage of the photogenic Lottie, with whom viewers found it easy to empathise. He won the award for best documentary at the 1951 Venice Film Festival.

Today, although his wandering intellect has led him to other interests, divers all over the world hold Hass in the highest esteem. The freedom and beauty he experienced and celebrated in his pioneering days will live with him forever. He last visited Sudan in 1979 to make a documentary for a German television channel, but if he were to visit today he would find that the marine environment is still a paradise – albeit one with fewer sharks. He will go down in history as the father of Red Sea diving.

◀ Fishing boats moor up as the sun sets over the Sudanese desert, a place largely unchanged since Hans Hass first visited in the early Forties.

▶ The large bumphead parrotfish favours the warm waters of Sudan and Eritrea, where it is a common sight.

▼ Sudanese reefs bristle with life, with a wide variety of coral species in evidence.

SHA'AB RUMI: SOUTH PLATEAU

Max depth: 40m optimum

Skill level: 20 dives

Access: liveaboard/support or dayboat

Current: low

Must see: grey reef sharks; bumphead parrotfish; great barracuda

Just 24 miles north east of Port Sudan is Sha'ab Rumi, one of the most productive spots for shark diving in the entire Red Sea. The southern edge of the reef ends in a long plateau that leads out some 180m from the shallows to the dropoff. Most of the plateau is at a depth of about 25m, though the reef flat is interspersed with coral-covered bommies.

As you come down the middle of the plateau you should find a raised hump and an unmistakable coral bommie with a bulbous green tip. If you don't want to push on to the end of the reef and the drop-off, this is a good place to sit and watch out for the resident grey reef sharks. There seems to be a highly active cleaning station in operation here: keep your distance until a shark has relaxed and is being cleaned, then try to sneak closer for a better view. Once the shark is preoccupied with the cleaning process, it will be less likely to spook.

Those who want to look for more sharks should continue to the end of the plateau, where there is a very obvious dropoff starting at about 30m and descending for hundreds of metres. If you're looking for hammerhead sharks (and if you have enough air to make your way back up the plateau), descend to about 40m and try to find the thermocline, where the warm surface water meets colder upwellings. This is where the hammerheads hang out.

In summer, the thermocline tends to be deeper than most recreational divers are qualified to venture. From January through to March, though, you stand a very reasonable chance of finding the elusive hammerheads anywhere from 20m to 50m. They are incredibly skittish, so control your breathing and stay close to the reef. If you're lucky, you may see a school swimming in formation.

Every element of this dive is world-class. As you ascend back along the reef, you should encounter sizeable schools of barracuda and bigeye trevally, and there's always a chance of meeting grey reef sharks along the cleaning station area. Jacques Cousteau was sufficiently concerned about Sha'ab Rumi's resident predators to install one of his shark cages here, and it still lies at a depth of 22m on the eastern side of the plateau.

You can continue along the eastern wall, but it's all rather tame compared to the tip. We recommend you spend as much time as possible in the vicinity of the plateau, then ascend along its shallow wall, where your support boat may in any case be moored. This is a fine place to look out for schools of bumphead parrotfish, another Sudan speciality.

Alexander Mustard

THE GUYS IN THE GREY SUITS

With a few exceptions, you have to dive quite deep to find grey reef sharks throughout most of the Red Sea. There is a theory that they are disturbed by the constant presence of divers, and choose to inhabit deeper waters during the hours in which divers normally visit the reef.

Whatever the case, Sudan's reefs offer the chance to view these elegant sharks at moderate depths and even in relatively shallow water. The most famous site is probably the southwest plateau of Sha'ab Rumi, where up to 40 grey reef sharks used to be seen at regular feeds. It all ended in 1995, when Yemeni fishermen moved into Sudan waters and wiped out most of the sharks in a single day. The sharks were used to taking bait, so it was easy to catch them on baited long lines.

Since then, other sharks have moved in to claim the rich territory of Sha'ab Rumi, but not in the numbers seen before 1995. If you're lucky, you may see a dozen or more on a single dive. The reef today has about 20 resident greys; we were encouraged by the sight of several pregnant females during the research trips made during the preparation of this book.

Getting close to grey reef sharks can be a matter of luck. They favour a few cleaning stations around the 25m mark on Sha'ab Rumi, but when divers close in, they tend to retreat towards deeper water. Some boats still feed sharks in Sudanese waters, a controversial practice that excites the animals, making their behaviour less predictable. Still, you do tend to see them close-up in such circumstances. Another tactic is to take a plastic water bottle (filled with water, or it will be super-buoyant!) and roll it around vigorously in your hands; the sound seems to excite the sharks and they can make fast approaches as a result.

Never forget that grey reef sharks are territorial animals, and as a diver you are a guest on their patch. The same species has been recorded displaying threat postures in the Pacific, with body contortions and exaggerated swimming patterns eventually giving way to full-blooded attacks. Such behaviour has not been officially recorded in the Red Sea, but if you see any shark swimming in jerky movements with its fins pointing down at an unnatural angle, our advice would be to get out of its way and leave the water at the earliest opportunity.

Charles Hood/oceans-image.com

SHA'AB RUMI: CONSHELF II

Max depth: 12m to the garage remains; 33m to the shark cage

Skill level: suitable for novices in the shallows

Access: liveaboard or dayboat

Current: none

Must see: the 'garage'; the 'toolshed'; the collapsed shark cage: the remains of the fish farm experiment

Here's a dive that polarises opinion. To some, it is an opportunity to witness first hand the historical remains of a bold experiment carried out by Jacques Yves Cousteau, the most famous diver of all time. To others, it's just a pretty reef cluttered with rusty mess. Our view is that the remains of Conshelf II, or Precontinent II, offer one of the world's most unusual wreck dives. To visit it is to touch the history of our sport, and at the same time to enjoy one of the prettiest reefs you will find anywhere.

Cousteau's team used dynamite to blast a channel into the lagoon, then settled on the west side of Sha'ab Rumi for the site of Conshelf II, a high profile experiment in underwater living carried out over four weeks in 1963. It was the perfect setting, as the reef is one of the richest in the Red Sea, with healthy coral and billowing schools of reef fish. With its blend of historical interest and natural serenity, this is a dive that lives up to the hype.

The classic dive here begins just outside the dynamited channel that links Sha'ab Rumi's lagoon with the open sea. If you keep the reef to your right, you will find a series of coral bommies leading to a structure that appears at first to be a perfectly round bommie sitting on the sand at 12m. In fact, it is the dome of Cousteau's underwater garage, in which his wet submarine was housed during the experiment. It was designed to resemble the body of a sea urchin, and the shape is still unmistakable.

The garage was so well constructed that it remains largely airtight even today: you can swim right into the bell of the urchin, where the exhalations of hundreds of divers have created an air space. Do not on any account be tempted to breathe this air. Aside from the fact that it has high carbon dioxide levels, the algae coating the inside of the structure suggests the presence of various toxins. It will not hurt to break the surface and have a squeaky conversation with your buddy inside the air bubble, but keep your regulator firmly clamped in your mouth and do not remove your mask.

Head further along the reef and you will come across more relics from the Conshelf II expedition, including a submarine tool shed that resembles an A-frame tent. It's a fun little swim-through, but be careful not to bump into the soft corals growing on either side or the table coral on the far side. As you progress down the reef, you will find more bommies covered in soft coral and some triangular structures that were part of an aquarium experiment.

Proceed beyond this area for about 30 metres, following the lip of the reef, and you will come to another group of triangular structures. If you choose to, you can go over the dropoff here and head down to 33m, where you will find a collapsed shark cage that is covered in encrusting sponges and soft corals. The cage's interior is now home to a school of glassfish, and it all makes for charming photographs.

Further down on the seabed at 40m, you will find more detritus from the fish farm experiment. It can be a very beautiful, serene dive, but your perception of it will change with the prevailing conditions. We have experienced this site with 40m visibility and bright sunshine, when the sunlit ripples dancing on the sandy bottom were visible at 40m. However, we have also dived here under dark skies and in limited visibility, when the reef took on a more sinister ambience and darkness enveloped the diver below 25m.

Whatever the case, it is an exceptional dive in any circumstances. So enjoy the reef and take a plunge into Red Sea history!

OTHER DIVE SITES

Dahrat Abid
Dahrat Qab
Karam Masamirit
Masamirit
Preserver Reef
Protector Reef

▼ This unusual structure, built to resemble the body of a sea urchin, was used by Cousteau as a garage for his submersible vehicles during the Conshelf II experiment.

Simon Rogerson

Simon Rogerson

CONSHELF II: A DESIGN FOR LIFE

Prior to Jacques Cousteau's famous Conshelf experiments, the notion of people living underwater for prolonged periods was considered the stuff of science fiction. Co-inventor of the demand valve, Cousteau practically invented scuba diving as a recreational sport, which he then went on to popularise in his classic book and film, *The Silent World*.

In the early Sixties, Cousteau began discussions with George Bond, an American navy doctor who envisioned underwater habitats in which people could live for weeks on end. The US Navy had rejected Bond's ideas, so he took them to Cousteau, who was even then regarded as something of a visionary. Together, Cousteau and Bond oversaw Conshelf I, in which, for a duration of seven days, two divers lived and worked from an air-filled chamber placed off the coast of Marseilles at a depth of 11m. The experiment was a success, so Cousteau devised a second endeavour that would increase the scale of the original Conshelf project. When he encountered difficulty in raising the money, he decided to fund the experiment himself and recoup the investment through a feature-length documentary.

Cousteau eventually settled on Sha'ab Rumi as the setting for Conshelf II. Its relative proximity to the logistical centre of Port Sudan was useful, and the reef itself was (and remains) one of the most productive in the Red Sea. He chartered a freighter, the *Rosaldo*, to transport the components of the starfish-shaped habitat to Sha'ab Rumi, where a channel was dredged through the shallow reef to allow access to the shelter of the inner lagoon. The 'starfish house' was eventually placed on a sandy area at 11m.

On 12 June, 1963, five divers took up residence in the habitat. The project was clearly influenced by the visual demands of documentary making, as Cousteau's team was decked out in silver wetsuits and given a futuristic-looking wet submarine to ride. The submarine was housed in an urchin-shaped underwater garage, which is still the major remaining artefact on Sha'ab Rumi.

A second, smaller habitat capsule was placed at 25m, from which two divers used Heliox (a specialist gas mix of helium and oxygen, often used by commercial divers for deep projects) to descend to depths of more than 100m. They made an important discovery: minor cuts seem to heal quicker under increased pressure. Decompression chambers are today commonly used to speed up the recovery process in sports injuries. The divers also noted that the growth of their hair slowed down while they were in the habitat.

The project came to a successful end on 15 July, when both teams safely returned to the surface. The 'starfish house' was broken up and transported back to France, while the remnants of the experiment were left on the reef, to be colonised by coral and fish. Today, they are part of the reef itself, a living testament to the imagination of diving's most charismatic leader.

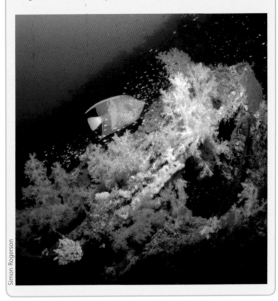

Simon Rogerson

▶ A diver swims by an A-frame structure known as the 'tool shed', one of many relics left by Cousteau when the Conshelf II experiment concluded.

Alexander Mustard

▲ An emperor angelfish hides in a coral overhang.

SHA'AB RUMI: NORTH PLATEAU

Max depth: optimum 40m

Skill level: 30 dives

Access: liveaboard/support or dayboat

Current: moderate, some care required

Must see: longnose hawkfish; schooling bigeye trevally and barracuda

This plateau is smaller and more exposed than the one on the southern side, but again it is a superb place to dive with sharks in a high-energy environment. Currents and swell tend to be more powerful here, so divers will often be asked to carry out negative entries from their inflatable support boats. The idea is to expel all the air from your BCD prior to rolling off the boat, so that you sink immediately instead of floating around at the surface where you may be carried away from the site. You then reconvene with your buddy at a depth of 5m, gather yourselves, and begin the dive proper.

The stronger currents hitting the north plateau create a favourable environment for schooling fish, so watch out for bigeye trevally, which often form into spectacular spiralling schools. Swim along the dropoff at about 30m and you'll find the perfect place to observe both the schooling fish and the famous grey reef sharks. It's also worth taking a close look at the gorgonian fan corals here: some are home to one of Sudan's most photogenic creatures, the longnose hawkfish.

Ask your boatmen to drop you in the middle of the plateau, then head towards the dropoff to look out for big fish. The optimum depth for shark spotting here is about 40m, so you can enjoy around eight minutes at depth before decompression becomes an issue. At this point, we recommend you turn around and swim along the western side of the plateau, where you stand a good chance of finding more bumphead parrotfish.

Aim to finish your dive close to the reef's shallow section on the western side, where inflatable boats are able to moor up. If the current is running, it is advisable to send up a delayed surface marker buoy or safety sausage, so that your boatman will know where you are – and, more importantly, in which direction you are likely to drift.

SANGANEB: SOUTHWEST PLATEAU

Max depth: optimum 40m

Skill level: 30 dives

Access: liveaboard or dayboat

Current: light to moderate

Must see: soft coral pinnacles; grey reef sharks cruising over the sandy plateau; hammerhead sharks at 40m from December to April; longnose hawkfish in the gorgonian fan coral

Around 14 miles northeast of Port Sudan, Sanganeb reef is the only true atoll in the entire Red Sea. It is an area of outstanding marine diversity, to the extent that a dive off one of its extremities has been likened to seeing the whole Red Sea in an hour. Accordingly, it is Sudan's only marine protected area and was in the running to become a World Heritage Site in 1994; the move was only stopped due to a lack of baseline scientific data on the reef. What we do know is that its sheer walls drop straight down to 800m, and that the reef acts as a magnet for a huge variety of marine life.

The south-western point is the most famous dive at Sanganeb. As with Sha'ab Rumi, you can expect to see plenty of grey reef sharks, but the challenge is to continue descending over the dropoff in order to find the elusive scalloped hammerheads. If the thermocline doesn't appear before you reach a depth of 40m, forget it; head up and enjoy the action on the plateau. The hammerheads will wait for another day.

Depending on the currents, your boatman should put you in somewhere on the western side, from where you can fin straight down to the plateau at 25m. This is no ordinary plateau, even by Red Sea standards. Interspersed among the sandy areas are some of the most beautiful coral pinnacles you will see anywhere in the Red Sea. Just at the tip of the dropoff is an especially beautiful bommie, the sides of which are coated in brightly coloured *Dendronephthya* soft corals. The corals here occur in vivid reds, pinks and purples, growing in a concentration that has to be seen to be believed; yet many divers swim straight past them, looking only for sharks.

To be fair to these divers, there is much to distract the eye on Sanganeb. Just beside the aforementioned bommie, you will find a clump of black coral, which (at the time of writing) is home to a couple of camera-friendly longnose hawkfish. Take a look in the sand and you may also find a large stingray that seems to have made the south-western point its home. There are scorpionfish, groupers, countless anemones and frequent sightings of schooling blackfin barracuda. Manta rays are also known to visit this atoll, so be aware of the blue and be ready for anything!

SANGANEB LIGHTHOUSE

Simon Rogerson

There is a handsome lighthouse on the southern section of Sanganeb, built by the British in the Victorian era and maintained by dedicated keepers in conjunction with the Sudanese Navy. In general the keepers seem to be indulgent of tourists, so you are welcome to climb to the top, from where you can photograph the snaking outline of the atoll as it plunges into deep water. It's worth the sweaty climb, but don't wear your best clothes for this excursion, as you'll have to do a fair bit of shimmying to get from your inflatable boat onto the pier, where generations of seabirds have left their inimitable mark!

▼ The southern tip of Sanganeb is blessed with some of the world's most extravagant soft coral growth.

Simon Rogerson

If you should hear a loud thudding sound while underwater, don't be fooled. It may sound like distant dynamite fishing, or even a first stage o-ring failing nearby, but it's more likely to be the resident bumphead parrotfish indulging in a spot of buffalo-style head banging. This is a natural way for male bumpheads to contest a territorial dispute, as can be seen from the white scarring around their bulbous foreheads.

Further up the plateau, you should find more pinnacles, including one shaped like a mushroom (at about 22m) that could just be the best soft coral pinnacle in the world. It's not as large as the others, but the top is swathed in the richest coral. It's a great place to take photographs of your buddy, as those soft corals really come to life under the bright light of a flashgun. Also, you may be lucky enough to have a grey reef shark come nosing around while you are snapping away.

Your dive will finish as you head up the wall towards the shallows. Even here, you should pay close attention to your surroundings. Great barracuda frequent this area and allow divers to approach very closely (being confident that we can't do them any harm). There's also a good chance of coming across the bumphead parrotfish. Many a seasoned diver will tell you that, on its day, Sanganeb South is the best dive in the entire Red Sea.

SANGANEB: NORTH PLATEAU

Max depth: 45m

Skill level: 50 dives

Access: liveaboard/support boat

Current: unpredictable, often strong

Must see: Napoleon wrasse; schooling jacks; wide diversity of soft and hard corals

It's a lengthy journey in an inflatable boat to get to Sanganeb Atoll's northernmost tip, and those little whitecaps you may have observed from the comfort of your liveaboard can turn into formidable walls of water by the time you are actually powering out over them. If sea conditions allow, however, a visit to Sanganeb North is well worth the effort. Schooling fish are guaranteed, and the coral here is pristine.

You'll typically be dropped in close to the reef shallows, and can then make your way down a series of shelves until you come across a raised mound, the top of which sits at about 15m. After this it's a fairly straight drop down to a plateau at 45–50m, where the shark action can be fantastic if there's enough of a current to keep them active. At about 50m the reef slopes away into blue infinity.

In the deeper sections of this dive, you'll find clumps of black coral and gorgonian fan corals. It's worth spending some time at 30m just beyond the mound,

Alexander Mustard

▲ Bigeye trevally pair off during mating, when males turn black.

where you are likely to run into tuna and other pelagics. Closer to the main reef, you will find grouper and Napoleon wrasse. As you ascend, the coral catches the light and becomes the focus of your dive. Look out for the pretty cave on the main reef wall at about 12m.

This can be a great dive, but its depth and unpredictability make it potentially dangerous for the inexperienced. If you're in any doubt about your physical capabilities, ask to go to the southwest plateau instead. The good news is that on a reef like Sanganeb, there's no such thing as a boring dive.

◀ A coral grouper pauses to yawn, displaying ridges of tiny, razor-sharp teeth designed to trap and hold small fish.

► Tiny humbug damsels use hard coral as shelter.

Simon Rogerson

MESHARIFA

Max depth: 15m

Skill level: novice

Access: liveaboard

Current: slight to moderate

Must see: manta rays (count them!)

Mesharifa is a small island of coral sand located in a sheltered bay close to the mainland and just in front of Mohammed Qol, a small fishing village. Here Sudan boasts a manta ray site to rival any in the world. Unlike the classic manta dives of the Maldives or Yap, the site is not centred around a deep cleaning station, but takes place in a shallow channel where the graceful rays gather to socialise and feed on plankton.

All along the shoreline, there is a protected bay running at depths of 6-15m and studded with little ergs. The ergs form channels through which a light current passes, bringing a rich soup of zooplankton for the rays to feed on. Visibility is not great here – you can expect 6–18m of water clarity – but when you've got a group of four-metre rays dancing right in front of you, you don't need to see far.

It is possible to use scuba here, but if the mantas should decide to move on from the spot you have picked (as they invariably do), then the task of getting in and out of the boat becomes laborious. Almost all the visitors choose to snorkel, as it offers an agreeable break from scuba diving and affords greater manoeuvrability.

Swimming with mantas may seem like a straightforward proposition, but it takes a degree of skill, not least guile. They may be big (an individual nearly 7m across was once caught in the Pacific), but these are shy animals with a curious nature. They gather near channels and passages where the current funnels plankton into a tight area, often maintaining a steady position against the moving water and allowing it to pass through their open mouths.

Manta rays need time to become accustomed to human presence. When you first see them, resist the temptation to swim directly at them. Keep your distance and maintain your position at the surface. They will swim towards you and then veer gracefully away when they get to within a few metres. If someone in your group cannot contain their excitement and swims right at the rays, ask your boatman to take you further away from the other snorkellers. Chances are that there are several different groups of manta rays feeding in the area, and a keen-eyed boatman will be aware of their position around the reef. If you are lucky enough to get a small group of mantas to yourself, enjoy every second of it!

The peak season for manta action at Mesharifa runs from June to October, when you should see hundreds of pectoral fins breaking the surface as you arrive. This is also a good time for flat calm waters - a definite bonus if you are snorkelling at the surface (snorkelling in chop is hard work). But there is a downside: the Sudanese summer is stiflingly hot, with temperatures sometimes reaching 50ºC. From November onwards the manta population thins out as the water cools, but there is evidence that between 15 and 20 rays are permanent residents here.

► As daylight fades on the reef, crinoid feather stars unfurl their arms to gather plankton from the water.

MANTA RAYS: ANGELS OR DEMONS

In fishermen's folklore, manta rays were characterised as 'devil fish', their reputation sealed by the two cephalic fins, which sit like demonic horns on either side of the animals' mouths. When Hans Hass prepared to make his first dives off Sudan in the 1950s, locals warned him that the 'devil fish' would devour him.

Of course, the great man was unmolested and the public soon had a very different idea of the way manta rays relate to human presence. Recently, the UK scuba magazine DIVE carried out a poll of the readers' favourite marine animals, and the manta ray, *Manta birostris*, emerged a clear winner.

Anyone who has seen mantas underwater will understand why these harmless, filter-feeding rays are so popular. For such large animals (most measure between three and four metres across their broad pectoral fins), they move with remarkable grace, yet you can tell they are also extremely powerful. These are highly social animals with a nature that is at once curious and cautious: on cleaning stations, they appear to form orderly queues while they wait for the attentions of the wrasse.

Each manta ray seems to respond to humans in a different way. It is now universally acknowledged that swimming directly at mantas causes them to flee. The best tactic is simply to remain as calm and still as possible. At first, try to observe the ray without looking at it head-on. As time passes it should become more curious and will make closer passes.

There have been several authenticated reports of rays enjoying a 'jacuzzi' bath in diver's bubbles, and at least one true instance where a ray took a diver on its back and swam her around. But for the most part these animals do not crave human contact. Simply to see them in their own environment is a privilege few can claim to have enjoyed. Those who have swum with manta rays speak of it as a humbling experience in which they feel they have been visited by a benign force of nature. In less then 60 years, manta rays have shed their demonic reputation, to the extent that they are now regarded as the angels of the sea.

► At once elegant and powerful, a four-metre manta ray smashes its broad pectoral fins into the water as it swims just under the surface.

Simon Rogerson

SHA'AB SUEDI: THE *BLUE BELT*

Max depth: 70m to bottom, optimum 40m

Skill level: 40 dives for the deeper section

Access: liveaboard

Current: unpredictable, can be strong

Must see: Toyota cars inside the *Blue Belt*'s hold and on the reef; giant table corals on the nearby reef

Head north from Sha'ab Rumi and you will come to the long reef of Sha'ab Suedi and the wreck of the *Blue Belt*, a cargo ship that sank in mysterious circumstances in the 1970s. The wreck turned turtle and now lies hull-up, with most of the interesting deck features hidden or buried in the sand. Large parts of the wreck are accessible, however, and its cargo of Toyota vehicles can still be seen in the holds.

In fact, a few cars fell off the ship when it sank and now sit conveniently in the shallows to provide photo opportunities after the deeper section of the dive. The wreck starts at 18m and goes as deep as 70m, but the classic route takes you to holds at 40m and 33m, which you can easily enter and explore. The deeper of these two has the more intact vehicles, but it's more than worth investigating the hold at 33m, where there is scope for a fair amount of exploration. You can ascend through the ship and exit via an opening at 22m, but be

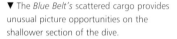

▼ The *Blue Belt's* scattered cargo provides unusual picture opportunities on the shallower section of the dive.

careful as you swim out, as there's a burgeoning growth of blueish soft coral around this area.

The upturned hull is undeniably impressive, and is often visited by passing jacks, snappers and dogtooth tuna. We have heard reports of tiger sharks on this wreck in the later stages of the afternoon, but such appearances are far from everyday. You're more likely to find a white-tip reef shark dozing on the sand.

There is an area at about 18m where several Toyota cars lie in various states of decay. For the classic photograph here you must persuade your buddy to get behind the wheel of one of them, but you'll have to find the steering gear from the big 4x4, which has been detached and now serves as a photographic accessory that is passed around the site before being discarded on one of the vehicles.

Continue with the reef to your left and you will come across some of the massive table coral structures that are so typical of Sudan diving. Elsewhere in the world, the remaining areas of hard coral tend to be rather monochromatic, but in Sudan the table and staghorn coral appears in vivid blues and yellows as well as the familiar skeletal grey. They grow to great sizes and there is a group of table corals that resembles a natural altar. Fish life is also well represented: you can expect to see plenty of anthias and pufferfish, alongside coral groupers and small schools of sweetlips.

Simon Rogerson

Alexander Mustard

ANGAROSH REEF

Max depth: optimum 30–35m

Skill level: 40–50 dives

Access: liveaboard/support

Current: moderate

Must see: schooling barracuda; silvertip sharks

Viewed from the air, Angarosh is a seemingly obscure patch of sand surrounded by waves breaking on a small fringing reef. Underwater, its full glories unfold. It is typical of what local guides call the 'christmas cake' reefs of northern Sudan, which tend to fall away evenly on all sides. Angarosh is the most spectacular of these, with perfect drop offs on three sides of the island and a series of sloping plateaus on the fourth.

Your boatman should drop you off on the eastern side of the reef, then you should descend immediately to a shelf at 30–35m. This is a high-energy area, so the coral itself is very healthy, harbouring shimmering schools of anthias and other territorial fish. Look out for resident Napoleon wrasse and marble groupers.

▲ Chevron barracuda swim in perfect formation, often in appearing in schools of thousands of fish.

Simon Rogerson

▲ A close-up view of a Napoleon wrasse.

▶ Though rusty, most of the *Umbria's* structure is intact.

From January to March, you may well come across scalloped hammerheads here on the second plateau, which levels out at around 45m and is also a productive area for soft corals. There is also an outside chance of finding silvertip sharks here. Silvertips are among the most beautiful of shark species, bulky yet elegant and characterised by bright white markings on their dorsal and pectoral fins. They are generally not aggressive, but when they first see divers they often approach in order to satisfy their curiosity, thereafter tending to keep their distance. They are sometimes mistaken for oceanic white-tip sharks, but you can tell the two species apart easily enough by looking at the first dorsal fin, which is rounded on the oceanic white-tip but angular on the silvertip. Silvertips are also generally bulkier than oceanics.

From the deepest section of your dive, simply follow the contours of the reef back up to shallower water. You may encounter grey reef sharks at any depth of this dive, and the coral cover is excellent at most depths, right up to the surface. On the way up, look out for Angarosh's own anemone city, whose host anemones close up in the later stages of the day, revealing their bright scarlet bodies. You can pass your last minutes on this dive admiring surgeonfish and other reef dwellers as you decompress in the shallows.

SHA'AB AMBAR

Max depth: 25–30m optimum

Skill level: 30 dives

Access: liveaboard/support

Current: low to moderate

Must see: resident spinner dolphins; giant groupers on the reef

The reef systems to the south of Port Sudan are subject to seasonal changes, which can make visibility very unreliable. But when the water cools down during the winter they can be worth a visit, particularly if you happen to be on a two-week liveaboard charter. Of these many reefs, Sha'ab Ambar stands out because of its sheltered lagoon and resident pod of spinner dolphins.

Only very fortunate divers encounter spinner dolphins while using scuba apparatus, but it can be worth trying to snorkel with them. If they are in a mood to play, try slipping off the side of your boat and swimming steadily in their general direction. Often, they speed off as soon as the boat stops, but sometimes they are inclined to frolic around swimmers at high speed. There are all sorts of tactics for persuading dolphins to play – we even know of divers who recommend singing into your mouthpiece. Perhaps the dolphins then approach just to make sure you haven't had too much sun!

The dive itself takes place on a sandy plateau on the five-mile reef system's south-east extremity. The idea is to concentrate on the eastern wall that faces open sea, where you can see large pelagics such as tuna and barracuda. Solitary hammerhead sharks have been seen here, but as yet the famous schools have not been observed off this reef. The sandy plateau at 25m has a few colourful raised sections and bommies; watch out for giant groupers and white-tip reef sharks cruising around their territory or dozing on the sand.

THE WRECK OF THE *UMBRIA*

Max depth: 33m to the seabed

Skill level: suitable for novices

Access: liveaboard or dayboat

Current: generally calm

Must see: the huge propeller; Fiat Lunga cars inside the first hold forward of the bridge; bombs – you can't miss them!; the engine room

You should ask to dive the *Umbria* at least twice, or maybe even three times. It is possible to cover the entire length of the 150m wreck in a single dive, but why hurry when you can explore its different facets at your leisure? The *Umbria* only reveals its secrets to those who take their time. Chances are you will be given the

Simon Rogerson

▶ The *Umbria's* massive propeller is the ideal starting point for a tour of the stern section of this unique shipwreck.

▼ A diver swims over some of the brightly coloured coral that grows on the wreck of the *Umbria*.

choice of dropping in either at the stern or the bow, so do one of each and concentrate on specific portions of the ship. Those who have no interest in wreck dives will find that the structure is also home to a diverse array of coral and fish, including resident lionfish and some large groupers.

If you begin your dive at the stern, the first feature to locate should be one of the two massive propellers (the other has sunk into the mud). The wreck is largely intact and covered in bright sponges and corals, though not to the extent that the features have become obscured. The wooden decking has rotted away, so there are plenty of entrances into lower decks. One atmospheric area is the galley and mess, where only the table supports remain and where faint light streams in through the portholes. The engine room is a delight, with many of the original controls still in place and plenty of ambient light.

The most interesting cargo sits inside the first of the bow holds, where three stately Fiat Lunga cars are slowly rusting away. These distinctive cars with their triple rows of seats are a compelling sight, a real reward for the diver prepared to explore inside a shipwreck. That said, they do not lie deep inside and you still have

a little ambient light in that area, so viewing them is not a dangerous undertaking. Elsewhere, the holds are filled with stack upon stack of bombs, and we have it on good authority that it is still possible to find bottles of wine.

The imposing bow is covered with an encrusting red sponge. In fact, underwater photographers should know that photogenic red sponges tend to thrive all over the *Umbria*, providing a welcome touch of close-focus colour to offset the structure of the wreckage.

The *Umbria* is a world-class wreck dive, and was listed among the top ten when Britain's DIVE magazine carried out a survey to celebrate the world's finest. In the Red Sea, it is second only to the *Thistlegorm*, which has an astonishing array of features and artefacts. However, the unique history, shallow depth and lack of crowds have led some to suggest that the *Umbria* is the superior dive.

Whatever your opinion, this site usually provides the climax to any visit to the Sudanese Red Sea. You can spend your final precious minutes exploring the sunlit gangways on the top of the wreck before surfacing and facing that dreary chore that comes at the end of every dive trip – rinsing your equipment in fresh water.

Simon Rogerson

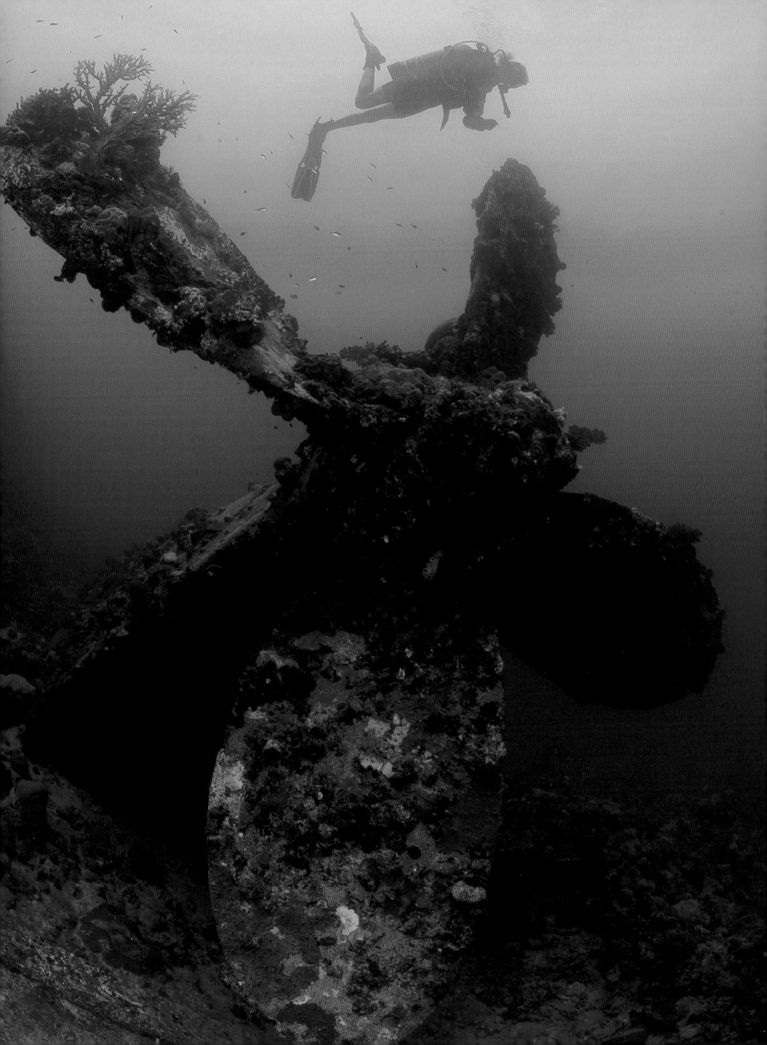

UMBRIA

Originally built as a freighter in Hamburg in 1912, the *Umbria* started off her life as the *Bahia Blanca* and underwent a name change when she changed hands a few years later. For her last voyage from Messina, she was loaded with around 360,000 individual bombs and incendiary devices, in addition to sacks of cement, vehicles and cases of wine. The idea was to deliver the bombs to Italian troops in Massaua, Eritrea, in the period leading up to Italy's entry into the Second World War.

The British, based at Port Sudan, knew exactly what the *Umbria* was carrying in her holds, so contrived a series of bureaucratic delays that kept the vessel moored on Wingate Reef while they waited for events to unfold. As soon as the announcement was made that Italy had entered the war, the British would seize the ship and its cargo.

Around midnight on 10 June 1940, Captain Muiesan was listening on his radio when Italy declared war, and made the decision to scuttle his ship rather than allow its cargo to fall into British hands. The problem was how to evacuate the ship without giving the game away to the British, who were keeping a very close watch on the *Umbria*. He staged a rescue drill, bringing the crew to the deck while a few saboteurs flooded the ship.

By the time the British realised what was happening, the crew was safe and the *Umbria* was on her way to the bottom of Wingate Reef. Accounts of the scuttling are often tinged with nationalistic prejudice – read an Italian account and you will likely be told of the brave and cunning manoeuvre which kept the cargo out of British hands, while British reports typically refer to the cowardly, underhand manner in which a captain gave the orders to sink his own ship.

Whatever your perspective, it was never considered feasible to carry out full salvage works on the *Umbria's* cargo. In a very cool and collected report to the British military, a salvage expert predicted that if one of the bombs were to detonate, the resulting explosion would create a tidal wave that would engulf nearby Port Sudan. The *Umbria*, meanwhile, settled with her port hull on the seabed, so that the starboard lifeboat davits broke the surface at low tide, which they still do. The explosives remain neatly stacked in the holds

As an addendum, it is worth considering the wreck of the SS *Richard Montgomery*, which lies off Sheppey in Kent, England and contains 13,000 bombs. The British military has expressed concern that a mass explosion on that wreck would result in coastal destruction and banned anyone from going near it. By contrast, the *Umbria* has 360,000 individual bombs, and there is no real control over the divers who visit it other than the briefings given by dive guides. Our advice is not to interfere with the bombs and simply enjoy the remarkable sights of this historical shipwreck.

1. Winch
2. Mast
3. Bombs in hold
4. Companionway
5. Fiat cars
6. Bridge
7. Funnel
8. Engine room
9. Machinery
10. Stern
11. Railings
12. Propeller

sea level
top of wreck 1m

lowest point 33m

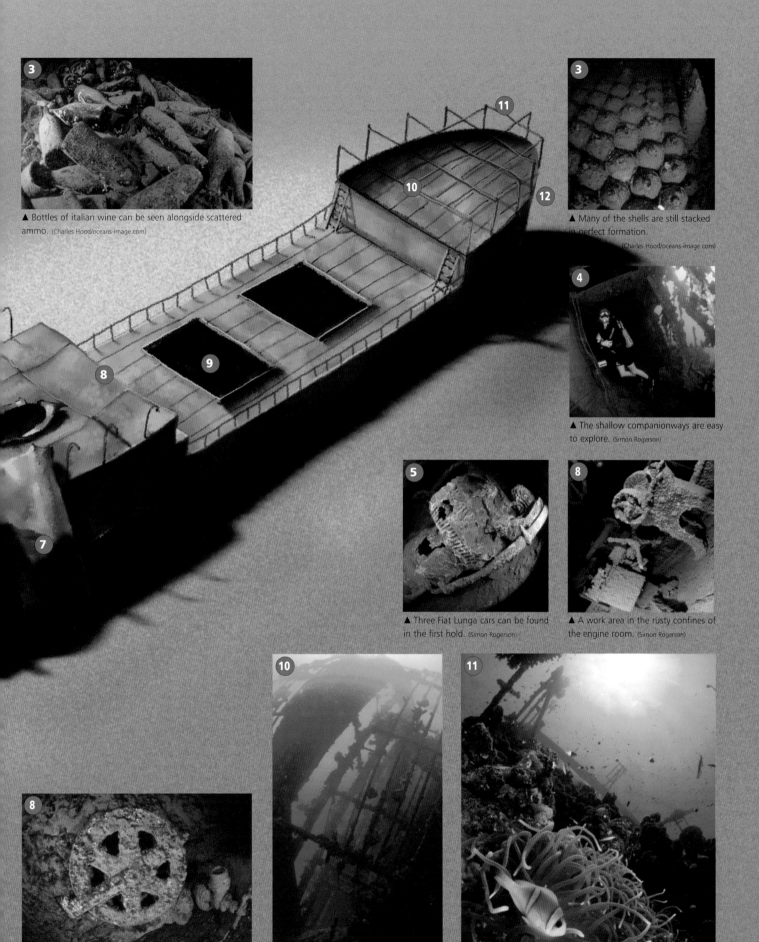

▲ Bottles of italian wine can be seen alongside scattered ammo. (Charles Hood/oceans-image.com)

▲ Many of the shells are still stacked in perfect formation. (Charles Hood/oceans-image.com)

▲ The shallow companionways are easy to explore. (Simon Rogerson)

▲ Three Fiat Lunga cars can be found in the first hold. (Simon Rogerson)

▲ A work area in the rusty confines of the engine room. (Simon Rogerson)

▲ Controls in the engine room are rusted fast. (Charles Hood/oceans-image.com)

▲ Wood has rotted away from the stern area, leaving a skeletal structure. (Charles Hood/oceans-image.com)

▲ The wreck's exterior has been colonised by corals and anemones. (Charles Hood/oceans-image.com)

ERITREA

ALTHOUGH IT IS CURRENTLY THE LEAST ACTIVE DIVING NATION IN THE RED SEA, THERE IS A STRONG TRADITION OF UNDERWATER EXPLORATION IN ERITREA DATING BACK TO THE PERIOD BEFORE THE 30-YEAR ETHIOPIAN CIVIL WAR.

The country has been independent since 1993, but periodic skirmishes with Yemen and a continued border dispute with Ethiopia have kept it well and truly off the tourism map.

Eritrea boasts an impressive 1,151km coastline and about 350 islands, most of which are in the Dahlak Archipelago (and only a few of which are populated). The Dahlaks have received continued protection as a marine park since the 1970s, and special permits are still required for visiting divers, who must be accompanied by a local guide. Guides are, however, not easy to find, and one of the few remaining operators closed shop as this book went to print, blaming the persisting conflict for lack of business.

This is a shame, as Eritrea has some unique features that would be of great interest to Red Sea connoisseurs, though conditions are in marked contrast to the blue water and sheer walls of the north. Boats can be chartered in the port of Massawa, but do not entertain visions of Egyptian-style gin palaces: expect, instead, to be sleeping on deck on the same kind of vessel used by local fishermen. Most diving takes place on the shallow Dahlak Bank, where the presence of super-heated water and sediment limits coral development. In the absence of international operators offering Eritrea diving packages, the onus is on visitors to find a local fixer, or to organise permits and transportation direct with Eritrean Shipping Lines (T124201, Asmara).

Sharks are not abundant in Eritrea, but it is possible to find dugong (on the seagrass beds of Norah) and manta rays, both of which thrive here. The sites offer typical southern Red Sea fish life, such as bumphead parrotfish, fusiliers and several species of butterflyfish. There is much to enjoy, but the country needs to stabilise before it can attract significant numbers of divers. Until then, Eritrea will remain the domain of the expedition diver, for whom the lack of an established infrastructure is a challenge rather than an irritation.

One important point: when you enter the country, you will most likely spend the night in the capital, Asmara, before being driven down to Massawa – a journey that takes you through the mountains, reaching heights of up to 2,300m. If you are heading to Massawa after your arrival, you can dive quite soon after you get there. On the way back, however, you should wait for at least 24 hours after your last dive before beginning the journey.

◄ Vast fields of seagrass cover the long shallow shelf that extends from the Eritrean mainland, creating a habitat for turtles and dugongs.

Alexander Mustard

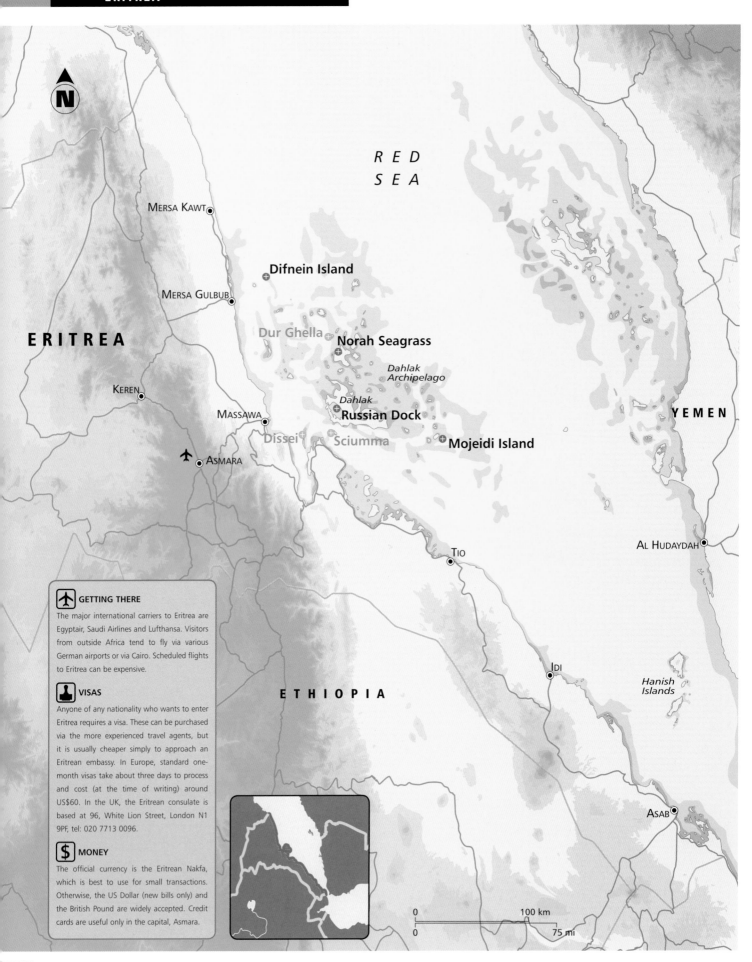

R E D
S E A

MERSA KAWT

Difnein Island

MERSA GULBUB

ERITREA

Dur Ghella

Norah Seagrass

Dahlak
Archipelago

KEREN

Dahlak

Russian Dock

MASSAWA

Dissei   Sciumma

Mojeidi Island

YEMEN

ASMARA

AL HUDAYDAH

TIO

IDI

Hanish
Islands

ETHIOPIA

ASAB

GETTING THERE

The major international carriers to Eritrea are
Egyptair, Saudi Airlines and Lufthansa. Visitors
from outside Africa tend to fly via various
German airports or via Cairo. Scheduled flights
to Eritrea can be expensive.

VISAS

Anyone of any nationality who wants to enter
Eritrea requires a visa. These can be purchased
via the more experienced travel agents, but
it is usually cheaper simply to approach an
Eritrean embassy. In Europe, standard one-
month visas take about three days to process
and cost (at the time of writing) around
US$60. In the UK, the Eritrean consulate is
based at 96, White Lion Street, London N1
9PF, tel: 020 7713 0096.

$ MONEY

The official currency is the Eritrean Nakfa,
which is best to use for small transactions.
Otherwise, the US Dollar (new bills only) and
the British Pound are widely accepted. Credit
cards are useful only in the capital, Asmara.

0   100 km

0   75 mi

DIFNEIN ISLAND, NORTHERN SIDE

Max depth: 20m

Skill level: 15 dives

Access: liveaboard or private charter

Current: slight to medium

Must see: pelagic fish, jacks and tuna

Shallow water and the presence of sediment inhibits hard coral development in Eritrean waters, but there is sufficient depth around Difnein Island for relatively good visibility. The proximity of this deeper water makes the northern side of the island a good bet, though there's no need to go deeper than 20–25m, after which the topography is featureless.

This area was once popular with Italian spearfishermen back in the 1970s, but they stayed away during the war of independence and the game fish are back in numbers. Here, you can find dogtooth tuna, great barracuda, almaco and snappers. On no account be tempted to venture onto the island itself, as mines were placed there during the war and have not been removed. Every now and then a turtle blows itself up when it hauls out of the water to lay its eggs, and there have been reports of fishermen receiving serious injuries.

Follow the slope down: there are some big coral formations here, an unusual sight in Eritrea. Look out to the blue, as manta rays are frequently encountered, as are grey reef sharks and batfish. There are unconfirmed stories of tiger sharks visiting this reef at night.

 VISIBILITY

Most dives take place on the shallow Dahlak bank, where routinely poor visibility can be made worse by plankton blooms. Accordingly, the visibility range is normally 8–15 metres.

 WATER TEMPERATURE

27°C in winter, 33°C in summer (up to 35°C in shallow lagoons).

 SEASONALITY

Winter is the time to escape the worst of the heat and humidity, but there can be short bouts of rainfall around the coastal region from December to February. For diving, the optimum months are held to be April and May, then October and November. The weather is extremely hot and humid during the summer months.

OTHER DIVE SITES

Dissei

Dur Ghella

Sciumma

Simon Rogerson

◀ A school of blue-lined snapper reflect the morning light at Difnein Island.

NORAH SEAGRASS

Max depth: 5m

Skill level: novice

Access: liveaboard

Current: none

Must see: dugong, seahorses, pipefish

This is a dive for macro photographers, providing something of an antidote to the traditional Red Sea open reef dive. Unlike a traditional coral reef, the animals are spread widely over a uniform environment, so you need to develop an eye for the camouflaged critters that lurk in the miniature underwater jungle.

You can expect to see juvenile versions of reef fish, plus the sort of macro creatures that can blend themselves effortlessly into this habitat. Pipefish are one of the first things you will find, but seahorses take a lot more commitment to track down – you have to get down low and almost become part of the environment. Even if you fail to find a seahorse, the search will turn up creatures you would never have spotted otherwise. Snake eels, boxfish, filefish and crabs can all be found in the seagrass.

The grass flats are also home to reclusive giants. The warm water and lack of divers is manna from heaven as far as dugongs are concerned. These bulky sea cows normally flee whenever they see divers, but every now and then you may come across one that will tolerate your presence. Maximise your chances by moving around it in a large circle, then advance slowly from in front. If it decides to swim away, you might at least get a lucky photograph.

RUSSIAN DOCK

Max depth: 15m

Skill level: novice

Access: private charter or liveaboard

Current: slight to none

Must see: the dry dock's cranes, coated in soft coral

This has to be one of the most unusual dives in the world, let alone the Red Sea. At the end of the Eritrean War of Independence, the Russian and Ethiopian navies pulled out of their base on the island of Nocra in the entrance of Ghubbet Mus Nefit. They had established a floating dry dock, but didn't want it to fall into Eritrean hands, so they scuttled the whole thing and the resulting wreckage still sits at 15m. Its rectangular structure has proved irresistible to corals and marine life, which have little else to latch onto. Soft corals thrive on the wreckage, though they may die off during plankton blooms and other periods of environmental stress.

Interest is not limited to the wreck of the old dock. A dive in the general vicinity can yield patrol boats, a supply ship and various heavy weapons, all of which were considered too useful to fall into the hands of the triumphant Eritreans. It is worth looking around the sandy areas between the items of wreckage, as all the life attracted to the Russians' impromptu artificial reef programme has in turn caught the attention of benthic predators such as stingrays, stargazers and crocodilefish.

MOJEIDI ISLAND SOUTH

Max depth: 15m

Skill level: 10 dives

Access: liveaboard or private charter

Current: moderate

Must see: eagle rays, soft coral, green and hawksbill turtles

This is very much the quintessential Dahlak reef, but its position at the extreme east of the archipelago means that deeper water is nearby, so visibility is better than

◀ Seahorses can be found at Norah Seagrass, but you need to either rely on a recent local sighting or be prepared for an exhaustive search.

▼ A moray eel waits patiently while a shrimp cleans its skin.

Simon Rogerson

► In shallow water, even hard corals appear colourful under the strong sunlight.

Jane Morgan

► This green turtle is carrying a passenger, a remora fish, which in addition to hitching a lift, may feed on scattered debris when the turtle feeds.

►► A big school of circular batfish sweeps in from the blue, accompanied by a lone surgeonfish. (JP Trenque)

elsewhere. The southwestern side of the reef is the spot to head for: you dive on a reef promontory that runs about 50m off the shore and attracts extravagant coral growth at depths of 10–15m.

Mojeidi is a great place to dive with green and hawksbill turtles, which arrive here to lay their eggs on the isolated shores. Think of a scaled down-version of Sipadan in Malaysia, with plenty of turtles relaxing on the reef, feeding on sponges and soft corals. The island is also known for a spectacular sight: eagle rays swim-

ming in formation, like a flock of submarine geese. The rays can be seen on the sandy bottom or mid-water, along with white-tip reef sharks and schools of blue-striped snapper.

As with most Dahlak dives, this one is quite simple: check the current and drop in the water just in front of the promontory; try to spend as much time there as possible before continuing with the current. Sadly, poor visibility can spoil the dive, and visitors are advised to avoid this site following periods of rough weather.

DJIBOUTI

JOURNEY SOUTH FROM ERITREA AND YOU ARRIVE AT THE SMALL REPUBLIC OF DJIBOUTI, FORMERLY THE COLONY OF FRENCH SOMALIA. ITS POSITION AT THE MOUTH OF THE RED SEA HAS MADE IT A STRATEGICALLY IMPORTANT BASE FOR MILITARY FORCES FROM BRITAIN, FRANCE AND AMERICA, ALL OF WHICH MAINTAIN EXTENSIVE BASES HERE.

As a result, Djibouti is a stable and relatively safe place in which to travel, although getting around is more expensive than in many African countries.

The English novelist Evelyn Waugh described this land in terms of: 'intolerable desolation ... a country of dust and boulders, devoid of any sign of life'. And it does indeed have a harsh topography, consisting mostly of volcanic rock and salt depressions – such as Lake Assal, one of the hottest places in the planet. The underwater scene is in complete contrast to the arid emptiness of the land: while coral cover is mediocre in the Gulf of Tadjoura, its fish life puts many sites in the north to shame. Still more impressive are the Seven Brothers islands, where fast currents provide the energy for a rich and complex reef habitat.

For decades, Djibouti has been overlooked by divers, with the exception of resident military services and a trickle of adventurous tourists. In the last few years, however, this tiny nation has attracted attention due to the discovery of a gathering place for whale sharks. People have always known that these enormous fish – the largest in the sea – pass through Djibouti's waters, but now a specific area has been identified in the Gulf of Tadjourah where they gather in significant numbers. The discovery of the whale shark aggregation at Arta Beach has occasioned much excitement in the diving press, leading an increasing number of divers to investigate the southernmost limits of the Red Sea.

Above the water, Djibouti offers plenty of wilderness to explore, and geologists will enjoy the volcanic scenery around Assal and a mysterious inland sea known as the Devil's Cauldron. Elsewhere, there is even a small area of cloud forest, a superb location for camping and hiking, and a cheetah sanctuary between the city and the border with Somalia. We recommend the latter for anyone who wants to fill an afternoon while waiting for the evening flight to

◄ Indian Ocean species such as these schooling oriental sweetlips can be found at the mouth of the Red Sea and around Djibouti's Seven Brothers Islands.

Simon Rogerson

Paris, not least because the owner is doing some worthy conservation work. Any taxi driver should be able to take you there, though the drive through the city dump is far from picturesque. This is Africa, where plastic bags live forever.

Although, technically, it lies outside the bounds of the Red Sea, we have included information on the Gulf of Tadjourah to the south, a large bay that defines Djibouti's coastline. Its dive sites are likely to be incorporated into any liveaboard itinerary visiting the Seven Brothers, and it is closely connected with the Red Sea. This is, after all, the area where waters from the Indian Ocean and the Red Sea mingle, and where many of the familiar Red Sea fish species still dominate the underwater scene. It is biologically, if not geographically, an important part of the Red Sea.

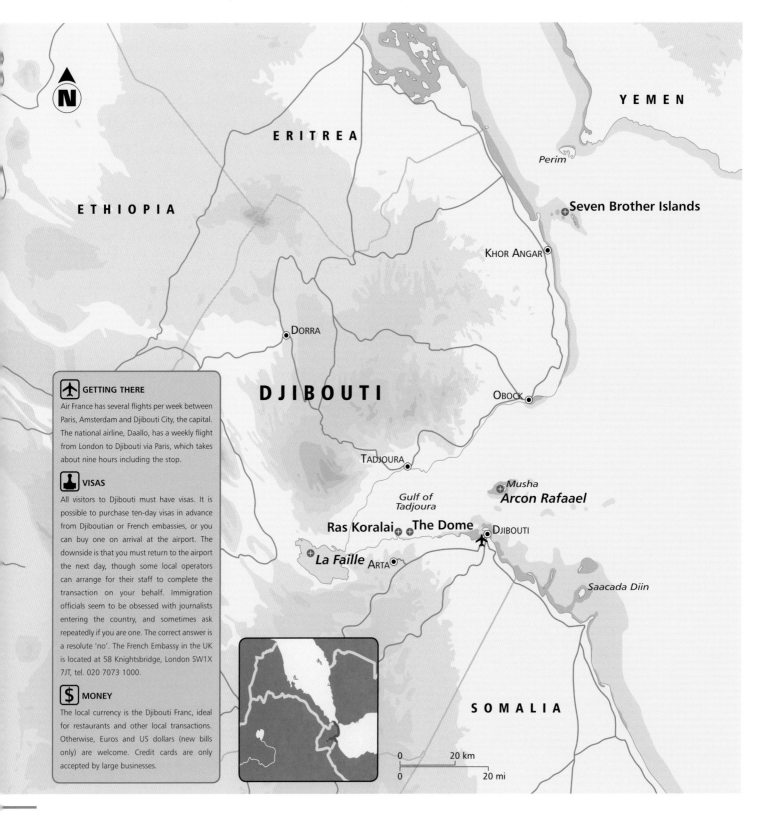

THE DOME

Max depth: 35m

Skill level: 20 dives

Access: liveaboard or dayboat from Djibouti city

Current: slight

Must see: white-tip and black-tip reef sharks

Situated just 100m off the southern coast of the Gulf of Tadjourah, the Dome is a coral mound with a shallowest point at about 15–17m and coral walls sloping down a sand flat at 35–40m. Whale sharks are known to pass by this site throughout the year, though water clarity can be so bad in the winter that they could swim by 20m away and you would never know they were there.

The goal on this dive is to find the white-tip reef sharks, which tend to occupy the deeper section and provide a counterpoint to the famous sightings of whale sharks elsewhere in the Gulf. There's also a decent chance of finding guitar sharks on the coral wall or the sand. All you have to do is follow the contours of the wall until you come to a path of white sand that looks strangely like an underwater wadi. Descend along the sandy 'road' until it gives way to scattered rocks at a depth of 35–40m: this is where the current hits the reef, every shark's favourite place to hang out.

As you descend, the sharks may swim towards you out of curiosity, but don't worry, as white-tips are not aggressive toward divers. The idea is to remain unobtrusive so that they continue to patrol the leading edge of the reef and hopefully they will not consider you a threat. Sometimes, you see the sharks lying motionless on the sand, allowing the moving water to flow into their mouths and over their gills. Grey reef sharks and black-tips also occur here, so you can in theory see five species of shark on a single dive. Are you feeling lucky?

Inevitably, it is all too easy to do this dive and see no sharks at all. The reef itself looks good by Tadjourah standards, but the coral cover is uninspiring. Still, there's an interesting mixture of Red Sea and Indian Ocean fish, and plenty of moray eels. If you're diving in December or January, the visibility here can be quite poor and you may be better off looking for scorpionfish on the reef than carrying out a deep dive. It is one of those decisions you can only make once you have hit the water, but it is nevertheless worth considering the option with your buddy and arranging a 'decision' signal prior to the dive.

 VISIBILITY

In the Gulf of Tadjourah, visibility is generally better during the stiflingly hot summer months. In winter, coastal waters can be very stirred up and visibility is typically 5–12m. Further up in the area of the Seven Brothers Islands, the water is blue, with potential for 40m visibility, depending on currents and other conditions.

WATER TEMPERATURE

Water temperature: 25°C in winter, 30°C in summer. The Seven Brothers is subject to cool currents and an average temperature of around 26°C.

SEASONALITY

The whale shark season in the Gulf of Tadjourah runs from October to late January, though it can be unpredictable. The sea is rougher in winter, but it is still possible to dive the Seven Brothers if you have a suitably hardy and well-equipped liveaboard. Humidity is lowest from June to August.

Alexander Mustard

◄ White-tip reef sharks have the ability to rest on the seabed, pushing fresh water over their gills by gulping through their open mouths.

Simon Rogerson

RAS KORALAI

Max depth: 34m

Skill level: 30 dives

Access: liveaboard or dayboat

Current: moderate to brisk

Must see: moray eels on the reef, swirling sardines and trevally

This dive is named after a nearby headland, though it actually takes place on the sloping reef that lies beyond, with a shallowest point at about 13m. We have given the dive a fairly advanced skill rating, but it is quite possible to stay in the shallow section, where the reef topography is sufficiently varied to be of interest.

The reef is 150m long and on average 30m wide, sloping gradually into deeper water. The idea is to drop in on its northern extremity, and then swim down the eastern side of the reef into deeper water, before returning up the western side until you reach shallow water.

Simon Rogerson

Such scenes are difficult to photograph, as the action is fast and the behaviour is not the same as formation schooling. There just happens to be lot of very busy fish in one place, and not much order to their movements. On the reef, you will find moray eels that try to find shelter amid the scrappy *Acropora* coral, but seem to spend much of the time in the open. Grey reef sharks and silvertips have also been seen in the deeper sections, where the reef meets a sandy sea floor.

'LA FAILLE'

Max depth: 50m
Skill level: 50 dives, including experience with currents and deep dives
Access: liveaboard
Current: unpredictable, occasionally powerful
Must see: the crack itself and the black coral that grows around it

This dive takes place in an eerie place at the western extremity of the Gulf of Tadjourah, the 'Ghoubbet el Kharab', or 'Devil's Cauldron'. Your liveaboard will steam through a narrow passage where the current rages at speeds of up to eight knots, bringing you into a miniature sea surrounded by foreboding brown hills. Weird volcanic domes rise from the water at the far side of the Ghoubbet, and you feel as though you have reached the end of the world. So what do you do? You dive it, of course!

La Faille translates as 'the crack', which tells you exactly what to expect: a long fissure in the reef. Only it's much more than that, because the crack is evidence of a unique geological scenario that centres on the Ghoubbet. This circular mini-sea is the beginning of the Africa's Great Rift Valley, where the Arabian and African continental plates are slowly moving apart, and the 'crack' shows how the immense forces at play are gradually splitting the seabed. When local guides explain the scenario, they draw a diagram of the fissure with 'Africa' written on one side and 'Asia' on the other. This may sound like a glib joke, but in essence it is true: you are diving in a tiny space between continents, and by exploring the crack you are witnessing the birth of an ocean.

The dive starts deep. There's nothing much to distract you as you descend the featureless wall, so you keep moving past the boulders as light gradually recedes and you find yourself at the opening of the crack at 40m. The reef here is practically devoid of hard coral, but large clumps of branching black coral sprout from the walls, providing shelter for hawkfish and basslets. There is a tunnel opening at 40m, but no exit; try and find the tunnel at 37m, which takes you right into the

◄ Schools of crimson soldierfish inhabit the long crack that is 'La Faille'

It sounds easy enough, but as you approach that deep section, you can feel the current pushing you away from the reef. It is not overly dangerous, but you need to stay close to the reef and remain alert.

On deep dives such as this, experienced divers can descend into turbid blue water and – as long as they do not have to work too hard – should feel only a slight twinge of nitrogen narcosis. But all divers must be conscious of the current at all times, not least during the gradual ascent up the western side of the reef, which can require a fair amount of effort against it.

Naturally, all this moving water promotes a generous amount of fish action. Dive guides describe this site in their briefings as being like an 'aquarium', and as you approach a depth of 25m, the promise is fulfilled. Wrasse, parrotfish and sweetlips pulse around the reef, joined by sardines, jacks, barracuda and basslets. It is a frenetic ballet of feeding, and the action does not let up when divers arrive. The fish swirl around with speed; it can be quite mesmerising as you descend.

◄ Squirrelfish regularly pass though the dive sites in the Gulf of Tadjourah.

Simon Rogerson

▲ Crumbling volcanic mounds appear in the far reaches of the eerie Ghoubbet, an inland sea beyond the Gulf of Tadjourah.

crack. There's not much to see inside, it's just an atmospheric space in which a diver's imagination can and will run riot. Dim light enters from above, but it's worth taking a torch. There's a large opening again at 20m, at which point you can rejoin the reef wall and follow it up towards a nearby islet.

It is hard to imagine many sea creatures venturing this far into the Ghoubbet, but you can have some impressive encounters on the reef if visibility allows. Schools of amberjacks, eagle rays and bigeye trevally can be found, alongside white-tip reef sharks and, in season, whale sharks.

On the subject of leviathans, the Afar people speak of monsters living in this eerie body of water. It was a legend Jacques Cousteau helped to perpetuate when he visited the area and claimed to have seen a giant shark in the depths around the gulf. Of course, it sounds like a typical sailor's story, but when you sail into the Ghoubbet and find yourself in the strangest of seas, anything seems possible.

THE WRECK OF *ARCON RAFAAEL*

Max depth: 28m

Skill level: 20 dives

Access: dayboat out of Djibouti City

Current: slight

Must see: big groupers under the bow (and we mean really big!)

Just a 30-minute sail north from Djibouti City lie Musha and Maskali Islands, the haunt of weekender divers, and of fishing trips for French expats and the various military forces based in Djibouti. Unsurprisingly, perhaps,

much of the coral has been trashed, but there are some interesting shipwrecks in the area, and this is the best of them. In a way, it sums up the Tadjourah experience: scrappy coral growth, but amazing fish life.

The *Arcon Rafaael* was a cargo ship that went down after striking the reef in 1983. It is hardly a satisfying wreck for the traditional metal-fancier: there's no great mystery about its sinking, little in the way of features and limited scope for exploring the interior. What it does have is a lot of fish, more so even than the *Umbria* in Sudan or the *Thistlegorm* in Egypt.

The wreck lies on its port side at a maximum depth of 28m. In case of current, divers should descend with a hand firmly on the shotline until they are practically on top of the wreck. Right in the middle of the 80m-long structure is a deep tear, which practically bisects the ship. There is scope for a penetration here, taking you forward into the wrecks superstructure – already you should be able to see that the wreck has a lot of semi-tame Arabian angelfish, a typical species of the southern Red Sea.

Carry on swimming forward, and descend to the trench in the sand below the bow. This area is teeming with fish – notably grunts, sweetlips, bigeye soldierfish and stingrays. Look up and you may also see the silhouette of a giant grouper. There is one absolute monster on this wreck; like all big groupers he can be a bit shy, but you can edge closer by pretending you haven't seen him. He is the highlight of the dive, and well worth seeking out.

The hull area is relatively dull, though you can treat it as a little wall dive. It is better to swim back into the breach and cross over to the deck, continuing until you reach the stern, where a propeller protrudes from the sandy seabed. Fans of non-ferrous metal can find a spare propeller on top of an accommodation block on the stern deck.

THE SEVEN BROTHERS ISLANDS

Max depth: 40m optimum

Skill level: 40 dives

Access: liveaboard

Current: powerful

Must see: mobula rays, schooling snappers, soft coral and sweetlips

The Seven Brothers Islands represent the best reef diving in the southern Red Sea. Don't expect silken beaches and palm trees: what you get down here are rocky shores, no trees and flocks of migratory birds. It is a problematic place for dive boats, as the islands lie exposed in front of the Bab el Mandab Strait and offer few reliable mooring places.

So what makes the Seven Brothers exceptional? Well, the large numbers of fish that occur on Djiboutian sites are tripled at these islands, coral cover is much more impressive and visibility often reaches 40m. The downside is that occasional and unpredictable plankton blooms can reduce water clarity to 10m, and that diving in such current-fuelled waters is strictly for experienced divers.

The eastern islands of the group are probably the most beautiful, featuring a soft coral-strewn slope that descends to 60m. Fish from both the Red Sea and the Indian Ocean are common here, so you can expect to see a Red Sea anemonefish one minute and a honeycomb moray the next. Many of the schooling fish will be familiar to those who have been to the Maldives: oriental sweetlips and blue-lined snapper are frequent sightings. The same species can be seen in the Gulf of Tadjourah, but in this high-energy environment they are bigger and more numerous.

One of the most famous sites here is Japanese Garden on Main Island, which has a picture-perfect mixture of soft and hard corals. Marine biologists have said it is the single richest area for coral in the whole Arabian Peninsula. Another 'must do' is the caves and arch at Tolka: the caves themselves are neither big nor deep, but they are very pretty, and you can often find nurse sharks or eagle rays sleeping on the sand. The arch is home to white-tip reef sharks; in fact this site would probably be home to many reef sharks were it not for the predations of Yemeni fishermen.

Spectacular marine life is a calling card of the Seven Brothers. There are some big pods of bottlenose and spinner dolphins, and many divers have seen schools of mobula rays here. Mobulas are best described as mini-mantas: they have similar bodies to manta rays and are also filter-feeders, but typically have a wingspan of 1.5m and are more likely to be seen in big schools. You sometimes see them soaring over the reef shallows, effortlessly riding the current as they search for feeding grounds. They have been seen at a site named Boeing, the island in question being shaped like an aeroplane.

The best time to visit the Seven Brothers is from mid-March to mid-October. It is hellishly hot from June to August, but a new generation of liveaboards is emerging in Djibouti, with many of the home comforts familiar to those who have been on Egyptian vessels. From January to the middle of March the Strait of Bab El Mendab has very rough seas, so most local boats tend to focus on the whale sharks and the diving in Tadjourah at this time.

▼ The lyretail angelfish is found on coastal reefs as well as drop offs.

Alexander Mustard

Simon Rogerson

WELCOME TO THE PLAYGROUND!
THE WHALE SHARKS OF ARTA BEACH

Arta Beach is an incongruous setting for one of the most spectacular events in the natural world. Overlooked by foreboding hills and a Foreign Legion rifle range, this low-key bay is rich in zooplanton, the tiny gelatinous organisms that make up the diet of the biggest fish in the sea: the whale shark. For years, divers have known that whale sharks pass through the Gulf of Tadjourah, but only recently has the aggregation at Arta Beach become known to the wider diving world.

Whale shark aggregations are the subject of intense interest and debate in the scientific world. The most famous one takes place off Ningaloo Reef in western Australia from April to July, when spotter planes find the sharks cruising along the coast and guide boatloads of snorkellers to the scene. Similar events take place at select locations all over the tropics: off the Seychelles; Tanzania; the Gujarat region of India; Gladden Spit in Belize; Yum Balam in Mexico and several other locations.

Every aggregation is different, but as more come to light, the hidden life of the world's biggest fish is slowly being revealed. While the whale sharks of Gujarat seem to be mature females, Djibouti's are almost all juveniles, giving rise to speculation that the area may be some sort of nursery. Sexually mature sharks have to be at least 6m long, and the average size at Arta is about 4.5m. To put all this into perspective, full-grown adults can measure a whopping 12m or more.

Divers in Djibouti have regular encounters with whale sharks throughout the year, but the Arta sightings become a certainty between October and late January. What makes this place truly special is that the sharks occur in large numbers inside a bay less than a kilometre in length. So while boat operators in the Seychelles and Ningaloo rely on spotter planes, it is sometimes quite hard to avoid the Djibouti whale sharks. Almost certainly, the bay creates an eddy that concentrates the sharks' favourite food into this relatively compact area. Recent satellite tagging studies carried out by local dive operator Dolphin Diving suggest that the sharks move around all over the Gulf and even into the Ghoubbet (see 'La Faille'), but never appear to leave the vicinity for long periods.

Photographic databases suggest that the whale shark is a slow growing species and does not mature until it is about 30 years old. Scientists are able to determine the age of dead sharks by counting growth rings in vertebrae samples; it is now thought that they can live to more than 100 years.

So why do these sharks need to group together? Feeding in a rich body of water is the obvious answer, but it could also be that this is a safe place for young whale sharks to socialise, for even these big fish have their predators. Whale shark flesh has been found in the guts of marlin and mako sharks, and orcas have been observed killing them in the Gulf of California. For Djibouti's sharks, the most serious threat comes from the Yemeni shark-finning industry, which sells to the Far East. Whale shark meat is a delicacy in Taiwan, and while the fins do not break down suitably for use in shark fin soup, they fetch a high price as adornments for seafood restaurants.

Swimming with whale sharks requires a degree of stamina and control. Under normal circumstances, you will be in a small skiff that will drop you in the water about 15m in front of a shark. You should swim gently towards it, then as it looms forward move sharply to one side, changing direction so that you can swim alongside it. Smaller individuals spook easily, so the 2.5m juveniles at Arta Beach tend to speed away, while larger ones are more tolerant and even curious. It is not the done thing to use scuba, as manoeuvrability is important during the encounter and the sharks dislike the sounds produced by scuba bubbles. In any case, you can count on climbing in and out of the boat at least a dozen times over the course of a 90-minute snorkelling session, so wearing full scuba kit would entail a lot of hard work!

Quite often, snorkellers find the sharks sitting virtually upright, treading water and gulping excitedly at the surface. This behaviour, which is rarely observed elsewhere, is known by scientists as 'ram-feeding': when the sharks come across a patch of water that is brimming with zooplankton, they just stay in one spot, forcing their great heads forwards and taking in gallons at a time. They are so focussed that a snorkeller can swim all around them as they gulp down the plankton soup; you can even approach them head-on and, provided you don't make physical contact, they really don't seem to mind.

YEMEN

IN THE WEST, THE MOST WIDELY PUBLICISED ASPECT OF YEMEN IS THE CULTURE OF KIDNAPPING, A TACTIC USED BY ANTI-GOVERNMENT GROUPS FOR GENERATING PUBLICITY. IT IS UNDENIABLY A THREAT TO TRAVELLERS IN CERTAIN PARTS OF THE COUNTRY, BUT HOSPITALITY RATHER THAN AGGRESSION IS MORE CHARACTERISTIC OF YEMENI CULTURE.

Yemen is the probable site of the ancient trading civilisation of Sheba, and one of its oldest traditions holds that someone with whom you have shared a meal will not be your enemy.

Yemen is also one of the most exciting and diverse countries in the Red Sea region. On land, it has varied landscapes ranging from the cool, mist-shrouded highlands to the flat coastal plains of the Red Sea coast, where summer air temperatures approach 50°C. At present, tourism is very much the domain of specialist adventure and expedition groups, but it is widely predicted that this culturally rich country will one day emerge to become the greatest attraction in the region.

The underwater scene presents a contrast to the blue water dropoffs of Egypt and Sudan. Inshore sites tend to be shallow and murky, a result of the Red Sea rift valley being much narrower in the south, and we do not recommend people come to Yemen to dive in such places. The Hanish Islands in the south and Zubayr Islands to the north are a different proposition: they are located in much deeper offshore waters, with steep dropoffs and clearer conditions. There is a great concentration of fish life here, including some sharks. Do not expect to see many sharks, however, as Yemeni fishermen have been systematically removing them from the water since the Eighties. Coastal Yemen has a strong fishing tradition, and this quickly turned to shark finning when agents representing the Far East soup trade first arrived to barter for fins. It was Yemeni fishermen who decimated the grey reef shark populations of Sanganeb and Sha'ab Rumi in Sudan, and they have been suspected of incursions elsewhere in the Red Sea.

The marine life inhabiting the Yemeni Red Sea has long been of special interest to marine biologists, as this area was one of the first to be studied back in the 18th century, a good 200 years before scuba diving was even invented. Corals are plentiful in many areas,

◄ The unblinking, camouflaged eye of a crocodilefish gazes upward, waiting for a suitable prey item to swim within striking range.

Alexander Mustard

and certain Red Sea fish seem to fare especially well – notably the blue-cheeked butterflyfish, which occurs here in great numbers.

Yemen sits on the eastern side of the entrance to the Red Sea, the shallow strait known as Bab el Mandab ('Gate of Lamentations'). This is where the waters and marine life of the Red Sea mingle with those of the Indian Ocean, an area of biological complexity that would be of great interest for divers – if they could only get there. Of course, the strait is one of the most strategically important waterways in the world, so it is practically impossible to gain permits to explore it. At present, the closest you can get is the Seven Brothers Islands of Djibouti.

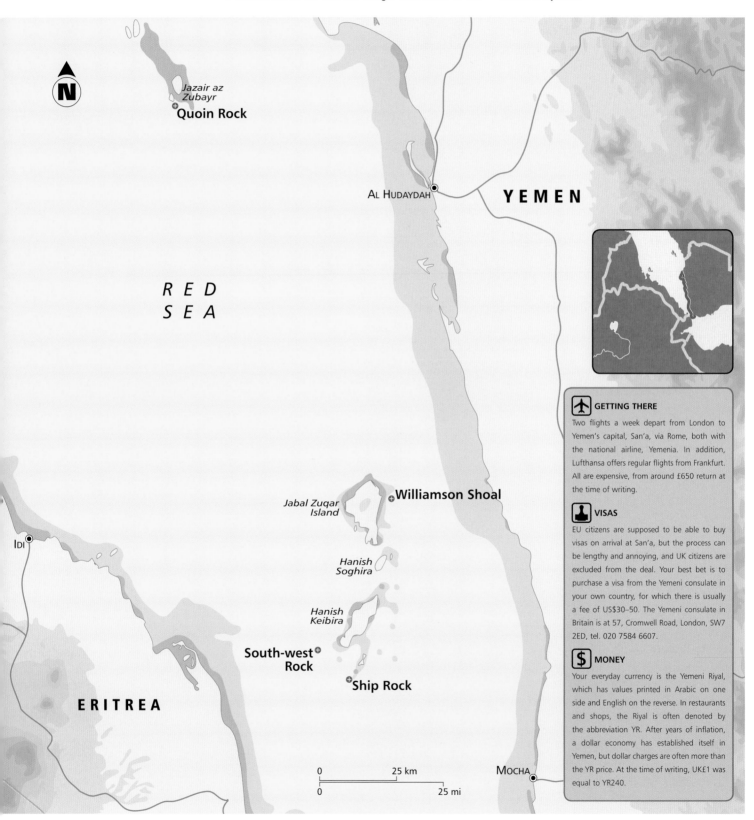

GETTING THERE

Two flights a week depart from London to Yemen's capital, San'a, via Rome, both with the national airline, Yemenia. In addition, Lufthansa offers regular flights from Frankfurt. All are expensive, from around £650 return at the time of writing.

VISAS

EU citizens are supposed to be able to buy visas on arrival at San'a, but the process can be lengthy and annoying, and UK citizens are excluded from the deal. Your best bet is to purchase a visa from the Yemeni consulate in your own country, for which there is usually a fee of US$30–50. The Yemeni consulate in Britain is at 57, Cromwell Road, London, SW7 2ED, tel. 020 7584 6607.

MONEY

Your everyday currency is the Yemeni Riyal, which has values printed in Arabic on one side and English on the reverse. In restaurants and shops, the Riyal is often denoted by the abbreviation YR. After years of inflation, a dollar economy has established itself in Yemen, but dollar charges are often more than the YR price. At the time of writing, UK£1 was equal to YR240.

SOUTH-WEST ROCK

Max depth: 40m
Skill level: 40 dives
Access: liveaboard
Current: often powerful
Must see: dogtooth tuna, jacks

The Hanish Islands combine the best of Yemen's teeming fishlife with corals that are still in good health. While inshore Yemeni diving entails shallow reefs and extremely poor visibility, the Hanish Islands (and the Zubayr Islands to the north) have steep slopes and dropoffs. Even so, there are plenty of oddities in this area, including giant nudibranchs similar to the Spanish dancer, believed to grow to an astonishing length of 50cm.

South-west Rock is one of the most isolated of the Hanish Island group, lying far beyond the rest of the archipelago. It was only opened up to divers in 1997, and access has been an unpredictable issue ever since.

Check with your local dive operator if you are intent on diving this site.

The reef dive is straightforward but challenging, with the prevailing current coming from the south. It may take some time to establish where to drop the divers in, but your aim should be to head for the western side of the reef, where you should find some colourful bommies and a slope that descends to 45m. Currents stream over this area, bringing in the pelagic fish that are the hallmark of the dive.

This is one of the best places to find dogtooth tuna. These powerful predators from the open sea drift lazily by the reef as they look for likely prey, then burst into action, fizzing along the reef like a heat-seeking missile that invariably finds the target.

Other big fish on this reef include great barracuda and giant groupers, which hide in a large crack in the reef or can be seen on the deeper sections of the slope. As usual, they are difficult to approach, but those beefy silhouettes are unmistakable.

VISIBILITY

In common with Eritrea and much of Djibouti, Yemeni dive sites are mostly found on relatively shallow banks and are subject to silting. You can expect 5–10m visibility for inshore dive sites, increasing to 15–22m for sites around Zubayr and the Hanish Islands.

WATER TEMPERATURE

Shallow coastal waters can reach high temperatures of 32°C in July and August. Otherwise, the Hanish Islands vary from 24–29°C over the year.

SEASONALITY

Wind is an important factor in Yemeni diving. From November to March there is a prevailing south to south-easterly wind that gusts at up to force four, and some local winds are even faster. Accordingly, the diving season in Yemen traditionally runs from April to October.

PIRATES

Travellers in Yemen should be warned that pirates have been known to operate in the Hanish Islands as well as along the country's Indian Ocean coastline. Assailants have fired on private yachts in the Hanish Islands, and Somali pirates have strafed passenger liners with gunfire outside Bab el Mandab. In one case, a skipper responded by hurling Molotov cocktails at the pursuing pirates. Inside the confines of the Red Sea piracy is far from being a persistent problem, but you should check government travel advice websites prior to visiting any remote reefs. Local diving operators should also be able to advise on risk assessment prior to a voyage.

Charles Hood/oceans-image.com

◀ Greasy groupers can be seen waiting motionless on the reef – approach slowly for a close-up portrait.

Simon Rogerson

▲ A rare sight in the Red Sea, the beautiful zebra shark (commonly and erroneously referred to as the leopard shark) feeds on crustaceans and can be seen resting on the seabed.

SHIP ROCK

Max depth: 30m

Skill level: 25 dives

Access: liveaboard

Current: moderate to strong

Must see: the stern section of the *Alma*; zebra sharks; potato cod

The southernmost dive site of the Hanish Islands, this reef lies just under the surface to the southwest of Siyul Hanish. On both sides of the reef are the broken-up remains of a 2,000-tonne English steamer, believed to be the passenger liner *Alma*. This P&O vessel came to grief after striking the reef in 1859 en route from Aden to Suez. The cargo and luggage were abandoned, but the crew and passengers escaped with their lives.

As an old vessel in shallow water, the iron wreck is extremely broken up, but the stern section is recognisable and a handsome bronze propeller is still there to be admired. This part of the wreck provides shelter for sand-dwelling predators, including some large stingrays, white-tip reef sharks and perhaps even a zebra shark or two. The structure of the wreck is swathed in hydroids and branching coral with white polyps, lending the scene a ghostly appearance.

Aside from these attractions, this site is noted as a good place to find the burly grouper known as potato cod. These bulky beauties occur throughout the Indo-

Pacific, but seem to be shy of divers in many places, possibly because they are targeted by spearfishermen from time to time. There are many of them around Ship Rock, but they tend to flee whenever divers approach.

WILLIAMSON SHOAL

Max depth: 30m optimum

Skill level: 30 dives

Access: liveaboard

Current: slight to medium

Must see: schooling snapper; grey reef sharks

This coral pinnacle lies about a mile to the east of the offshore island of Zubayr. If you look on Admiralty chart 453, you will see quite a few pinnacles of this type. The close contours around them suggest steep sided walls rising from relatively deep water, clearly a recipe for adventurous diving. Williamson Shoal is a classic of its kind, representing the best of the archipelago.

From the moment you submerge, you enter an explosion of fish. Nutrient-loaded water ensures the presence of thousands of plankton-feeders, which in turn attract predatory fish such as snapper, barracuda and tuna. Grey reef sharks have also been seen in this area, but given the Yemeni fishing industry's propensity for catching and finning sharks, it seems unlikely there are many left. There is a downside to this impressive concentration of life, in that the water is often murky due to the amount of suspended plankton; expect typical visibility of 10–15m on the reefs off Zubayr.

This reef has some fine hard corals that seem to have escaped the ravages of the El Niño coral bleaching event of 1997/98, but the overall impression is of monochrome stony coral. It is possible to swim all the way around the pinnacle, so try to head into the current for a while, as it is likely to lead to areas where fish are aggregating. The swirling, shifting schools of snapper and sardine are typical of the southern Red Sea, but be cautious if you choose to swim away from the reef, as the current can pick up pace in open water.

QUOIN ROCK

Max depth: 40m optimum

Skill level: 40 dives

Access: liveaboard

Current: medium to strong

Must see: schooling tuna and manta rays

This obscure outpost of the Zubayr Islands is held by many to be the best dive in Yemen, and is certainly a contrast to the inshore dives, in that the surrounding deep water attracts a great many pelagic fish. It is a challenging dive on a long ledge that slopes down from the reef's northeast point, leading to a dropoff at 40m. The proximity to open water, coupled with some frisky currents, make Quoin Rock (Quoin is French for 'corner') a magnet for silver fish. Expect to see giant trevally, barracuda and schools of juvenile tuna, which stop by to pick off the plankton grazers.

It is worth going deep to look for sharks and enjoy the black coral scenery, but do not neglect the main reef. Swim around the island and you should find a gulley, which completely bisects the reef. You can swim through this in most conditions, but beware the swell, which can drag you onto coral or – worse – a lurking scorpionfish. All over the reef you will find magnificent sea anemones, which close to reveal their red bodies at the end of the afternoon.

There is a manta ray cleaning station on the southern side of the reef, marked by a series of small bommies from 15–10m. As ever, the rules of manta diving should be strictly adhered to: first, a cautious approach, let them see you keeping your distance; then edge closer if they seem to be relaxed. Keep clear of the area where the cleaner wrasse flit about. If you spook them, the mantas will move further away to another spot where the cleaners are still in operation.

▶▶ A school of blackfin barracuda, the most common species of barracuda in the Red Sea, swims in tight formation. (JP Trenque)

▼ The best way to spot a bearded scorpionfish is to look out for the shape of the open pectoral fins – then the rest of its form will become apparent.

Simon Rogerson

SAUDI ARABIA

SAUDI ARABIA HAS THE LONGEST COASTLINE OF ALL THE RED SEA NATIONS. STRETCHING 1,800KM FROM THE BORDER WITH JORDAN IN THE GULF OF AQABA TO THE SHALLOW FARASAN ARCHIPELAGO AND YEMEN TO THE SOUTH, THIS HUGE NATION LAYS CLAIM TO THE VAST MAJORITY OF THE EASTERN RED SEA.

Yet despite this immense resource, relatively little diving takes place in Saudi waters. For years, the strict Muslim government refused to allow tourists to enter the country, so the only divers were resident Saudis or expatriate workers who formed their own clubs. Since the year 2000, however, the Kingdom (as it is usually called) has begun tentatively issuing a small number of tourist visas. So what awaits us behind diving's Iron Curtain?

With liveaboard operations now taking place courtesy of the pioneering Desert Sea Divers, three principal offshore areas have opened up: the reefs to the north-west of the natural harbour of Yanbu; the islands and reefs south of Jeddah known as the Farasan Banks; and the Farasan Islands in the far south, opposite the city of Jizan. Of these, the Farasan Banks and Yanbu reefs rise from very deep water and consequently they generally enjoy better visibility.

Diving still takes place around the city of Jeddah but, while there are a few good quality sites, the overall story is one of degradation. In the late Seventies, the shallow reef and inner lagoon in this area was refilled to build the prestigious 'Jeddah Corniche', a broad, 48km highway. Marine life was smothered by the sheer amount of sediment that was swept into the sea. Today, the reefs close to Jeddah suffer pollution from the city's sewage outflow, but there are some pretty reefs to be found if you take time to travel out beyond the pollution zone. Jeddah's reefs have also suffered from a strong and ongoing tradition of spearfishing: big fish are rare, and territorial creatures such as grouper are conspicuous by their absence.

North of Jeddah – about 400km – is the industrial city of Yanbu. Saudi-resident divers hold this to be one of the best places for shore-based diving, but you need to obtain permits from the regional

◀ Saudi waters have plenty of drop offs, where deep water corals such as these large gorgonians flourish.

Simon Rogerson

GETTING THERE

Direct flights are available from most European capitals to Jeddah, the gateway to diving in the Saudi Red Sea. Several airlines fly in and out, but there's no point buying tickets yourself. You will need a sponsor (see 'visas'), and this means buying a package tour in which flights, transfers, accommodation and diving are all included. Jeddah airport is located about 40km to the north of the city – your sponsor should have arranged for transport to come and collect you, or may even be waiting for you in person. From Jeddah, it is possible to fly to Jizan (for the Farasan Islands) or Yanbu (for the northern reefs). For the Farasan Banks, dive operators usually bus their clients down to a convenient port closer to the reefs.

 VISAS

Saudi Arabia remains one of the most insular societies on Earth and visas are extremely difficult to obtain. As a foreigner entering the Kingdom you must have a local sponsor, who will vouch for you and your conduct. Until recently, the only way divers have been able to visit Saudi is under a visitor's visa issued to people who have legitimate work in the Kingdom – expatriate engineers in the oil industry being a typical example.

In 2000 Saudi Arabia began issuing so-called tourist visas. For a while, there were visions of a new era of Red Sea tourism, but these visas are equally tricky to obtain. While there are elements within Saudi society who wish to share the marvels of the Kingdom's reefs, there are many more who resist any notion of foreigners entering the country.

Applications for tourist visas may be made direct to Saudi embassies. The embassy in Britain is at 30 Belgrave Square, London, SW1, tel. 020 7235 0303. The first step is to obtain a letter of permission from your sponsor, the local diving operator who will be your host in the Kingdom. Next, you must fill in an online form on the Saudi Ministry of Foreign Affairs website (http://visa.mofa.gov.sa) in order to be issued with a password. Finally, you must fill in a form detailing the purpose and dates of your visit, enclosing two passport-size photographs and a payment of around £40. You can post these to the embassy, or attend in person. Either way, even if you fill in all the correct forms, there is a fair chance that your application will be turned down without any clear explanation. So while it is true to say that Saudi Arabia is opening up to divers, this is hardly taking place with universal enthusiasm.

$ MONEY

The official currency is the Saudi Riyal (SAR), which is divided into 100 halalas. The Riyal is linked with the US Dollar, but exchange rates with other currencies will fluctuate. Tipping is not part of Saudi culture, though taxi drivers and waiters will certainly appreciate a small tip.

► A 'ship of the desert'.

authorities. The fallout of the 9/11 terrorist attacks made the security situation in Saudi Arabia more volatile and membership of expat diving clubs began to fall. Since the attacks on foreigners that took place in 2004 and 2005, many restrictions on travel have been introduced and the expat social scene has lost much of its vibrancy. These days, most diving takes place from the privacy of liveaboards or private beaches.

While 'local' reefs are popular with expatriates and other weekenders, the people who travel to Saudi Arabia specifically to dive are best advised to concentrate on Yanbu's offshore reefs and the Farasan Banks. These are blue-chip dive destinations, both capable of delivering the same level of colour and life you would expect of the best Sudanese or Egyptian reefs. Still, tourism remains a tiny industry in Saudi; holidays here are more expensive than elsewhere in the region, and the restrictive laws still dissuade many people from visiting. A local guide must always accompany dive groups, alcohol is completely banned and women must wear the traditional black chador when going into town or travelling.

Saudi Arabia's northern reefs and the Farasan Banks sit in the central Red Sea, where tidal movement is minimal, the water is clear and currents are seldom fierce. This stands in sharp contrast to the southerly reefs of the Farasan Islands, where there is a vertical tidal range of two metres, and where powerful currents sweep over the shallow sea floor, stirring up sediment. Many pelagic fish prefer these high-energy, nutrient-rich waters, and indeed the Farasans support a sizeable fishing community.

As this book was being researched, the only recompression facility on the Saudi west coast was declared to be defunct, and the private hospital that looked after it has no plans to spend the money that would make it operational again. For now, there are no public recompression facilities on the Saudi Red Sea coastline. With such limited safety backup, conservative diving and long safety stops are essential.

So, after decades of isolation, is Saudi Arabia ready at last for diving tourism? While there is no denying the enthusiasm of the pioneering operations and the quality of the reefs they have discovered, a visit to Saudi is unlike anywhere else in this book. During our research, we spoke to expatriate divers who warned that the emergency services are too slow to react and that local infrastructures are not adequate to meet the needs of visiting divers. In fairness, this could also be said of Egypt, where cash payments must be made up front to the air force before they will conduct an aerial search for lost divers, yet hundreds of thousands of divers still choose to go there.

Diving in Saudi Arabia is certainly more complex and costly than in some of the other nations in this book, but there will always be a market for places that have pristine reefs such as those highlighted in this chapter. For now, this country is likely to remain a curiosity for Red Sea connoisseurs with the requisite money and patience. It is a destination for those who like to be ahead of the pack, or who want to enjoy a reef in the knowledge that they are on the only dive boat for miles around. Perhaps, then, we should savour Saudi Arabia's underwater delights while every visiting diver remains a pioneer of sorts.

Interestingly, dive guides in Saudi Arabia do not use the traditional Arabic terminology for reef structures, preferring the Australian 'bommie' to erg. Equally, there are few references to 'sha'abs' or 'habilis' during dive briefings. This may partly be explained by the presence of Filipino dive guides on some of the boats. Anyone who learns to dive in the Philippines tends to adopt the diving argot of Australia and the Pacific Rim, and it seems to have become established in this most unlikely of settings.

Dave Lucas

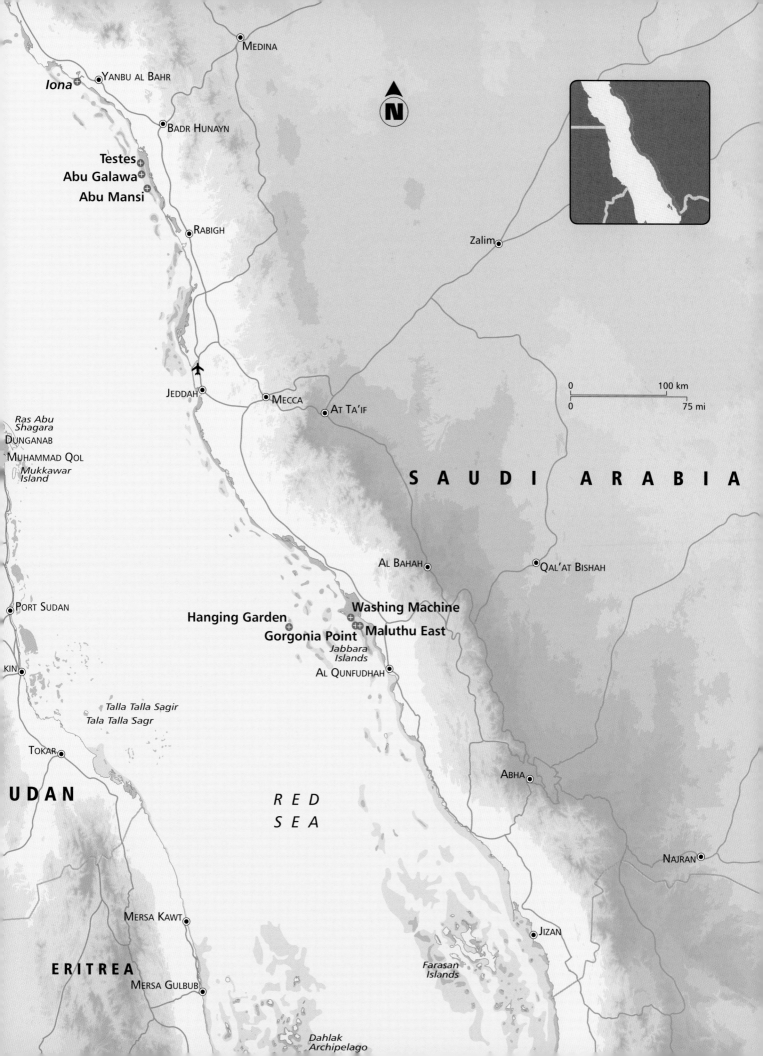

MEDINA

Iona ⊕
● YANBU AL BAHR

⊙ BADR HUNAYN

Testes ⊕
Abu Galawa ⊕
Abu Mansi

● RABIGH

ZALIM ◉

✈

JEDDAH ●
● MECCA
◉ AT TA'IF

Ras Abu
Shagara
DUNGANAB
'MUHAMMAD QOL
*Mukkawar
Island*

SAUDI ARABIA

AL BAHAH ● ◉ QAL'AT BISHAH

● PORT SUDAN

Washing Machine ⊕
Hanging Garden
⊕ ⊕ **Maluthu East**
Gorgonia Point ⊕
*Jabbara
Islands*
AL QUNFUDHAH ●

KIN ◉

Talla Talla Sagir
Tala Talla Sagr

ABHA ◉

TOKAR ◉

UDAN

*R E D
S E A*

NAJRAN ◉

MERSA KAWT ◉

JIZAN ◉

ERITREA

MERSA GULBUB ◉

*Farasan
Islands*

*Dahlak
Archipelago*

VISIBILITY

25–30m on the Farasan Banks and northern reefs; 10–15m around the Farasan Islands.

 WATER TEMPERATURE

26°C minimum in winter, 30°C maximum in summer. Dive sites to the far south are 1–2°C cooler than those in the central and north regions, with shallow water around the Farasan Islands reaching 34°C in July and August.

 SEASONALITY

The best diving in the Yanbu region and the northern reefs is from May to September. For the Farasan Banks, January to April is the best time for big fish action.

▶ Large schools of trevally can be around the reef.

▼ The blacktip grouper, a common species on coral and rocky bottoms.

WASHING MACHINE

Max depth: optimum depth 35m (drops to 500m)

Skill level: 40 dives

Access: liveaboard

Current: medium to extreme

Must see: scalloped hammerhead sharks; bumphead parrotfish

Seen from above, Mar-Mar island looks like a giant egg, with the dry section representing the yolk and the fringing reef the white. This volcanic, low-lying island only attains an altitude of 4m above sea level, but it is covered with vegetation and attracts more topside life than offshore islands in Sudan or Egypt. From December to March, Mar-Mar is visited by hundreds of birds, including ospreys and brown boobies.

Underwater, the wildlife is even more intense. The Washing Machine, as its name suggests, is the current-blasted northern tip of the fringing reef, where you will encounter large numbers of pelagic fish when conditions are amenable. The reef sits just 1.5m underwater, and drops to a plateau at 30m. From there it slopes gradually away to depths of 500m or more.

With such deep water and currents, it will come as little surprise to learn that this is shark country. If the current is moving across that northern point, you are likely to see solitary hammerhead sharks and silky sharks, occasionally swimming together. Hammerheads seem to be quite bold in Saudi waters, and quite often make a point of changing direction to inspect divers at close quarters.

The point is also a good place to find schooling fish, including bigeye trevally and other members of the jack family. The resident school of trevally is unusually diver-friendly and will open up to allow divers to join their school. A local guide told us that sometimes the fish even allow divers to stroke them, although we do not recommend this as some of the natural oils from our hands can cause delicate fish flesh to become infected.

In the words of the same dive guide: 'If the current is moving here, hang on to your regulator and kiss your buddy goodbye'. For the most part, the currents are manageable, but if they get too feisty you should stay close to the reef and allow yourself to be taken on a drift along the western or eastern walls. The reef is of volcanic origin, so the wall is punctuated with characteristic caves and overhangs, lending the environment

Alexander Mustard

a complexity you would not associate with sheer walls. Here, you will find many of the classic Red Sea reef fish, including grouper, anthias and squirrelfish. You may also find white-tip reef sharks dozing in the shelter of the overhangs; they are abundant in Saudi waters, but remain typically skittish and do not allow divers to approach closer than a few metres unless they are being cleaned.

Your final safety stop should be entertaining, as the reef is home to a large population of bumphead parrotfish, which tend to favour the shallows. Bumpheads are very difficult to approach in Egypt, but do not seem to have such a fear of divers in Saudi waters. They thrive in the slightly warmer temperatures of the Farasans, and are often seen moving across the reef in schools, led by an alpha male. These herbivorous fish feed on the hard coral, deriving nutrition from the algae and polyps inside the stony skeleton, which they break down into fine sand and 'redistribute' across the reef once it has passed

through their digestive system.

We have heard reports of baby turtles hatching around this island from March to April, including one of the sea's great rarities, the leatherback turtle. Predictably, the hatching season in March and April attracts predators, who can easily pick off the defenceless hatchlings. Jacks and snappers account for most of them, but this is also the time when you might encounter tiger sharks on Saudi reefs.

Whether the tigers come to predate on young seabirds or turtles is unclear, but they certainly add a frisson to your dive! These are potentially the most dangerous of Red Sea sharks, but they do not automatically attack people, and if they have come to this reef to feed specifically on small turtles then they are likely only to make a few passes before returning to this easier food source. If the sharks show signs of aggression, stay close to the reef, move away from the area (they may be guarding a kill) and try to exit the water as soon as possible.

GORGONIA POINT

Max depth: 35m optimum

Skill level: 25 dives

Access: liveaboard

Current: slight to medium

Must see: oceanic white-tip sharks; scalloped hammerheads; forest of gorgonian fans

Gorgonia Point is the southern tip of a submerged reef between Maluthu and Jadir islands in the Farasan Banks. The reef rises from 550m to within 1.5m of the surface. Unlike many such reefs, the shallows are not spoiled by silty runoff when the weather is rough: the reef top is clean bedrock with virtually no sand, and visibility on the site is as good at the surface as it is at depth.

There's a good chance of finding hammerheads anywhere on this dive, but the southern point is the best place as it seems to attract aggregating oceanic triggerfish, barracuda and various jack species. The inflatables should drop you in close to the tip, so it's just a case of heading south and descending until you reach a plateau that stretches out for about 120m, eventually leading you down to about 45m. It's very similar to the southern point of Sha'ab Rumi in Sudan.

On the plateau, you are likely to find hundreds of black surgeonfish and seething schools of fusiliers, which pulse so beautifully that they can amplify the symptoms of nitrogen narcosis (a sensation familiar to anyone who dives Saudi Arabia's offshore sites!). There can be quite a few white-tip reef sharks lying on the bottom or drifting along the outer edges of the reef, but the stars of the show here are the oceanic white-tip sharks that visit from September to November.

▼ The Sohar surgeonfish is typical of this region, and lives in small territories on the outer edge of shallow reef flats.

Alexander Mustard

Simon Rogerson

No one knows exactly what brings the sharks in from the open sea at this time of year, but it seems to coincide with similar events in Egyptian waters, and most of the sharks seem to be mature females. This encounter is a little different to the classic oceanic meeting, as the sharks seem to favour the deeper sections of the reef, possibly because they prefer the cooler water. Still, it is possible to find them at the surface, particularly if any local boats have been emptying food into the sea.

This site is named after a forest of gorgonian fan corals that starts at about 30m on the southern plateau and runs as deep as 65m. You will find some of the largest gorgonians in the Red Sea here, and they are in pristine condition. Fish life is not profuse among the fan corals, but they provide an unearthly backdrop in golden brown tones that look their best when lit by a diver's torch. When you have used up your planned bottom time, swim back up along the plateau and on the right side of the reef at about 20m you should arrive at a large area of bubble coral. It's a curious microenvironment, providing cover for many small crustaceans and juvenile fish.

In February and March, the reef is visited by mating squid, most of which die of exhaustion after completing the act that will perpetuate their species. It is an eerie time to visit the reef, as the pale corpses of the squid gather on the shores of the nearby islands and can be seen bobbing in the swell. Most of them are eaten by jackfish or seabirds, but the eggs have already been laid and the next generation of cephalopods is on its way.

Again, it is easy to find bumphead parrotfish on the shallowest portion of this dive. They seem to enjoy grazing on the reef shallows at 2m, where the sun's rays heat up the water an extra 1–2°C. Of all the Red Sea's fish, these seem to be the ones with the greatest tolerance for super-hot water.

▲ Octopus are seldom seen in the open, but may stay in place if approached slowly.

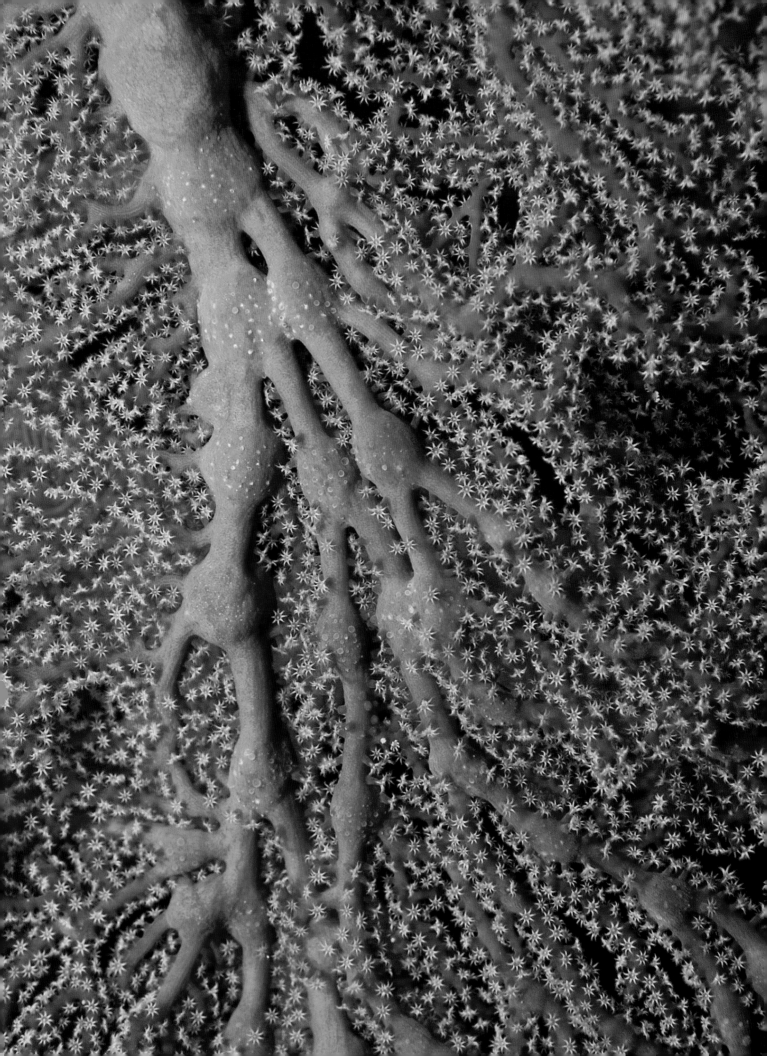

MALUTHU EAST

Max depth: 35m optimum

Skill level: 20 dives

Access: liveaboard

Current: moderate

Must see: scalloped hammerheads; dogtooth tuna; bonito; potato cod

This reef runs east to west, and the idea is to drop in close to the eastern point and follow a 30m-wide, sandy gully (local guides call it the 'sand highway') down to 30-35m, to a point where scalloped hammerheads are often seen. Although these sharks do not occur in big schools here, this site offers good encounters with small groups of them – usually no more than seven at a time.

If there are no sharks here, do not despair. The point at the base of the highway is the focus for aggregating fish, especially dogtooth tuna, bonito and some bulbous potato cod, which tend to keep their distance from divers. Schooling barracuda are also found here, though they seem to enjoy meandering all over the reef and tend to visit Maluthu East when the current is running.

On the sand, you will find several different species of ray. As ever in the Red Sea, there are plenty of blue-spotted stingrays, but here you may also come across something rather rarer, the blacktail bull ray. This is a much larger, more classically proportioned stingray, a very rare sight in the Red Sea and more typical of the Indian Ocean. These impressive creatures have also been found in Sudan and Djibouti, but the full extent of their range in the Red Sea remains a mystery. Saudi Arabian dive operator Erik Alexander Mason was stung by one while this book was being researched: the sting went through his neoprene boot and into his ankle and, in his words: 'put me down like a pole-axed steer'. He was ill for a month.

HANGING GARDEN, MUDDAR REEF

Max depth: 30–35m optimum

Skill level: 30 dives

Access: liveaboard

Current: slight to moderate

Must see: the hanging garden, with its sponges and black coral; the wall

Muddar is a 400m-long submerged reef with a small sand island just breaking the surface on the southern tip. The reef runs east to west, with steep walls descending almost straight down to 340m. On the southern point there is a plateau at 25–30m; head out 100m or so along this area and you will come to a cut in the reef that forms a cavern. This is one of the most colourful

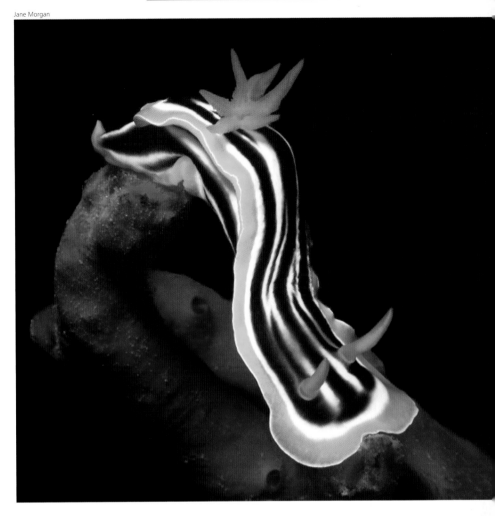

Jane Morgan

crannies you will find in the Saudi Red Sea, with yellow, white, blue and red sponges hanging from the ceiling among great bushes of black coral. Only a few divers have ever visited this 'hanging garden', since it was only recently discovered and lies far out on the most exposed part of the reef. There is room enough for a good number of divers to enter simultaneously, as the cavern is at least 70m in length. It provides a home to various fish and nudibranch species, including the familiar cave-dwelling soldierfish and squirrelfish, which turn their heads as if in embarrassment when they see divers heading their way.

On the northeast point you are likely to encounter scalloped hammerheads, schools of trevally and yellowfin barracuda. Currents are generally light, but if the water is running, there tend to be more fish on the tip. Settle down at 35–40m and wait for a while to see if the sharks will come to you. In February, March and April, tiger sharks are known to frequent this part of the reef. Later in the year, the water starts to warm up and the cool water favoured by the sharks sinks lower, so that eventually they are patrolling at 70m. The upper slopes of the reef wall host a big school of bumphead parrotfish, which must be responsible for excreting all the white sand that now makes up the beach.

▲ This nudibranch's bright colours indicate it is too poisonous to be eaten.

◀ The intricate latticework of a 'splendid knotted fan coral', with the white feeding polyps clearly visible.

Jane Morgan

▲ A banded cleaner shrimp.

▼ This grey reef shark is possibly pregnant, and further encumbered by two huge remoras.

As with most offshore Saudi dives, this is a big wall and you will need good buoyancy control skills if you are to visit the deeper sections with confidence. Apart from anything else, you should aim to have enough air in reserve to explore the different facets of this reef. On the southern plateau, there are two coral heads at a depth of 30m, with just about enough space for a diver to squeeze between them. You should then emerge into a seaweed garden where various small creatures can be found hiding among the fronds of the plant life.

Recently, a diver discovered a ghost pipefish here. This is a familiar species in the shallow, super-heated waters of the Arabian Gulf, but was previously unheard of in this part of the Red Sea. It is a relative of the seahorse and is equally hard to find, favouring black coral, soft coral and seagrass as the perfect backdrop for its camouflage. Ghost pipefish are not powerful enough to flee across open water, and stay close to the protection of their chosen habitat. They make excellent subjects for macro photographers, but they have an annoying habit of retreating from view. Do not be tempted to chase them out with your finger, as these are among the most delicate animals in the sea.

With its mixture of soft corals, shark action and small fish, Muddar is one of the most diverse reefs in Saudi Arabian waters and can be the highlight of a visit to the Farasan Banks. If possible, try to stay here for at least a day to see how the reef changes as the day progresses.

ABU GALAWA

Max depth: 30m optimum
Skill level: 20 dives
Access: liveaboard
Current: slight to moderate
Must see: grey reef sharks, coral pinnacles, fusiliers

Galawa is one of the most easterly reefs of the Seven Sisters system, and offers safe anchorage on a fixed mooring. The reef is about 1km long and runs east to west, submerged just 30cm beneath the surface. On the eastern side is a plateau that starts at 20m and stretches out a further 60m before dropping away into deep water. The name of this site, 'Abu Galawa', refers specifically to the plateau and is not to be confused with the site of the same name in Egypt's Fury Shoal system.

The Seven Sisters are a haven for marine mammals. Bottlenose and spinner dolphins can be seen in superpods, composed of hundreds of individuals, while pilot whales and even humpbacks have been known to make an appearance. If you do have the opportunity to enter the water with whales, take careful stock of the situation. Humpbacks can be defensive of their young, while pilot whales are contemptuous of human contact at the best of times.

Whale sharks arrive with the plankton blooms that occur through May, June and July, but they seldom appear on the dive sites. Instead, they are sighted from the boat in open water, and it may be possible to snorkel with them for a while. The form for snorkelling with the sharks is very much the same as described in the Djibouti chapter, but whale shark sightings are more a matter of luck in Saudi Arabia, as there is not a contained area where aggregations are known to take place.

Grey reef and black-tip reef sharks patrol the far edge of the dropoff, while the plateau is the domain of groupers and fusiliers. As with so many offshore reefs in this chapter, there is a very good chance of seeing scalloped hammerheads, although they and the other sharks move into deeper water from May to October, when the surface temperatures are too warm for their liking. The plateau itself is similar to the south side of Sanganeb in Sudan, in that it has sandy highways punctuated by coral outcrops and beautiful pinnacles.

The pinnacles and many other areas of the plateau and walls are covered in soft corals, the most common of which is a curious grey/green colour, although they also occur in reds and blues. At first, these soft corals appear to offer little in the way of shelter for reef life, but it can be worth taking a good close look: they are sometimes used as a habitat by tiny crabs, which mimic the appearance of the coral, right down to having 'polyps' growing on their bodies.

Simon Rogerson

The dive is designed to return you on an easy drift in the direction of the liveaboard, but the inflatable tenders should be on standby to collect you if you don't find your way back.

ABU MANSI

Max depth: 40m optimum

Skill level: 20 dives

Access: liveaboard

Current: slight to moderate

Must see: aggregating fish at the thermocline; manta rays; caverns and eagle rays on the northern point

South of Abu Galawa lies this circular reef of about 500m in diameter, where sheer reef walls drop straight down to a depth of 450m. So much for the topography; what about the dive? Well, it's a classic: as varied as anything in Sudan or Egypt, yet only experienced by a handful of divers. This is close to being the total reef diving experience, delivering electrifying shark encounters, colourful scenery, more fish than you would ever believe and still with the promise of something more.

There's no plateau to find on this reef, so divers usually head from the east to the south after dropping in. On this dive, it's very much a case of finding a depth that you are comfortable with – anywhere between 20 and 40m at the beginning of the dive. The southern side is the place to look for scalloped hammerheads: you may find them in schools of 18–20 here, if you're lucky, and it's hard to finish a dive on this site without seeing at least one.

Fun as the sharks are, don't let them take up too much of your attention, as too much time gazing hopefully into the blue will mean missing out on the other attractions, in particular the massed ranks of reef fish that swirl around the thermocline, the area where the deeper, cool water meets the warmer water of the surface. This is the sweet spot, where nutrient-rich waters dance in a haze before your eyes (and if the thermocline happens to be deep, nitrogen narcosis will play its own role when it comes to haziness). More to the point, it's the zone where fish swarm with remarkable vigour. When the right conditions come together, you will find schools of snapper, batfish, grouper, black surgeons and jacks; even the territorial, coral-eating parrotfish join in the excitement generated by the thermocline. This sort of aggregation is the first sign of the frenetic fish behaviour that typifies reefs from the Farasans down to the Seven Brothers in Djibouti. Guides sometimes refer to aggregation zones as 'aquariums', reflecting how numerous and densely packed the fish are in such spots.

Despite all this action, it's not an especially difficult dive in terms of current. When the water is really running, you can get two knots here, but for the most part currents are slight. On the east wall, these currents promote the growth of soft coral, while on the north side they bring in eagle rays. It will not always be possible to dive the northern side of the reef, but it is worth investigating its pretty coral caverns, where small fish and crustaceans peer from the shadows.

With all this action around the reef, you could be forgiven for neglecting the western side, but that would be ruling out your best chance of finding manta rays. Mantas appear seasonally throughout Saudi Arabia's reefs, but the two rays seen regularly here appear to be permanent residents. As ever, approach them slowly or even stay still, and you have a much better chance of a sustained encounter.

JP Trenque

▲ Unicornfish and grouper swim alongside each other.

Alexander Mustard

▲ A cleaner wrasse services a Red Sea fusilier – trust is essential!

▶ Blue spotted stingrays are common in Saudi Arabia, but they are nevertheless easily missed.

TESTES

Max depth: optimum 30m

Skill level: 20 dives

Access: liveaboard

Current: moderate

Must see: grey reef sharks resting on the sandy bottom

Testes is the easternmost of the Seven Sisters, a reef shaped almost exactly like a teardrop. with an expansive plateau on the eastern point, starting from a depth of about 20–25m. Under normal conditions, divers will jump off the back of the liveaboard near a marine marker, then swim in an easterly direction with the reef on their left and blue water to the right. After visiting the plateau, the idea is to continue around the reef and head north, ending up at another plateau on the western side of the reef.

The seabed here is composed of coral heads and sand. Unusually, grey reef sharks can sometimes be seen resting here with their mouths open, allowing oxygen-rich water to flow over their gills while cleaner wrasse peck away at any parasites around their mouths. Although grey reef sharks have been observed resting in submerged caves off Mexico, such behaviour is extremely rare and this is the only example of it to be regularly observed in the Red Sea. Contrary to popular belief, several shark species can breathe while lying still on the seabed, notably nurse, zebra and white-tip reef sharks. These are regarded largely as bottom-dwelling sharks, but the grey reef is a different case. While this species is certainly a territorial shark, it is designed very much for mid-water existence, and it can only lie still in the presence of flowing, richly oxygenated water that nourishes the blood. Why the water here is so well enriched is still a mystery, though it may be attributable to deep upwellings or volcanic activity.

There is also a good chance of seeing two silky sharks that are reputed to frequent a coral pinnacle in this area. One of them has a deformed dorsal fin, possibly a result of an enthusiastic mating session. There are plenty of surgeonfish and trevally, but the familiar bumphead parrotfish of the Farasan Banks do not live this far north.

The best time to visit this site is from May to September, when the seas are relatively calm. There is a coral ridge on the western plateau that is said to lead to Abu Galawa, but this is at least a 5km swim, so it is highly unlikely that the two sites will ever become linked – unless the Saudi dive operators invest in some extremely fast underwater scooters. It could happen!

THE FARASAN ISLANDS

The shallow coral shelf of the Farasan Islands is found 48km off the southern coast of Saudi Arabia, opposite the city of Jizan. It is the largest group of islands in the Red Sea, encompassing 85 islands and straddling the border with Yemen. The average depth here is only about 10m, but these shallow seas are loaded with nutrients carried along by powerful currents. Manta rays are common, and the area is home to a large population of skittish dugong.

The islanders are more relaxed than mainland Saudis, and you may even see women driving some of the small boats used to get around (women are banned from driving cars in Saudi Arabia). To get here, you must fly or drive into Jizan and take a speed ferry or the military ferry to Farasan Khabir, where a hotel and dive shop have recently been built. Still, this is an extreme place: air temperatures often reach the high forties or low fifties, and even the seawater hits a bath-like 33ºC in summer. Thanks to the nutrients, the water appears blue-green and visibility is typically 10–15m.

You will encounter pelagic fish all over the Farasans, but in the periods after a storm, when all that silt is still suspended in the water, you may not be able to see much at all. With conditions on your side, you should expect to see plenty of white-tip reef sharks, snappers, jacks and barracuda. On the seabed, you will find blue-spotted stingrays, guitar sharks, moray eels and grouper. The mangrove trees that dominate the shallowest areas form an important habitat for juvenile fish, which find shelter among the tangled mass of submerged roots.

When diving here, as with the areas around Yanbu and Jiddah, you need to report in to the local military coastguard. The local operators should be able to help you dive without incurring the wrath of the authorities, but be prepared to change your plan, as a given area may be declared off-limits at any time. The three-star Hotel Farasan (email: farasanhotel@yahoo.com) should be able to offer support in arranging a workable itinerary.

▼ Stony coral provides shelter for juvenile basslets and damsels.

Simon Rogerson

THE WRECK OF THE *IONA*

Max depth: 32m

Skill level: 20 dives

Access: liveaboard or private vessel out of Yanbu

Current: none

Must see: the stern section; masses of reef fish

This shipwreck lies just outside the extensive natural harbour of Sham Yanbu, and is used as a checkout dive before liveaboards head on to dive the outer reefs. It seems that the ship blundered right into a submerged reef known as Shib Ash Sharm and sank along the sloping wall, with the bow section smashed up and ground into the reef at a depth of 15–20m.

The reef is relatively uninteresting, but life has taken a hold on the wreck in the form of corals and clouds of anthias fish. The full story of the sinking is not known, but the vessel was an open-hold Greek container ship and it seems to have hit the reef while seeking shelter at Yanbu. The wreck is about 80m in length and lies sideways across the reef, with the single propeller resting at the deepest point at 32m. Judging from the level of deterioration of the wreck and the amount of coral growth, it has probably been underwater for a good 50 years or so.

Being relatively close to land, the wreck occasionally receives the attention of spearfishers. You can tell when they have just visited, as the fish tend to be skittish. There is a theory that if a fish is killed by spearfishers using scuba gear (as opposed to free-diving), then other fish in the area begin to associate the sound of scuba bubbles with danger, and give divers a wide berth.

Local operators are not confident about the stability of the wreck, and discourage divers from carrying out ambitious penetrations into its interior. The open holds allow plenty of light to enter, though there is not much to find inside. The *Iona* had either already emptied its cargo, or was salvaged after sinking. The most satisfying part of the ship to explore is the stern, where a large funnel still stands proud of the wreckage.

Aficionados of ancient wrecks may be interested in three amphora wrecks, which lie approximately 10km to the north of Shib Ash Sham. The wooden ships that once held the amphorae have long since rotted away. They hardly make for the most interesting dive, and it would be extremely unwise to remove any of the amphorae, as all historical sites are protected in Saudi Arabian law. These waters probably hide thousands of undiscovered wrecks, both ancient and modern, and with liveaboard diving finally opening up the outer reefs of Saudi Arabia, amazing discoveries are certain to be made.

▶▶ During night dives, look closely at the fire coral, which is home to tiny Red Sea squat lobsters, about 1–2cm in length. (Alexander Mustard)

▼◀ The Red Sea anemonefish, in all its glory.

▼ A redstripe fairy basslet.

JP Trenque

Jane Morgan

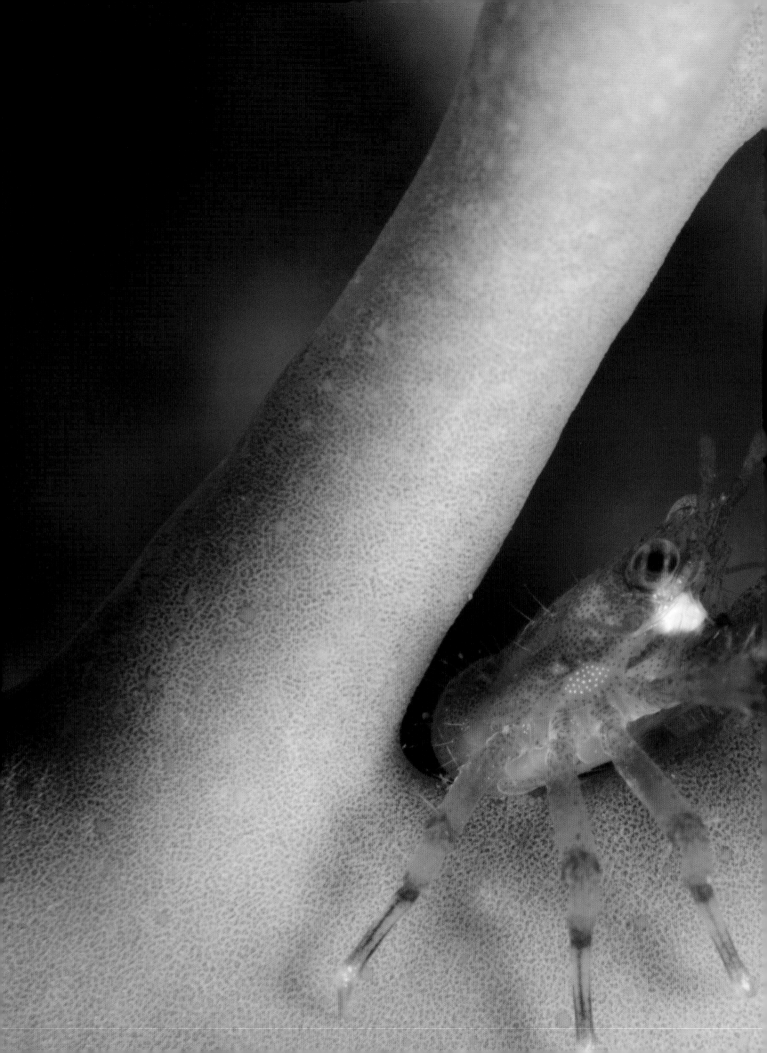

MARINE LIFE IDENTIFICATION GUIDE

SO WHAT WAS THAT FISH? HERE, WE LIST THE RED SEA'S KEY SPECIES: WHERE TO FIND THEM AND HOW TO APPROACH THEM. THIS LIST INCLUDES MOST COMMONLY ENCOUNTERED REEF FISH, AS WELL AS SOME OF THE OTHER MORE SPECTACULAR AND UNUSUAL CREATURES THAT EVERY DIVER WANTS TO SEE.

Alexander Mustard

Scalefin anthias, *Pseudanthias squamipinnis*

If a single fish could be said to represent the Red Sea, it would be the anthias, also known as the fairy basslet. These ubiquitous fish live in massive schools, enjoying the protection of the coral reef but also billowing out into the water column to feed on plankton. This vision of bright orange fish set against the deep royal blue of the water has become a visual archetype of the Red Sea. Indeed, seasoned photographers can usually tell if a photograph has been taken in the Red Sea simply by looking at the colour of the background water and checking to see if there are any orange fish in the foreground. Anthias reportedly grow to 15cm long, though most individuals are about 5cm. They can be found on coral reefs from the surface to a depth of 45m.

Charles Hood/oceans-image.com

Napoleon wrasse, *Cheilinus undulates*

Growing to 2m and more, the Napoleon wrasse (also known as Napoleon fish, or humphead wrasse) is another signature fish of the Red Sea. Curious and well disposed towards divers, these robust fish are found on dropoffs and (to a lesser extent) lagoon reefs, where they feed principally on molluscs. You can identify them by their sheer size, the telltale 'hump' and the ornate markings behind the eyes. Until the early Nineties, there was a regrettable trend of feeding these fish hard-boiled eggs, and although the practice has now largely ceased, some large individuals in the northern Red Sea will approach divers very closely – coming even closer if you begin to search demonstratively in your BCD pockets. You can find Napoleon wrasse anywhere from the surface to 50m; they have a habit of following groups of divers.

Simon Rogerson

Whale shark, *Rhincodon typus*

An oceanic wanderer, the whale shark is the biggest fish in the sea, growing to 12m and beyond. Due to their immense size and rows of prominent white spots, these filter-feeding sharks are unmistakable. They seem to swim at a variety of depths, but most encounters take place at the surface, where they can sometimes be seen ploughing through plankton-rich water with their huge mouths wide open. Whale sharks can be either curious or timid when they meet divers or snorkellers, depending on the individual, but most tend to dive deep or swim off at speed if confronted head-on. Encounters with whale sharks are possible practically anywhere, with offshore reefs being the most likely places. The best location is off Djibouti's Gulf of Tadjoura, where sub-adults gather from October to late January.

White-tip reef shark, *Triaenodon obesus*

If you're new to the Red Sea, these sharks will probably be the first you'll see. You can find them at anything from 5–50m, resting on the sand or in caves. They can grow to 2m in length, but most are smaller. White-tips are quite timid and do not pose any threat to divers, but you should not get in their way when they start to hunt on the reef at night, since they may attack if harassed or cornered: author Simon Rogerson once fended off a small individual that had developed an unhealthy interest in his underwater flashgun.

Simon Rogerson

Grey reef shark, *Carcharhinus amblyrhynchos*

Growing to 1.8m in length, this is a beautifully proportioned shark, typically found in reef areas exposed to current. The greys are the royalty of the reef, feeding on bony fishes and dominating most of the other resident predators (with the exception of the largest groupers). You can identify them by the black markings on the tail fin and the small white marking on the first dorsal fin. Greys tend to move away if you swim towards them, but they show curiosity towards divers and are known to be occasionally aggressive: if a shark is swimming in a jerky, exaggerated way with its pectoral fins pointing down, you are best advised to swim away.

Jane Morgan

Scalloped hammerhead shark, *Sphyrna lewini*

With a maximum size of about 4m, this is a shark to reckon with. It is one of the Red Sea's more elusive residents, favouring the deeper portions of offshore reefs, but is easily recognised by the trademark 'hammer', thought to be a means of spreading the shark's sensory apparatus over a greater area – like a living metal detector. These imposing sharks can be encountered singly or in schools of up to 40, which appear on the thermocline where cool, deep water meets the warmer water of the surface. They are not aggressive to divers, and feed mostly on crabs, squid and rays.

Simon Rogerson

Great hammerhead shark, *Sphyrna mokarran*

Growing exceptionally to 6m, though usually much less, this magnificent shark closely resembles the scalloped hammerhead, but its behaviour is quite different. Great hammerheads are solitary alpha predators, and feed on a variety of large prey, including eagle rays and smaller reef sharks. They have been known to approach divers fearlessly, though there has never been any record of an attack in the Red Sea (most recorded attacks have been on spear fishermen in the Western Atlantic). Great hammerheads are occasionally seen at the Brother Islands and Elphinstone, but sightings are very rare. The best way to differentiate them from scalloped hammerheads is by the first dorsal fin, which is extremely tall and sickle-shaped.

Alexander Mustard

Simon Rogerson

Zebra or variegated shark, *Stegostoma fasciatum*

This bottom-dwelling shark seems to be declining in the Red Sea. This is a great shame, because it has such memorable markings. The gold skin and black spots sometimes earn it the name 'leopard shark', but since that name is already taken by a species in California, we are obliged to call this one the zebra shark (even though it may seem a rather less accurate description). Divers tend to encounter individuals on the more remote reefs and lagoons, often sleeping on the sand. They will tolerate you as long as you move slowly and steadily, and keep your hands to yourself; venture too close, too soon and they simply swim away. Zebra sharks grow to 3.2m and generally feed on crustaceans.

Alexander Mustard

Tiger shark, *Galeocerdo cuvier*

Tigers are not common in the Red Sea, but we know that they are present from the frequent sightings reported by divers from parts of Egypt, Sudan and, recently, Saudi Arabia. This is a huge shark, growing to 7m (though most measure 3–4m). It can be recognised by its vertical stripes (which fade with age) and bluntly rounded snout. Its coxcomb teeth are designed to tear through a wide range of prey. If you see one, stay close to the reef and, if it shows any sign of aggression, move away as calmly as possible and leave the water at the earliest opportunity. These sharks are not generally aggressive towards divers, but there are a few scattered reports of attacks. Tiger sharks do not have territories as such, but range across large areas of sea, usually timing their appearance to coincide with a seasonal event.

Simon Rogerson

Black-tip reef shark, *Carcharhinus melanopterus*

This small, timid shark grows to no bigger than 2m and tends to favour shallow areas, mangroves and some reef dropoffs. It can be identified by the prominent black markings on the tips of all of its fins, in addition to a relatively large second dorsal fin. Black-tips have been greatly reduced in number by coastal fisheries throughout the Red Sea, though they range throughout the tropics and are relatively common in the central Pacific. They feed on mid-sized reef fishes and occur singly or in small groups.

Simon Rogerson

Silky shark, *Carcharhinus falciformis*

This shark is an oceanic species that can be identified by its tapered snout, classical shark shape and lack of dorsal fin markings. Silkies grow to 3.3m in length and can be found at any depth, though they seem to enjoy swimming close to the surface between moored boats, perhaps hoping for leftovers from the galley. Left to themselves, they feed on bony fish such as tuna and are usually inquisitive rather than aggressive towards divers. However, there have been cases of silkies threatening divers towards the end of the afternoon – a time when shark behaviour seems to shift up a gear. Silkies often appear at the surface in the Brother Islands and at Daedalus, but don't be tempted to snorkel with them alone: take a buddy, if only for your peace of mind.

Oceanic white-tip shark, *Carcharhinus longimanus*

The most distinctive of the requiem family of sharks, this ocean-going predator is also one of the most beautiful denizens of the offshore islands. It grows to an impressive 3.5m and is easily recognised by its long, rounded pectoral and dorsal fins, each sporting the eponymous white markings. These sharks are as powerful as they are elegant, and have been implicated in several famous attacks on shipwreck survivors. When they encounter divers they seem to be extremely curious, to the extent that they may even bump people with their snouts. Such behaviour is usually a good signal that it is time to leave the water, but full-blooded attacks are rare, as these sharks mostly feed on bony fish. Still, they are very much sharks to respect. The best place to find them is around Elphinstone during October and November.

Simon Rogerson

Blue-spotted stingray, *Taeniura lymma*

You can find these cute little rays throughout the Indo-Pacific, but the reefs and lagoons of the Egyptian Red Sea are the best places to look, to a depth of around 25m. 'Blue-spots' reportedly grow up to a metre in diameter, but most are no more than 30–45cm across. They tend to be nocturnal, resting on sandy areas below coral heads during the day and hunting for worms and small crustaceans at night. When approached by a diver, they may briefly hold their ground before retreating into deeper cover. Though not aggressive, they can inflict a nasty wound with a poisonous spine on the end of the tail, so it is best to allow them plenty of space.

Alexander Mustard

Spotted eagle ray, *Aetobatus narinari*

Some divers regard this ray, which grows to a maximum width of 3m, as even more beautiful than the manta. Whatever your opinion, there's no denying that the spotted eagle ray is a spectacular animal. In the Red Sea, this species generally grows to 2m and is found around coastal and offshore reefs. The hotels with snorkelling access on Ras Nasrani, Sinai, often tell their guests to look out for juvenile eagle rays, which hunt along the sand in very shallow water. When they are mature, they become formidable predators, feeding mostly on crustaceans and molluscs. Perhaps their most distinctive feature is that angular face, a contrast to the expressionless maw of the manta. They tend to be shy of divers, so a good photograph of an eagle ray is something to treasure.

Alexander Mustard

Manta ray, *Manta birostris*

One of the most spectacular of all marine animals, the manta is the king of the ray family, a filter-feeding giant that can reportedly grow to nearly 7m across its broad pectoral fins. Most individuals, however, seem to be more like 3–3.5m. These rays lead a pelagic existence in the open sea, but resident groups have established themselves around certain places, including the Mesharifa area in northern Sudan. Generally, you stand a better chance of finding mantas in the southern Red Sea than in the north, as they favour the plankton-rich shallows of the Dahlak Archipelago rather than the super-clear water of the Sinai Peninsula.

Simon Rogerson

Striped remora, *Echeneis naucrates*

If you see a large animal in the Red Sea, there is every chance that one of these characters will be in attendance. The striped remora is the most common shark sucker in our area, and can be seen on manta rays, grey reef sharks and sea turtles. It grows to a surprisingly large size of 80cm – surely large enough to slow down its host. Remoras are hitchhikers rather than parasites, using a modified dorsal fin to attach themselves to larger animals and feeding on the unwanted detritus of their host's meal. Unlike similar species in the Pacific, they do not leach blood from their host's body.

Giant moray, *Gymnothorax javanicus*

Often unfairly portrayed as a monster, the giant moray only represents a threat to its natural prey and any diver foolish enough to tease it. This impressive eel grows to 2.5m or longer, and is armed with needle-sharp teeth, the better to trap slippery fish. During the day, giant morays rest in cracks in the reef, gazing out at the world with impassive eyes. You can identify them by their size (they are the biggest eels in the Red Sea) and the distinctive yellow/brown head. During the day it is an enjoyable challenge to find them, while on night dives there's nothing more thrilling than watching them foraging on the open reef.

Peppered or Grey moray, Siderea grisea

A pretty and photogenic eel, this species is found only in the Red Sea and the Arabian Sea, from the shallows to a depth of 40m. Much smaller than the giant moray, it grows only to about 40cm long, and groups of smaller individuals can often be found occupying the same crevice. Peppered morays make very rewarding subjects for beginner photographers and occur in good numbers in the Gulf of Aqaba. They feed on small fish, and can be identified by their pale yellow skin and 'pepper' spots.

Yellow margin moray, *Gymnothorax flavimarginatus*

A good eel to find but easily confused with the giant moray (see above). You can identify this species by the more prominent yellow on its skin, along with brown spots and a dark patch close to the gill opening. As with many morays, the saliva of these eels contains chemicals that prevent wounds from clotting and healing, so you are advised not to try their patience.

Regal angelfish, *Pygoplites diacanthus*

You can show non-divers endless photographs of schooling pelagics, but if you really want to get their attention, remember to snap an angelfish. The angels look very similar to butterflyfish; to tell them apart, look for the spine on the angelfish's gill cover. This species is common throughout the central Red Sea, where it feeds on sponges from the surface down to 50m. As with anthias, these fish occur all over the Indo-Pacific, but for some reason look more vibrant in the Red Sea.

Alexander Mustard

Arabian angelfish, *Pomacanthus maculosus*

Growing to 40cm, this is one of the largest and most beautiful of the angelfish. It occurs all over the Red Sea and the Arabian Peninsula, favouring both the prettiest reefs and the drabbest mud flats. Whatever its backdrop, this is a fish that stands out. It is especially abundant in Sudanese waters, and can usually be seen grazing on algae-covered rocks, when it is relatively easy to approach with a camera.

Charles Hood/oceans-image.com

Emperor angelfish, *Pomacanthus imperator*

The attractive markings of this angelfish make it instantly recognisable. This is a common species which can be encountered in all reef environment where it can be seen continually on the move browsing on the reef. Males tend to be larger than females and often have a dark face. Juveniles have very different colouration, with vertical white stripes on a dark blue background, which become circular towards the tail.

Alexander Mustard

Sohal surgeonfish, *Acanthurus sohal*

The large and distinctively patterned surgeonfish is endemic to the Red Sea. A herbivorous species that is highly territorial, it defends its algae gardens from other vegetarian species with sharp scalpels in the base of its tail. This species is very common on shallow reef flats, although divers more commonly see them on shipwrecks, where the large exposed sheets of metal provide ideal growing conditions for their food.

Alexander Mustard

Alexander Mustard

Painted frogfish, *Antennarius pictus*

Also known as the anglerfish, because of its use of a dorsal spine (or 'esca') as a fish lure, this fish is a master of camouflage and extremely hard to find on a crowded reef. Typically, divers come across one by accident when the 'sponge' they are looking at proceeds to surprise them by yawning or blinking! Frogfish are weak swimmers, preferring to push themselves around the reef with modified pectoral fins that resemble elbows. They are the quintessential ambush predators, waiting patiently until a suitable fish happens by, then lunging forward and sucking the unfortunate victim into their distended maw in a movement so fast it can only be recorded with specialist film equipment. Frogfish generally grow to about 25cm.

Alexander Mustard

Crocodilefish, *Cociella crocodiles*

Also known as the carpet flathead, this species resembles a large, flat lizardfish. In fact, it's a member of the Platycephalidae flathead family, ambush predators that lurk on sandy or seagrass bottoms, waiting for small fish to swim within striking range. Crocodilefish are common throughout the Red Sea, but can be hard to find. They grow to a maximum length of 100cm and make excellent photographic subjects, being so confident of their camouflage that they keep perfectly still even when you and your camera are only inches away.

Alexander Mustard

Devil scorpionfish, *Scorpaenopsis diabola*

Even a dive around an area of coral rubble can be rewarding if you keep an eye out for this heroically ugly scorpionfish, which dwells on reef flats, lagoons and coastal reefs. You can recognise it by the round hump that rises from behind the eyes and extends to the middle of the body. If you disturb these fish, they have a habit of raising the underside of their pectoral fins, displaying the colourful markings beneath. This could be a means of advertising their poisonous defences without having to abandon their camouflage. This species grows to 23cm.

Alexander Mustard

Bearded scorpionfish, *Scorpaenopsis barbata*

Though quite common, this ambush predator has especially effective camouflage and represents a real challenge to reef watchers. It grows to 22cm and appears bright red to dull grey under artificial light. By day it rests on crowded areas of reef and is very hard to spot; by night it seems to become more active and conspicuous – or perhaps that's more to do with divers having a torch! Named after the camouflaged fronds that protrude from under its mouth, this fish can inject poison through spines on its dorsal fin. While the poison is not as powerful as that of the infamous stonefish, a sting is sufficiently nasty to cause serious problems. Fortunately these fish are not aggressive and such incidents are rare.

Common lionfish, *Pterois volitans*

Related to the scorpionfish, the lionfish is more fantastic than ugly, though it retains the venomous spines. Growing to 17cm, this is the most common species of lionfish in the Red Sea and an arresting sight for any diver. During the day it mostly hunkers down in coral crevices or in the shadowy protection of shipwrecks, but as the sun starts to set it emerges to hunt small fish in the open. This is the best time to appreciate the surreal form of these fish, as they hover effortlessly with delicate manipulation of their fins. On night dives, some even take advantage of divers' lights to stalk dazed fish. The best place to see them is around Aqaba, Eilat and Nuweiba, where they appear under jetties and hunt close to the surface. If you find a similar-looking species in deeper water, it is likely to be Russell's lionfish, *Pterois russelli*.

Alexander Mustard

Clearfin lionfish, *Pterois radiata*

Found in lagoons and reefs, the clearfin is more afraid of divers than the common lionfish, and has the habit of turning its back as soon as a diver approaches. It then raises its long spines in an unambiguous gesture, inviting the unenlightened to receive a painful education. Still, a very beautiful fish.

Alexander Mustard

Giant squirrelfish, *Sargocentron spiniferum*

The largest of the squirrelfish, this species grows to 45cm and lives at depths of up to 100m. You often find giant squirrelfish in caves or overhangs, or lurking inside shipwrecks. Although they are shy of divers, they can become habituated to your presence, so if you want to observe them closely you should really spend a few minutes pretending not to look, while all the time sneaking gradually nearer. There comes a point when they seem to accept you are not a threat, and then allow you to approach to within a couple of metres to take a photograph. The spine is venomous.

Simon Rogerson

Coral grouper, *Cephalopholis miniata*

Also known as the 'coral trout', this is a signature fish of the Red Sea. It grows up to 100cm in length and favours a variety of coral habitats, to depths of 50–60m. In the northern Red Sea, these fish are a common sight on practically every reef, each individual having its own territory. They occur in different colorations, from deep scarlet to a very pale pink and sometimes nearly white, but always with the blue/green elongated spots. This species and several close relatives are highly photogenic, but they seem suspicious of divers' bubbles. Serious photographers have devoted entire days to gradually insinuating themselves into the coral grouper's trust, staking out cleaning stations and waiting for an amenable individual to pose.

Alexander Mustard

Simon Rogerson

Greasy grouper, *Epinephelus tauvina*

Common in the Red Sea and the Arabian Sea, this grouper is worth getting to know because it allows divers to approach quite close. You find it on reefs at depths of 7–70m, where it can most often be seen sitting on coral, watching out for both predators and prey. It is similar to the marbled grouper, but can be distinguished by its paler scales. Individuals differ in their tolerance of divers, but as with all groupers, this species seems to dislike the sound or vibrations of scuba bubbles.

Alexander Mustard

Giant grouper, *Epinephelus lanceolatus*

The biggest of the groupers, reaching a colossal 2.5m and 300kg, this solitary giant is one of the Red Sea's most timid fish, brooding in coral caves or the most inaccessible reaches of shipwrecks down to 100m. Most individuals flee as soon as they see divers, but a few have been known to stand their ground as long as the diver does not approach head-on. Perhaps the only way to get close to this species is to corner it against a reef – though we strongly advise against harassment – or to attract it with bait, an outlawed practice for most operations. Thus the giant grouper remains a distant spectre on the deeper recesses of the reef, where it feeds mostly on lobsters and crabs.

Alexander Mustard

Longnose hawkfish, *Oxycirrhites typus*

A longstanding favourite of serious macro photographers, the long-nose hawkfish normally occupies the deeper end of the reef, favouring gorgonian fans or black coral as a habitat. Widespread throughout the Indo-Pacific region, it is nevertheless considered a 'find', and dive guides should brief you if they know of a resident pair (they tend to come in twos). Sha'ab Rumi and Sanganeb Reef in Sudan both have good photo opportunities with these skittish fish. If you want to take a photo, it really is a case of settling down and waiting until they swim onto a portion of coral from where you can get a clear shot. Do not be tempted to harass or prod them into position, as they will invariably disappear into the deepest folds of the coral. Longnose hawkfish feed on small crustaceans.

Alexander Mustard

Bigeye trevally, *Caranx sexfasciatus*

A Red Sea reef only enters the upper echelons of dive sites when it is sufficiently productive to attract a school of bigeye trevally. This size-able trevally grows to about 80cm and can be found in channels, on dropoffs and along reef promontories. Often referred to by dive guides by the generic tag 'jacks', you can find these fish at classic sites such as Ras Mohammad and Sha'ab Rumi. Schools move from reef to reef, hunting for small fishes and forming some of the most impressive aggregations in the Red Sea. In certain currents, these form into the classic spiral formation, one of the Red Sea's most dramatic sights. When mating, the schools break down into pairs and the males' scales turn black.

Goldbody trevally, *Carangoides bajad*

Of the 140 species of trevally, the goldbody is possibly the most beautiful. Streamlined, pelagic swimmers, these fish can be seen in small groups near coral walls and other exposed spots. They mostly appear in a dazzling gold phase, but have also been observed in silver with gold spots. They frequently show an interest in divers, swimming close for a brief inspection; but they don't hang around, so you have to be prepared to take your photograph quickly and get it right first time. The Straits of Tiran seem to be a hotspot for this species.

Alexander Mustard

Giant trevally, *Caranx ignobilis*

If you want to see some spectacular reef predation, keep an eye on this whopping trevally, which grows to 1.7m and can appear in any Red Sea habitat to strike terror into the hearts of the local fish. The giant trevally is the bully of the reef, threatened only by the biggest groupers and sharks. It is fast, hungry and utterly determined to feed on smaller fishes, even if that means moving into shallow water. The appearance of a school seems to create a completely different atmosphere on a reef: gobies retreat into their holes and anthias cling to the protection of the coral. The trevally move over the reef, looking out for a straggler, then burst into action, streaming over the coral like heat-seeking missiles as they close in on their prey. Sometimes, they move so quickly that they produce a sound like thunder.

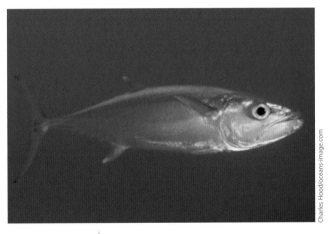
Alexander Mustard

Dogtooth tuna, *Gymnosarda unicolor*

While it is not regarded as the finest of the Red Sea's eating fish (that unwelcome honour goes to the yellowfin tuna, which is rare in these waters), the dogtooth is a formidable predator, growing to 2m. The adults are solitary, patrolling the deeper portions of high-energy reefs close to deep water. You're more likely to see juveniles, which develop in shallow reef flats and coastal areas. They prey on reef grazers and can move with fierce speed. While it is true to say that dogtooth tuna are unafraid of divers, they do not appear to be curious either, so getting close to an adult can prove challenging.

Charles Hood/oceans-image.com

Red Sea garden eel, *Gorgasia sillneri*

Although garden eels can be found all over the world, this species – which grows up to 38cm – is endemic to the Red Sea. It lives in colonies of hundreds, each individual occupying a specially constructed hole from where it rises into the current to feed on passing plankton. The sandy areas of coastal Sinai are prime garden eel habitat. Divers can usually see the eels from about 10m away, but they have a habit of lowering themselves into their burrows as you approach, so by the time you actually reach the 'garden' it looks just like any other featureless sand bed. The only reliable way to photograph garden eels is by using a remote control camera release. Videographers sometimes set up their cameras and leave them recording inside the colony, while they retreat and hope the eels overcome their natural shyness.

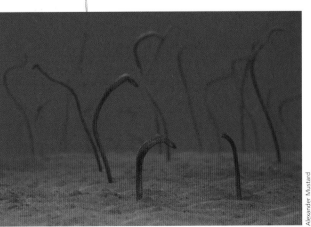
Alexander Mustard

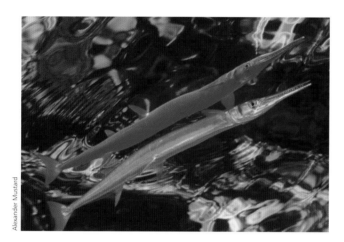

Alexander Mustard

Lizardfish, *Saurida nebulosa*

Named for their saurian heads, lizardfish are diminutive but effective predators, lying still until a small shrimp or fish blunders within striking distance. Then they strike with a rapid darting movement, bursting into action before settling down just as quickly to await the next victim. Lizardfish often occupy sand or rubble areas where photographers can hunker down and approach them without fear of damaging any coral. The trick is to make yourself comfortable a good distance away from the fish, get down low and approach slowly, controlling your breathing and taking a photograph when you can fill the frame with that impressive head. This species grows to 20cm.

Alexander Mustard

Red Sea needlefish, *Tylosurus choram*

If your liveaboard is moored close to a reef overnight, take a torch and look down into the dark water. Chances are a few of these super-streamlined surface hunters will be congregating not far from your vessel, hoping to catch a small fish attracted by the ship's lights. Common throughout the Indo-Pacific, they grow to around 80cm and use the surface reflections for camouflage. They can swim at incredible speed, and have been implicated in several bizarre injuries in which their armoured snouts have pierced a person's flesh, like a living bullet. Thankfully, such accidents are rare, and this species poses no threat to divers. Watch out for large aggregations above habilis and other reef systems.

Alexander Mustard

Striped eel catfish, *Plotosus lineatus*

They may appear vaguely comical when bundling over the reef in those tight little schools, but do not be tempted to touch striped eel catfish. The dorsal and pectoral spines can inject a nasty toxin, and are themselves barbed and difficult to remove. The sting is apparently very painful, and must be treated in the same way as that of a stonefish or scorpionfish, breaking up the proteins by plunging the affected area into hot water (as hot as the victim can stand). Adults grow to 25cm, but the schools are composed of juveniles. They occur just about anywhere in the Red Sea.

Common bigeye, *Priacanthus hamrur*

An unusual-looking reef fish, the bigeye can be found in caves, overhangs and wrecks all over the Red Sea. Although it is shy by nature, it is sufficiently confident to allow divers to approach to within a few feet. Stay in the vicinity for a few minutes and the fish will get used to you, but you will not get close if you steam in straight away. These fish grow to around 35cm and feed on small crustaceans. An eye-catching bright scarlet, they sometimes congregate in photogenic formations.

Alexander Mustard

Black-spotted sweetlips, *Plectorhinchus gaterinus*

There are about 120 species of sweetlips, reef fish that feed by night on sand-dwelling fish and crustaceans. This colourful species is the most common in the Red Sea and is a favourite with divers, as it forms into synchronised, tightly packed schools. The fish seem confident in their schools and can be approached quite closely, but any erratic movements can alarm the school into breaking up and retreating. Sweetlips seem to enjoy the services of cleaner wrasse, and it is possible to get good close-up photographs of them at cleaning stations.

Charles Hood/oceans-image.com

Blue-striped snapper, *Lutjanus kasmira*

The snappers are among the most colourful of the schooling fish, and the blue-striped snapper is the most abundant species in the Red Sea. It clusters in schools of 40–50, often accompanied by unrelated species, which for some reason choose to join the security of the snapper shoal. Blue-striped snappers grow to 35cm and are found at 8–30m. They are a typical feature of the Fury Shoal reefs in Egypt.

Simon Rogerson

Black snapper, *Macolor niger*

Growing to 60cm, the black snapper is often found in aggregations in the upper levels of coral walls and channels. This species, also known as black-and-white snapper, has an annoying knack of dispersing from its schools at the approach of a diver, so you need to be lucky to get a good photograph. Even with a powerful flashgun, it tends only to show up as dull grey in photographs.

Alexander Mustard

Bigeye emperor, *Monotaxis grandoculis*

A very common fish that you are likely to encounter on most northern Red Sea dives, the bigeye emperor grows to about 40cm. It occurs both singly and in aggregations during the day, and is often seen above 'garden' style reefs where there is a sandy bottom. This appealing fish has an inquisitive nature and sometimes approaches divers closely, albeit briefly. You find bigeye emperors at depths of up to 50m.

Alexander Mustard

Alexander Mustard

Longfin batfish, *Platax teira*

With their expressive face and bold temperament, batfish are among the most popular fish in the Red Sea. This and a similar species, *Platax orbicularis*, are seen in pairs or schools. The classic batfish dive is Ras Mohammed, where large schools can be seen in the summer months at 5–50m. This species eats jellyfish and, in common with the hawksbill turtle, can be attracted to large camera domes in the mistaken belief that it has found a meal. It grows to 50cm, and is also common around shipwrecks.

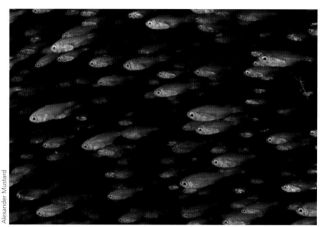

Alexander Mustard

Yellow sweeper or glassfish, *Parapriacanthus ransonneti*

A real treat for the cavern diver or wreck explorer, yellow sweepers form dense schools, which shift hypnotically as the fish respond to the subtle rhythms of their environment. Each is no bigger than 8cm, but they move as one, with a sinuous beauty that rivals that of any big animal. Some divers would happily watch them until they drain. The alternative name of 'glassfish' reflects the fact that these fish seem to have light organs in their stomachs, and look especially beautiful under torchlight or with flash photography. The yacht wreck at Abu Galawa has a fine school, which appears to have taken up permanent residence.

Charles Hood/oceans-image.com

Yellowfin goatfish, *Mulloides vancolensis*

There is something endearing about the slightly idiotic look of the goatfish, a sand feeder that sometimes mingles with sweetlips and snapper schools. The yellowfin is the most common species in the Red Sea: if you see a big school of yellow fish with barbels and big eyes, the chances are that it's this species. It grows to 40cm and is found throughout the Red Sea to a maximum depth of 25m. If you want to see these fish in action, watch the sand during a night dive: they use those barbels to forage for benthic animals.

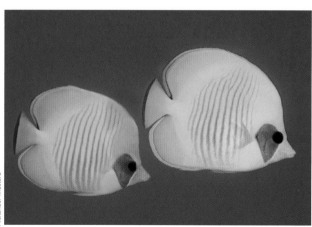

Alexander Mustard

Masked butterflyfish, *Chaetodon semilarvatus*

If you haven't seen any of these brightly coloured fish during your time in the Red Sea, you need to book another week! Growing to 22cm and commonly found from the reef top to 25m, the masked butterflyfish can be seen swimming delicately between coral heads, feeding on the soft polyps and hydroids. There is something in the flitting movements of these fish that recalls the insect after which they are named. They are often encountered in pairs, but are also seen in eye-catching aggregations that are easier to approach than individuals. At least 20 other butterflyfish species occur in the Red Sea.

Red Sea bannerfish, *Heniochus intermedius*

Another species of butterflyfish, this endemic species often swims in schools, feeding on plankton in its familiar territory. When resting, bannerfish seek shelter under table coral, so they are understandably common in areas rich in hard coral, such as the St John's system in southern Egypt or Sha'ab Suedi in Sudan. Though photogenic, these fish have a habit of swimming close to coral, so it is hard to capture their colours against a blue background.

Red Sea anemonefish, *Amphiprion bicinctus*

Possibly the Red Sea's most popular fish. Growing to 10cm, it lives in pairs or groups, almost always in symbiosis with a sea anemone. The dominant adults are famously territorial, always staying close to their anemone and fearlessly fending off intruders. The fish keep the anemone clean and defend it from some predators, while receiving protection and shelter within the stinging tentacles. They are immune from harm, as they are covered in a mucus which renders them 'invisible' to the stinging cells of the anemone. The largest fish in a group is always the female; if she dies, the dominant male will change sex and one of the smaller fish will grow to take his place. Although there are around 30 species of anemonefish in the Indo-Pacific, this is the only one found in the Red Sea.

Three-spot damselfish, *Dascyllus trimaculatus*

While you're looking at the anemonefish, you may see a few of these low-key characters sharing a nearby anemone. Adults grow to 8cm and can be found anywhere from the surface down to 40m on any coral reef or sand flat. Although juveniles are often associated with anemones, this species can utilise a wide variety of sheltered environments, including wreckage and litter.

Humbug damselfish, *Dascyllus aruanus*

This abundant damsel is commonly seen in shallow coral garden-type environments, where it uses various species of Acropora coral to shelter from predators. As you approach the coral head, you will see the little fish (no longer than 6cm) flitting up into the current, feeding on plankton. But as you approach, they move closer to the coral and eventually hide inside its 'fingers'. They can be found from the shallows down to 25m.

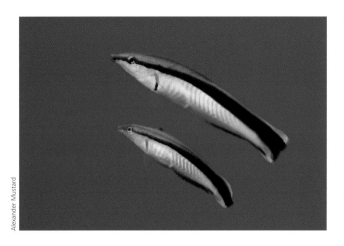

Alexander Mustard

Sergeant major fish, *Abudefduf vaigiensis*

A well-known algae-feeder, the sergeant major is usually associated with the shallowest portions of the reef, where it occurs in schools of up to 50. This species used to be one of the most popular photo subjects, possibly because in the old days it was one of the species most commonly encountered at fish feeds. It derives its common name from the prominent triple stripe pattern across its body.

Alexander Mustard

Common cleaner wrasse, *Labroids bicolour*

The most abundant of the Red Sea's cleaner fish, this industrious character is the workhorse of the cleaning station. Advertised by their striped bodies, small colonies occupy areas of reef where they are visited by a procession of 'client' fish seeking to have parasites removed from their skin. Cleaner wrasse swim with wriggling and swooping gestures, which possibly help other fish to identify them. Often, a fish in need of a clean will approach the station and come to a dead halt, angling its body to 45° as if to signal a truce in the normal 'predator–prey' relationship between large and small fish. With so many fish in need of skincare, the cleaner wrasse is an important figure in reef circles.

Alexander Mustard

Bumphead parrotfish, *Bolbometopon muricatum*

A signature fish of southern Egypt and Sudan, this is the largest of the parrotfish, growing to 1.5m. Due to its size, it can only really be confused with the Napoleon wrasse. The way to tell the two species apart is to look for the trademark beak of the parrotfish, a pair of fused teeth capable of chomping through rock coral. Parrotfish can be found sleeping in caves during the night, swimming on their own during the day or in large schools. With their bullish foreheads and grazing lifestyle, a lot of divers think of them as reef buffalo – an image reinforced by the males' habit of knocking heads during challenges for control of a harem. Bumphead parrotfish are normally shy towards divers, but it is possible to get close to them at Sanganeb and Sha'ab Rumi in Sudan.

Charles Hood/oceans-image.com

Blackfin barracuda, *Sphyraena qenie*

A highlight of any dive is to run into a school of these fish, the most common species of barracuda in the Red Sea. Typically encountered on the exposed northern tips of offshore reefs, they gather in schools that can number anything from 15 to 500 or more. These are among the largest, most dense schools in the Red Sea, a treat for any diver and a challenge for underwater photographers. You can identify this species from the dark vertical stripes along its flanks and the black marking on the trailing edge of the tail fin. Barracuda can be timid when faced with divers, but become easier to approach as they get used to your presence.

Great barracuda, *Sphyraena barracuda*

Growing to 2m in length and armed with a fearsome array of teeth, the great barracuda is sometimes incorrectly characterised as a threat to people. The misunderstanding probably stems from its fearsome countenance, coupled with an insouciant attitude towards divers. This is a large, confident fish, aware of its own speed and ability to see off all but the biggest predators. Occasional stories of attacks come from Florida, where this and other fish species have been known to bite people wearing bright jewellery, which in low visibility they mistake for baitfish.

Malcom Nobbs

Bluebelly blenny, *Alloblennius pictus*

At the smaller end of the fish scale, the bluebelly blenny is an example of the Red Sea's exoticism in miniature. Growing to just 4cm, it lives in coral or rock holes, emerging only to feed and breed. The male uses his blue belly to display in courtship dances. Divers need to control their breathing carefully to avoid spooking these fish when photographing them at close quarters. To get a good image, you'll need a specialist macro lens.

Charles Hood/oceans-image.com

Unicornfish, *Naso unicornis*

A ubiquitous figure on many reefs, this fish grows to 70cm and can be found from the reef top down to 60m. A relative of the surgeonfish, it feeds on algae and sand-dwelling animals, and can often be seen frantically foraging at night. You can identify it by its pale green colour and protruding spine, which is shorter than that of the similar long-nose unicornfish, *Naso brevirostris*. Juveniles lack the 'horn'.

Alexander Mustard

Redtooth triggerfish, *Odonus niger*

A common and numerous fish, this species is often seen in large schools, particularly in Sudanese and Eritrean waters. The fish are actually dark blue or purple, the scientific name being derived from a specimen that had been removed from the water and lost its colour, and the two protruding fangs have a reddish appearance. Some divers know this species colloquially as the 'bad viz' fish, as large aggregations have a habit of churning up silt while feeding on benthic animals and algae. They can be found at most depths, but are most common at around 10–15m.

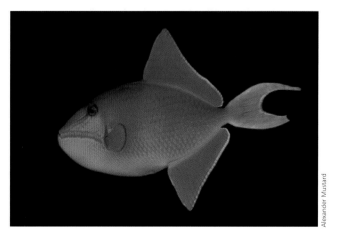

Alexander Mustard

Charles Hood/oceans-image.com

Titan triggerfish, *Balistoides viridescens*

Although it is one of the more colourful reef fish, the titan triggerfish is not popular with divers. This is due to its powerful protective instincts when defending a nest of eggs during breeding season. This fish usually grows up to 75cm, but the authors are aware of a few 'super-triggers', which definitely exceed 1m in length. The fish's aggression is legendary: it is prepared to attack animals far larger than itself, though other fish often help themselves to the eggs while the titan is busy chasing something. Divers are frequently assaulted by triggerfish, which have been known to bite fins and ram into people's heads with their armoured mouths. To escape, fin quickly away – but not upwards, as the titan's territory is vertical and it will continue to chase you.

Charles Hood/oceans-image.com

Scribbled filefish, *Aluterus scriptus*

Growing to 90cm, these shy fish are common throughout the tropics. With their psychedelic body patterns, they are eminently photogenic, but you need to be lucky to get close to them, or find them when they are sleeping on the reef at night. Filefish as a group derive their name from the roughness of their scales, which stick up like tiny spines. They can be found down to 60m.

Alexander Mustard

Masked pufferfish, *Arothron diadematus*

An endemic species that is synonymous with Red Sea diving, you are liable to come across the masked puffer in practically any environment, to a maximum depth of 35m. Like all pufferfish, it can inflate itself with water in order to appear more threatening to predators. Uninflated, it is about 30cm long. The skin is impregnated with a powerful tetrodotoxin, making it an unattractive option for predators. On rare occasions, this pufferfish can be seen in mass aggregations associated with breeding behaviour.

Malcolm Nobbs

Dugong, *Dugong dugon*

One of the most surprising animals to appear in the Red Sea, the dugong is a sea cow, a large mammal of the order Sirenia. Seldom seen by divers, about 4,000 are thought to live in the Red Sea, mostly around the shallow seagrass beds of Sudan, southern Egypt and the Dahlak archipelago. These mammals grow to 3m in length and weigh up to 250kg, bulking up on 40kg of sea grass a day. Sometimes, if you are moored in a shallow area, you can see them feeding intently in the shallows. They will even tolerate the presence of divers, though in general they are more timid than their cousins, the famous manatees of Florida. Several dugongs live in coastal areas close to Port Galib and Marsa Alam in Egypt.

Spinner dolphin, *Stenella longirostris*

One of the most pleasing aspects of a Red Sea trip is the possibility of your boat being escorted by spinner dolphins, which ride the bow waves and throw themselves acrobatically into the air. Spinners live in large pods in fairly sheltered areas, but venture out into the open sea to hunt fish. Sha'ab Samadai in southern Egypt is one of the best places to find them, though access to the reef is now strictly controlled. The best strategy for an encounter is simply to snorkel in the water and hope the dolphins will decide to approach you. They grow to about 1.8m in length.

Bottlenose dolphin, *Tursiops truncates*

An extremely successful species, the bottlenose dolphin is found as far north as the Firth of Forth in Scotland. The Red Sea's bottlenose dolphins are slightly smaller than their cold-water cousins, growing to a maximum of 2.4m and feeding on a variety of fish and crustaceans. They are often seen in Egyptian waters, though they do seem to have an aversion to underwater flashguns, so natural light photography is advisable. Dolphins are normally well disposed towards people, and there is anecdotal evidence that this species has defended swimmers from aggressive sharks in the Red Sea. They are sociable animals and live in pods, though there have been well-documented cases of 'solo' dolphins surviving on their own.

Green turtle, *Chelonia mydas*

These big reptiles are the genial (if occasionally grumpy) old men of the Red Sea. They live almost permanently at sea, except for a brief time when the females haul onto beaches in order to lay batches of eggs into meticulously excavated holes. Green turtles are widely distributed throughout the Red Sea, but you tend to find more of them in the north. Mature adults are occasionally eaten by passing tiger sharks, but populations seem to be steady. This species is slightly larger than the hawksbill, and has just one pair of scales between its eyes. It feeds on jellyfish, sponges and tunicates, and is easy to observe while feasting on the reef. It remains to be seen how the mass shoreline development of southern Egypt will affect turtle nesting in future.

Hawksbill turtle, *Eretmochelys imbricata*

The hawksbill is the most common turtle species in the Red Sea and can be differentiated from the green turtle by having two pairs of scales between its eyes. It is also rather smaller. If you run into a turtle at one of Egypt's offshore islands, the likelihood is that it is a hawksbill. One individual at Little Brother has a habit of approaching the dome ports of large camera systems head-on, in the myopic delusion that the shiny dome is a jellyfish. Never be tempted to ride on a sea turtle: remember that they, too, have to surface periodically, so being held down is a traumatic experience.

Charles Hood/oceans-image.com

Crown-of-thorns starfish, *Acanthaster planci*

A voracious feeder that feeds on hard coral, this starfish inverts its stomach to digest the polyps. Measuring up to 60cm in diameter and armed with stinging spines, it is a formidable invertebrate. Though by no means common in the Red Sea, there are occasional explosions in the population, which appear in great concentrations and can kill off large swathes of hard coral. In all likelihood, this is a purely natural phenomenon, and may benefit the long-term health of the reef. In the short term, a crown-of-thorns 'plague' can cause panic among dive operators, who feel they are losing an asset. During such an infestation in 1999, dive guides in Sinai were sent off on killing missions and burned thousands of starfish on the beaches.

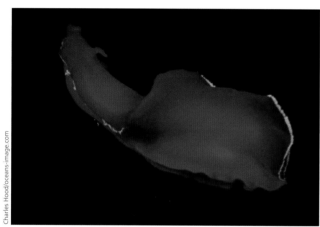

Charles Hood/oceans-image.com

Spanish dancer, *Hexabranchus sanguineus*

One of the largest and most spectacular of the nudibranchs, or sea slugs, the Spanish dancer is the ultimate find on a Red Sea night dive. Growing to 40cm and more, it appears bright scarlet under torchlight and can be found foraging on reef rubble. The name derives from its ability to swim by undulating its body and 'flying' to more productive patches of reef, where it feeds on sponges. Look closely at the feather-like external gills, and you may find a pair of emperor partner shrimps, *Periclimenes imperator*.

Charles Hood/oceans-image.com

Common red octopus, *Octopus cyaneus*

Also known as the big red octopus, this is an intelligent but reclusive animal. By day, it hides in reef crevices (the lair's entrance is strewn with empty shells), all the while keeping an eye on the reef. If it spots a diver looking at it directly, it retreats immediately back into the hole and will not re-emerge until the 'danger' has passed. Growing to 1.2m, this octopus is a night hunter; the best time to observe one is while it is preoccupied hunting or mating on the reef.

Charles Hood/oceans-image.com

Bigfin reef squid, *Sepioteuthis lessoniana*

Another shy cephalopod, this squid is common throughout the Indo-Pacific. You can find it anywhere from seagrass fields to lagoon reefs, where it hovers above the coral, looking to catch a crustacean or fish with its two long hunting tentacles. As with the cuttlefish, it has an ability to change colour and patterns by manipulating millions of tiny pigment cells on its skin. Scientists are only beginning to decipher the thousands of pattern combinations, but it is universally acknowledged that these are intelligent animals, capable of complex communication. They grow to about 60cm, including mantle and tentacles.

Hooded cuttlefish, *Sepia prashadi*

This cuttlefish grows to about 15cm and is found over seagrass beds, where it preys on small fish. It's easy to tell cuttlefish apart from octopus or squid: they are much more confident and curious with divers, and their bulbous body shape is defined by the flat, oval cuttlebone. When threatened, they raise their long tentacles in a defensive posture and flash bold colours to signal their displeasure.

Alexander Mustard

Christmas tree worm, *Spirobranchus giganteus*

One of the first tricks a dive guide shows his charges will involve waving his hand close to a colony of these coral dwelling worms, which feed by raising a pair of spiral fans into the water and trapping plankton. When so threatened, each worm immediately retracts its delicate tentacles into its tube-shaped home, and then snaps shut the lid. This species is found on stony corals, and occurs in a variety of colours.

Charles Hood/oceans-image.com

Magnificent sea anemone, *Heteractis magnifica*

The most beautiful of the anemones occupied by the Red Sea anemonefish, this species is found on reef dropoffs and areas exposed to current. The combination of its neon green tentacles and bright red body make it a popular photo subject, particularly in the late afternoon, when the anemone contracts into a ball, exposing its colourful body. Large colonies may form, the most famous of which is Anemone City on Ras Mohammed.

Alexander Mustard

PHOTOGRAPHY

WE ARE LIVING IN THE DIGITAL AGE, AND UNDERWATER PHOTOGRAPHY IS NO LONGER THE PRESERVE OF A SELECT FEW. WHETHER YOU ARE USING A COMPACT CAMERA IN A PLASTIC BOX OR THE LATEST STATE-OF-THE-ART PROFESSIONAL MODEL, A FEW SIMPLE GUIDELINES CAN MAKE A BIG DIFFERENCE TO YOUR RED SEA PHOTOGRAPHY. FOLLOW THESE STEPS AND GET AHEAD OF THE OTHER SNAPPERS.

▶ Buoyancy skills must be fine-honed before any photography can be attempted.
(Charles Hood/oceans-image.com)

1. MASTER YOUR BUOYANCY CONTROL

You may be the best photographer in the world, but if you can't dive properly, you can't take decent underwater pictures. To capture complex scenery and work closely with wild animals, you need to be able to control the way you move through the water. You, the diver, are the most important element in the whole equation. Indeed, the basic skills of buoyancy control should not even be something you have to think about: they should come naturally and instinctively, allowing you the freedom to concentrate on your subject.

When are you ready to take underwater photographs? As a general rule, it's best to leave your camera at home until you have successfully completed your first diving course, plus at least five to ten open water dives. You need to familiarise yourself with the marine environment, its hazards and your own safety drills. Then, when you feel you are ready to dive without relying on your hands to steady yourself, carry out an experimental dive with an empty housing (most compact cameras come with their own plastic cases). This is an opportunity to find out whether the housing is indeed leak-proof and also whether you have the skill to handle it safely.

"Prepare your camera system well in advance - preferably the night before the dive, ensure all batteries are charged and take a few test exposures to ensure everything is working."

2. GET TO GRIPS WITH YOUR CAMERA

Just as your buoyancy control has to be an automatic skill, so your mastery of the camera should be instinctive and well informed. Whether you are using a relatively cheap compact or the latest digital single lens reflex, you should read the instructions until you understand them, then use the camera until you can make rapid decisions about which setting to utilise in any given situation. You should not be using your camera for the first time when you take it underwater: take days or even weeks of 'dry' use to familiarise yourself with its functions.

Every modern camera has complex specifications that can befuddle the first time user. It is much easier to work through these at home in front of the instruction booklet than on a swaying boat under the blinding sunlight of the Red Sea. Ultimately, when you are swimming towards the big grouper at the cleaning station, you need to know that the camera will do what is necessary to capture the best possible photograph. Once you're in position, often with a very brief window of opportunity, you should not be struggling to locate the 'on' button.

3. 'GET IN CLOSE, SHOOT UPWARDS'

These are the fundamental rules of underwater photography, and they are as true today as they were in 1949 when Hans Hass first picked up a camera and went swimming with manta rays off the coast of Sudan. All water contains suspended particles, no matter how clear it may appear, and the more space you allow between your camera and the subject, the more these particles reduce the clarity and definition of the photograph. By moving closer to a subject, you reduce the amount of particles and so achieve a clearer image. Unless you are taking a big scenic photograph in natural light, you should never really be further than two metres from your subject.

On coral reefs, natural light comes from above and the seabed is a jumbled clutter. To make your subject stand out against that beautiful blue background, you need to position yourself so that you can angle the camera upwards at your subject. If you shoot downwards, the subject will more often than not be lost amid the clutter. Then you lose the benefit of the blue background, which helps to put your image in an 'underwater' context. You should meter your camera for the blue background and then, if possible, use a modicum of artificial light (see below) to highlight the foreground subject.

4. GET SNEAKY

In underwater photography, as in so much else in life, sneakiness is a virtue. Coral reef photography is really not that dissimilar to hunting. You have to choose a target, and then adopt an approach that will allow you close enough to capture it. Your approach should be based on knowledge of the animal, its likely behaviour and the environment it inhabits. This is all part of the challenge of underwater photography: you have to marry your technical knowledge with your diving ability, then you need to apply both skills in the pursuit of creatures that can be both fast moving and shy.

There are plenty of strategies for getting close to the animals you will find in the Red Sea, though each individual has its own personality and tolerance of divers.

The species identification chapter (see page 292–311) has key information on most of the creatures you are likely to encounter and the way in which they react to divers. Ultimately, the goal is to convince your subject that you do not pose a threat: only then will it start to behave naturally in front of your camera.

5. CHOOSE THE RIGHT SUBJECT

Different cameras have different capabilities, and they all have limitations when used underwater. When you first explore the Red Sea, you will see great vistas of coral and fish and you could be forgiven for being awe-struck. The natural reaction for anyone with a camera is to point it at a pretty scene and hope the camera sees it the same way as your eyes. This approach seldom works. Cameras and lenses are tools designed for specific jobs; ask them to do something vague and you get a vague result. More to the point, no camera lens can match the scope of human vision, so you have to reconcile yourself to the limitations of whatever system you are using.

Experiment with your camera, whichever model you choose, and quantify its strengths and weaknesses. For instance, the less expensive compact cameras can pro-

"Concentrate on one subject, flitting from close-up to wide angle for instance yield poor images."

▼ Only venture this close to the reef if you are truly able to control your movements.

Charles Hood/oceans-image.com

► External flashguns prevent flash from illuminating particles in front of the lens.

(Charles Hood/oceans-image.com)

"Don't chase. Creatures will simply swim away. Back-off and most marine critters curiosity will get the better of them."

▼ This photographer is using a wide-angle attachment to allow her to capture a scene without going too far back

(Charles Hood/oceans-image.com)

duce crisp photographs of a coral head or an eel from a distance of a metre or less, but their zoom lenses are seldom up to the job of capturing a large area of reef or shipwreck. Similarly, if you are taking photographs with the macro setting, you must first establish how close you can have the camera to the subject. Start off with modest subjects and then move forward to test the scope of your system.

6. USE A WIDE-ANGLE ATTACHMENT

Whether you are using a digital compact in a housing, or an underwater film camera, you soon begin to appreciate the advantages of using a wide-angle lens. Such lenses allow you to get closer to the scene you are photographing without simply zoning in on a small area. The problem is that most compact cameras are not really designed for advanced underwater use – the attached lenses on such cameras are normally no wider than around 5–6mm (equivalent to 24–35mm on a 35mm film camera), whereas you really need something like the equivalent of a 20mm wide angle or 16mm fisheye lens to capture underwater vistas.

To achieve this, you need to invest in a specialist piece of kit, a supplementary lens that clips to the outside of your housing and allows you to photograph big scenes without having to back off so far that the image loses clarity (remember rule three!). Such lenses are available at specialist underwater photography outlets; make sure you buy a model that is compatible with your camera and that it will attach to the housing. One disadvantage of using wide-angle lenses is that they sometimes open up such a large area that you find fellow divers straying into the frame. There's no point in becoming impatient (after all, they have as much right to be there as you), so either think of another way to frame your image, or perhaps use the divers to enhance the finished picture. Think of them as unpaid models.

7. USE AN EXTERNAL FLASHGUN

Underwater photography becomes more complex with the introduction of external flashes, but these can really add depth to your photography. Purpose-made underwater flashes (also called 'guns' or 'strobes') are attached to the camera by an arm that can be adjusted to aim the direction of the flash. The trick is to arrange the flash so that it lights your subject from an angle above and to one side of the camera. Above all, you should not allow it to fall on any area between your lens and the subject, as it will light up particles in the water, obscuring your image with reflected specks of light known as 'backscatter'.

You need to experiment with your camera to achieve images in which the flash lights the subject rather than the plankton in front of it. The preview on digital cameras can help, but you can only really assess the quality of an image when it has been opened on a sizeable screen. When you position your flashgun, try to aim slightly to one side of your target, as the beam will be broader than you imagine. Many compact cameras come with automatic flash settings that can be imitated by external flashes, but the best approach is to experiment with manual settings, as this allows for greater precision. There is an alternative to using flash: in shallow water and with good light, it is possible to use red filters that highlight subjects as well as, if not better than, artificial light. Such filters are inexpensive and can be bought online or in specialist underwater photographic outlets.

8. USE AN SLR SYSTEM

Almost all the images you see in diving magazines (and definitely all the ones in this book) have been taken by what is known as a single lens reflex (SLR) camera. Professionals and serious amateurs favour these cam-

eras because they produce images of high quality and allow for a range of specialist, high-quality lenses to be used for different functions. Digital SLR systems became instantly popular with serious underwater photographers because of the benefit of instant feedback on the LCD screen, in addition to their enhanced ability to perform well in low light conditions. Many leading underwater photographers have said that their new digital systems have quickly paid for themselves, because they no longer have to spend so much money on films in order to obtain good results. The complexity of underwater photography produces an exceptionally high error rate, but on digital we do not have to pay for all our mistakes! Nonetheless, a few traditional snappers still enjoy using film cameras.

SLRs afford underwater photographers freedom in choosing how to approach a dive, and offer picture quality and functionality beyond that of any compact camera. But they can be limiting at the same time. While there is little doubt that they help photographers achieve great shots, the cameras and their housings are both expensive and bulky. They can thus be awkward to handle in a current and more prone to damage in transit. Invariably, those who go down the route of buying an SLR camera system tend to allow photographic concerns to dictate their diving. If you do not want the fuss of a large camera system (serious photographers also use twin external flashguns with their bulky housings), do not despair. It has been said that top-end digital compacts can achieve 90 per cent of the things you can do underwater with an SLR – as long as you know which buttons to press.

9. BREAK THE RULES!

Being a good underwater photographer is an achievement to be proud of, but being an original one is rare indeed. The photographers who really stand out are the ones who have the ability to look at a scene and 'see' a photograph that puts it in a unique context. Underwater photographers have freedoms land photographers can scarcely imagine. With a flick of a fin, we can move around a subject in three dimensions, photographing it from every conceivable angle as we float in a liquid world.

As a consequence, the rules in this chapter – with the firm exceptions of 1, 3 and 10 – are all there for the breaking. Sure, you can obtain great images by understanding the basic principles of underwater photography. But in the final analysis, a good picture is a good picture, and if you can make one while breaking a rule, the chances are you will have something original in your viewfinder. It's the same with writing or painting, or indeed any art form: you learn the basics as part of the learning curve, and in doing so you gain an understanding of how and when you can depart from them. The people who have truly made a mark in underwater photography are those with the confidence to break the rules. In doing so, they create a vision that is uniquely theirs.

10. THE ONE RULE YOU CANNOT BREAK

No matter what sort of photographer you are, your first responsibility is to your subject. This holds especially true with underwater photography, in which we are privileged guests in a fragile environment. Accordingly, the welfare of the wildlife and its environment should be your paramount concern. If you cannot take a photograph without touching live coral, do not take the photograph. If by taking a photograph you could injure a creature, move on and look for a different opportunity.

Unfortunately, the dynamics of underwater photography can lead to coral damage if photographers lose sight of this priority. Sometimes, when approaching close and trying to get beneath a subject, it is all too easy to kick or otherwise damage coral. You need a realistic understanding of your own skill levels, and you need to know when the best course of action is to back off and find a different way to approach your subject. Respect wildlife: do not, for instance, harass puffer fish in order to make them 'inflate'; do not repeatedly blast sensitive creatures such as turtles with flash photography; and do not encourage people to manhandle any marine animals. It's mostly just common sense. Improve your buoyancy and general diving skills, and you will find yourself getting closer to the amazing animals of the Red Sea. Inflict damage in the pursuit of a picture and you will not be made to feel welcome.

"Remaining in one location for several dives will allow you to get better images, you will get to know what's down there and how it will be lit prior to diving."

◀ This photographer is using a full SLR system with twin flashguns – a professional quality camera configuration.
(Charles Hood/oceans-image.com)

Net

Hyper Crystal LCD

Catch

Olympus DSLRs are the only ones to offer full live view on the LCD so you can see clearly exactly what you are trying to catch. Olympus cameras and underwater housings – comprehensive, affordable, innovative. At Cameras Underwater and other Olympus specialists. For your nearest Olympus underwater specialist call 0800 072 0070 or visit www.olympus.co.uk

OLYMPUS

Accept No Limits

VIDEOGRAPHY

AS THE POPULARITY OF UNDERWATER PHOTOGRAPHY INCREASES, MORE DIVERS ARE TURNING TO VIDEO AS THE NEXT STEP. WITH SUPERIOR CAMERAS AND HOUSINGS NOW AVAILABLE, THE CHALLENGE IS TO MAKE HOME MOVIES THAT PEOPLE WILL WANT TO WATCH.

John McIntyre

CHOOSING THE GEAR

Underwater video has undergone a revolution, fuelled by the startling progress of digital technology. This revolution has brought down the price of cameras and inspired the growth of an industry catering for everyone from the broadcast professional to the once-in-a-while holidaymaker. Supply and demand have led to a multi-million dollar business in housings and lighting systems. Add to this the plethora of computer editing and DVD authoring systems, which allow users to turn their holiday video into an entertaining narrative, and you have the ability to deliver a finished piece of television in the comfort of your own home.

If we start with the camera, the most significant development has been the introduction of the three-chip system – or 3CCD ('Charge Coupled Device'). Prior to this, there was the clunky VHS or latterly Hi-8, which wasn't bad – though if you look today at the pictures recorded in this way, you'll wince. Film has never really gone away and is still the preferred choice of Hollywood filmmakers. If anything, the holy grail of video is to match the superlative images of film.

Today, video picture quality is excellent in consumer models. The size of the chip and the precision of the optics determine just how good the end result actually is. So the lines between professional and consumer cameras have blurred, to the extent that there are now cameras aimed at a middle market often referred to as 'prosumer'.

Once you have your video camera, you need a housing. Some are little more than strong metal or moulded tubes with perspex at either end and manual levers or switches to gain access to the controls. These sound basic, but they work. Essentially, there are two schools of thought when it comes to housings: some prefer electronic controls through a 'lanc' connection; others prefer fully manual housings. As with so many things in life, you get what you pay for. But remember: the pictures are usually only as good as your camerawork.

As long as they are working, electronic housings can be much more user-friendly. 'Lanc' connections allow

◄ Co-author John McIntyre enters the water with his professional video system, lights blazing.

access to a wider range of the camera's functions, depending on its housing design. The downside is that if something goes wrong while you are filming the trip of a lifetime, there is usually nothing you can do except curse the controls. Hitting it doesn't tend to solve the problem (I've tried). Repairs to electronically controlled housings also tend to be more expensive.

The biggest change in video over recent years has been the move from 'standard definition' to 'high definition' (HD). In the latter, the amount of information being recorded is much greater. Picture quality is nothing short of sensational when recorded on high-end professional cameras. HD is recorded using the same process as used for DVD recordings, called MPEG-2. Even this is constantly being developed to improve compression techniques and playback quality. There will come a time when all television is digital HD.

So what are the essentials when buying your kit? The first thing to decide is how you intend to use the footage. If it is purely for personal interest, then there are many consumer models that will suffice. Any camera that has a wide range of housings available must be a popular model for underwater use. And, of course, a wider choice means a more competitive price.

It is crucial to choose a housing that allows the use of a wide-angle adapter or lens, as well as a colour correction filter. A very useful feature is having access to manual white balance (In basic terms, the white balance feature assesses how colours should be represented, based on letting the camera know exactly what white looks like in ambient conditions).

Get used to your camera's features: use it on land until you are familiar with its functions. Then get used to how it feels in the water and work out the best position in which to hold it. This can be improved by adding an external colour monitor, which allows you to keep an eye on your subject as well anticipating its next move – such as a shark looming into view. It is far better to let the animal come into shot than you suddenly turning the camera onto the subject and following it everywhere. Try letting the animal move through the lens, say from left to right. The shot will look better and be much easier to edit.

MAKING THE MOVIE

You can get some good ideas for making your own video by watching television programmes to see how the professionals do it. Observe carefully how their shots are made: you will not see sudden movements or jerky pans and zooms. The important thing is to let the action do the talking and keep the camera still, or at least make any moves as smooth as possible. None of this will be possible if your diving is not up to scratch: in underwa-

Charles Hood/oceans-image.com

▶ Video cameras can be awkward to wield underwater, so it can help to pre-plan a sequence with fellow divers.

(Charles Hood/oceans-image.com)

ter videography, buoyancy is absolutely crucial.

Try to work out a rough storyline. Take a wreck dive, for example: shoot a series of sequences, starting with people jumping off the boat on the surface, and then film other divers jumping from the underwater perspective. For the next sequence get ahead of the dive party and video them arriving at the wreck, again letting them swim through the shot.

To make your pictures easy to edit, follow the simple rule: 'wide and tight'. If, for example, you record a diver shining a torch on an object, record this wide, then get the diver to do exactly the same again, and shoot much tighter. You will then have the equivalent of a two-camera shoot. Construct a journey around the wreck. Never simply keep the same person in shot the whole time, as this is impossible to edit.

The other shot to remember is the 'cutaway'. This often consists of the subject seen from the diver's point of view. So for example, if you video a diver looking at a coral, when the diver has moved away, video the subject matter close up. You can then edit this as part of your sequence. The point of having a series of sequences is to allow you to compress the journey into a shorter space of time, so when people watch your final production they will see the entire wreck and feel as if they are part of the journey.

White balancing is important to master. Assuming you can do this manually, a simple but effective trick is to paint one of your fins white. This will give you an excellent white balance. You need to check white balance whenever you change your depth. Point the camera at your fin and hold down the white balance until it locks. Below about 10m you should always have the red 'blue water' filter in place when you adjust white balance. Red disappears with depth, so all you are really doing is trying to restore some of this colour and to make it appear as natural as possible. If, on the other hand, you are using lights, do not use the red filter: instead, point the lights at your fin and re-white balance.

You may need to experiment to get the best results from your camera. When using the external monitor

you will also have to get used to the colours appearing slightly pink. This will usually appear normal when you view your pictures on the surface.

The autofocus function can be extremely useful, but it is preferable to be able to switch between auto and manual. This helps prevent the camera's autofocus 'hunting' while filming. With a wide-angle lens, you may get away with leaving the camera on infinity, but it is better to use the auto function to get the focus right, then switch to manual for that particular shot.

As for how you video the marine life, it is best to observe behaviour and thus anticipate a move. For example, a turtle may be swimming along the reef. Rather than get a shot of its retreating rear end, swim ahead and allow the subject to come to you. Some animals are actually drawn to the camera lens because of the reflection; this can make for excellent head-on shots.

Once you have your footage 'in the can', log it by making make sure the tapes are numbered and given brief descriptions of dive site and content. Since most people now use digital editing software, good housekeeping will pay dividends when loading your material onto the computer.

When you are making the edit, try to imagine you are telling the story of the dive. Keep up the pace and never let shots run on too long. One word of warning: don't overdo the special effects that often come with editing software, as these can be distracting. Most natural history programmes tend only to use cuts and transitions. A few special effects may be okay for the titles, but after that they can ruin a film. Above all, it is the pictures people want to see. Appropriate music can help set the mood and the pace: try laying the music on the timeline first and then cutting to the beat.

If you are brave enough to include a voice track, use a reasonable quality microphone and ensure the levels are reasonable. Never let the levels peak into the red, as this kind of distortion is impossible to remove. Get a rough idea of the narrative and keep the sentences short and simple. Remember: your images will tell much of the story, so you don't have to describe everything you see. For example, there's no need to say: 'The divers jumped in the water.' People can see that for themselves. It may instead be better to say: 'Divers entered the water just a short distance from the mooring line.' The trick is to impart a little pertinent information that is not immediately obvious. If it is obvious, then you don't need to say it.

Finally, all you have to do is convert your footage into a form that people can watch, the most common being DVD. Don't make your audience suffer an eternity of the same type of shots: show them something short, fresh and structured. And leave 'em wanting more.

▶ The Red Sea is a treat for videographers, with sets that Hollywood directors can only dream of.

GETTING THE BEST FROM THE RED SEA

Image courtesy of ScubaPro

IN SEARCH OF THE PERFECT DIVE BAG

When you are on the road, your dive bag is your world. Bags suitable for carrying diving equipment come in different guises, but the two standard types are either the classic zipped holdall or the heavier upright travel bag, which tends to come with wheels and an extending handle for pulling it along. The upright-style bag usually has greater capacity and more compartments for stowing items, but most of them weigh 5–8kg even before you have put any diving equipment inside. The holdall-style bags, meanwhile, offer less protection for your kit and do not have wheels. Ultimately, the choice between the two is down to your personal preference, with the obvious influence of luggage restrictions.

Whichever bag you choose, the challenge is in limiting your overall hold luggage, as airlines are now stricter than ever on the amount that their clients can carry. Officially, the weight limit for most charter flights operating between Europe and the Egyptian Red Sea is 20kg, but most leading tour operators have agreed 10kg extensions with the charter companies and in any case, few are likely to impose fines unless you exceed 30kg. It becomes more difficult with scheduled or national carriers, as the official weight limit is likely to be set in stone and not subject to negotiation.

For the most part, you should be safe with hold luggage of up to 30kg, and even if you do get fined for this amount, the sum should not be too much. Do bear in mind that many airlines levy fines of UK£5–15 per kilogram for excess luggage. Weight limits vary dramatically from one region to another: whereas BA and most transatlantic flights offer 46kg of hold luggage for economy passengers, 23kg per bag maximum. In practice, most of the agents will allow you to travel with around 30kg, but venturing much beyond this level will entail a sizeable surcharge. Ironically, you can take as much as you like for the onward flight to Port Sudan.

So, weight considerations are paramount when packing your bags for the Red Sea. The good news is that even if you choose to travel with a full set of conventional scuba kit, your hold luggage should not really weigh in at much more than 25kg, and you are still allowed an additional 4–7kg hand luggage, depending on the rules of your carrier. If you have relatively lightweight kit, a full set (see box) in a roll bag should not weigh much more than 18kg. That still gives you the option of carrying your regulator in your hand luggage in order to ensure it is not damaged in transit.

Everyone has a favourite way of packing a dive bag, and we recommend the following. First, open your bag fully and lay your wetsuit down flat along the base so that it covers as wide an area as possible without bulking up in height – it will act as a further layer of padding without taking up too much volume. Then, over this, place an open BCD and position your regulator (if it's going in the hold) in the middle. Next, fold up your BCD so that the side wings envelop and protect the regulator, which also has the protection of the bag and the wetsuit. Now it's simply a question of filling the remaining spaces with fins, boots and the rest of your equipment, plus however many T-shirts you can fit in. The rest of your clothes can either go in a separate bag (two hold items are permitted on most flights) or, if you have a large bag, in one of the external compartments.

If you have prescription lenses in your mask, you should bring a spare and carry it in your hand luggage. Trivial though the mask may seem, it is key to your enjoyment of a diving trip and prescription lenses are not widely available – though some Egyptian dive centres may be able to help. If your entire luggage is lost, you can always borrow or hire the kit, but a prescription mask is irreplaceable.

Most Red Sea travellers pack too many clothes. The basic requirement is a T-shirt and appropriate underwear for each day, plus a comfortable pair of shorts, a selection of swimwear, something smarter for the hotel lobby and something to keep you warm in the evening. In winter, it is essential to bring a fleece and, if you really feel the cold, some sort of extra jacket for chilly nights. Even for the dedicated clothes-horse, all this need not add up to more than about 7–8kg, and a basic wash bag with contents is only about 1kg. If you are staying in a hotel, you can use the laundry services and bring even fewer clothes.

Weight issues only become serious if you have a specialist interest within diving that necessitates additional kit. Photographers and technical divers are both accustomed to flirting with excess charges, often because of heavy-duty kit (technical BCDs can weigh two or three times as much as the lightweight models favoured by travellers) or delicate items transported in padded cases. In Egypt, it is possible to hire twin sets or extra cylinders, so there's really no point in taking your own unless you are going somewhere like Yemen or Eritrea, where bail-out cylinders are generally not on offer. In many cases, it is easier to twin up a pair of 12-litre aluminium cylinders than to find a small 'pony' cylinder. Good tour operators should be able to facilitate requests for additional cylinders if you make the request in advance.

Image courtesy of ScubaPro

As for underwater cameras, digital compacts should fit neatly into hand luggage, even if you have an external flash. This may mean relegating your regulator to hold luggage, but if you follow the packing system outlined above, your regulator should survive the rough treatment meted out by some ground handlers. The issue becomes more serious if you have a complicated camera system: the average digital SLR system weighs around 18kg, with carrying cases, arms, flashes, additional lenses, laptop computers, chargers and other accessories. This clearly puts you well over the weight limit, and seasoned underwater photographers have come up with a series of tricks to get their kit to the Red Sea without paying surcharges. Those truly committed to the cause buy photographer's jackets and fill the pockets with lenses and other heavy items. We have heard of photographers boarding the aeroplane with 7kg of hand luggage and 15kg packed into their jackets!

Airlines are, of course, aware of such ruses, and what you get away with will be subject to the agent, the day, and your own luck. The best way around the problem for the serious photographer is to accompany someone who tends to travel light: the extra weight of the photographic gear should be absorbed into the shared limit, and any infringement is likely to be minor.

Organise your luggage carefully: wash bags contain shampoos, gels, creams and foams that will make a terrible mess if they leak in transit. If possible, stow your toiletries in a separate compartment and always wrap them up in a plastic bag to provide another layer of protection. Try to keep a separate source of cash and identification somewhere in your hand luggage in case you lose your wallet and have to scrape by until you can arrange emergency funding. If you are visiting one of the Red Sea's more obscure destinations, you may want to consider hiding some emergency money in your clothing. One trick is to slip two US$50 bills under the soles of a typical pair of trainers. No matter where you are, US$100 is more than enough to see you safely to a friendly embassy, should you find yourself in need of emergency help.

▲ A state-of-the-art dive bag with wheels, dry compartments and a choice of strap systems.

DIVE BAG CHECK LIST

- mask
- fins
- snorkel
- swimming costume
- regulator
- wetsuit
- BCD
- fins and boots
- safety sausage (delayed surface marker buoy) plus reel or line
- dive computer
- weightbelt (with no weights!)

N.B. Cylinders and weights are provided by all Red Sea diving operations. In the course of our travels we have come across a few fastidious types who travel with their own lead weights, but we do not recommend going down this rather unnecessary path.

HEALTH ESSENTIALS

- sunblock cream – always a higher factor than you think!
- rehydration salts
- sunglasses
- hat, or some other head protection

SPARES AND ACCESSORIES

While most dive centres are well equipped with spares, it may be worth bringing the following:
- spare fin strap with clips
- extra mask – if you use prescription lenses
- lightweight hood to stow in your BCD
- spare batteries for cameras/laptop

◄ Dive bags are available in all shapes and sizes – but will it take all your kit?

Neil Beer

ARRIVAL IN THE RED SEA

Landing in a foreign country can prompt a degree of uncertainty, but there's really not much to worry about, as long as you don't mind waiting while the wheels of bureaucracy turn at their own pace. In all cases, you will have to clear immigration before collecting your luggage. When dealing with immigration officials, keep your answers simple and polite, and never show any sign of exasperation (even if they show plenty).

Egypt is easy these days. If you have booked your holiday with a tour operator, you should have the services of a local agent or fixer, who will help you purchase the correct visa stamps and point you in the correct direction. Even without the assistance of a tour guide, the airport officials will show you where to buy the visa stamps. Then it's just a question of collecting your bags from the luggage carousel.

There is always a small chance that your luggage may have been misdirected, in which case you should inform your local agent and ask to speak to a representative of the airline to arrange for it to be sent on. If you have a lot of luggage, it is worth hiring a trolley. We recommend carrying a quantity of small change in order to pay for trolley hire (the going rate is about a dollar), but do not feel obliged to hire the annoyingly persistent porters. Keep a firm hand on your trolley and just say 'la'ah' (no) repeatedly. They'll get the message and find someone else to hassle.

Of the other Red Sea countries, Sudan, Eritrea and Saudi Arabia are the trickiest to enter. You should expect lengthy if directionless luggage searches, endless form filling and plenty of time waiting in disorderly, spirit-sapping queues. These are the hoops you have to jump through in order to dive in these countries, where tourism is still a novelty. Djiboutian immigration officials are either very easy or very difficult to deal with; they only speak in French and ask a lot of quite strange questions, but if you smile politely and reiterate the truth – that you are an adventurous diving traveller – there shouldn't be any problem.

Every now and then in Djibouti and Sudan, an official may decide to block someone's entry. This welcome is usually reserved for local dive guides whose faces have become a little too familiar in the immigration queue. In such circumstances, it is sometimes better to agree to be transported back on the next outward flight and begin mentally filling in your insurance claim form. Alternatively, if you have a local fixer or agent with good connections, you may wish to consider paying a little *baksheesh* to smooth the way. Do not be tempted to offer this yourself, as it might be construed as bribery and your advances may simply be too clumsy. Leave any negotiations to your fixer.

Wherever you land, there will be no shortage of people outside the terminal offering various services. In most cases, local representatives of your dive operator will be willing to turn up and collect you personally, so don't get into any vehicle unless the driver is an employee of your boat or hotel. You should ask your agent for the local operator's telephone number in case no one turns up to collect you, but invariably the pick-up system works perfectly.

THE LIVEABOARD SCENE

Certain sites are only accessible by liveaboard boat, and with a few exceptions, they offer the most exciting diving in the Red Sea. Liveaboards or safari boats are exactly what the name implies, large vessels that act as floating hotels. The advantages of liveaboard diving are mostly for the committed diver: simply, all the elements of a holiday that are not closely related to actual diving are removed from the equation. There are no hotels, no shopping, no evening strolls around the bay. For the duration of the voyage, your life is reduced to a blissfully simple mantra: dive, eat, sleep.

The most luxurious liveaboards operate in Egyptian waters, unless you count the private super-yachts that ply Saudi waters. Jordan and Israel are so small that to run a liveaboard there would be laughable, while the vessels that operate out of Port Sudan tend to be the older Egyptian boats. The liveaboard scene in Yemen and Eritrea changes on a regular basis, but the boats that occasionally operate there are small yachts belonging to adventurers. There are only a few boats in Djibouti, including some stylish Turkish-built *gulets* and a couple of Egyptian-built vessels, which specialise in trips to the Seven Brothers Islands.

Liveaboard diving first began on the Great Barrier Reef in the early 1970s, but in the Red Sea the concept has its roots in the pioneering 1950s expeditions of Jacques Cousteau, whose research vessels were arguably the first liveaboard dive boats. The first Red Sea liveaboards started operating in the Eighties, when there were fewer restrictions on tourist vessels moving between different territorial waters. Today, liveaboards tend not to cross borders (at least, not on purpose), though there is talk of getting permission to run liveaboards across from southern Egypt to northern Sudan.

For many divers, liveaboards are the first taste of life at sea. These are relatively small vessels, and you feel the waves far more than you would on a big ferry. If you suffer from seasickness, consider taking pills or wearing pressure patches, but you should also question whether the whole liveaboard experience is really for you. In many cases, the weather will be calm and your motion tolerance will not be tested. But if the wind is howling as you step onto the boat, you may want to swallow those pills as soon as possible. Seasickness tablets work best if you take them before the motion begins, so don't wait until you're feeling queasy: by then it will be too

◀ Egyptian hotels have excellent facilities, so make the most of the pool and take the opportunity to relax.

▼ Recent years have seen Egyptian liveaboards getting bigger and better, though it can entail diving in bigger groups.

Tony Backhurst

Blueotwo

▲ The top deck of a liveaboard is the place to relax and catch some sun.

late. Thankfully, most people overcome the nausea quite quickly. Even if you feel a bit rough, see if you can do that first dive. The effects of breathing air underwater are curiously restorative, and you may well find yourself looking forward to breakfast.

So, what should you expect from your liveaboard? The classic Egyptian-built vessel is changing from the 25-metre, 12-person model to a 40-metre gin palace. Wooden hulls are giving way to steel hulls, which afford greater stability in the water. Spacious twin-bed cabins with panoramic windows, televisions and minibars are replacing the narrow bunk cabins of old. The Egyptian businessmen who construct and manage most of the leading liveaboards now compete in terms of opulence and size, investing money in bigger boats that make more money by getting more people on board. Today, the leading vessels are 35–40m long and take 20 or more diving guests.

Layout varies depending on the concept of the liveaboard and how many customers it aims to accommodate, but there is a generic pattern that applies to most of the Egyptian variations on this theme. The first thing you should see as you step onto the stern is the dive deck, where rows of cylinders are secured on long benches. You can leave the BCD on your cylinder for the whole trip (though it will need to be checked and secured periodically), and the immediate area around it is your domain. Most boats provide a plastic crate, stowed under the bench, in which you can keep your fins, mask and other essentials. Superior liveaboards even have camera tables, and dip tanks for testing housings prior to a dive (and rinsing afterwards). Leading down from the dive deck is the dive platform, just above

sea level. On some sites, the skipper may request that divers enter via a giant stride from this platform; in most cases, though, it is used as the best way to step onto inflatable boats.

A word about inflatable boats: while it is much easier to dive off the back of the liveaboard, inflatables (also known as RIBs or Zodiacs) are far more practical, not to mention safer, for dropping off and collecting divers. They ensure that divers can be dropped in on the exposed northern edges of offshore reefs, where manoeuvrability is crucial. Today's generation of 35m-plus liveaboards is fine for the open sea, but even the best skipper in the world would feel dubious about sailing them within metres of a reef. The quality of your ship's inflatables is key to your overall enjoyment of the diving: they should be powerful, well maintained and equipped with radios in case of a breakdown. Sizeable liveaboards need at least two big inflatables. Your dive guides will brief you on how to step from the liveaboard onto the inflatable; the best method is to enlist a helping hand from one of the boatmen, who will tell you where to sit.

Inside the vessel, the interior forward of the dive deck is usually an all-purpose saloon, the place where you will eat and laze around when you aren't diving. Some large liveaboards have reserved this space purely as a dining area, which can be a bit of a waste of space, but it does make mealtimes easier to organise for the crew. Most cabins are located below deck level, and divers are fond of arguing which is best. Few liveaboards have guest cabins in the bow, as this is the area where you feel the motion most acutely. On larger boats, a few cabins may be located on or above deck level; these are sometimes more spacious, and come with smoked windows that allow you to enjoy the view, while no-one can see in.

When you first embark on your liveaboard, you should receive a ship briefing, including emergency drills and safety information. The one feature that all briefings share is their emphasis on the proper use of the toilet facilities. It boils down to this: never put toilet paper in the toilet. The basic plumbing on board most boats cannot handle paper: when toilets get blocked, some poor devil has the unpleasant task of cleaning out the pipes. So pay heed to the briefing and deposit yours in one of the little bins provided. The basic rule is not to put anything down the toilet unless it has been through you first!

The engine room is always below deck level. Guests are normally excluded from the engine room, but many dive guides will be happy to show you around if you are interested in the mechanical workings of the vessel. In addition to housing the ship's engines, this is also where you find the generators that keep everything working, from the air conditioning to the compressor. Good liveaboards should have one or two emergency generators.

Moving upstairs, the bigger vessels have an open deck with seating, as well as a further lounge and bar. Every boat has its own policy when it comes to drinks: coffee and tea are always free, but beware how many caffeine drinks you indulge in, as these have a diuretic effect and can thus contribute to dehydration. Bottled soft drinks and mixers tend to be free as well, but there is usually a charge for beers and spirits. We know of at least one liveaboard selling alcohol in Sudan, and the French-run vessels running out of Djibouti would rather scuttle themselves than leave port without a decent stock of wine. Dive boats in Saudi Arabia, however, are 100 per cent dry – and don't even think about bringing your own!

Forward on this deck is the bridge, which often comprises the captain's quarters. Unless you are told otherwise, this area is off-limits to guests. All the same, many skippers enjoy a chat with the divers; it's just a question of asking the dive guides for advice on a good time to approach him. Many skippers use the flying bridges on the top deck and welcome the pleasure of conversation, especially if they are sailing through the night. The bow area tends to be the working part of the boat and is traditionally the place where crew can escape from guests.

Whatever the size or layout of a liveaboard, there are certain points of etiquette to observe if you are to make the most of your time on board. A boat has a specific place for everything, so try to avoid leaving your possessions lying around. Dive kit should be stowed in your crate, cameras should be placed in a dedicated area, and bulky dive bags should be emptied and handed to the crew for storage below. Egyptian boats have responded to the digital age by supplying 24-hour electricity and dedicated areas for charging. You will be dissuaded from charging electrical equipment in your cabin, as this is considered a fire risk. If you leave watches, dive computers, books and bottles of suntan lotion lying around the boat, the crew will move them somewhere out of harm's way, then they will forget where exactly and you will have to wait for the items to turn up. The best place for a dive computer is either on your wrist or tied to your BCD: that way, if you forget to put it on your wrist before a dive, it will still come with you.

▼ Most liveaboards have an all-purpose saloon area where you can eat and relax when you not diving.

Blueotwo

Blueotwo

▲ A group of divers preparing to leave the M/Y Amelia on a dive.

The boat's 'dry areas' must be respected. Don't sit down to breakfast in your bathing costume if it is going to leave a damp patch on the seat. Similarly, once that wetsuit is on, don't be tempted to run below to pick up that computer from your cabin. The cardinal sin is to run through the dry area of the boat in your wetsuit to fetch a towel after a dive. This always results in a telltale set of sopping footprints leading right to your cabin.

Mercifully, there aren't too many rules when it comes to life on a liveaboard. You are on board to dive, eat and sleep, so all you really need to do is turn up on time for the diving and the eating. If you plan to miss a dive, tell someone else and save the guides the effort of searching for you prior to the dive briefing. Try and get kitted up in good time so that you are ready to step into the inflatable as soon as it is ready to go, and stick to the time limits stipulated for the dive.

The choice facing prospective Egyptian liveaboard guests is whether to go for one of the big boats or choose a smaller boat. The larger vessels offer more home comforts and greater stability at sea, but you can end up diving in some fairly large groups. If your liveaboard takes only 12 and has two inflatable tenders, you will dive in groups of six, which can be handy if you are looking for hammerheads or other large animals likely to be intimidated by a wall of bubbles.

Finally, the secret to a really successful liveaboard trip is to relax and make the boat your home. Arabic people have a great tradition of hospitality and they love nothing more than seeing their guests enjoy themselves. You will meet all sorts of strangers while liveaboard diving, and it is an easy way to get to know people and make friends with whom you will have much in common. For real diving enthusiasts, there is simply no alternative to liveaboards.

▶ A moment of glorious anticipation before hitting the water.

GETTING THE MOST FROM DIVE GUIDES

Good dive guides are to be treasured. It is they who decide which sites should be dived, and if you have the good fortune to sail with knowledgeable guides who want to share their love of the Red Sea, you are assured of a fine time, whether diving from a liveaboard or a day boat.

In theory, guides have a simple job. They brief you prior to the dive, accompany the group underwater and perform head counts to make sure everyone is collected afterwards. It sounds easy, but in reality the job is far more complex. The guide will also be responsible for the care of out-of-practice or newly qualified divers, who may need more than a helping hand once they are in the water. They will be on hand to perform impromptu repairs on faulty kit, dispensing advice and reassurance when necessary.

On liveaboards, the guides are on duty 24 hours a day. While the captain remains the ultimate authority, they work with him to determine the daily timetable. The liveaboard dive guide has to be an expert diver, instructor, diplomat, host, medic, bartender, hotelier, plumber, electrician and linguist – all in one. Some even find time to film and edit a DVD of the trip.

Due to the size of its diving industry, Egypt is where people go to learn how to be a Red Sea dive guide. Almost all guides work on a tourist visa, so it is something of an unofficial trade in Egypt, but the system seems to work well enough. There is a definite hierarchy in the instructor/guiding scene: young hopefuls typically spend a few weeks networking, doubtless buying plenty of rounds at popular instructors' hangouts such as the Camel Bar in Na'ama Bay.

The best jobs are with the well-established schools that have a reputation for quality instruction and guiding, but half the game is getting your face known around town while working odd-jobs for dive businesses. That should lead to the first full-time job, after which it's a case of climbing the greasy pole and getting a job with one of the blue chip operations. In addition to the usual instructor's qualifications, language skills are seen as a major asset for a jobbing guide – and anyone with mechanical or boat-related skills has an immediate advantage when it comes to the liveaboard scene.

Liveaboard jobs tend to go to the more senior instructors, but some instructors prefer to remain land-based, partly due to the fact that liveaboards are unrelentingly hard work, and partly because of the lack of bars and clubs at sea. Often, the most contented liveaboard guides are couples (who can keep each other sane), or those who are trying to save money and want a working arrangement that includes all their meals and accommodation.

Charles Hood/oceans-image.com

The average age of a Red Sea dive guide is somewhere between 20 and 35. After three or fours years of hard work, most retire from the business and go off to start a career that preferably will not involve any sort of service industry. Some move up to become skippers and go to work in the Mediterranean; others get jobs working for American-promoted operations in the Pacific and the Caribbean, where there is the lure of big tips and a different dive scene.

But for most guides, the advantages of the job far outweigh the disadvantages. For single male dive guides, the promise of romance is renewed each time a new planeload of clients touches down. We spoke to several guides while preparing this section, and at first some of them made the serious point that their employers do not encourage 'fraternising' with the guests. None of them, however, were able to keep a straight face for long. It is well known but seldom stated that holiday romances go with the territory.

Equally as important is the crew, those hard-working men whose constant labour allows you to relax. Put simply, dive boat crews are the unsung heroes of the Red Sea scuba industry. They are the ones who will prepare your meals, fetch your drinks, clean your cabin, drive the inflatables and help you lift your equipment on and off the boat. Crewmembers tend to be nationals of the country in which the vessel is based, although there are some fairly international crews in Saudi Arabia, Yemen and Djibouti. Remember, a liveaboard is the crew's home, so you will be expected to keep your shoes off.

On Egyptian liveaboards, the crew tend to be split between engineering duties, diving duties and galley work. Sometimes, a senior member of the crew is being trained by the captain – you often see such an individual at the helm when the skipper is catching up with his sleep. The guides are there to act as intermediaries between guests and crew staff, but you are welcome to chat with them when they are not busy. Indeed, most crews appreciate a spot of light-hearted banter with the guests, and if they remember you as a friendly face, chances are you will be well looked after.

Dive boat crewing is hard work, so it is traditional for guests to leave the crew a cash tip at the end of each voyage. On liveaboards, the benchmark trip is UK£30–40 for the crew, and guests have the option to tip the dive guides privately. For day boats, it can be more difficult to tip if you are moved around from one vessel to another, but it is always worth leaving a tip with a central manager. If you want to ensure a particular crewmember gets a certain amount, you can give it to him personally, but try to be discreet in order to avoid any discontent among the others.

TRAVEL TIPS AND HINTS

ARRIVING IN EGYPT

When you arrive in Egypt, prepare to be greeted by armies of porters, trolley pushers and bag handlers who have the challenge of persuading you to part with your cash. They are usually extremely polite, if a little over-friendly. If you accept a trolley from someone, you will be expected to pay, so have the right money on you – preferably in the local currency. They might ask for an English Pound, which is worth ten times the local money, when in fact you should only be giving them two or three Egyptian Pounds. Dollars, Euros and Sterling are all accepted, as are many other currencies. The best way to avoid being unwittingly over-generous is to ask the price first. If you don't like it, don't accept it. Or try haggling, if you have the energy. Tour guides will usually have a good idea about the going rate. Having a pocketful of single Egyptian pound notes helps you to tip without excess.

TAXIS

Tourists can make life difficult for dive guides who live and work in Egypt, especially around Sharm el Sheikh and Hurghada, by paying top dollar for taxis instead of finding out in advance what a journey should cost. Non-Egyptian guides end up dealing with sporadic and bizarre price-hikes. The simple rule is to ask the fare before getting into the taxi – and remember it! Check with hotel staff what is a reasonable price for your journey. Another good way of ensuring you don't get ripped off is having the right amount of change. Always try to keep some small notes handy.

SECURITY

Tight security is a fact of life these days and Egypt is no exception, having recently learned a tragic lesson in both Taba and Sharm el Sheikh. Both resorts were bombed, killing dozens of people and injuring hundreds more. Almost simultaneous explosions in Sharm on July 23, 2005, caused widespread revulsion and horror. Locals and tourists, including 11 British nationals, were killed. The Egyptian authorities reacted quickly to restore confidence and the evidence is plain for all to see on arrival, with highly visible policing and

a ban on taxis driving up to hotel lobbies. Some inland tours are now given a police escort – often in coach convoys.

Advice about the security situation is available from government foreign offices. A good website is that of the British Foreign Office, which offers advice country by country (www.fco.gov.uk).

Otherwise general crime is relatively low, but holidaymakers are advised to take care of passports, valuables and cash and where possible to make use of a hotel safe.

EXCESS BAGGAGE

Many but not all of the airlines allow divers up to 30kg for hold luggage and 7kg for hand luggage. Some restrict all passengers, diver or not, to 20kg, and the charges for any excess can be quite steep, especially on long haul flights. For those divers carrying heavy photographic equipment, and increasingly, tekkies, taking rebreathers, it is worth finding out in advance what the allowances are. Some carriers charge a modest upfront fee for, say, an extra 10kg. This can be a lot less painful than paying at the check-in desk. Another option is to team up with a large group. Chances are that when all the weights are added up the excess will be waived. The charter companies know that they rely on divers and, providing that you have not massively exceeded your quota, you may be able to ride out your luck. No single bag should be more than 23kg, because of airport health and safety regulations.

DIVING INSURANCE

It is an unacceptable risk to go on a diving holiday without insurance. There are numerous cases of divers needing expensive recompression treatment in the Red Sea and a few who have had to pay out of their own pocket. As the insurance market is fiercely competitive, it is well worth shopping around. Depending on your qualification, it is also worth bearing mind that many policies cover divers only to a depth of 30m. Many accidents occur when diving deeper than this. You may be required not only to pay for a chamber but also for any rescue by air or sea. There are companies offering policies covering divers to

50m on air and increasingly extended risk for divers using trimix (though again there is usually a depth limit). If you travel more than once a year, seek out the best deals for multiple trips, which can also include your partner. Once you've bought insurance, be sure to keep your contact details and policy number with you.

TUMMY TROUBLE

It goes under any number of names, from 'gyppy tummy' and 'Tut's trot' to 'mummy's tummy' and 'Tutenkamen's Revenge'. Whatever you call it, diarrhoea was until recently a dead certainty when travelling to Egypt's Red Sea coast. Nowadays food preparation is a lot better, but you have to remember that the local people are far more resilient: what they eat might not affect them, but it sure will affect you. Even the elegant buffets in the hotel can conceal the dreaded bugs. So the first rule is never to travel to Egypt without a supply of rehydration sachets, and anti-diarrhoea tablets such as Imodium or the like.

Avoiding salads that might have been washed in tap water is another good way to stay healthy. The more well-cooked the food you eat, the better your chances of avoiding problems. Drink only bottled water, as this is the only really safe supply, and drink plenty of it. Remember, too, that you will dehydrate during a dive because your air is dry, so drink plenty before and after dives. Fingers crossed, you'll have a tummy trouble-free holiday.

WHAT NOT TO WEAR

Since the majority of people in the Middle East are Muslim, you risk causing offence by wearing skimpy clothing or sunbathing topless. The latter is not permitted in Arab countries. In the big resort hotels in Sharm el Sheikh and Hurghada, however, visitors are pushing the boundaries, and many owners turn a blind eye to topless bathing on the private beaches. Some may tolerate this, but during the month of Ramadan you are best advised to be more considerate. This also goes for dive boats and liveaboards: crew members observing this holy month may take offence.

Otherwise, T-shirts and shorts or skirts are sufficient during the summer months. A baseball cap or floppy hat is also a good idea to keep the sun off your head. During the winter months, especially at night, temperatures can drop into the teens, so sweat shirts and long trousers are recommended. On dive boats you will be expected to remove footwear.

HAGGLING

Stallholders will try to use all their powers of persuasion to get you to buy something from their stall, whether a carpet, papyrus or some other souvenir of your visit. They will generally accept notes in most European currencies. Often the opening line will be: 'Where do you come from?' followed by a silent appraisal of your wealth. You'd be amazed how much you can lower the price by haggling. Don't be scared to suggest a figure way below the asking price. And don't just settle for the first reduction: keep haggling, especially if the item is expensive. Try walking away: if the price is right you will be called back.

RAMADAN

Whether you spend your holiday on a dive boat, in a hotel or lounging on a beach, a little respect for the local culture can go a long way. Arabic countries are steeped in religious traditions, which are extremely important to them. One in particular is Ramadan. This is a holy month in which Muslims observe a strict spiritual routine of abstinence during the hours of daylight. From dawn until dusk, adults will not eat, drink, chew gum, use tobacco or have any kind of sexual contact. There are exceptions, such as, for example, when someone is ill, but the majority of Muslims pride themselves on a strict adherence to tradition.

Ramadan commences with the new moon in the ninth month of the Islamic Calendar, and is informed by the philosophy of discipline and prayer inspired by the Holy Quran. As a tourist, having a simple understanding of this tradition should help you to avoid any *faux pas* – just as, for example, it would be insulting to talk about sex or make a rude gesture while the call to prayer is being made. It is impolite to offer alcohol in most circumstances, but during Ramadan this would confirm a particular degree of ignorance.

Most local people will not make a fuss: they realise that you are a tourist and prefer not to show that any offence has been caused. But, although it is fine to carry on your daily routine as normal, a little diplomacy never hurts. Ostentatiously eating

and drinking in front of someone who wants to pray, for example, might be pushing things a bit far. Ramadan may also affect the opening times of certain attractions and, in some places, may mean alcohol is not served.

Muslims break their fast soon after the sun goes down, and at the end of Ramadan (otherwise known as the *Eid ul-Fitr*) there is a something of a festival atmosphere, with plenty of wholesome food and socializing. Do remember during Ramadan to spare a thought for your Muslim dive guide: the level of exertion and dehydration while diving is onerous, especially if you are not even drinking water.

CAMELS

Believe it or not, Egypt is nowhere near the top of the pile when it comes to camel populations. The country's 120,000–170,000 camels make it a mere 19th in the world camel ratings. Sudan, according to one reputable list, is number one, with well over three million. Camels are amazing creatures: they can go for a week without drink, then guzzle 20 gallons of water in ten minutes; they can also carry loads of up to 500kg. Nomadic tribes domesticated the camel and continue to use them as transport. For tourists, they are part of the fun of coming to Egypt. Beware: always negotiate the price before mounting a camel. And once you're up, hold on tight!

QUAD BIKING

Camels may be *de rigueur* in the desert, but quad bikes are the thrill-seeker's choice for rattling over the sand dunes. They have become big business, with quad bike operations opening up in Sharm, Hurghada and Taba Heights. There are purpose-built tracks and the option to take guided tours into the desert. You can usually arrange rental through your hotel. Two tips: don't wear your best sunglasses, as they are likely to get damaged by the sand; and wear a scarf over your mouth to avoid swallowing half the desert.

FERRY RIDES BETWEEN SHARM EL SHEIKH & HURGHADA

When the ferry/catamaran service is running to schedule and the weather is reasonable, this is a fun way to get between the two big resorts. You will need to buy tickets in advance and arrive at the terminal at least an hour before departure.

Though the service is advertised as taking 90 minutes, it usually takes closer to three hours, since the full engine power is rarely used. The service usually operates on Mondays, Thursdays and Saturdays.

ELECTRICAL SUPPLY AND ADAPTERS

Egypt uses 220 volts AC, 50Hz. You will need adapters for round two-pin plugs. The same applies on liveaboards. If you have a few electrical devices it can be worth taking an extension lead with multiple sockets.

EGYPTIAN WINE

Though Egyptians have been making wine for thousands of years, the kindest of critics could not suggest it is among the world's finest. Egypt's climate is far from the best for grapes. Modern production methods, however, are at least helping to improve standards from the days when it could be best described as either 'four-star or unleaded'. There is a red, a white and a rosé, the latter being the least bad. Imported wines are expensive, but make excellent gifts for Egypt-based dive professionals if you want to curry favour on the boat.

EGYPTIAN BREAD

Pitta bread is one of the most common types, and is served with most meals. There are essentially three types: *aasah shamy*, which is white and made from wheat flour; *aasah balady*, which is darker and made from a mixture of wheat flours; and the darkest of the three, crisp *aasah makamar*, which is baked for longer. Fresh bread is available every day and is perfectly good to eat. In markets you will see locals carrying warm bread on trays high above their heads. Bakeries, which use traditional cooking methods, are sometimes happy to invite you in to see the bread being made.

TIME ZONES GMT

At midday in Cairo, the following times apply:

San Francisco: 2am
New York: 5am
London: 10am
Paris: 10am
Rome: 11am
New Delhi: 3.30pm
Bangkok: 4.30pm
Tokyo: 7pm
Sydney: 8pm
Times vary in those coutries where the clocks change for daylight saving.

ROSETTA

DUMAIT

PORT SAID

EL MATARIYAH

DAMANHUB

EL MANSURA

KHAN YUNIS

MASADA

DEAD
SEA

BEER SHEVA

TANTA

ISMAILIYA

EL ARISH

Kara

SHIBIN EL-KOM

N E G E V

ISRAEL

Shobak

Great
Bitter
Lake

Petra

GIZA   CAIRO

Memphis

Suez

EGYPT

JORDAN

MA'AN

Pyramids of
Dahshur

Wadi Rum

*Lake
Qarun*

EILAT
TABA

AQABA

Philadelphia

S I N A I

MEDINET EL-FAIJUM

HAQL

BENI SUEF

Monastery of
Saint Anthony

NUWEIBA

GULF OF AQABA

Monastery of
Saint Paul

SAUDI
ARABIA

St Catherine's
Monastery

DAHAB

RAS GHARIB

Mount Sinai

*Gebel Umm
Shawmar*

EL-MINYA

Gebel Gharib ▲

EL TUR

Gebel el Thabt ▲

rmopolis

MALLAWI

NABQ

ASH SHAYKH
HUMAYD

GULF OF SUEZ

E A S T E R N

SHARM EL SHEIKH

NA'AMA BAY

D E S E R T

GEMSA

RAS MOHAMMED

ASYUT

EL GOUNA

HURGHADA

Nile

*Gebel Sha'ib
el Banat* ▲

AKHMIM

SAFAGA

*R E D
S E A*

Abydos

QENA

EL QUSEIR

Qasr el Banat

⊕ place of interest

Valley of the Kings   Karnak

0   60 km

LUXOR

0   50 mi

ATTRACTIONS AND EXCURSIONS

THE RED SEA REGION IS A CRADLE OF CIVILISATIONS, AND IT IS POSSIBLE TO VISIT SOME OF THE KEY HISTORI-CAL SIGHTS IN CONJUNCTION WITH A DIVING HOLIDAY. HERE WE PRESENT THE MOST POPULAR EXCURSIONS TO ARCHAEOLOGICAL SITES, FORGOTTEN CITIES AND DESERT AREAS OF SPECTACULAR NATURAL BEAUTY.

▲ The Luxor Temple was constructed for the ancient Egyptian god Amon Ra and is a great place to visit from any of the southern Egyptian resorts. (Egypt Tourism Board)

▲ The Egyptian Museum in Cairo houses over 250,000 ancient artefacts including mummies, sarcophagi and the treasures from Tutankhamen's tomb. (Egypt Tourism Board)

▲ The Dead Sea, the lowest point on earth and the largest "Natural Spa" in the world. Just a short day-trip from Eilat and Aqaba. (Israeli Tourist Board)

▲ Karak is an ancient Crusader stronghold a day's drive north of Aqaba. It has a maze of stone-vaulted halls and passageways to explore. (Jordan Tourism Board)

PETRA

THERE CAN BE FEW MORE INSPIRING SIGHTS THAN WHEN THE MORNING SUN BURNS BRIGHT RED ON THE ANCIENT SANDSTONE TREASURY AT PETRA.

Built over a period of about 100 years, this remarkable facade carved into the rock face rightly deserves its reputation as one of the archaeological wonders of the world. Standing proud at 43m high and 30m wide, it is without doubt the most instantly recognizable tourist attraction in Jordan, attracting hundreds of thousands of visitors every year. From Aqaba, the journey takes a little over two hours and trips are easily arranged at most hotels. From the small neighbouring town of Wadi Musa, visitors can either walk for about half an hour through the narrow gorge known as the Siq, or pay a modest fee to enjoy a traditional, if bumpy ride on an Arabic horse.

To see the famous Treasury in all its sun-drenched glory you will need to make an early start. The aim is to arrive when the aspect of the sun beams into the enclosed rocky opening, which happens some time between 9am and 11am, depending on the time of year. For this reason, the mornings can be extremely busy, with some half a million visitors a year pouring through the Siq. Tickets are available either at the visitor centre or through agents at most hotels.

It is a journey of some 3km to the main attraction. This can be pretty arduous, especially during the heat of summer, so remember to take plenty of water with you. Along the narrow, steep sided passage you will pass the remnants of ancient waterway channels that once carried water supplies to the old city.

When the majestic Treasury, known as the al-Khazneh, looms into view, visitors are often overwhelmed by the impressive scale and condition of the carvings. These have lasted over two thousand years – a testament to the workmanship of the industrious Nabatean people, who clearly set out to create a monument to last.

Equally impressive is the way in which the Treasury was built: craftsmen began their titanic efforts at the top of the structure and painstakingly carved their way to the bottom over a century or so. They left behind them a marvel of stone-carved eagles, an Egyptian goddess and a myriad impressions depicting the lives and beliefs of the Nabatean people.

Despite making a significant cultural impact on the region, Petra fell into ruin and was lost to the outside world for many

Neil Beer

hundreds of years. In 1812, a Swiss traveller, Johann Louis Burckhardt, rediscovered the site's hidden treasures. It is now believed that the Treasury was built as an imposing tomb for a great king.

Petra has been classified as a UNESCO World Heritage Site for its outstanding historical significance. Today, however, many visitors are also drawn by its association with the silver screen, for Petra is the setting and inspiration for the final, dramatic sequence in the Hollywood blockbuster *Indiana Jones and the Last Crusade*. It is now impossible to overlook this fact, since a giant *Indiana Jones* billboard greets visitors on arrival at the ticketing gates. Petra's international renown received an enormous boost as a result of the film, and this in turn enhanced its importance to Jordan tourist economy.

Along from the Treasury, many more tombs and caves punctuate this historic enclave, which is also known today – in the words of the 19th century poet, John William Burgon – as the "Rose Red City". There is also a vast classical open theatre, which once seated 7,000 Nabateans, and more determined tourists can take a somewhat arduous walk to the giant monastery, about four kilometres from the Treasury. Those with the stamina can also take in another of Petra's historic sites, the High Place of Sacrifice, which requires a fairly steep climb near the Treasury. This provides an excellent high

▲ The first sight of Petra's ancient wonders is visible through the narrow rock passageway as you approach the site.

▶ This spectacular building carved into the sandstone is known as the 'Treasury'.

vantage point atop the mountainous scenery where religious ceremonies used to take place.

An hour or so from the Treasury is the equally stunning 1st century monastery, known locally as Al Deir. Be prepared, however, for a challenging trek. At 45m high and 50m wide, the façade is even larger than the Treasury's and was also built as a tomb. The views from here are spectacular.

For many tourists, the experience of Petra and its ancient architectural treasures is all the more enjoyable at night, when Bedouin music and food creates a more traditional, even magical atmosphere, with up to 2,000 candles lighting the façade. Visitors were once allowed to travel back in time by sleeping among the tombs and caves. Nowadays, with concern about the protection of the monuments, night tours can only be arranged with the accompaniment of a local guide. They usually start around 8.30pm and last for a few hours. If you're looking for a night under the stars, then the vast desert plains of nearby Wadi Rum offer the perfect addition to sightseeing in Jordan.

There is plenty of information about the sites and tours operators on the internet. Good starting places are the official websites: www.see-jordan.com & www.aqaba.jo. It is worth noting that certain tourist attractions are closed during big religious holidays.

▲ The interiors of most of Petra's buildings are mostly dark and undecorated, but lights are occasionally placed inside for special occasions.

WADI RUM

WADI RUM IS A BREATHTAKING WILDERNESS, EVOKING THE ROMANCE OF THE DESERT AND THE POWER OF NATURE OVER HUNDREDS OF MILLIONS OF YEARS.

TE Lawrence, immortalised on the silver screen as the legendary *Lawrence of Arabia*, described the landscape as 'vast, echoing and god-like'. Today, visitors passing under the shadow of the Seven Pillars of Wisdom, named after Lawrence's written account of the Arab revolt of 1917–18, are overwhelmed by the majesty of these natural mountain sculptures.

The whole area covers some 720km^2 and lies just over one hour's drive from the port city of Aqaba. Tours are easy to arrange through most hotels. A sturdy 4x4 jeep is one of the best ways to explore this dramatic landscape. But the more adventurous may decide to join one of the many camel trains that weave a dusty trail over the red, scorched desert, surrounded by sheer-sided mountainous valleys of granite and sandstone towering to over 1,700m. A good guide will ensure that you see the Seven Pillars of Wisdom close up. Other significant features include the amazing natural rock bridges spanning the network of canyons and gorges. A small, crumbling collection of sandstone brickwork and rocks marks the place where TE Lawrence once lived: no wonder David Lean chose this stunning backdrop for his epic Oscar-winning movie.

Wadi Rum, also known as the Valley of the Moon, is also home to a precious desert eco-system. Though the wildlife is not easy to find, lucky visitors may encounter the Syrian wolf, striped hyena or Nubian ibex. But the popularity of the site has also taken its toll: the Jordanian government is now concerned about damage to the environment and has taken steps to protect the more fragile areas by coordinating routes for vehicles and persuading people not to drop litter.

Most people conclude their visit at the place known as the 'Sunset Site', where hundreds clamber onto the rock peaks as the sun slides behind the mountains, leaving behind a searing red and yellow glow. The full experience, however, is best appreciated by camping out in the desert overnight to enjoy a bewildering starlit sky without the slightest hint of light pollution. Bedouins, who once roamed this vast landscape as they plied their trade, now secure their livelihoods from tourism. Although some changes have been made for the benefit of western-style appetites, visitors can still enjoy authentic Bedouin fare in this unique corner of Jordan.

▶ The majestic mountains of Wadi Rum dwarf the camels as they cross the desert.

▶▼ Wadi Rum is noted for its bizarre sandstone formations, which can be seen on walking or climbing tours.

▼ A night in the desert is best spent in the company of those who know it best – the Bedouin.

Jordan Tourism Board

Jordan Tourism Board

Jordan Tourism Board

CAIRO

Neil Beer

▲ Africa's biggest city is built around the continent's longest river – the Nile.

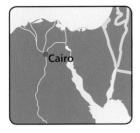

▶▲ The pyramids at Giza loom from the edge of the desert, timeless monuments of a bygone era.

▶ Cairo is the most populous city in Africa and the cultural centre of the Arab world.

AS EGYPT'S RED SEA COASTLINE IS SOME DISTANCE FROM THE CAPITAL, MOST DIVING VISITORS TEND TO STAY NEAR THE SEA AND MISS THE OPPORTUNITY TO VIEW THE FAMOUS SIGHTS OF CAIRO.

However, for an additional cost it is relatively easy to arrange flights that will include a layover in Cairo, where it is possible to visit two of the most famous sites in one day. These are the pyramids at Giza and the Museum of Egyptian Antiquities, home of the world-famous Tutankhamen exhibition.

Cairo is a vast and complex city, and while it has many rewards for the seasoned traveller, it can be a confusing place when visiting for the first time. If you are visiting Egypt

principally to dive, but want to include Cairo on your itinerary, it is possible to conduct a whistle-stop tour of the key attractions over the course of a single day before flying on to a Red Sea airport the next morning. For divers enroute to Port Sudan, Cairo is an obligatory stop-off, presenting an excellent opportunity to incorporate a day of culture into an already adventurous trip. It is possible to travel from Cairo to Sharm el Sheikh on a Superjet bus (from the Turgoman garage in Bulaq district), but the journey takes at least five hours.

We recommend incorporating flights into your holiday package and hiring a guide (your hotel or travel agent can arrange this) to help you make the most of your brief time in Cairo. Your day should start as early as possible with a visit to the Pyramids of Giza, the last standing of the Seven Wonders of the ancient world. Tickets for the pyramid site can be purchased at a tourist office at the entrance, but be warned that queues are long and disorderly – a good guide will be

Neil Beer

able to secure your tickets while you wait out of harm's way (and the sun) in your tour car. Your ticket allows you exterior access to the pyramids of Mycerinus and Chephren and the Great Pyramid of Cheops, as well as Sphinx and Chephren's valley temple.

Cairo is the biggest city in Africa and the Middle East, with a population of about 15 million people and a history that spans nearly 5,000 years. Today, the star of the show is the oldest and largest of the pyramids – that of the fourth dynasty pharaoh Cheops, who reigned around 2,586-2,564 BC. It is thought to weigh six million tons and contains more than two million closely packed blocks weighing between 2.5 and 14 tonnes apiece. It is possible to explore inside the pyramid and access the Great Gallery and the various chambers, but you must buy a special ticket, as visitor numbers are controlled to keep down humidity.

You could spend a week wandering the corridors of the Museum of Egyptian Antiquities, but an afternoon is sufficient to take in the Tutankhamen exhibition and a few other highlights. The boy king's funeral treasures can be viewed across a series of galleries on the museum's upper floor, including the gilded shrines that housed Tutankhamen's sarcophagus. Finally, there is a room devoted to his gold, the centrepiece of which is the beautiful funerary mask, a beautiful if sinister icon linking modern Egypt with its extraordinary past.

Dave Lucas

MOUNT SINAI AND ST CATHERINE'S

IT IS SOMETHING OF AN IRONY THAT THE LESS ADVENTUROUS SUN SEEKERS OF SHARM SIT IN THEIR AIR-CONDITIONED RESTAURANTS OR POOL BARS, BARELY AWARE THAT THEY ARE ON THE LIMITS OF ONE OF THE WORLD'S MOST DESOLATE WILDERNESS REGIONS.

▼ The sandstone peaks of the Sinai Mountains shine golden in the morning light.

The Sinai Peninsula's interior is an inaccessible desert of wind-scarred mountains and wadis, yet there are patches of desert where life springs defiantly from the sand, fed by precious spring water.

The place to visit is Mount Sinai and St Catherine's Monastery, supposedly the site where Moses heard God speaking from a burning bush. Established in 337AD, the monastery is run by the Greek Orthodox Church and is regularly visited by pilgrims. There are usually between 20 and 25 resident monks, most of whom came from the monasteries of Mount Athos in Greece.

It is easy to arrange excursions to Mount Sinai and St Catherine's Monastery from Sharm or any of the seaside resorts of the Sinai Peninsula. Your hotel should be able to

Egypt Tourism Board

recommend a suitable guide. The monastery is open to visitors from 9am until noon, so most trips leave Sharm at about 6am in order to cover the three-hour journey. Be aware that the monastery is closed on Fridays, Sundays and all Greek Orthodox holidays.

The monastery complex is housed behind 15m-high, 3m-thick walls. Visitors are led through a small gate in the northern wall and taken to Moses' Well before being shown to a thorny bush. This is the Burning Bush itself, or at least a relative of the original, from which clippings were apparently taken. It may sound all very fanciful, but it is the only bush of this species in the whole of the Sinai, and attempts to grow cuttings from it outside the monastery have all failed. The bush itself is of the type *Rubus sanctus*, a kind of wild raspberry that grows primarily in the mountains of Central Asia, and is extremely rare in the Middle East. The monks say the bush was moved several hundred years ago to accommodate a new chapel. Incidentally, the monks may seem a foreboding bunch, but there are signs they have a desert-dry sense of humour, as a fire extinguisher can sometimes be seen close to the bush.

Otherwise, the obvious highlight is the Church of St Catherine, a granite basilica erected between 424 and 551. The monks say that the basilica's doors are the oldest functioning ones in existence and that they lead to what is the world's oldest continually operating monastery – seven services are held, three times a day, in the Byzantine Greek language.

St Catherine's has a library containing 4,500 manuscripts, 7,000 early printed books and 6,000 modern tomes. The collection includes some of the world's oldest Bibles, plus copies of the first printed editions of Plato. Its most famous manuscript was the *Codex Sinaiticus*, an ancient Bible dating from the 4th Century. It was housed at St Catherine's for 1,500 years before a scholar took it away – he claimed for copying – and it found its way into various collections, including the British Museum. A few pages were hidden in a wall in the monastery library, though, and are still on display there in a specially designed archive.

Mount Sinai itself is a 2,300m slab of granite, which is possible to ascend with the help of local guides. You can rent a camel or carry out the climb on foot (it takes between two and three hours, depending on your level of fitness) along one of two routes. The Camel Path is seen as the easier option, while the Steps of Repentance represent a steeper route – they were apparently hewn by a penitent monk, and are extremely steep.

For those who cannot schedule a visit to this area, it is easy enough to book desert excursions closer to the coast – the highlight is often tea or a meal at a Bedouin camp. Quad bike trips have become popular in the past few years, but be aware that the guides will limit your speed in the interest of safety.

Egypt Tourist Office

▲ St Catherine's Monastery lies behind a formidable set of walls, 15m high and 3m thick.

Dave Lucas

◄ One of the local Bedouin.

THE VALLEY OF THE KINGS

Valley of the Kings

▶ A statue of Ramses II and his wife Nefertari is situated at Karnak temple in Luxor, east of the Valley of the Kings.

▼ The Luxor temple was constructed for the worship of the god Amon Ra whose marriage to his wife Mut was celebrated once a year.

LOCATED IN THE SHIMMERING HEAT OF THE THEBAN HILLS TO THE WEST OF LUXOR AND THE RIVER NILE, THE VALLEY OF THE KINGS IS PROBABLY THE WORLD'S MOST IMPORTANT ARCHAEOLOGICAL SITE.

It was here that lavish tombs were built for the Pharaohs and nobles of the New Kingdom, which comprised the 18–20th dynasties of Ancient Egypt. In 1922, the valley came to worldwide prominence with the discovery of the treasure-packed Tomb of Tutankhamen.

So far, 62 different tombs in the valley have been excavated by Egyptologists, and found to be in differing states of preservation. Those belonging to nobles rather than Pharaohs lacked the elaborate decoration, while it appears that some of the tombs were never completed. During the 20th Dynasty, some tombs were looted, and at this time the mummies and funerary treasures were reburied in two secret places.

Visitors are allowed to view some of the tombs, but hundreds of years of tourism, combined with pollution and rising groundwater, has caused some deterioration within them. At the time of writing, access was being determined on a rotational basis. Many of the decorated walls are set behind glass, and 11 tombs have been rigged with electrical lighting. The tombs were cut into the local limestone, incorporating three corridors, an antechamber and a sunken space for the sarcophagus.

Egypt Tourist Office

Tours approach the valley along a twisting road that was once the route of funeral processions. Coaches set down at a restaurant, from where it is no more than a 500m walk to the necropolis. Most visitors try to take in between three and five tombs in a day. Surrounded by limestone hills, the valley is a natural suntrap and can be uncomfortably hot even during winter. As ever, the rule is to drink plenty of water.

On the day of your visit, your choice of tomb will be dictated by the rotational system. The tomb of Tutankhamen is obviously a big draw, but it is unimpressive compared to other tombs in the valley, and may have been hastily ordained as a Pharaoh's tomb. Its fame stems from the boxes of treasure and funerary mask recovered, and the lateness of its discovery by archaeologist Howard Carter and his backer Lord Carnavon. The tomb's wall paintings are now behind glass and visitor numbers are naturally suppressed by the EG£45 entry fee.

One of the best tombs is that of Ramses IV, where a huge pink granite sarcophagus is guarded by carved representations of the gods Isis and Nephthys. It is one of the more colourful tombs, with bright inscriptions still evident despite the Geek and Coptic graffiti. Probably the most spectacular tomb is that of Ramses III, where intricate sunken reliefs depict everyday life of the time. The deepest tomb is that of Amenophis II, where a famous starry sky is painted onto the ceiling, representing the heavens.

Egypt Tourist Office

Egypt Tourist Office

▲ Queen Hatshepsut's temple is composed of three stories which can be accessed by the ramp at the front. Queen Hatshepsut was the only woman to rule ancient Egypt.

◄▼ Details of some of the wonderful wall paintings that can be found in the burial chambers at the Valley of the Kings at Luxor.

Egypt Tourist Office

Egypt Tourist Office

Start your underwater adventure here

Whether you are looking to experience breathing underwater for the first time, taking the initial steps towards becoming a qualified diver, or would like to brush up on your skills, our highly qualified instructors are here to help you along.

The London School of Diving brings together the best instructors, equipment and facilities in London with the patience that will guarantee your satisfaction.

Outstanding facilities with on-site pool

Conveniently located in West London the centre is well served by rail, road and tube.

- heated on-site training pool
- state of the art classrooms
- modern changing and shower facilities

london school of diving

London's premier dive school

Courses

London school of diving, a member of PADI, the professional association of diving instructors, offers high quality scuba instruction from entry level courses through to instructor level training.

PADI Courses
- Try Diving
- Open Water Diver
- Advanced Open Water Diver
- Rescue Diver
- Divemaster
- Instructor

Junior PADI Courses
- Junior Open Water
- Junior Advanced Open Water Diver
- Junior Rescue Diver

020 8995 0002
www.londonschoolofdiving.co.uk

GLOSSARY

Barbel

Tactile feeler around the mouth of some fish species.

BCD

Buoyancy control device, a jacket worn by divers to adjust trim underwater.

Benthic

Describes a bottom dwelling marine creature.

Bommie

A coral pinnacle or boulder rising from the seabed, see also erg.

Cleaning station

An area of reef populated by cleaner fish and established as an area where they can tend to larger fish (largely) without fear of being eaten.

Demand valve

Mechanism within a divers regulator that enables air or breathing gas to be supplied at ambient pressure when a diver inhales.

Dive computer

A personal, battery powered computer that advises the user on an array of essential diving data, usually wrist-mounted.

Downcurrent

An eddy which has the effect of dragging divers downwards, potentially dangerous but rare in the Red Sea.

Drop off

Diving term for the area where a reef plateau gives way to a steep wall, leading immediately to deeper water.

Hyperbaric chamber

Also known as decompression chamber or recompression chamber, this is an airtight room or capsule in which pressure can be controlled externally. Used for treatment of divers suffering from decompression sickness.

Negative entry

A descent technique used in powerful surface currents, in which divers empty all air from their BCDs and sink towards the reef immediately on entering the water.

Nitrox

An increasingly popular blend of breathing gas, in which the proportion of oxygen is normally increased against the nitrogen, allowing longer bottom times.

Pelagic

Describes a marine creature that lives in open sea, as opposed to territorial fish that associate with a particular reef.

Regulator

The name given to a diver's breathing apparatus.

RIB

Stands for rigid-hulled inflatable boat, a convenient mode of transport for divers that is valued in the Red Sea for manoeuvrability, speed and durability. Also referred to as an inflatable boat or by the popular manufacturer's name 'Zodiac'.

Shot line

A weighted or anchored line deployed in order to guide divers to a specific area of seabed, especially a shipwreck.

SMB

A surface marker buoy, used to indicate a diver's position to boat cover and traffic at the surface. A delayed SMB, or safety sausage, can be deployed from underwater by attaching it to a reel and inflating from a regulator.

Soft coral

Corals that lack a hard covering (exoskeleton).

Symbiosis

An association of two different organisms living close together, or one within the other, in a relationship that is mutually advantageous. A classic example is the anemonefish living with its host anemone.

Technical diver

Diver trained in the use of mixed gas systems and techniques.

Tender

A small, easily manoeuvrable support boat, typically used by liveaboards to drop off and collect divers, usually a RIB.

Thermocline

The area in which warm surface water meets cooler water welling up from the deep, creating a hazy visual effect.

Trimix

A mixture of three different gases (usually oxygen, helium and nitrogen) for use in deep or technical diving.

Wetsuit

A body suit fashioned from neoprene and worn by divers for heat retention and protection against coral cuts.

Zooplankton

Plankton consisting of animal rather than plant matter.

ARABIC DIVING TERMS

Erg

A coral tower, round or oval in shape, rising close to the surface.

Habili

A submerged coral pinnacle that does not rise to the surface, literally 'unborn'.

Must

A small erg.

Ras

A headland.

Sha'ab

Simply, a reef.

Sharm

A large bay.

Wadi

A dry valley, usually created by floodwater.

USEFUL RESOURCES

HOSPITALS, HYPERBARIC CHAMBERS & DIVE SAFETY

● **AQABA**

Princess Haya Hospital
Tel: +962 03 201 4111

● **EILAT**

Yoseftal Hospital
Tel: +972 07 635 8011
Chamber direct line: +972 07 635 8067

● **EGYPT**

El Gouna Hospital and Hyperbaric Chamber
El Gouna
Tel: +20 065 580 012/017 or 065 580 011

Hughada Naval Hyperbaric and Emergency Medical Centre
Hurghada
Tel: +20 065 449 150/151

Marsa Alam Hyperbaric Chamber
Marsa Shagra
Tel: +20 195 100 262
24 hr Emergency tel: +20 12 2187 550

Hyperbaric Medical Centre
Sharm el Sheikh
Tel: +20 069 660 922/923
24 hr Emergency tel: +20 12 2124 292

Sharm el Sheikh International Hospital
Sharm el Sheikh
Tel: +20 069 660 894

Sharm el Sheikh, Sea Search & Rescue (SSR)
Sharm el Maya
Tel: +20 12 3134 158
Radio: Channel 16

● **ERITREA**

Orota Referral Hospital
Asmara
Tel: +291 20 29 14/20 19 17

Massawa Hospital
Massawa
Tel: +291 55 26 44

● **DJIBOUTI**

Peltier General Hospital
Djibouti City
Tel: +253 35 07 50

● **YEMEN**

Yemeni-German Hospital
San'a
Tel: +967 418 000

Modern German Hospital
San'a
Tel: +967 608 888

● **SAUDI ARABIA**

United Doctors Hospital
Jeddah
Tel: +966 2 653 2423

Abuzinadah Hospital
Jeddah
Tel: +966 2 651 0652

King Abdul Aziz University Hospital
Jeddah
Tel: +966 2640 1000

RESCUE AND EMERGENCY

e-Med
www.e-med.co.uk

U.K. Sport Diving Medical Committee
www.uksdmc.co.uk

American Academy of Underwater Sciences
www.aaus.org

Dive Rescue International
www.diverescueintl.com

Divers' Alert Network (DAN)
www.diversalertnetwork.org

International Association of Dive Rescue Specialists
www.iadrs.org

British Diving Safety Group
www.bdsg.org

DIVER TRAINING

PADI
Unit 7 St Philips Central Albert Road, St Philips, Bristol, BS2 0PD, U.K.
Tel: +44 117 300 7234
www.padi.com

Sub-Aqua Association
Space Solutions Business Centre,Sefton Lane, Maghull, Liverpool, L31 8BX, U.K.
Tel: +44 151 287 1001
www.saa.org.uk

The British Sub-Aqua Club
Telford's Quay, South Pier Road, Ellesmere Port, Cheshire CH65 4FL, U.K.
Tel: +44 151 350 6200
www.bsac.com

The Scottish Sub-Aqua Club
The Cockburn Centre, 40 Bogmoor Place, Glasgow, G51 4TQ, Scotland, U.K.
Tel: +44 141 425 1021
www.scotsac.com

Irish Underwater Council
78a Patrick Street, Dun Laoghaire, Co. Dublin, Ireland
Tel: +353 1 284 4601
www.cft.ie

National Assoc. of Underwater Instructors
P.O. Box 89789, Tampa, FL, 33689-0413, U.S.A.
Tel: +1 800 553 6284
www.nauiww.org

Scuba Diving International
18 Elm Street, Topsham, MN, 04086, U.S.A.
Tel: +1-888-778-9073
www.tdisdi.com

Diver Certification Board of Canada
Suite 503, 5121 Sackville Street, Halifax, Nova Scotia, B3J 1K1, Canada
Tel: +1 902 465 3483
www.divercertification.com

MARINE ORGANIZATIONS

OCEANS

www.savethehighseas.org
The Deep Sea Conservation Coalition brings together around 30 conservation groups worldwide in an attempt to halt trawling and damage to seamounts, cold water corals and other deep sea ecosystems.

www.fish4ever.org
Fish 4 Ever is a global email campaign calling for the urgent implementation of sustainable fisheries and the creation of a network of marine parks to safeguard the future of the world's oceans.

www.greenpeace.org
Greenpeace runs international campaigns on a variety of marine issues including pollution, whale and dolphin conservation, and deep sea trawling.

www.oceana.org
Oceana works in North America, South America and Europe on issues including oil pollution, destructive trawling and seafood contamination.

www.oceanconservancy.org
The Ocean Conservancy coordinates international coastal clean-ups (covering 90 countries) and campaigns on a range of marine issues.

www.oceanfutures.org
Jean-Michel Cousteau's Ocean Futures Society focuses on four main areas: clean water, coastal marine habitats, marine mammals and sustainable fisheries.

www.panda.org
WWF (formerly World Wildlife Fund) runs a Global Marine programme that sponsors research and publications as well as campaigning on a wide range of marine conservation issues.

CORAL REEFS

www.coralreefalliance.org
Coral Reef Alliance works with divers, snorkellers, local communities and governments to protect and manage coral reefs and promote marine parks. It produces an excellent and comprehensive set of guidelines on good environmental practice for diving, snorkelling, and managing an 'underwater clean-up'.

www.reefcheck.org
ReefCheck, founded in 1996, is dedicated to saving coral reefs globally and temperate reefs in California. It works in over 80 countries with volunteers, governments and businesses to monitor, restore and maintain coral reef health.

www.reef.org
The Reef Environmental Education Foundation is a fish monitoring programme for divers, in which information is fed into a publicly-accessible database.

www.reefguardian.org
ReefGuardian International focuses on reefs and marine life.

SHARKS AND WHALES

www.csiwhalesalive.org
The Cetacean Society International campaigns on whale conservation.

www.sharktrust.org
The Shark Trust works to promote the study, management and conservation of sharks, skates and rays in the UK and internationally.

www.wdcs.org
The Whale and Dolphin Conservation Society is one of the leading international voices for the protection of whales, dolphins and their environment.

www.whalesharkproject.org
The Whale Shark Project is a joint campaign by the Shark Trust and PADI Project AWARE to create a Whaleshark photo-identification database.

REGIONAL ORGANIZATIONS

www.deepwave.org
Deep Wave is a German ecology group working on a range of marine issues.

www.livingoceans.org
Living Oceans campaigns on fisheries, aquaculture and marine protected areas in British Columbia, Canada.

www.mcsuk.org
The Marine Conservation Society is a UK-based charity dedicated to protecting the marine environment and its wildlife. MCS organises an annual beach clean up and publishes the Good Beach Guide and the Good Fish Guide.

CONSERVATION EXPEDITIONS

www.amca-international.org
Access to Marine Conservation for All helps disabled divers participate in conservation expeditions.

CONSUMER ISSUES

www.bite-back.com
Bite-back has successfully campaigned to persuade supermarkets and restaurants in the UK to stop selling shark products. It has since also campaigned on other non-sustainable fisheries, including those for marlin, swordfish, monkfish and Orange Roughy.

www.fishonline.org
The UK-based Marine Conservation Society has an on-line guide to help consumers choose fish from sustainable sources. (Internet version of their Good Fish Guide.)

www.msc.org
The Marine Stewardship Council is an independent, non-profit organization that promotes responsible fishing practices through the MSC sustainably-fished labelling scheme.

www.mbayaq.org/cr/seafoodwatch.asp
The Monterey Bay Aquarium publishes seafood guides.

www.oceansalive.org/eat.cfm
US-based Oceans Alive publishes another seafood selector guide.

www.seafoodchoices.com
The US-based Seafood Choices Alliance helps fishermen, chefs and restaurant-goers make sound seafood choices.

CARBON OFFSET SCHEMES

www.carbonneutral.com
Formerly known as Future Forests, the CarbonNeutral Company also allows you to calculate your emissions from flights, domestic travel or from your home, and to offset them in various ways.

www.climatecare.org
Climate Care allows you to calculate the carbon cost of flights or the day-to-day emissions from your car and home. You can then offset your carbon usage by donating to reforestation or projects to reduce greenhouse gas emissions at source.

PHOTO CREDITS

CHARLES HOOD

Charles Hood is a freelance underwater photojournalist currently under contract to DIVE magazine in the UK. When he is not testing diving equipment he is usually travelling the world photographing news stories or on commission for various publications and tourist boards. His work has recently been seen on the front cover of TIME magazine, Sunday Times, Guardian, Daily Mail and Independent as well as being twice highly commended at the Natural History Museum Wildlife photographer of the year competition. He has written his own book on diving in Cornwall, edited various manuals for BSAC and supplied numerous books with underwater images.

Website: www.oceans-image.com

JANE MORGAN

Jane is the Online editor of DIVE Magazine and an award winning committee member of BSoUP (The British Society of Underwater Photographers). Jane learned to dive in 1991 and is an open water instructor and an International Association for Handicapped Divers instructor. Passionate about the underwater world she has worked on conservation projects with Coral Cay in both the Philippines and Borneo.

Jane discovered underwater photography during a trip to the Southern Red Sea in 2001 and never looked back. In 2006 she was awarded a Palme D'or at the Antibes World Festival of Underwater Photography for black and white photography.

Website: www.morganreefphotography.com

ALEXANDER MUSTARD

Alexander Mustard is both a marine biologist and a highly talented underwater photographer, with multiple awards from the BBC Wildlife Photographer of the Year and the World Festival of Underwater Photography in Antibes.

Alex was an early adopter of digital cameras and pioneered many of the specialist techniques of digital underwater photography. His is Digital Officer for the British Society of Underwater Photographers and Co-Administrator of Wetpixel. com. His first book "The Art Of Diving" also published by Ultimate Sports has been described by David Doubilet as "the best book about diving since Jacques Cousteau's The Silent World".

Website: www.amustard.com

JP TRENQUE

Originally from France, he learnt to dive in 1980 to follow his father's fin strokes.

He moved to London in 1994, where he became a diving instructor. After some time shooting video underwater, he took up digital still photography in 2003. He now spends much of his spare time capturing the beauty of the aquatic environment, either in the UK or abroad with his wife Jane Morgan.

In 2004, JP was awarded a third place at the Antibes World Festival of Underwater Photography in the black and white prints category, and in 2005, he won the BBC News Photographer of the Year competition with a shot of schooling barracuda taken at Ras Mohammed in Egypt (see page 80).

Website: www.jptrenque.com

MALCOLM NOBBS

Malcolm Nobbs, an enthusiastic amateur underwater photographer and member of BSoUP, took up diving in 1995. Malcolm regularly travels to renowned dive sites around the world, compiling photographs and reports for his website.

Website: www.malcolmnobbs.com

PETER COLLINGS

Peter Collings has been a writer/author and explorer of shipwrecks since 1982, logging over 6500 dives and has received several international awards for his work. His images appear regularly in the international diving press and he has led over 600 wreck safaris in the Egyptian Red Sea.

Website: www.deeplens.com

NEIL BEER

Having sidestepped a career in Graphic Design Neil now specialises in photographing tribal peoples, ancient sights and wild landscapes. To date Neil has visited over a hundered countries.

Website: www.neilbeer.com

DAVE LUCAS

Dave Lucas has been the main activist in new climbing development within the Sinai Desert. He has also achieved hundreds of new climbing routes in many far-flung corners of the globe.

Website: www.verticalworld.co.uk

OTHER USEFUL WEBSITES

www.bsoup.org
www.photosub.co.uk
www.artofdiving.com
www.divemagazine.co.uk
www.divernet.com
www.scubadiving.com
www.wetpixel.com
www.divester.com
www.divephotoguide.com
www.divingindex.com
www.ukdiving.co.uk

INDEX

Wrecks are shown in *italics*.

SEVENTENTHS®

THE ORIGINAL DIVE THREADS

Europe • Asia Pacific • Red Sea   worldwide online store **www.seventenths.com**

continue
your
adventure
in the
underwater
world

www.artofdiving.com

The Art of Diving website has been created to enhance your enjoyment of **Dive Red Sea** and other scuba diving books from Ultimate Sports.

Visit **www.artofdiving.com** and enter the activation code below when registering to activate your **FREE** membership.

Your **FREE** activation code for the members only zone is: **vnx6 3bmd 95ys**

Already a member? If so there is NO need to re-activate membership

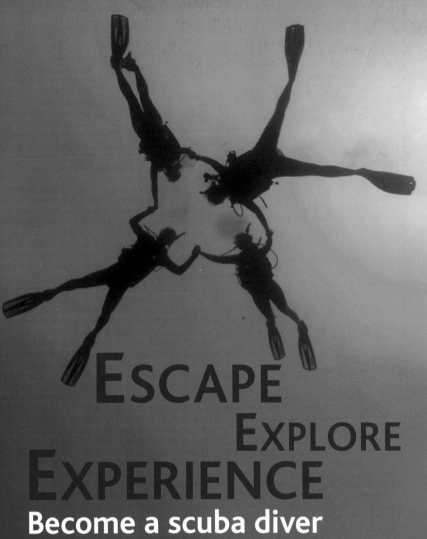

ESCAPE EXPLORE EXPERIENCE

Become a scuba diver

Thank you for purchasing DIVE RED SEA. As you will already be aware by reading this book, a wonderful underwater world full of beauty and adventure awaits you. Consider the purchase of this book as an investment in the life- changing experience of becoming a scuba diver.

From 1st March 2007 until 28 February 2008, when you complete a PADI Open Water Diver course, PADI will refund you the purchase cost of DIVE RED SEA (£20) towards the purchase of your PADI Open Water Diver programme.

To take advantage of this offer simply go to www.artofdiving.com and register using the activation code "vnx6 3bmd 95ys" then complete and return the voucher.

The great thing about becoming a scuba diver is that the beauty and imagery in DIVE RED SEA can be experienced first hand by completing the PADI Open Water Diver programme.

If you are already a diver we encourage you to share this special offer with your friends, family or significant other, or better yet, buy them a copy of DIVE RED SEA of their own.

For more information about this and other special offers from PADI, and a list of PADI dive centres around the world, visit: www.padi.com

PADI
padi.com

By taking a PADI Open Water Diver course from now* until the 28th February 2008, this voucher entitles the newly qualified PADI Open Water Diver named below to receive a cheque from PADI International Limited of twenty pounds sterling. Please provide the information requested below and return this voucher to Marketing, PADI International Limited, Unit 7, St Philips Central, Albert Road, BS2 0PD, United Kingdom.

Name:

....

Address:

....

....

....

Post code:

....

E-mail:

....

Telephone number:

....

Your PADI Open Water Diver certification number:

....

Date you commenced the course:

....

Date of completion:

....

Name of the PADI Dive Centre/Instructor where the course took place:

....

*To qualify for this offer the PADI Open Water Diver course taken must have started after the date of publication of Dive Red Sea (1st March 2007).

www.artofdiving.com

The Art of Diving website has been created to enhance your enjoyment of DIVE RED SEA and other scuba diving books from Ultimate Sports.

Visit **www.artofdiving.com** for:

- Photographers' tips
- Guest photographers
- Photo galleries
- Free desktop pictures downloads
- Dive news
- Red Sea Dive centre directory
- Conservation listings
- Forthcoming NEW publications
- Partner offers & promotions
- Competitions & prizes

Go to **www.artofdiving.com** now and enter the activation code below when registering to activate your **FREE** membership and gain access to the members only section.

Enter email address and preferred personal password then when asked enter the activation code: vnx6 3bmd 95ys

Already a member? If so there is NO need to re-activate membership.

continue your adventure in the
underwater world

Red Sea PADI Dive Centres

EILAT
Aqua Sport International, Aqualine, Divers Village, Marina Divers, Prodive, Red Sea Lucky Divers, Sea Sport Club, Siam Divers, Snuba.

AQABA
Aqaba Gulf Dive Center, Aqaba International Dive Centre, Aquamarina Dive Center, Dive Aqaba, Sea Dive Centre, Royal Diving Club, Seastar Watersports.

TABA
Aqua - Sport International Ltd, Diving Centers Werner Lau, Red Sea Water World - Radisson SAS, Sea Water World - Taba Heights.

NUWEIBA
Emperor Divers and Scuba Schools, Scuba College - Diving Camp.

DAHAB
Barakuda Dahab, Bedouin Divers, Big Blue Dahab, Blue Beach Dive Club, Club Dahab Diving, Club Divers, Dahab Divers, Dahab Divers Lodge, Dahab-Club, Daniela Diving Center, Deep Blue Divers, D ert Divers Co. Ltd, Dive Urge, Divers Down Under, Diver's House, Emperor Divers and Scuba Scho Fantasea Divers, Inmo Divers Home, Nesima Diving Center, Octopus Divers, OK Club, Orca Dive C Orca Dive Club, Planet Divers, Poseidon Divers - Pro Dive, Red Sea Relax, Reef 2000, Sinai Di "Backpackers", Sinai Divers Dahab - Red Sea, Sphinx Divers, Sub Sinai, Sunsplash Divers, Torch Div

SHARM EL SHEIKH
Action Sport, African Divers, Albatros Top Diving Coral Beach, Aqua Sharm Diving College, Aqua Diving Club - Sheraton, Azure Diving College, Blue Sea Diving Centre & Scuba College, C Fun Div Camel Dive Club, Colona Dive Center, Dive Africa Watersports, Dive In Sharm, Diver's Dreams, Div International, Divers Lodge, Divers United, Diving & Discovery Dive Centre, Diving Centers Wer Lau, Dolphin, Easy Divers Sinai, Egyptian Divers, Emperor Divers and Scuba Schools, European D ing Centre, Go Dive El Fanar, Maxi Diving, Moon Divers, Mr.DIVER Marriott, Mr.DIVER Pyramisa, M Waves, Ocean College, Only Six, Oonas Dive Club, Orca Dive Club, Pirate Divers, Red Sea Diving C lege, Red Sea Water World - Hyatt Regency, Scubadreamer Diving College, Seasoul, Sharks Bay Div Club, Sheikh Coast Diving Center, Sinai Blues, Sinai Dive Club, Sinai Divers, Sun-n-Fun Divers, Diving Sharm, The Wave Diving Center, Tornado Marine Fleet- M/Y Typhoon, Tornado Marine Fle M/Y Cyclone, Tornado Marine Fleet: M/Y Tempest, Tornado Marine Fleet: M/Y Whirlwind, Valturdiv Sharm El Shiekh, Ventadiving Faraana, Ventadiving Reef Oasis, Ventadiving Sharm, Vera Sub, Viag Nel Blu, Xaloc Egypt, Xwander.

HURGHADA
Aquanaut Red Sea, Aquarius Diving Club, Blue Water Dive Resort, blueotwo, Bubbles Diving Coll Colona Dive Center, DC Aliav, Dive In Hurghada, Dive Point Red Sea, Divers International, Div Lodge, Diving World Hurghada, Dream Divers International, Emperor Divers and Scuba Schools, Gr Orca Diving Center, Hor Palace Diving Center, James & Mact, Jasmin Dive Center, Kawarty 2, Kawa 3, Pirates Diving Network, Pirates Diving Network, Red Sea Association for Diving & Wtspts., RedS Divers, Seafari Hurghada, Seawolf-Diving Safari, Sub Aqua DC Sofitel, The Crab, Undersea Adventu Voodoo Divers Ltd.

SAFAGA
Alpha Red Sea, Barakuda Diving Center, Barakuda Safaga, Duck's Dive Center, Dune Diving Cen Emperor Divers and Scuba Schools, MenaDive, Orca-Red-Sea, Shams Safaga, Sharm el Naga Resor Diving Centre, UTS Tauchcenter.

EL QUSEIR
Marina Divers

MARSA AL ALAM
Aquarius Diving Club, Blue Heaven Holidays, Emperor Divers and Scuba Schools, Global Divers, S fari Marsa Alam, TGI Diving Marsa, Tornado Marine Fleet: M/V Hurricane, Wadi Gimal.

DJIBOUTI
Dolphin Excursions SARL, Lagon Bleu.

SAUDI ARABIA
Scuba Club, Sharky Dive Center, Al Khorayef Sea & Sun, Blue Reef Divers - Jeddah, Blue Reef Diver Riyadh, Desert Sea Divers, Dream Divers, Red Sea Divers, Saudi Divers, The Arab Circumnavigator, B Reef Divers - Jubail, Al Khorayef Sea & Sun, Makkah Diver, Red Sea Divers, Blue Reef Divers - Yan Tornado Marine Fleet: M/V Royal Emperor.

For a full listing and contact details visit: